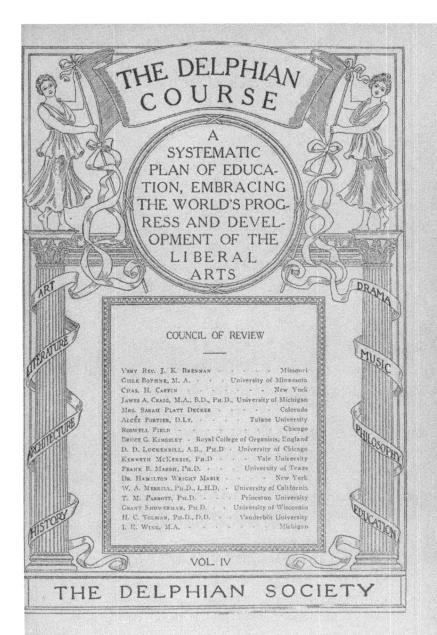

Roman Social Life and Literature
Age of Chivalry
Delphian Reading Course
Part Four
Plus Study Guide

Copyright © 2018 by Libraries of Hope. All rights reserved. No part of this publication may be reproduced, stored in a retrieval system, or transmitted in any form or by any means, electronic, mechanical, photocopying, recording or otherwise, without prior written permission of the publisher. International rights and foreign translations available only through permission of the publisher.

Compiled from:
The Delphian Course, by the Delphian Society, Chicago: The Delphian Society, (1913).

Study Guide, by the Delphian Society, Chicago: The Delphian Society, (1911).

Cover Image: God Speed by Edmund Leighton (1900, from Wikimedia Commons

Libraries of Hope, Inc. Appomattox, Virginia 24522

Website: www.librariesofhope.com
Email: support@librariesofhope.com

Printed in the United States of America

TABLE OF CONTENTS
PART IV:

THE ROMAN PRINCIPATE.

Chapter XV.
The Establishment of the Principate.................................... 1

Chapter XVI.
The Deeds of Augustus.. 7

Chapter XVII.
Rome Under the Julian Princes... 15

Chapter XVIII.
The Flavian Princes... 22

Chapter XIX.
Five Good Princes; The Decline of the Principate...................... 27

Chapter XX.
The Reforms of Diocletian and Constantine............................. 34

Chapter XXI.
Early Christianity 40

Chapter XXII.
To the Fall of Rome... 47

Chapter XXIII.
From the Fall of Rome to Charlemagne.................................. 54

SOCIAL LIFE IN ROME.

Chapter I.
The Roman Family 59

Chapter II.
Houses of the Ancient Romans 66

Chapter III.
Wearing Apparel 73

Chapter IV.
Food, Meals and Banquets.. 77

Chapter V.
Birth and Childhood... 83

TABLE OF CONTENTS—PART IV.

Chapter VI.
Schools and Education 87

Chapter VII.
Sports and Pastimes 93

Chapter VIII.
Books, Letters and Libraries 102

Chapter IX.
Business Activities 106

Chapter X.
Slavery in Rome 113

Chapter XI.
The Army 121

Chapter XII.
Tombs and Funeral Customs 125

LATIN LITERATURE.

Historical Review 130

Chapter XIII.
Beginnings of Latin Literature 137
The Chant of the Arval Brothers 143
Ennius 143
Plautius 145
Terence 173
Tarquin's Dream 179

Chapter XIV.
The Age of Cicero 181
Lucretius 186
Cicero 191
Catullus 204
Laberius 214
Sallust 216
Caius Julius Caesar 222

Chapter XV.
The Age of Augustus 233
Virgil 244
Horace 261

Chapter XVI.
Later Writers 269
Ovid 275

TABLE OF CONTENTS—PART IV.

	PAGE
Tibullus	291
Propertius	294
Livy	296
Tacitus	313
Phaedrus	322
Persius	323
Seneca	323
Lucan	337
Petronius Arbiter	345
Pliny the Elder	354
Martial	361
Pliny the Younger	365
Juvenal	367
Suetonius	374

Chapter XVII.

Architectural Wonders of Rome 380

Chapter XVIII.

Italy of Today 387

THE MIDDLE AGES.

The Forest Children 398

Chapter I.

Introduction; The Teutons; Charlemagne 408

Chapter II.

The Early Church; Beginnings of the Papacy..................... 418
The Monk as a Civilizer 425
The Rule of St. Benedict 434

Chapter III.

The Feudal System 442

Chapter IV.

Religious Wars; The Crusades; Ordeals........................... 451

Chapter V.

Schools and Education in the Middle Ages........................ 469
Institutions of the Middle Ages 476
Description of Illustrations... 485

FULL PAGE ILLUSTRATIONS

PART IV.

	PAGE
ROMAN CHARIOT RACE (Water Color)	Frontispiece
THE COLISEUM	47
BATHS OF CARACULLA	82
ARCH OF TITUS	181
TEMPLE OF VESTA—RESTORED	224
PANORAMA OF ROME FROM ST. PETER'S	296
DEATH AND THE PLOWMAN	360
MOSAIC—WORSHIP OF THE MAGI—SIXTH CENTURY	398
FARMING IN LUZON—AS IN MIDDLE AGES	414
MINIATURE—QUEEN OF SHEBA BEFORE SOLOMON	432
KNIGHT IN ARMOR	459
MAP OF ANCIENT ITALY	VIII

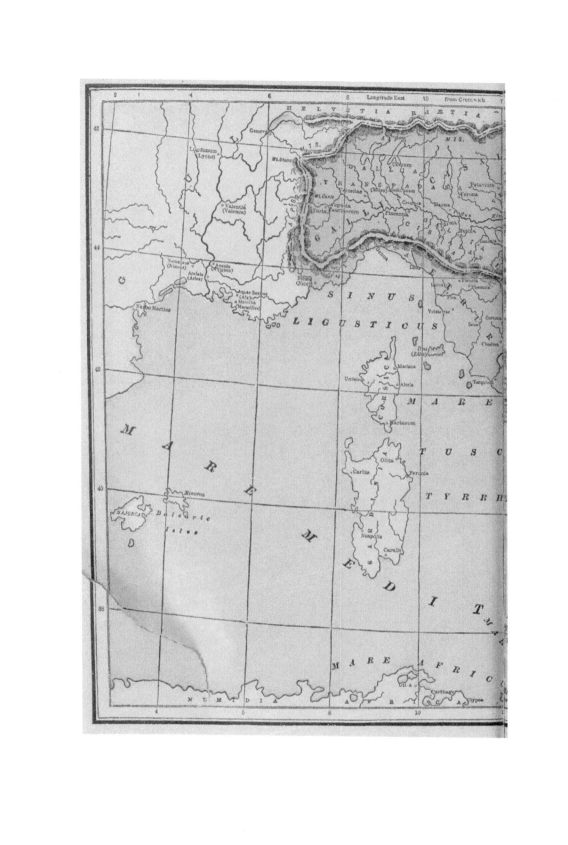

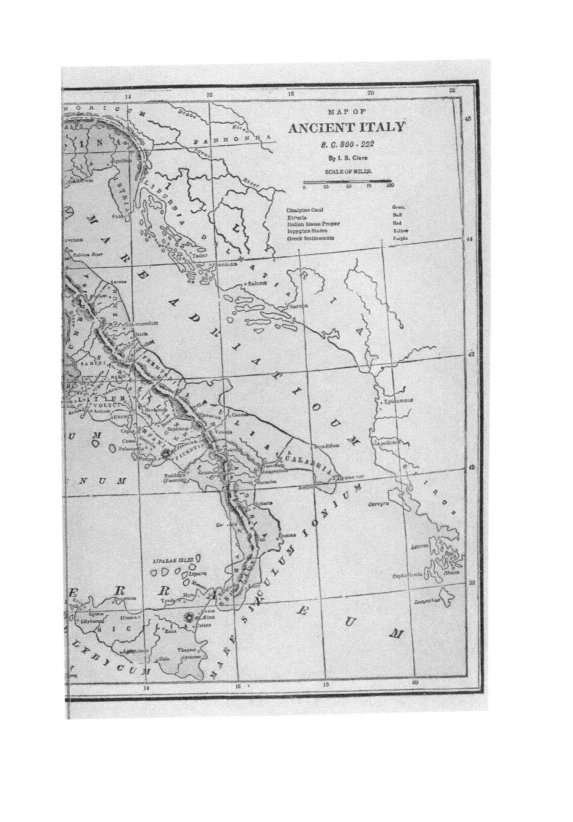

THE ROMAN PRINCIPATE

CHAPTER XV.

The Establishment of the Principate.

In 27 B. C. Octavius returned to Rome and surrendered to the senate and the Roman people any extraordinary power he had exercised under the stress of civil and foreign war. In gratitude to one who, possessing great authority and wide influence, yet held himself bound by the Roman constitution, the senate conferred upon him the title *Augustus*—one worthy of reverence. In addition to this merely honorary title, he was made prince of the senate, pontifex maximus, and imperator, or commander of the army. Ere long he was given the proconsular imperium, whereby his authority was made greater than that of any other proconsul, and finally the people bestowed upon him perpetual tribunary power. This amounted to preserving the form of the republic, while in reality final control was in the hands of the princeps, or prince.

Augustus at once restored to the senate its former dignity, of which it had been stripped by Caesar when he augmented its membership to 900 and gave senatorial seats to Italians and provincials. Those who felt themselves unworthy to hold senatorial office were first invited to withdraw, some fifty voluntarily leaving. Then the senatorial list was revised and those who were unfitted for this high honor were dismissed. The rule of the prince and the senate which was now inaugurated has been called a *dyarchy* by certain German historians, meaning the rule of two powers; recently it has been called the principate, or rule of the prince, with the aid of the senate. Either term is preferable to that of *empire,* which implies absolute power in the hands of one man. While there is no question but that Augustus actually held supreme control, he nevertheless retained the forms of the old republic. Maintaining the magistrates established by the republic, he caused their titles to become chiefly honorary, while new servants of the principate, answerable to himself, absorbed many of their functions.

Restoring the senate and making it an advisory body, Augustus also perpetuated the assemblies of the people. These had, however, become too large to conduct the lawmaking for the realm. Laws were occasionally submitted to the people for ratification, but their principal duty came to be the election of magistrates from names presented to them. These names were generally submitted by the prince. It would seem vain to contend that one who largely controlled the finances, whose opinion, being asked first in the senate, as a natural result, largely influenced the expression of that body; who could control all elections and all actions of the legislative bodies; and who, above all, commanded the army, was not possessed of absolute power. However, it pleased Augustus not to offend the people, as his illustrious uncle had done, by brushing aside their prejudices, but, preserving the skeleton of the republic, to develop beneath it a strength that no longer needed support.

We have seen that since the time of the Gracchi disorder had been the rule rather than the exception in Rome; discontent and unrest had harassed the peninsula, and the provinces had been disgracefully plundered. All this was now changed. City, state and provinces received attention and were so thoroughly organized that prosperity attended them for many years.

In Rome the old officials were retained, but three important additions were made. A praefectus urbis, a sort of mayor or chief of the city, was appointed to see that order was maintained. A praefectus vigilum was chosen to organize a city fire department, and a praefectus annonae, or grain commissioner, was assigned the duty of supervising the grain supply for Rome. It will be remembered that during the second Punic war the farms of Italy had been plundered and Rome grew to depend upon foreign grain. Later, the conditions were such that agriculture largely declined in Italy, especially after the passage of laws which required the government to supply grain to the poor for less than cost. For some time Rome had looked to Egypt for her grain supply. During part of the year the sea was rough and vessels were not infrequently obliged to lie over for weeks at a time, while this delay of grain caused great suffering among the poor, who were accustomed to receive rations from the state once a month. This officer now appointed by the prince was commissioned to provide enough grain to prevent temporary famine to which Rome was subject. The city was divided into fourteen wards, and henceforth city administration was carefully supervised.

For purposes of government Italy was divided into eleven districts, each having a magistrate to direct affairs within its territory. To facilitate rapid communication between the various districts, existing roads were repaired and others built. A post system was organized between Rome and Italian centers, and military patrols were stationed in lonely places where highwaymen might be concealed. Of course such measures as these were highly important in building up the commerce of the land, which had suffered severely in the last hundred years. Another successful effort was made to fill up unsettled parts of the peninsula with colonists from Rome or discharged veterans.

The provinces of Rome were divided into two classes: senatorial and imperial. The senatorial provinces were those where troops were no longer required. Appointments to these were made by the senate and the proconsuls sent thither were accountable to the senate for their conduct. Moreover, the revenues from these provinces were controlled by the senate. Those provinces yet unsettled, requiring still the presence of an army, were under the control of the prince, to whom their governors were answerable and who managed the yearly taxes. The governors in the imperial provinces now received a stated salary and were strictly watched to see that no oppression of the people might occur.

Augustus was not himself a strong military leader, and he inaugurated a peace policy, striving only to defend the boundaries of the Roman empire. There was but one exception to this general rule. When he became prince, the Roman world extended from Asia Minor to the Atlantic ocean, from the North sea to the Sahara. On the east the Parthians marked the eastern boundary of the Roman empire. On the north alone was there opportunity to expand, and Augustus tried to make the Elbe and the Danube Rome's northern frontier. To win the territory south of these rivers, Tiberius and Drusus were sent and remained until the death of Drusus in 9 B. C. Tiberius completed the work and the Elbe-Danube boundary was secured. However, Tiberius was succeeded by Varus, a most inefficient general. Quite incapable of understanding the German tribes, Varus felt a safety unwarranted by the circumstances. He allowed himself to be led into a trap and lost almost the whole Roman army. This was one of the worst disasters in the whole history of Rome. Thereafter the Rhine, not the Elbe, constituted Rome's northern frontier.

It was in the works of peace, however, that Augustus' peculiar ability for executive control was most apparent. It was his boast that he had found Rome in brick and left it in marble. By brick we think of the substantial material today supplied under that name. The bricks which formed the early Rome of Augustus, however, were, for the most part, sun-dried bricks, neither very substantial nor attractive. To a large extent, the public buildings of the city were replaced by splendid marble edifices, far worthier of the capital of a wealthy empire. One of the most beautiful buildings erected by Augustus was the temple of Apollo, vowed to the Sun-god if he would give Augustus success in the battle of Actium. This was erected on Palatine hill and, beautiful in outline, the temple was surmounted by a statue of Apollo, his head surrounded by rays of the sun. Other temples were constructed and many were repaired, as Augustus has left record in his famous inscription, reprinted in the following chapter.

The literary history of the Augustan Age will be considered elsewhere. It remains here to consider the moral and religious reforms enacted by Augustus Caesar.

One hundred years of civil war had brutalized Italy, and a recklessness was now apparent among the upper classes of society. Foreign gods had replaced the earlier divinities of Rome, and eastern cults had superseded the simplicity of worship. Unparalleled accumulations of wealth gave rise to excessive extravagance. The aristocracy had taken on a scale of living that made it necessary for them to control heavy financial interests. The wealthy had villas everywhere. From one hundred to one thousand slaves were kept where a few should have sufficed. Cooks were imported for thousands of dollars. Men ransacked the known world for delicacies for the table. Banquets represented fabulous sums, as indeed, they have been known to do in modern times. Marriage was no longer regarded as a sacred institution; divorces were as easily secured as they are today in America. Those who married did not wish the care of children.

Augustus sought to revive the moral condition of early times, wherein the family had been pure and the moral tone of the country remarkably good. To this end he secured the passage of the so-called sumptuary laws. These imposed the duty of marriage upon men and women, and prohibited those who refused to wed from receiving inheritances from any but those of whom they were direct heirs; even so, part of such inheritances went to the state. Divorces were no longer easy to obtain. Favors were extended to fathers and mothers with more than three children. Severer than these were the regulations which shut unmarried men and women out of the national celebrations of games and festivals. Held only now and then, these were the great social functions of the state, and not to be allowed to witness them was a heavy penalty.

Limits were placed upon the building craze; banquets were regulated so that the recent extravagance could no longer obtain. The dress of the women was considered and efforts made to restrict the vast outlays lavished upon costume. Quite naturally these laws called forth greatest indignation and protest on the part of the wealthy, yet, nevertheless, they received the sanction and approval of a wholesome class of people who had never viewed reckless expenditures with patience. It is certain that the new conditions in the provinces which prevented rapid accumulations of wealth had more to do with working a social reform than all the legislating upon the subject; nevertheless, some good results accompanied the enforcement of these regulations.

The Prince wished especially to restore the early gods of Rome to their old-time favor. To this end he repaired little shrines erected at the intersection of streets, at cross roads, and where four farms met, for the worship of the Lares. His own figure he caused to be placed between the two figures of the Lares. These domestic gods had remained closely interlinked with family worship throughout the centuries, and it was easier to reach the hearts of the people through them than by any other means. Foreign gods were driven out and in their places the worship of Apollo, Vesta and Jupiter was substituted. Julius, Augustus' great uncle and adopted father, was also deified, and a temple erected in his honor.

In spite of all Augustus could do, however, the days of the early divinities had passed, and Greek philosophies were taking their places in the minds of thinking men.

Augustus died in 14 A. D., having given the Romans such an era of peace and prosperity as had been unknown for long years. Future ages have conceded him to have been a man of wonderful executive ability and remarkable statesmanlike qualities.

AUGUSTUS.—VATICAN MUSEUM.

CHAPTER XVI.

THE DEEDS OF AUGUSTUS—AS TOLD BY HIMSELF.

Below is a copy of the deeds of the divine Augustus, by which he subjected the whole world to the dominion of the Roman people, and of the amounts which he expended upon the commonwealth and the Roman people, as engraved upon two brazen columns which are set up at Rome.

I.

In my twentieth year, acting upon my own judgment and at my own expense, I raised an army by means of which I restored to liberty the commonwealth which had been oppressed by the tyranny of a faction. On account of this the senate, by laudatory decrees, admitted me to its order, in the consulship of Gaius Pansa and Aulus Hirtius, and at the same time gave me consular rank in the expression of opinion, and gave me the *imperium*. It also voted that I, as pro-praetor, together with the consuls, should see to it that the commonwealth suffered no harm. In the same year, moreover, when both consuls had perished in war, the people made me consul, and triumvir for organizing the commonwealth.

II.

Those who killed my father I drove into exile by lawful judgment, avenging their crime, and afterwards, when they waged war against the commonwealth, I twice defeated them in battle.

III.

I undertook civil and foreign wars by land and sea throughout the whole world, and as victor I showed mercy to all surviving citizens. Foreign people who could be pardoned with safety, I preferred to preserve than to destroy. About five hundred thousand Roman citizens took the military oath of allegiance to me. Of these I have settled in colonies or sent back to their *municipia,* upon the expiration of their terms of service, somewhat over three hundred thousand, and to all these I have given lands purchased by me, or money for farms, out of my own means. I have captured six hundred ships, besides those which were smaller than triremes.

IV.

Twice I have triumphed in the ovation,[1] and three times in the curule triumph[2], and I have been twenty-one times saluted as imperator. After that, when the senate decreed me many triumphs, I declined them. Likewise I have often deposited the laurels in the Capitol in fulfillment of vows which I had also made in battle. On account of enterprises brought to a successful issue on land and sea by me, or by my lieutenants under my auspices, the senate fifty-five times decreed that there should be thanksgiving to the immortal gods. The number of days, moreover, on which thanksgiving was rendered in accordance with the decree of the senate was 890. In my triumphs there have been led before my chariot nine kings, or children of kings. When I wrote these words I had been thirteen times consul, and was in the thirty-seventh year of the tribunitial power.

V.

The dictatorship which was offered to me by the people and the senate, both when I was absent and when I was present, in the consulship of Marcus Marcellus and Lucius Arruntius, I did not accept. At a time of the greatest dearth of grain I did not refuse the charge of the food supply, which I so administered that in a few days, at my own expense, I freed the whole people from the anxiety and danger in which they then were. The annual and perpetual consulship offered to me at that time I did not accept.

VIII.

In the fifth consulship, by order of the people and the senate, I increased the number of patricians. Three times I have revised the list of the senate. In my sixth consulship,

---

[1] The lesser triumph, generally entering city clad as ordinary magistrates.
[2] The General, dressed in purple, rode in four-horse chariot.

with Marcus Agrippa as colleague, I made a census of the people. I performed the lustration after forty-one years. In this lustration the number of the Roman citizens was four million and sixty-three thousand. Again assuming the consular power in the consulship of Gaius Censorius and Gaius Asinius, I alone performed the lustration. At this census the number of Roman citizens was four million, two hundred and thirty thousand. A third time, assuming the consular power in the consulship of Sextus Pompeius and Sextus Appuleius, with Tiberius Caesar as colleague, I performed the lustration. At this lustration the number of Roman citizens was four million, nine hundred and thirty-seven thousand. By new legislation I have restored many customs of our ancestors which had now begun to fall into disuse, and I have myself also committed to posterity many examples worthy of imitation.

IX.

The senate decreed that every fifth year vows for my good health should be performed by the consuls and the priests. In accordance with these vows games have been often celebrated during my lifetime, sometimes by the four chief colleges, sometimes by the consuls. In private, also, and as municipalities, the whole body of citizens have sacrificed at every shrine for my good health.

Janus Quirinus, which it was the purpose of our fathers to close when there was peace won by victory throughout the whole empire of the Roman people on land and sea, and which, before I was born, from the foundation of the city, was reported to have been closed twice in all, the senate three times ordered to be closed while I was *princeps*.

XV.

To each man of the Roman *plebs* I paid 300 sesterces, in accordance with the last will of my father; and in my own name, when consul for the fifth time, I gave 500 sesterces from the spoils of the wars; again, moreover, in my tenth consulship, I gave from my own estate 400 sesterces to each man by way of congiarium; and in my eleventh consulship I twelve times made distributions of food, buying grain at my own expense; and in the twelfth year of my tribunitial power, I three times gave 400 sesterces to each man. These, my donations, have never been made to less than 250,000 men. In my twelfth consulship and the eighteenth year of my tribunitial power I gave 320,000 of the city plebs 60 denarii (about $12) apiece. In the colonies of my soldiers when consul for the fifth time, I gave to each man a thousand sesterces from the spoils; about 120,000 men in the colonies received that triumphal donation. When consul for the thirteenth time I gave 60 denarii to the plebs who were at that time receiving public grain; these men were a little more than 200,000.

XVII.

Four times I have aided the public treasury from my own means, to such extent that I have furnished to those in charge of the treasury 150,000,000 sesterces. And in the consulship of Marcus Lepidus and Lucius Arruntius I paid into the military treasury, which was established by my advice, that from it gratuities might be given to the soldiers who had served a term of twenty or more years, 170,000,000 sesterces from my own estate.

XVIII.

Beginning with that year in which Gnaeus and Publius Lentulus were consuls, when the imposts failed, I furnished aid sometimes to 100,000 men, and sometimes to more, by supplying grain or money for the tribute from my own land and property.

XIX.

I constructed the Curia, and the Chalcidicum adjacent thereto, the temple of Apollo on the Palatine, with its porticoes, the temple of the divine Julius, the Lupercal, the portico to the Circus of Flaminius, which I allowed to bear the name Portico Octavia, from his name who constructed the earlier one in the same place; the Pulvinar at the Circus Maximus, the temples of Jupiter the Vanquisher and Jupiter the Thunderer, on the Capitol, the temple of Quirinus, the temples of

Minerva and Juno Regina and of Jupiter Libertas, on the Aventine, the temple of the Lares on the highest point of the Via Sacra, the temple of the divine Penates on the Velian hill, the temple of Youth, and the temple of the Great Mother on the Palatine.

XX.

The Capitol and the Pompeian theatre have been restored by me at enormous expense for each work, without any inscription of my name. Aqueducts, which were crumbling in many places by reason of age, I have restored, and I have doubled the water, which bears the name Marcian, by turning a new spring into its course. The Forum Julian and the basilica, which was between the temple of Castor and the temple of Saturn, works begun and almost completed by my father, I have finished; and when that same basilica was consumed by fire, I began its reconstruction on an enlarged site, inscribing it with the names of my sons; and if I do not live to complete it, I have given orders that it be completed by my heirs. In accordance with a decree of the senate, while consul for the sixth time, I have restored 82 temples of the gods, passing over none which was at that time in need of repair. In my seventh consulship I constructed the Flaminian Way from the city to Ariminum, and all the bridges except the Mulvian and Minucian.

XXI.

Upon private ground I have built with the spoils of war the temple of Mars the Avenger, and the Augustan Forum. Besides the temple of Apollo, I built upon the ground, bought for the most part at my own expense, a theatre, to bear the name of Marcellus, my son-in-law. From the spoils of war I have consecrated gifts in the Capitol, and in the temple of the divine Julius, and in the temple of Apollo, and in the temple of Vesta, and in the temple of Mars the Avenger; these gifts have cost me about 100,000,000 sesterces. In my fifth consulship I remitted to the *municipia* and Italian colonies the thirty-five thousand pounds given me as coronary gold on the occasion of my triumphs, and thereafter, as often as I was proclaimed imperator, I did not accept the coronary gold, which the municipia and colonies voted me as kindly as before.

XXII.

Three times in my own name and five times in that of my sons or grandsons, I have given gladiatorial exhibitions; in these exhibitions about 10,000 men have fought. Twice in my own name, and three times in that of my grandson, I have offered the people the spectacle of athletes gathered from all quarters. I have celebrated games four times in my own name, and twenty-three times in the turns of magistrates. In behalf of the college of quindecemvirs, I, as master of the college, with my colleague Agrippa, celebrated the Secular Games.... Twenty-six times in my own name, or in that of my sons and grandsons, I have given hunts of African wild beasts in the circus, the forum, the amphitheatres, and about 35,000 beasts have been killed.

XXIII.

I gave the people the spectacle of a naval battle beyond the Tiber, where now is the grove of the Caesars. For this purpose an excavation was made 1,800 feet long, and 1,200 feet wide. In this contest 30 beaked ships, triremes or biremes, were engaged, besides more of smaller size. About 3,000 men fought in these vessels in addition to the rowers.

XXIV.

In the temples of all the cities in the provinces of Asia, I, as victor, replaced the ornaments of which he, with whom I was at war, had taken private possession when he despoiled the temples. Silver statues of me, on foot, on horseback, and in quadrigas, which stood in the city to the number of about 80, I removed, and out of their money value, I placed golden gifts in the temple of Apollo in my own name, and in the name of those who had offered me the honor of the statues.

XXV.

I freed the sea from pirates. In that war with the slaves I delivered to their masters for punishment about 30,000 slaves who had fled from their masters and taken up arms against the state. The whole of Italy voluntarily took the oath of allegiance to me, and demanded me as leader in that war in which I conquered at Actium. The provinces of Gaul, Spain, Africa, Sicily and Sardania swore the same allegiance to me. There were more than 700 senators who at that time fought under my standards, and among these, up to the day on which these words are written, 83 have, either before or since, been made consuls, and about 170 have been made priests.

XXVI.

I have extended the boundaries of all the provinces of the Roman people, which were bordered by nations not yet subjected to our sway. I have reduced to a state of peace the Gallic and Spanish provinces, and Germany, the lands enclosed by the ocean from Gades to the mouth of the Elbe. The Alps from the region nearest the Adriatic as far as the Tuscan sea, I have brought into a state of peace, without waging an unjust war upon any people. My fleet has navigated the ocean from the mouth of the Rhine as far as the boundaries of the Cimbri, where, before that time, no Roman had ever penetrated by land or sea. . . .

XXVII.

I have added Egypt to the empire of the Roman people. Of greater Armenia, when its king, Artaxes, was killed, I could have made a province, but I preferred to deliver that kingdom to Tigranes. .

XXVIII.

I have established colonies of soldiers in Africa, Sicily, Macedonia, the two Spains, Achaia, Asia, Syria, Gallia Narbonensis and Pisida. Italy has also 28 colonies established under my auspices, which, within my lifetime, have become very famous and populous.

XXIX.

I have recovered from Spain and Gaul, and from the Dalmatians, after conquering the enemy, many military standards which had been lost by other leaders. I have compelled the Parthians to give up to me the spoils and standards of three Roman armies, and as suppliants to seek the friendship of the Roman people. Those standards, moreover, I have deposited in the sanctuary, which is in the temple of Mars the Avenger.

In my sixth and seventh consulships, when I had put an end to the civil wars, after having obtained complete control of affairs by universal consent, I transferred the commonwealth from my own dominion to the authority of the senate and the Roman people. In return for this favor on my part I received, by decree of the senate, the title Augustus, the doorposts of my house were publicly decked with laurels, a civic crown was fixed above my door, and in the Julian Curia was placed a golden shield, which, by its inscription, bore witness that it was given to me by the senate and Roman people on account of my valor, clemency, justice and piety. After that time I excelled all others in dignity, but in power I held not more than those also held who were my colleagues in any magistracy.

XXXV.

While I was consul for the thirteenth time the senate and the equestrian order and the entire Roman people gave me the title of father of the fatherland, and decreed that it should be inscribed upon the vestibule of my house and in the Curia, and in the Augustan Forum beneath the quadriga which had been, by the decree of the senate, set up in my honor. When I wrote these words I was in my seventy-sixth year.[3]

[3] From the Pennsylvania Reprints, V. 5, 1898.

CHAPTER XVII.

ROME UNDER THE JULIAN PRINCES.

Augustus was succeeded by four princes related to his family and to the family of Julius Caesar; none were equal to either of these illustrious ancestors. Tiberius and Claudius ruled in accordance with the constitution; Caligula and Nero governed with the caprice of madmen—the first being merely capricious, the second, depraved.

In 14 A. D. Tiberius was called to Rome by the death of Augustus. He was now a man of fifty-five years, having already given thirty-eight years to the service of his country. It is quite impossible to judge correctly of his later life unless one takes into account the course of his earlier career, and it is impossible to understand the monster of whom Rome stood later in terror without following the sequence of events which evolved the monster.

In 22 B. C. he was appointed to take charge of the corn supply of Rome. Two years later, he went to Parthia to establish a new king upon the throne and to receive back standards previously taken by the Parthian army from the Romans. Not long after, he and his brother Drusus were dispatched to the northern frontiers, along the Rhine and Danube, to subdue the Germans and make sure this territory for Rome. This required hard fighting. In 9 B. C. Drusus was killed and the remainder of the conquest was conducted by Tiberius alone. Always sharing the soldiers' lot, never requiring of his men what he himself would not do, Tiberius was popular with the army. He was an able general and did much to Romanize this portion of the empire.

Like all the Claudian family, Tiberius was fine looking. He was, however, excessively sensitive, and was never able to mingle freely among men. His private life tended to make him even more sensitive and susceptible to adverse criticism. For reasons of state, Augustus compelled him to divorce his wife, whom he fondly loved, and marry Julia, Augustus' daughter. The misbehaviour of Julia was the comment of the age, and Tiberius found it very hard to face a scandal in his family. Moreover, upon the birth of his two sons, these were promptly adopted by Augustus as his heirs, while Tiberius was obliged to see himself passed by and preference given to his little children. Unable to bear humiliations longer in public life, he retired in 6 B. C. to the island of Rhodes. Here for ten years he lived in retirement. Even now he was not free from embarrassment, for Augustus lost no opportunity in showing his partiality for his grandsons. At length, wearying of quiet life, Tiberius expressed a desire to return to Rome, but he was at once informed that his presence at the capital was not desired. Conscious that he was closely watched, Tiberius had to be careful lest by misconstruction, some word or act might arouse the suspicions of the prince. However, the two grandsons died early in life, and in 4 A. D. Tiberius was needed to defend the frontiers. Probably he welcomed the change to army life, and found no greater dangers in the field than surrounded him at home.

Deprived of other heirs, Augustus was finally obliged to adopt Tiberius, although he did so rather ungraciously. During his life Tiberius was given tribunary powers, and was looked upon by all as Augustus' natural successor. In 14 A. D., upon the death of the first princeps, there was no rival to dispute Tiberius' succession.

Tiberius, however, was weary with long service and hostile criticism. There is probably no doubt but that he would have gladly escaped the assumption of princely duties had there been any apparent way of escape. The senate was in favor of bestowing absolute power upon him, but this he would not accept. Finding no way to shift state responsibilities, Tiberius accepted the office of Prince of the Roman people which the senate conferred upon him, and took up the administration where Augustus had left it.

No page in provincial history is more gratifying than that devoted to the age of Tiberius. He was the first to point out that Rome had some obligations in regard to her provincial possessions—that in exchange for tribute or taxes, she ought to insure good administration. He put an end to the farming out of taxes and made towns directly responsible for their own share of the tax. Again, until this time the nobles had regarded the provinces as spoils, to be passed around from one to another. It naturally took a man some little time to become familiar with his duties as governor, and no sooner had he grown accustomed to the province he was appointed to govern, than he was sent elsewhere, while the territory became the charge of another. Naturally, it was the provincials who paid dearly for such a policy. Tiberius largely ended this rotation of office. He made comparatively few changes, and proconsuls were left in control during good behavior.

In connection with his attitude toward the provinces, the following instances may be cited: An earthquake occurred in Asia, destroying whole towns and leaving a large number of people without homes. Immediately, from his own funds and those of the state, Tiberius sent aid to the stricken districts. Such an action was unprecedented in Roman colonial history.

Tiberius found the state treasury empty, and he left it full. Nor were heavier taxes imposed; in some instances they were lightened. To be sure, Augustus' tremendous building enterprises had made heavy inroads upon the national funds.

Sejanus was appointed by the new prince as Praefect of the Praetorian Guards, and his disposition toward duties of government caused Tiberius gradually to shift many affairs of state to him. He gave such faithful attention to responsibilities and proved himself so efficient withal, that presently Tiberius retired to the isle of Capri, leaving Sejanus in a position comparable to that of a modern prime minister. His confidence, so thoroughly given, was most basely betrayed. Suddenly, like a thunderbolt from a clear sky, Tiberius was made aware of a bold plot on the part of the praefect to dispose of him and establish Sejanus in his place. After a life of disappointment and humiliation, wherein little had fallen to awaken confidence and trust, he had now to face the most disillusionizing betrayal of faith, and the strain proved too great. Tiberius became almost mad, taking delight in the punishment of those who had plotted against him. Sejanus and his companions were put to death, and a series of investigations were begun by the senate with a view to ascertaining what nobles had been implicated in the plot. Instead of having prosecutions regularly conducted, as they are at the present time, anyone in Rome was at liberty to enter complaint against his neighbor. Since rewards were given for information leading to the conviction of any who had aided Sejanus, the most atrocious crimes were committed. Slaves fabricated stories about their masters, thus gaining their freedom, and often, some share in their property. Families divided, and unscrupulous ones invented reports which would compromise others. Hearings were made before the senate, but each senator was so afraid lest any leniency he might show would be interpreted as personal interest in the plot, that death-sentences were promptly given, even where the guilt of him accused was by no means proven. A reign of terror followed the downfall of Sejanus and ceased only with the death of Tiberius.

In spite of all this, however, only the upper class in the city of Rome was concerned. In the provinces, the administration of government went on justly, as before. The reign of Tiberius, which was viewed with such dismay by the nobles in Rome, was regarded by the provincials as an unalloyed blessing. Even in the capital itself, only the aristocracy was affected by the reign of terror. For the common people, life went on as before.

It is charitable to pass over Tiberius' closing years with little comment. Many were responsible for making him the sort of being he became, and when the end grew near, there can be no doubt that it was received with thanksgiving in Rome. Caligula had been designated by Tiberius as his successor, and no rival opposed his claim.

Caligula had been trained by Antonia, daughter of Mark Antony; and several oriental princes, while being educated in Rome, were his boyhood companions.

There is no doubt but that he was molded by Eastern influence while his ideas were taking definite form. For awhile all promised well. Caligula was delighted with the praise and honors bestowed upon him. But his judgment soon gave way. He probably wished to restore the government of Julius Caesar —setting aside the examples of Augustus and Tiberius, to make himself an absolute ruler after the fashion of the Orient. To this end he commanded that he should be worshipped as a god, at once, during his lifetime. Hitherto the princes had been worshipped only after death. Caligula connected his palace with the temple of Jupiter, since he also was divine.

Considerable trouble was brought on with the Jews because of Caligula's attitude toward his own divinity. It was against the Hebrew teaching to offer sacrifices to any but the one God. The Jews insisted that they sacrificed *for* the emperor—but not *to* him. This was not enough to satisfy Caligula, and but for the intercession of Agrippa, king of the Jews and once a boyhood companion, a religious war would have broken out in the empire.

It would be folly to follow all the caprices of Caligula. Like Julius Caesar, he filled the senate with all kinds of people, greatly augmenting its membership. He also conceived of the world-conquest idea, and fitted out a great expedition against Britain. The preparations were so great and the results so small that the whole thing was absurd. Fortunately for Rome, Caligula's unsettled mind remained at the head of affairs but four years.

In 41 A. D. Claudius succeeded Caligula. He was the brother of Germanicus, a famous Roman general. In his childhood Claudius had suffered from a disease which caused his body to develop abnormally. He had always been kept in the background, and while the soldiers were ransacking the royal palace at will, after Caligula's death, he was found hiding behind a curtain. The soldiers carried him out to their camp and the army proclaimed him imperator. The senate did not consider him fit to rule, but it was notorious now that the army, not the senate, was strong enough to name the emperor.

Although Claudius was inexperienced, and, because of his failings, had always been withheld from public life, he nevertheless ruled far better than anyone would have imagined. He kept the example of Augustus ever before him and emulated him so far as possible. The government of the provinces was carefully supervised and many improvements were made in Rome. One of the most picturesque ruins in Rome today is the Claudian aqueduct, which this emperor constructed to bring water many miles, in order to supply Rome with pure water. In his personal vanity, in his devotion to literature, and in several other respects, Claudius might well be compared with James I. of England.

Upon the death of Claudius in 54 A. D., Nero was proclaimed ruler by the army. He was a grandson of the great Germanicus. During his early years the management of affairs was left almost wholly to Seneca and Burrhus, while Nero devoted himself to his love affairs and to various sorts of amusement. He was naturally gifted in an artistic way, and some of his caprices are attributable to his artistic susceptibility. Upon the death of Burrhus and retirement of Seneca, the course of affairs underwent a change. The treasury, thus far sufficient, was drained to provide amusements for the people and the prince. The easiest way of replenishing it was to confiscate the property of some wealthy citizen. Since life was at the will and disposition of the emperor, no one felt himself secure, and many were summarily disposed of and their property seized.

During the reign of Nero, some small shops accidentally caught fire, and, owing to a fierce wind, the flames rapidly spread through the city, until out of fourteen wards, four alone escaped injury. Nero was out of the city at the time, but because he had often expressed dissatisfaction at the narrow streets of Rome, the rumor spread abroad that the city was burned by his command. Then different people remembered that his servants and officers had been seen moving about in the burning districts, which was quite true; they had been trying to stay the ravages of the flames. Instead of meeting the foolish accusation and disclaiming any part in the conflagration, Nero looked around for some scapegoat and found it in the Christians, a despised group of people, who were very unpopular because they refused to conform to the requirements of the Roman faith. Nero was too much of an artist to allow the city to be rebuilt upon the old plan, and his care in supervising its reconstruction gave color to the story that he had planned the fire.

Believing himself to be gifted as a poet and musician, Nero performed frequently before audiences which were wise enough to appreciate him. However, he believed that the Greeks alone could fully understand ability such as his, and he toured Greece one summer, playing before many a wondering audience. He was suddenly recalled by one of his ministers because of the growing discontent in Italy. The army now made and unmade emperors. It was composed at this time of Italians, and these cared less about Nero's scandalous conduct in Rome than his undignified appearance touring Greece as a fiddler. Tacitus says that in the year 68 A. D. a new discovery was made—that not alone the praetorian guards, but the army as well, could make emperors, and that not alone in Rome, but wherever they happened to be stationed. When this idea got abroad, it was bound to work great havoc. The army proclaimed Galba emperor, and Nero, learning that a price had been put upon his head, took his own life.

"If we would get a correct idea of the Roman world under the Julian line, we must distinguish between the character of the emperors and the condition of the empire. When we consider the severe and tyrannical methods of Tiberius, the wild vagaries of Caligula, the weakness and timidity of Claudius, and the cruelty and wickedness of Nero, we can find little to admire in the personal character of these princes. But when we turn from the princes themselves to the world over which they professed to rule, we find that the empire itself was little affected by their peculiarities. While the palace and the capital may have presented scenes of intrigue and bloodshed, the world in general was peaceful and prosperous. This condition of things was no doubt due to the thoroughness of the work done by the great founders of the empire, Julius and Augustus. The imperial system, which had for its purpose the welfare of the people, was not overthrown. The empire prospered in spite of the emperors. But it should be said that when the emperors or their advisers seriously considered the needs of the empire at all, they generally followed the policy of Augustus, and when they were oblivious of these needs, the world moved peacefully on without their aid."

CHAPTER XVIII.

The Flavian Emperors.

Upon hearing that Galba had been accepted by the Praetorian Guards as imperator, Nero had inflicted a wound upon himself that caused his death. For two years following, civil war waged in Rome. Opportunity for anarchy at the close of each reign was given because no definite law of succession was recognized. To be sure, it was theoretically the duty of the senate to name the succeeding prince, but since the time of Tiberius the Praetorian Guards had simply set aside this senatorial privilege by proclaiming the prince themselves. Now the armies in the provinces felt that they, as well as the Praetorians, were able to name the prince, but the question was, which army would prove most powerful? The army in Spain proclaimed Galba; the Praetorian Guards chose Otho as their leader; the army of the Rhine declared in favor of Vitellius; and the army in Syria and the East put forward their general, Vespasian.

Upon the immediate accession of Galba, no rivals appeared at once. Galba, however, was an old man, crippled with the gout. Even the soldiers who supported him were not particularly enthusiastic about him, and he estranged the Romans at once by his attitude toward games, races and gladiatorial shows. He soon showed plainly that he was greatly under the influence of three favorites. The army of the Rhine refused allegiance, while the Praetorians came forward with Otho.

While Rome was torn by factions, espousing now one, now another candidate, Vespasian was being urged by his soldiers and his son to come to the front and make himself first in the empire. He proceeded cautiously at first, but finally his son Titus proclaimed him as Nero's successor. His name having been compromised in this way, he saw the need of definite action. The praefect of Egypt put the corn supply of Rome in his hands, and when the granaries of the city were within ten days' of famine, Vespasian went to Rome, driving out the candidate supported by the armies of the north and establishing himself as prince in 69 A. D.

Four lessons had been taught by these two years of civil war: first, that the rural strength of the empire lay in the army; second, that the armies of the provinces would no longer stand quietly by while the Praetorian Guards named the prince; third, family connections were no longer vital, since the man who at last succeeded in making himself supreme came from humble origin; and lastly, military renown was to be the road to power.

Vespasian was primarily a man of the people. He had no proud name to live up to; he preferred his simple home to the gayeties of the court. An able, upright man, he was so economical in his tastes and so guarded in his expenditures from state funds, that numerous stories were circulated by those who disliked him to show that he was extremely penurious. Many of them were doubtless true. Vespasian found an empty treasury. He governed wisely and left many splendid evidences of architectural beauty to perpetuate his name in Rome. To accomplish his purposes without inflicting heavy taxes, it was necessary that expenditures be carefully supervised.

Two revolts occurred during this administration—one in Gaul and one in Asia. Civilis, a Gallic chief, thought the time opportune to rally the Germanic nations to regain their independence. Most of the soldiers had been recalled from the northern frontier during the period of civil strife, and it was thought possible that those who remained might join with the Germans. This revolt was not serious, since the Gauls were quickly won back to Rome and the German tribes, as a whole, did not participate in the revolt.

In Syria a war with the Jews had been some time in progress. While Nero lived he had sent Vespasian into the East to put down a Jewish revolt, caused by general dissatisfaction with the provincial administration. It will be remembered that Caligula had very nearly precipitated a religious war by insisting that his statue should be set up in the Jewish temple for worship. Owing to the intercession of Agrippa, and to the wisdom of the proconsul of Syria, a break did not occur at this time. However, the Jews were hated by the Romans because they proved such an obstinate race and were so unyielding in their attitude toward the customs of others. Their province had been repeatedly plundered by the Roman governors, and at last the people rose up in rebellion. Vespasian had put down the trouble except in the city of Jerusalem. When he departed for Rome, he left the siege of that city to the management of his son, Titus. The siege lasted seven months, and the Jews carried on a defense that was greatly out of proportion to their numbers. At last, however, greater numbers of Roman soldiers, as well as superior machines for attacking the walls, resulted in the destruction of Jerusalem. Titus, it is said, wanted to spare the temple, and several times offered to show mercy if the Jews would yield, but many refused to do so. At last the fury of the soldiers knew no bounds and the slaughter and destruction of the city was fearful. Every stone was removed and the people taken captives to Rome. Only a handful remained of these who earlier had fought for their temple and their homes. A splendid triumph was celebrated by the victorious Titus. The spoils of many cities passed before the wondering people, followed by trains of captives. Various scenes from the besieged city were pictured before the Roman crowds. Finally, and most disheartening to the mournful Jews, the sacred possessions of the temple—vessels for the sacrifices, the golden table for the shew-bread, and the candlestick, were paraded before the eyes of the Gentiles.

"That triumph, earned with more toil and peril than any one perhaps of the three hundred and twenty which had preceded it, has been rendered memorable to posterity by monuments still existing. Even in the confusion of the storm and the conflagration, some of the choicest ornaments of the temple may have been seized and saved by the conquerors. Many of them had, perhaps, been hidden by pious hands before the last crisis of disaster. But after the capture of the city, certain priests emerging from their hiding-places had saved their own lives by delivering the treasures they secreted. The sacred furniture of the Holy Place was borne before the Imperators to the Capitol—the candlestick with seven branches, the golden table, the trumpets which announced the year of Jubilee, the Book of the Law and the Vessel of Incense. When, some years later, an arch was erected to commemorate the victory of Titus, these illustrious trophies were sculptured upon it, with figures of Jewish captives surmounted by an emblem of the victor's apotheosis. These witnesses to the truth of the history are scanned at this day by Christians passing to and fro between the Coliseum and the forum."[1]

Vespasian's age was characterized by peace and general content. To be sure, there was merely a pretense of government by the people any longer, but, on the other hand, those who years before had held tenaciously to the republican forms, had passed away. Their places were taken by many who owed their positions to the favor of the prince; naturally, therefore, they were inclined to support his measures and to approve, as a rule, of his administration. With the exception of fifteen years, during the rule of Domitian, the prince and the nobles were in harmony. The provinces were well governed, generally speaking, and at home much was done to beautify Rome. The Coliseum today, in its ruins, testifies to the gigantic building enterprise of Vespasian.

Titus had been associated with his father in the government for several years, and when Vespasian died in 79 A. D., no break occurred in civil affairs. The vast majority of the people were unaware of any change in the course of Roman life. There was little difference in the character of the two administrations, save, indeed, that Titus was more lavish in his expenditures than his economical father. A destructive fire occurred in Rome during the two years Titus reigned, but of far greater importance was the destruction of Pompeii and Herculaneum, caused by an eruption of Mount Vesuvius. The two cities were completely covered by the ashes and lava that poured out from the burning crater. These enclosed the towns, and shutting out air and action of the elements, thus preserved the ruined cities, which have only in the last few years been revealed by the spade of the excavator. Great light has been thrown upon the life of antiquity by articles recovered in Pompeii.

Titus was succeeded by his brother, Domitian. Although of the Flavian family, Domitian was wholly unlike his father

[1] Merivale: Roman Empire, V. 6, 471.

and his brother. Naturally moody, he became oppressive and harsh when power passed into his hands. He wished to renew the military activities but lacked sufficient military skill to accomplish his desires. A successful expedition was made into Britain by his able general, Agricola, but his own expedition against the Germans proved a failure, and when he led an army in the direction of the Danube to quell an uprising, he accomplished so little that stories of victory had to be fabricated to satisfy the citizens of Rome. In course of time the truth was known and Domitian's later years were clouded by his military failures.

In his efforts to raise the moral tone of Rome he was no more fortunate. Angered by his failure to accomplish his purpose in this regard, he revived the methods of Tiberius, resorting to illegal arrests and trials and confiscating the property of those he wrongfully put to death. In the fifteenth year of his reign he was murdered by one of his servants.

Great social changes had come about in Rome. There had been a strong tendency to break away from the old class distinctions. The prince was no longer of necessity from an old Roman family. The accession of the Flavians had shown that family connections were not essential. The friends of the prince, naturally, were those to whom he had been previously attached, and those to whom he chose to give positions of influence. The senatorial class remained, but senators, like the friends of the ruler were men put forward by him because of wealth or special ability evinced by them. The great mass of people included the professional class, the tradesmen, artisans and farmers. These possessed equality with those of the upper class. Finally there was a large slave class, whose general condition was better than it had been during the late republic.

ARCH OF TITUS (ROME).

CHAPTER XIX.

FIVE GOOD PRINCES; THE DECLINE OF THE PRINCIPATE.

Upon the death of Domitian in 96 A. D., the army had no candidate, so the senate was allowed to elect the prince. Its choice was Nerva, a man about sixty-five years of age. His reign was marked by a return to the administration of Vespasian and Titus. Nerva at once abolished the system of illegal arrests and trials, revived by Domitian, recalling those whom the last prince had sent into banishment. Excessive taxes were removed and the peace and prosperity which had characterized the early principate came again, to the gratification of the Romans. The senate was restored to the dignity which had been wholly impaired by the crimes of Domitian. Funds were provided for sending colonies of the idle from Rome to country districts, where industry might restore men to usefulness and self-respect. The treasury had been drained during the previous rule, and the economy of Nerva would not allow large sums to be expended in mere pastimes for the city mobs.

It soon became apparent to Nerva that his health was no longer equal to the task of holding the legions and Praetorian Guards in check, so he took as his colleague a man who was high in command on the German frontier. Having associated Trajan with him in the government, Nerva died, after ruling but sixteen months.

Trajan was by birth a Spaniard. His succession to the principate marked an end of that sharp distinction between Italians and provincials, which Augustus had endeavored so long to maintain. He waited until his authority had been recognized by the legions and came to Rome in 99 A. D. Two years were spent in superintending the affairs at home. Special care was taken to revive and preserve the old forms of the republic. The senate was treated with marked consideration, and the people were allowed to elect their own magistrates for the first time since the rule of Tiberius. In one regard Trajan departed from the policy of Augustus, whose example he generally followed. He abandoned the frontier policy and extended the territory of Rome, giving the state a military character it had not assumed since the days of Julius Caesar. Dacia, the country north of the Danube, was subdued and made a Roman province.

"Still he was not content; year after year he poured Roman colonists, builders and artisans of every sort into the country; bridges, roads and fortresses, towns, temples and baths grew up on every side, so that within one generation the land was transformed into a completely Romanized province. Thenceforth Dacia, a land more than a thousand miles in circumference, lay as a barrier against the rapidly advancing German hordes; and the province which Trajan had created stood for a century and a half as a buffer against the northern barbarians."[1]

To commemorate this great victory, a monument was given Rome. "To find room for it a space was cleared on the high ridge which ran between the Capitoline and Quirinal hills. Within this space a new forum was laid out, and the skill of Apollodorus, the great designer of the age, was taxed to adorn it worthily. At the entrance rose the triumphal arch, of which some of the statuary and bas-reliefs may still be seen in the arch of Constantine, although disfigured by the tasteless additions of a later age. Opposite was built the great basilica, one of the covered colonnades which served then for an exchange and law-court. In the center of the forum, as in the place of honor, was a statue of the emperor on horseback. All around in every corner were statues and warlike emblems of the conquest, to which the later emperors added in their turn, till art sunk under Constantine too low to do more than spoil the ornaments which it borrowed. Close by was the great library, rich above all others in statute law and jurisprudence, and graced with the busts of all the undying dead in art and literature and science.

"Far above all towered Trajan's famous column, the height of which, 128 feet in all, marked the quantity of earth which had been cleared away below the level of the hill in the place

---

[1] Wolfson: Essentials in Ancient History, 423.

of which the forum stood. Twenty-three blocks of marble only are piled upon each other to make up the column's shaft, round which winds in spiral form the long series of sculptured groups, which give us at once a lively portraiture of the details of Roman warfare and all the special incidents of the Dacian campaigns. Though we have often little clue to time or place or actual circumstance, still we can follow from the scenes before us the invading army on the march, see them cross each river on their bridge of boats, force their way through rock and forest, storm and burn the strongholds of the enemy, and bring the spoils of war to grace the triumph of their leader. We can distinguish the trousered Dacians with their belted tunics, skirmishing outside their quarters, over which flies the national symbol of the dragon. We see them sue for pardon with their outstretched hands, or wend their way in sad procession from their homes, with wives and children, flocks and herds, turning their backs upon their devastated country, or when driven like wild beasts to bay, crowd round the poisoned goblet and roll in the agonies of death upon the ground.

"This monument, the crowning glory of the splendid forum, is left to us well-nigh unscathed by the ravages of time, save that the gilding and the colours have faded almost wholly from the sculpture, and that Trajan's statue, which once took its stand by natural right upon the top, has been replaced by that of the Apostle *Paul."[2]

Seven years of peace followed, wherein Trajan gave attention to the government of Rome and the provinces. During the disordered rule of Domitian, officers had taken advantage of the times to make their salaries off those they governed. Fixed salaries put an end to this oppression. New roads to various parts of Italy aided the work of administration. Aqueducts, baths and theatres were built in Rome.

For two centuries it had been the policy of the city to provide grain for free distribution among thousands of idle. The policy had been adhered to through no spirit of charity, but rather, to keep the rabble quiet. To provide sufficient supply, those provinces which were grain-producing were required to

[2]Capes: The Age of the Antonines, 38.
*This is a statue of Peter instead of Apostle Paul.

pay their taxes in grain and were forbidden to sell it in other than Italian ports. Officials at Rome had arbitrarily fixed a price for it, and altogether interfered with the natural law of supply and demand. Trajan abandoned this policy and left natural conditions to work out their own results.

In 114 A. D. an expedition was made against the Parthians. This was followed by great success to the Roman arms, and armies penetrated beyond the Tigris-Euphrates. Trajan himself died while commanding this campaign, leaving the largest empire Rome ever knew. From Scotland to the deserts of Africa, from the Atlantic to the Euphrates the name of Rome was supreme.

In 117 A. D. Hadrian became prince of the Roman people. He was well fitted to rule. He saw at once that Rome's greatness could not depend upon military power alone, and he promptly abandoned any territories won beyond the Euphrates valley. Thorough administration of territory which was unquestionably Roman was the task Hadrian set himself, and, regarding Rome as merely the capital of a mighty empire, he spent the greater portion of his time elsewhere, looking after the welfare of his subjects.

Hadrian had been named by the Praetorian Guards as Trajan's successor, but he insisted that his election be ratified by the senate—thus indicating his intention to rule in a constitutional manner. No Roman prince ever gave himself more completely to the work of ministering to his people than did he, living temporarily in many cities that he might become the more familiar with conditions common to each. A series of garrisons were planted along the northern frontier, and a wall was erected by this ambitious imperator to protect Britain from northern invasions. So long away from Rome, Hadrian was better loved in the provinces than at the capital. His last years were stained by excesses, which one is inclined to pass by out of consideration for his long continued rule of peace.

A mausoleum was constructed by Hadrian for his final resting place. "A stately bridge across the Tiber, in the neighborhood of the Campus Martius, decked with a row of statues on each side, was made to serve as a road of state to lead to the great tower in which his ashes were to lie. Above the tower stood out to view the groups of statuary, whose beauty moved the wonder of travellers of later days; within was a sepulchral chamber, in a niche of which was stored the urn which contained all that the flames had left of Hadrian. The tower was built of masonry almost as solid as the giant piles of Egypt, and with the bridge it has outlived the wreck of ages. For almost a century it served only to enshrine the dust of emperors, but afterwards it was used for other ends, and became a fortress, a papal residence, a prison. When the Goths were storming Rome, the tide of war rolled up against the mausoleum, and when all else failed, the statues which adorned it were torn from their pedestals by the besieged, and flung down upon their enemies below. Some few were found long centuries after, almost unhurt, among the ruins, and may be still seen in the great galleries of Europe. The works of art have disappeared with the gates of bronze and with the lining of rich marble which covered it within, and after ages have done little to it save to replace the triumphal statue of the builder with the figure of the Archangel Michael, whom a Pope saw in his vision sheathing his sword, in token that the plague was stayed, above the old tower that has since been called the castle of St. Angelo." [3]

In 138 A. D. Antoninus Pius became prince of the Roman people. Although he ruled until 161, his reign has been called uneventful. The prosperity of later years attended him; no serious wars disturbed the country and at home life went on as it had for many years. Because so little of importance occurred during Antoninus' age, we know comparatively little about him. His was a simple nature, refined, calm and kindly, devoted to the interests of the people and the welfare of his country.

In 161 A. D. Marcus Aurelius succeeded. He was a philosopher as well as a statesman, and his "Meditations" embody the highest expression of Stoicism. While in every way an able man, quite the equal of his predecessors, his age was harassed with troubles of various kinds. On all sides the frontiers were assailed and Marcus Aurelius, naturally a man of peace, was forced to live in camp during the greater portion of his

[3]Capes: The Age of the Antonines, 74.

later life. It has often been pointed out that his persecution of the Christians was the only stain upon his name. His attitude in this regard can be understood only when it is viewed, not from the standpoint of the Christian, but the Roman.

"The century from the accession of Vespasian to the death of Marcus Aurelius is a century of the greatest prosperity in all antiquity. Men were at last content to live under the imperial government without opposing its head. Even in the reign of Domitian the provinces prospered, though discontent was rife in the city; and from the death of Domitian to the death of Antoninus Pius, all was peace and contentment within the empire. Though Trajan carried the Roman arms into lands far removed from the center of the empire, his wars resulted in nothing but good; and when he died, there began an era of peace such as the ancient world had never known before. The reign of Marcus Aurelius marks a transition to other times; though a man of the same type as Hadrian and Antoninus Pius, he was forced by the growing pressure of the German tribes to spend most of his days in the field. If his reign was less prosperous than those of his predecessors, it was not because of any lack in himself, but because disintegrating forces were already at work within the empire."[4]

After the death of Marcus Aurelius, civil war destroyed the peace which had so long blessed the empire. One man after another was brought forward by the legions, only to be destroyed by them when he failed to carry out their desires. During the 104 years intervening between the death of Marcus Aurelius and the accession of Diocletian, twenty-nine men were put up by the legions as emperors. Of these, some few were capable, clear-sighted men, but the great majority were weak, wholly unable to cope with the problems before them.

Various influences combined to produce the anarchy that ruled in the Roman empire. No law of succession being recognized, unrest harassed the country at the close of each reign. Sometimes this trouble was averted by the naming of a successor by the dying prince, but even so, there was always question as to whether his choice would be acceptable to the soldiers.

The German tribes which had disturbed the reign of Mar-

[4] Wolfson: 429.

cus Aurelius continued to assail the frontiers, and a policy of allowing them to come peacefully into the empire and settle unappropriated lands grew up. Not only were the northern boundaries attacked, but the Parthians on the east and tribes upon each borderland began to press against the frontiers which had long held them at bay. This restlessness was to end only after long years of invasions and centuries of readjustment in Europe.

General after general was proclaimed imperator by the legions. All but four died in revolts. With frequent changes in the headship, administration suffered throughout the realm. The capital was no longer in Rome, but wherever the camp of the present imperator was pitched. Lack of consolidated strength lessened the defense of the empire and aided the assailing barbarians. Trade was no longer secure; taxes grew heavier each year and industry was crushed out. Not only did commerce decline but the population itself diminished rapidly.

One act of importance during the period of the so-called "barrack emperors" was the extension of Roman citizenship to every free man in the empire. While we note the anarchy and disorder that prevailed, we must nevertheless keep in mind the fact that Roman civilization had been widely diffused and was still spreading throughout the known world.

CHAPTER XX.

The Reforms of Diocletian and Constantine

The third century witnessed the utter prostration of government in the Roman empire. Internal and external wars afflicted the land. The principate during this century was a failure. The election of the prince and the independence of the armies were responsible for this condition. There had come to be four separate armies—the army of the Rhine, of the Danube, of the Euphrates and the army of Rome, or the Praetorian Guards. Each had grown to think that it had interests apart from the rest. Four centers of control arose, instead of one. Not only had these conditions resulted in many rulers who attempted within a few years to gain supremacy, but often two or three were ruling at the same time.

Such a collapse of authority brought about a speedy decline in the standards of culture. The effect of the accompanying wars was terrible upon the 50,000,000 people who dwelt within the empire. All districts were pillaged by fast succeeding armies; hardships were great and industry died out. Uncertainty of life and prosperity made men indifferent to matters of lesser importance. Commerce was crushed out by excessive taxes. Altogether, it would be difficult to find a more depressing picture than that presented by the third century of the Christian era.

In 285 A. D., Diocletian gained possession of the principate. Having overcome all opposition, he stood forth as the most powerful man in the Roman empire. Understanding the danger that would still threaten Rome upon the death of the imperator under the existing system, he determined to give each army a leader, as had long been desired. He associated with himself another, one Maximian, who possessed power second only to his own. These two Augusti, as they were called, controlled civil affairs, one in the East, the other in the West. At the same time two Caesars were appointed to supervise the military affairs. Constantius was chosen as the Caesar of Maximian; Galerius, a rough soldier who had proved his efficiency on the field of battle, became the Caesar of Diocletian.

Diocletian found the provinces large. Because he saw plainly that this allowed ambitious governors to gain unwonted power, he divided the provinces into smaller districts. Whereas Gaul had previously been divided into six provinces, Diocletian left it in fifteen; whereas Egypt had comprised but one province, it was separated into six. Similarly, each was cut up into several districts. Moreover, the armies were no longer at the command of the proconsuls, but were rather massed under the four rulers—the two Augusti and the two Caesars.

Hitherto the princes who followed the example of Augustus Caesar had been content with worship after death. To be sure, Caligula had brought the country very close to civil war when he insisted that the Jews should erect his statue in their temples, and Nero had likewise sought deification during life. However, these rulers had temporarily set aside the principate and for the time brought in the customs of Persia. The case was somewhat different with Diocletian. He thought that the imperator had hitherto been too little reverenced. Worship of the prince would tend to exalt him, and Diocletian caused the idea to be carried out for this reason. Everything which tended to elevate the prince, to set him apart from other men, was to be eagerly adopted and developed. It is significant to note also that a god would be above any constitution—the mere instrument of men.

A god should be suitably arrayed. A regal robe of purple, ornamented with pearls and precious stones, was consequently donned. It was left for Constantine to add the diadem. This kingly apparel so evolved, has been adopted in some modified form by monarchs since the age of Diocletian.

A prince who was addressed as " thy divinity," was worshipped as a god, and wore garments befitting one of such exalted state, ought of necessity to be withdrawn from the easy approach of men. This resulted in the creation of a court, organized in a somewhat military fashion. This conception of a court, as well as the regal robes, has been perpetuated by modern sovereigns. In these ways Diocletian departed wholly from the example of the first prince, who took great care to give himself no mark distinguishing him from any other noble in Rome.

During the time of the republic it had been the custom for a man to spend some time in frontier service, in military life, before he settled down to a magistrate's career at home. In course of time men lost their taste for frontier service, and a legal training took the place of the earlier military experience required of candidates for office. At the same time, men for command in the army were taken from the ranks. This opened a new career to the soldier, as one might start from the bottom and gradually receive promotion. The Germans were fond of fighting, and they grew to make up quite a portion of the Roman army. This opportunity for advancement allowed them, moreover, to reach positions of highest responsibility. Diocletian made his praetorian guard a training body for commands on the frontiers. He withdrew the legions from the frontiers, leaving mere detachments to police the borders. The four armies were massed at the capitals of the Augusti and the Caesars. By thus removing the military command from the provincial governors and by lessening the territory over which any one governor had civil authority, danger of uprisings on the part of ambitious proconsuls was removed.

During the third century a large number of coins had come into use and metal was lessened in them as the alloy increased. Gold quite generally disappeared, while silver coins contained much copper. Of course it quickly came about that the purchasing power of money fell. This made it necessary to require provinces to pay tribute in kind rather than money. An *annona,* or the pay of a soldier, became the basis of computation. Diocletian did not understand economic causes and effects as they are today understood. He noticed that his soldiers were required to pay much more money for supplies than had formerly been the case. Failing to see that this was the natural result of the depreciation of coinage, he attempted to establish an arbitrary scale of prices, which should be binding alike, on the buyer and seller. When no one would longer sell, and business came to a standstill, he was obliged to abandon his position and let matters take their natural course.

Desiring to unite his empire into a consolidated state, Diocletian continued the persecutions of the Christians, who seemed to be forming a state within a state. This effort will be noted again in the chapter on Early Christianity.

In 303 Diocletian visited Rome and celebrated a triumph. This was his only visit to the city. It was then agreed that when he and his colleague had reigned twenty years they should resign in favor of their Caesars. This plan was actually carried out, but instead of allowing the sons of the Caesars to fill the places their promotions left vacant, others were chosen for them. This gave opportunity for civil strife again, and only in 313 A. D. did Constantine put down the rivals and become prince of Rome.

Constantine was undoubtedly a great statesman. He at once abolished the four centers of power created by Diocletian, making himself the sole ruler of the empire. He continued the ceremony and pomp of Diocletian's court, and added certain contributions of his own. Like his able predecessor, he continued to divide the provinces, making the territory of each governor comparatively small. The only objection to this and to the elaborate court system was the great number of state employees now dependent upon the revenues for support. Taxes were of necessity heavy where three men did the amount of work hitherto done by one, and became a grievous burden to the people.

Constantine abolished the praetorian guards, believing that they constituted a constant menace to the government. He was himself a good general, and a triumphal arch still stands in Rome, testifying to one of his victories.

Unlike his predecessors, Constantine was friendly to the Christian religion There was already a strong element in the realm espousing this faith, and it was a diplomatic stroke to grant toleration to the Christians.

Rome was so thoroughly associated with the history of ancient worship that Constantine felt that never could he give Christianity sufficient prominence here as a favored religion. Moreover, for other reasons he desired to found a new capital, which should be located more centrally for both east and west than was Rome. He chose as a site for his new city a spot once settled by a Greek colony, and known as Byzantium.

"Constantine, with all the Roman world at his feet, and all its responsibilities weighing on his mind, was far too able a man to overlook the great need of the day—a more conveniently placed administrative and military center for his empire. He required a place that should be easily accessible by land and sea—which Rome had never been, in spite of its wonderful roads—that should overlook the Danube lands, without being too far away from the East; that should be so strongly situated that it might prove an impregnable arsenal and citadel against barbarian attacks from the North, that should at the same time be far enough away from the turmoil of the actual frontier to afford a safe and splendid residence for the imperial court.

"Byzantium was thoroughly well known to Constantine. For months his camp had been pitched beneath its walls; he must have known accurately every inch of its environs, and none of its military advantages can have missed his eye. Nothing, then, could have been more natural than this selection for his new capital. Yet the Roman world was startled at the first news of his choice; Byzantium had been so long known merely as a great port of call for the Euxine trade, and as a first-class provincial fortress, that it was hard to conceive of it as a destined seat of empire.

"The southeastern part of the old town was chosen by Constantine for the site of his imperial palace. The spot was cleared of all private dwellings for a space of 150 acres, to give space not only for a magnificent residence for his whole court, but for spacious gardens and pleasure-grounds.

"To fill the vast limits of his city, Constantine invited many senators of Old Rome and many rich provincial proprietors of Greece and Asia to take up their abode in it, granting them places in his new senate and sites for the dwellings they would require. The countless officers and functionaries of the imperial court, with their subordinates and slaves, must have composed a very considerable element in the new population. The artisans and handicraftsmen were enticed in thousands by the offer of special privileges. Merchants and seamen had always abounded at Byzantium, and now flocked in numbers, which made the old commercial prosperity of the city seem insignificant. Most effective—though most demoralizing—of the gifts which Constantine bestowed on the new capital to attract immigrants was the old Roman privilege of free distribution of corn to the populace. The wheat-tribute of Egypt, which had previously formed part of the public provisions of Rome, was transferred to the use of Constantinople, only the African corn from Carthage being for the future assigned for the subsistence of the older city."[1]

[1] Oman: Story of the Byzantine Empire, 16.

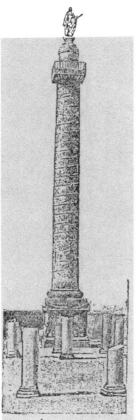

TRAJAN'S COLUMN TO-DAY.

CHAPTER XXI.

Early Christianity.

The history of Christianity begins with Christ, the founder of the faith. Given first to the Hebrews, it spread through them to the Greeks and Romans. Each of the three nations contributed something to the new religion, which by the fifth century had assumed a definite form and scope.

Christ was a Jew. We do not know just what were all his teachings, for he left no writings, and nothing was committed to writing by his followers until some time after his death. While there exists no complete record of his teachings today, yet we know much of his wonderful personality, which the greatest students of Christianity admit to be the essence of the faith. It was this striking personality which gave such a pulse of life to his teachings.

Such Hebrews as accepted the tenets of Christ held that Gentiles could become Christians only by first becoming Hebrews—being received into the nation by the rite of circumcision. Paul was of Hebrew-Roman extraction, and had received a Greek education. He took the stand that it was not necessary to become a Jew in order to become a Christian. The Hebrew followers of Christ were incensed by his position. Probably as early as 52 A. D. a council was held in Jerusalem to consider this question. Paul's influence proved the stronger and it was forever determined that Christianity should be universal rather than local—for all the world, not merely confined to one small nation. Henceforth the Hebrew Christians separated from the Gentiles who were Christians. They fell into many little sects, not unlike those of the later Christians. They called themselves Ebionites, or the Poor. In the seventh century they lost their identity.

Christ came to the lowly. His followers needed no creed. Their religion was something to be felt rather than expressed in words. For the first hundred years they held to their faith in one who had dealt fairly with them, one who was just and kind; and they awaited his return. The first hundred years has been called the *waiting age*. In the second century a realization came that Christ would reveal himself in the next world rather than here. When this idea once spread among his followers, organization soon took form. It was necessary to have some one to provide for the poor, to cheer the aged and encourage and train those recently received into the faith. From the first the Christians had celebrated the Agape, or love-feast. The old man who sat at the head of the table at this love-feast was called the *presbyter*. As the number of worshippers increased, more tables were needed. Before long, he who presided at the head table, the head presbyter, was called the *bishop*. By the end of the second century, the bishop presided over a city congregation, received alms for the poor, led the people in their meetings and continued to preside at the Agape. However, he did not give himself exclusively to these religious duties, but still had some trade whereby he supported himself. In time the importance of the bishop depended upon the size of the city in which he lived.

As we have noted, a change had made itself felt in the second century. Those persons who had come into personal touch with Christ or his apostles had passed away. New duties appeared as the number of worshippers grew, and new officers were provided to meet them. Gradually a separation took place between the religious officers, or the clergy, and the congregations, or the laity. In 325 A. D., at the council of Nicaea, an attempt was made to enforce celibacy upon the clergy. This movement started in the West and was unquestionably influenced by the moral laxity of the times. Virginity was emphasized and confirmation was given to the belief in the virginity of Mary, mother of Christ. As compared with the life of the celibate, there was thought to be something sullied about the relation of husband and wife.

In 60 B. C. the first Jews were brought as captives to Rome. They came to Rome as slaves, but because of their absolute refusal to adopt the customs of their masters, they proved to be unsatisfactory as house servants. They would not eat food prepared in the Roman fashion. They would not worship after the manner of Rome. In many ways their peculiarities as a race manifested themselves and in a short time the great majority of them were set free and banished across the Tiber—the first Ghetto. Here they became traders and gradually won some adherents among the Romans.

People from all parts gathered in Rome. As they came and went, Christianity was carried to the Eternal City. This religion appealed to the poor—to the slave. The comparatively few who were wealthy felt no special need of a new faith. They had the means and freedom to do as they would. The slave had a blank outlook. He reached out for this new religion. There were many, many hopeless ones in Rome who turned gladly to a belief that held out *hope*. The old deities had failed to satisfy.

"God as a tender father replaced the gods demanding worship for themselves as the price of holding their hands from afflicting men. Confidence in a blissful life after death replaced the old gloomy and shadowy future. The obligation of pure and helpful living was substituted for the duty of minute ceremonial. Christianity made hope, love, and mutual helpfulness the essence of religion for the masses of men, and it replaced the lofty but trembling aspirations of the noblest philosophers by a sure and glowing faith."

Even the upper classes were forming societies for the study of new religions, and Christianity was considered among them. By means of these *societies* and of this *hope* held out to the hopeless, Christianity spread in the Roman empire. The morality of Rome was bad; that of Asia was worse. This was an age of scepticism and doubt. Had the Romans been satisfied with their own religion at this time, there would have been no opportunity for Christianity to gain a foothold. Two reasons made it easy for the Romans to take on this new faith: they already believed in immortality, and in a judgment after death.

Coming first to the simple people, it required three hundred years for the faith to reach any considerable number of the upper classes. When it finally did penetrate to the thinking people, they had to first put it into language they could understand. The poor people had needed no creeds, no expositions to prove to them something they *felt* to be true. The thinking people of the empire,—particularly of the large cities,—influenced by their Greek learning, had to translate the religion into terms familiar to them before they could comprehend it. Terms had to be defined; statements established. This was truer of the Greek than the Roman—of the easterner than the man of the west. These discussions resulted in the production of written material. Before 70 A. D. nothing had been committed to writing regarding the faith. Before another century had passed. twenty-one of the present books of the New Testament had been produced.

When Constantine espoused the cause of Christianity he found the Christians divided over this question: Was Christ of the same essence as God? Some said: Christ was mere man; others, Christ is the same as the father; still others, Christ is subordinate to the father. Constantine called a council to decide upon the matter in 315. The decision reached by this body was that God is one and God is three. Christ is alike, yet different. Here is rather a difficult distinction for a westerner to grasp, but the argument-loving, hair-splitting mentality of the East understood it perfectly well and found the solution satisfactory.

To understand the early persecutions of the Christians it is necessary to view the matter from the standpoint of the ancient Roman. Rome welcomed all religions; each conquered people was invited to bring its gods to the capital, provided, always, that they were national gods. Rome tolerated no sects. That meant division, and Rome stood for unity. Moreover, it was always understood that the new comers would do reverence to the Roman gods, who were so closely interwoven with the state that it was not possible to distinguish between the two. Emperor worship obtained at Rome. Not that the people worshipped Caesar as Caesar, but in worshipping him, they worshipped the spirit of Rome. As we talk of Columbia, they talked of the genius of Rome. After the republic was gone, the emperor embodied the spirit of Rome, and it was this they worshipped in him. The deference which we show to our flag today was shown in Rome by reverence done to the bust of the emperor. All this the Christians refused to recognize. They said it was contrary to their tenets to worship any but the true God. Again, the Romans put the state first, religion second. The Christians put Christianity first and held Roman law in contempt. They had a code of their own which they felt to be greater than the law of Rome. Their attitude seemed to the Roman to be mere treason; he believed that the Christians were forming a state within a state. The Christians met in secret, and the Romans objected to secret organizations. Nevertheless, these had long flourished in the capital and for them alone the Christians would not have been disturbed, but they were opposed to fighting and did not want to take the usual oaths to defend the national gods. The standards carried into battle often had emblems upon them peculiar to the religion of Rome. Under these the Christians did not want to march. Finally the Romans learned that the Christians were not Jews and had not the religion of the Jews—that their religion was not a national religion. That sealed their fate, for Rome never tolerated little sects splitting off from national faiths. Persecutions followed as the princes tried to root out the religion that they deemed dangerous to the welfare of the state. The first of these persecutions occurred under Nero, who did not seek any such excellent reasons for considering Christianity a danger to his state. After the burning of Rome, finding the responsibility of the disaster laid at his door, he cast about for someone to throw the blame upon. The Christians were hated by the masses and were regarded as objectionable citizens, so he quickly accused them of having set fire to the capital. Many were cast into the arena and others were burned alive.

Trajan, Hadrian, Antoninus Pius and Aurelius each attempted to crush out the growing faith. Disabilities were placed upon the Christians and it was made a crime to profess Christianity. In spite of these efforts, the adherents increased, and men and women glorified in a death which brought them at once to a life deemed far more desirable than life on earth. Finally, in the reign of Constantine, this farsighted statesman regarded it as wise to make use of the strength of Christians; and he extended favor to them. Placing his sword above the cross, he converted the religion of peace into a religion of war and rallied to his support an element of the population thus far either ignored or persecuted by the state. Soon the tables turned, and the Christians, instead of being longer persecuted, proceeded to persecute those whose faith differed from their own.

Persecution Under Nero.

(This took place in 64 A. D. Tacitus' account is the best known and the most important. As a boy, he may have witnessed the fire and the persecution. An account of the fire immediately precedes the passage here quoted.)

Account by Tacitus.

"Therefore to check this rumor, those who were called Christians by the mob and hated for their moral enormities, were substituted in his place as culprits by Nero and afflicted with the most exquisite punishments. Christ, from whom the name was given, was put to death during the reign of Tiberius, by the procurator Pontius Pilate. Although checked for the time, this pernicious superstition broke out again, not only in Judea, where the evil originated, but throughout the city, in which the atrocities and shame from all parts of the world center and flourish. Therefore those who confessed were first seized, then on their information a great multitude were convicted, not so much of the crime of incendiarism as of hatred of the human race. The victims who perished also suffered insults, for some were covered with the skins of wild beasts and torn to pieces by dogs, while others were fixed to crosses and burnt to light the night when daylight had failed. Nero had offered his gardens for the spectacle and was giving a circus show, mingling with the people in the dress of a driver, or speeding about in a chariot. Although they were criminals who deserved the most severe punishment, yet a feeling of pity arose since they were put to death, not for the public good, but to satisfy the rage of an individual."

Account by Suetonius.

"In his reign many things were severely censured and suppressed and many also instituted; a limit was set to lavish expenditure; public dinners were reduced to doles; cook shops were forbidden to sell any prepared food except pulse or herbs, whereas formerly all kinds of relishes had been offered; Christians, a class of men of a new and vicious superstition, were subjected to severe punishments; the quadriga races were forbidden, because the charioteers wandered about, and by long license assumed the right to make a jest of cheating and stealing; the partisans of the pantomimes were banished, together with the actors themselves; to prevent forgery, means were first devised by which no document was to be sealed until it had been perforated and a thread run through three times."

SOLDIER WITH FULL ARMOR.

The Coliseum.

CHAPTER XXII.

To the Fall of Rome.

Constantine left three sons to quarrel over the well organized empire he had restored. Constantius reigned for eight years, during which period he was obliged to wage continual war with the Germans and Parthians. He was followed in 361 by Julian, frequently called "the Apostate."

For fifty years Christianity had been allowed to take its own course. The old religions had been discouraged and preference given the followers of Christ. In order to secure the emperor's favor, many had publicly espoused Christianity, although in secret they held to the gods of their fathers. The masses clung to the ancient faith. The adherents of Christianity had weakened their cause by quarrels among themselves. They had taken sides in heated discussions regarding the definition of their terms and their conception of the Father and Son, and the relation between the two. When they were favored by the sanction of law and the emperor's patronage, the change in the national faith made surprisingly small difference in the world. To be sure, suicide was considered a crime, charity was extended to the poor and the gladiatorial games were abolished, but the Christians unfortunately adopted too many methods of their opponents to produce any decided difference in popular estimation.

The new emperor had been brought up as a boy amid Christian surroundings, but was later sent to the schools of Athens. Here he became fascinated by the old philosophy as revived by the Neo-Platonists. As an offset to Christianity, certain Greek scholars revived the teachings of Plato, bringing these up to the thought of the day. It is not strange, when we contrast the religion of the third and fourth century Christians with the highest expression of Greek philosophy, that certain temperaments found the latter the more pleasing of the two. The present world would find life bleak and barren were it patterned after the ideals of early Christianity as interpreted by the contemporaries of Julian. They held this world to be only a preparation for the next. They enjoined one another to care not at all for any pleasures and comforts this world might offer. Attention was to be centered upon the next existence, and death was welcomed as a means of coming at once into a glorified state. Opposed to this was the old Greek conception and worship of beauty. Pleasant ceremonies connected with the old deities took the place of the doleful hymns of the Christians. Julian turned back the pages of progress and reinstated the pagan gods. All laws placing disadvantages upon the adherents of the old faith were removed. The temples which had fallen into decay or had been appropriated by the Christians were now restored. Christians were no longer given preference for office. In the army, the standards bearing the symbol of the cross were replaced by those sacred to the old divinities. Christians were no longer allowed to teach in the public schools. Julian required the pagan priests to adopt many of the methods of Christianity. They were admonished to set examples to their followers by the purity of their lives; they were instructed to dispense charity, to found hospitals and care for the needy.

On the contrary, Julian was friendly to the Jews. He recognized theirs as a national religion. He supplied money and men for the reconstruction of the temple at Jerusalem, although the Christians believed because of certain prophecies in the Old Testament that it would never be rebuilt. To disprove these Julian was anxious that the enterprise be undertaken, but explosions within the earth alarmed men sent to do the work and the scheme was abandoned.[1]

In 363 Julian died while conducting a campaign against the Persians. The soldiers proclaimed Jovian emperor. During his brief rule he restored the Christians to favor, and undid the work of his predecessor. He was followed by Valentinian, who established himself in the West, with his capital at Milan, while he appointed his brother Valens to preside over the East and reside at Constantinople. After twelve years, during which time he stayed the restless barbarians, Gratian, his son, succeeded him.

[1] See Ibsen's Emperor and Julian the Apostate.

Henceforth the story of the declining empire is no longer the story of emperors. Two great forces exceed all others in importance: the Germans, who struggle to break through the frontiers of the dying empire, and Christianity, soon standing triumphant over the religions of antiquity which had lived their appointed time.

For centuries the Goths and Germans had been held behind the Rhine-Danube frontier. As children outside the Troll garden, in the happy comparison of Kingsley, the barbarians look longingly across the frontier beyond which lay all the wonders they had heard about from the few of their numbers who reached Rome and returned. In 376 the Visigoths, a people who lived north of the lower Rhine, about 1,000,000 strong, asked permission of Valens to come peacefully into his empire, since they were being harassed by a strange, wild tribe, the Huns, whose attacks they could not withstand. This permission was granted, provided they would give up their arms and offer some of their children as hostages. Many days were spent in transporting their great numbers into the Roman empire. Not long after the Ostrogoths sent a similar request to Valens, who grew alarmed at the prospect of having so many strangers within his realm and refused their entreaty. However, between two dangers the East Goths chose the lesser and with their arms in their hands, crossed the frontier without the emperor's permission. Suddenly it appeared that the officers who had been sent to accept the arms of the Visigoths —West Goths—had been bought off by the chiefs and had left the weapons in the hands of the recent arrivals. Now the two Gothic peoples united and began to overrun the territory south of the Danube. Without waiting for the army of the West, Valens offered battle at Adrianople and was defeated. Nothing could now stay the zeal of the Goths. Since Valens had fallen in the fatal battle, Gratian appointed Theodosius in his place. He proved an able general. Reducing the Goths to submission, he settled the Visigoths in Thrace, the Ostrogoths in Asia Minor. These last became allies and 40,000 were received into the eastern army.

Gratian and Theodosius were both Christians; Gratian refused the title *pontifex maximus,* since, he said, it was a pagan office. For some years the new religion and the old had flourished side by side. In 341 an edict had gone forth that the heathen worship must cease; in 392 Theodosius forbade even the worship of the Lares and Penates. Nevertheless, paganism did continue in out-of-the-way places, hence the word pagan, from *Paganus,* a dweller in a *pagus,* or village.

Theodosius ruled both empires from 392 to 395. Before his death he gave his sons dominion over them. Arcadius, aged eighteen, took the East; Honorius, his eleven-year-old brother, was given the West. Henceforth it is necessary to follow the history of two empires. The Eastern Empire lasted from 395 to 1453 A. D. The early centuries were less disturbed in the East than in the West, because the eastern emperors did their best to turn the barbarians westward, thus sparing their own land.

In the beginning of the fifth century, under their leader, Alaric, the Visigoths left Thrace and passed into Greece, plundering as they went. Honorius sent his general Stilicho to meet them and he drove them out of Greece. They next invaded Italy. Here again Stilicho defeated them at Verona, after which Honorius and his efficient general, Stilicho, celebrated in 404 the three hundredth and final triumph seen in Rome. Somewhat later, Honorius grew jealous of Stilicho and foolishly ordered his execution. The followers of Alaric knew well that the only general who could defeat them was gone. In 410 Alaric accordingly appeared again and asked Honorius for lands within his empire, but Honorius had no desire to establish the Visigoths in his immediate vicinity. He refused the request, whereupon the Gothic king marched upon Rome, pillaging the city for five days and nights.

"Finally they entered the city of Rome and sacked it at Alaric's command. They did not, however, set fire to the city, as is the custom of the wild peoples, and would not permit that any of the holy places should be desecrated. They then proceeded into Campania and Lucania, which they likewise plundered, and came then to Britii.

"Alaric, the king of the West Goths, also brought hither the treasures of all Italy which he had won by plunder, and determined to cross from here over to Sicily and thence to

Africa, which would offer him a final abode. But a number of his ships were swallowed up by that dreadful sea, and many were injured; for man is unable to carry out his wishes when they are opposed to God's will.

"While Alaric, discouraged by this misfortune, was considering what he should do, he was struck down by an early death and departed this world. His followers mourned the loss of him they had so dearly loved. They diverted the river Busento from its ordinary bed near the town of Consentia and had a grave dug by captives in the middle of the channel. Then they permitted the water to return once more to its old bed. Moreover, in order that the place might never be found, they killed all those who had helped dig the grave." [2]

During this period of the so-called *Wanderings of the Nations,* the Vandals, related to the Goths, came from Pannonia into Spain; after some period here, they crossed into Africa and upon the ancient site of Carthage established a stronghold for their piracies upon the Mediterranean. The Burgundians located in the land still called by their name, while the Franks laid the basis of the present French nation.

For forty years Rome escaped further disaster, then came the Huns in 451. These were the people before whose destroying breath the Visigoths had appealed to Valens for protection, and to escape whom the Ostrogoths dared even face the Roman emperor, who had refused them entrance. They were a fierce nomadic tribe of horsemen, belonging to the Mongolian race. They had ravaged the lands north of China, and to protect their country from attacks, the Chinese had built a mighty wall, fifteen hundred miles in length, across their northern border. Crossing into Europe under their leader Attila, they defeated the army of the East and compelled Constantinople to pay tribute. Seven hundred thousand strong, they pushed into Gaul, whereupon the Germans and Romans united to defeat them in the battle of Chalons. Fleeing before them, the Veneti took refuge in the islands which since have formed their city. Advancing to the very walls of Rome, Leo I. came out to meet Attila and implored him to spare the city.

[2] Jordanes. Quoted by Robinson: Readings in European History, v. I.

"Then Leo had compassion on the calamity of Italy, and Rome, and with one of the consuls and a large part of the Roman senate he went to meet Attila. The old man, of harmless simplicity, venerable in his gray hair and his majestic garb, ready of his own will to give himself entirely for the defense of his flock, went forth to meet the tyrant who was destroying all things. He met Attila, it is said, in the neighborhood of the river Mincio, and he spoke to the grim monarch, saying: 'The senate, and the people of Rome, once conquerors of the world, now indeed vanquished, come before thee as suppliants. We pray for mercy and deliverance. O Attila, thou couldst have no greater glory than to see suppliant at thy feet this people, before whom once all peoples and kings lay suppliant. The people have felt thy scourge; now as suppliants they would feel thy mercy.'"

The ancient account continues to narrate how Peter and Paul now appeared before Attila and threatening him with death unless he gave heed to the prayer of the venerable Leo; Attila was appeased and quietly withdrew. As a matter of fact, the Huns now passed beyond the Danube. Just why they spared Rome has never been known, but it is not improbable that their numbers were being wasted by a pestilence.

Spared by the Huns, Rome soon suffered at the hands of the Vandals—such destroyers that their name has ever since signified wanton waste and destruction. Under Genseric they left their African kingdom, sailed up the Tiber and plundered Rome for fourteen days.

"This is the second sack. More dreadful far than the first—455 is its date. Then it was that the statues, whose fragments are still found, were hurled in vain on the barbarian assailants. Not merely gold and jewels, but the art-treasures of Rome were carried off to the Vandal fleet, and with them the golden table and the seven-branched candlestick which Titus took from the Temple of Jerusalem.

"How had these things escaped the Goths forty years before? We cannot tell. Perhaps the Gothic sack, which only lasted five days, was less complete than this one, which went on for fourteen days of unutterable horrors. The plunderers were not this time sturdy honest Goths; not even German slaves, made to revenge themselves on their masters: they were Moors, Austrian black savages, and all the pirates and cut-throats of the Mediterranean.

"Sixty thousand prisoners were carried off to Carthage. All the statues were wrecked on the voyage to Africa, and lost forever.

"And yet Rome did not die. She lingered on; her Emperor still calling himself an Emperor, her senate a senate; feeding her lazy plebs, as best she could, with the remnant of those revenues which former Emperors had set aside for their support—their public bread, public pork, public oil, public wine, public baths,—and leaving them to gamble and quarrel, and listen to the lawyers in rags and rascality, and to rise and murder ruler after ruler, benefactor after benefactor, out of base jealousy and fear of any one less base than themselves."[3]

But Rome was not to live on much longer—not as before. In 476 there was little left of the Western Empire. The Roman senate sent an embassy to Constantinople to signify the willingness of the West to serve Zeno, Emperor of the East, if Odoacer, a German leader, might rule in Italy as his regent. The request was granted and Italy became a province of the Eastern Empire in 476.

The true cause of Rome's downfall is of course to be found in Rome herself. Had she been able to retain her early strength, Rome might have held the barbarians beyond the Rhine and Danube in check for many years and perhaps effected a gradual union of Roman and Teuton. However, it was not wholly a loss that the children of the northern forests broke into the coveted land. It took them many years to assimilate Roman civilization, but they brought with them a moral purity and a nobility of character which the civilized world sorely needed.

[3]Kingsley: The Roman and the Teuton, 90.

CHAPTER XXIII.

From the Fall of Rome to Charlemagne.

For fifty years after the so-called "fall of Rome," weak men occupied the throne in the East, and they found it difficult indeed to withstand the dangers threatening from the barbarians. Their capital itself was in frequent danger, and the empire merely kept alive. In 527, however, Justinian gained control of the government and soon showed himself to be a man of ability. Having established himself at home, he turned to those portions of the empire which had fallen away in late years, gradually bringing them back again.

The Vandals, as we have already noted, had established themselves in northern Africa. Here they were very objectionable because of their piracies and unusual destructive policy. Justinian was implored to save Africa from their wanton waste and sent the army of the East to conquer them. Those who survived the war waged against them became absorbed with the native population and their identity was lost.

The Ostrogoths had appropriated Italy, and under Theodoric had set up a strong kingdom. During the years this able king ruled Italy, peace and prosperity unknown since the time of Aurelius returned to bless the land. Yet the kingdom so well organized lasted but twenty-seven years after the death of Theodoric. In 554 Justinian sent his general to free Italy from Gothic rule, and it was reunited to the empire.

Small wonder that the great treasures of Italy disappeared during those centuries which followed the invasion of the barbarians. Rome was plundered and pillaged, held now by one, then by another, people. This struggle between the Goths and Justinian's army was itself a terrific one for Rome.

"Five times during the war the unfortunate capital changed hands. In the year 537 it was invested by the barbarians under the command of their king, Witiges. During this siege, which proved unsuccessful, the city suffered irreparable damage. All of the eleven aqueducts constructed under the Consuls and Caesars were destroyed by the barbarians, and, with the exception of three, have remained in a ruined state ever since. The stately Mausoleum of Hadrian was converted by the Roman garrison into a fortress, and the masterpieces of Greek and Roman art which embellished it were used as missiles and flung down upon the heads of the assailants."

Greater than any of his conquests was the compilation of the Roman laws made under the direction of Justinian. The famous Justinian Code contained a collection of Roman laws, extracts from opinions of thirty-nine noted Roman jurists, and a treatise upon the principles of Roman law. This has proved one of the richest legacies left by Rome to posterity, and most modern law codes have been based upon it. "Every one of us is benefited directly or indirectly by this legacy of the Roman people—a legacy as valuable as the literary and artistic models which we owe to the great writers and sculptors of Greece."

In spite of the benefits of Justinian's rule, the country suffered serious calamities. A fire raged for five days in the city of Constantinople; a famine and pestilence afflicted the land. Justinian was a prolific builder, and his building enterprises and various other undertakings required vast outlays. To provide sufficient funds, heavy taxes had to be imposed, and the drain upon the country during the reign of this efficient emperor caused a reaction later which was far-reaching in its effects.

East of the Adriatic the empire had always been more Greek than Roman. As time went on, Orientalism permeated more and more, and after the first few centuries the student of Roman history is but slightly concerned with the Eastern, or Byzantine, Empire. One great benefit it conferred upon Europe: while Italy was being ravaged by tribe after tribe and was being fast despoiled of her treasure and her beauty, the learning of the ancients was stored away in the eastern empire, to be preserved until restored peace and safety should give time and impulse for its revival. Moreover, the idea of empire was kept alive in the East until the western world should be ready for the creation of an empire under Charlemagne.

While the Vandals were being driven from northern Africa, and the Ostrogoths from Italy, the Visigoths were maintaining a strong kingdom in Spain—ended only by the Saracens. The Burgundians had settled in Burgundy, but soon were overcome by the Franks. The Lombards, from Pannonia, entered Italy and appropriated the fertile valley of the Po. For assistance rendered him, Pope Gregory I. gave the Lombard king an iron crown, but later, because they were endangering the safety of church lands, Charlemagne was asked to drive out the Lombards, and he broke their strength in 774. The Saxons settled around the mouth of the Rhine, the Angles and Jutes in northern Europe, and all three tribes early secured a footing in Britain. Most important for some time were the Franks, a Teutonic nation, who produced several able kings. Merowig, an early chieftain, established a line of rulers known as the Merovingians. Clovis belonged to this line. He is remembered as having vowed to accept the God of the Christians if this God enabled him to win a battle. Victorious, he compelled his tribe to be baptized at once in the new faith—so that they who at sunrise had worshipped a Teutonic deity, at night were pledged to fight for another. This story indicates very clearly the superstition of these centuries and the blind impulse which led sometimes to the acceptance of a new religion. Clovis extended his authority over much of Gaul. His sons proved less able than he, and soon the Merovingian line gave way to the Carolingian kings.

The seventh century saw the birth of a new faith which was to prove important in the history of mediaeval Europe. It is not possible to give any considerable treatment to the life of Mohammed and the religion he taught at this time, but to understand the great peril which later confronted Europe it is necessary to note briefly the rise and spread of Mohammedism.

Mohammed was an Arab, born about 570 in the city of Mecca. His tribe had long had charge of a certain shrine located in the vicinity of Mecca. As a youth, Mohammed tended his flocks and herds, and, like the patriarchs among the Hebrews, was subjected to the mighty influence of the desert wastes, the limitless sky and mysteries of southwestern Asia. It is a fact worth deep consideration that all the great religions of the world have had their rise under similar circumstances, and those who have devoted long study to the matter insist that the life of the shepherd in the desert is conducive to religious contemplation. Mohammed remained alone much of the time, and shortly began to have trances or visions. As a result of his reflections and contemplations, he began to teach that there was but one God, Allah, and Mohammed was his prophet. For some years only a few of his immediate friends gave any heed to this teaching, but gradually it spread among the Arabians, particularly when the leader taught his followers that they were justified in putting to the fire and sword such as failed to accept their faith.

"The sword," said Mohammed, "is the key of heaven. A drop of blood shed in the cause of God is of more avail than two months of fasting and prayer; whoso falls in battle, all his sins are forgiven; at the day of judgment his wounds shall be resplendent as vermillion and odoriferous as musk."

A religion that was to spread by means of the sword appealed to the Arabians. Within a few years, many of these desert men, wholly disunited before, espoused the faith of Mohammed and found in it a bond of union. However excellent or misguided the new teaching, it was singularly suited to western Asia. Thence it spread rapidly into Egypt and northern Africa and across into Spain. Roderic, king of the Visigoths, was defeated and killed and his kingdom forever ended. Reaching over the Pyrenees, zealots tried to establish Mohammedism in France. It seemed as if European civilization was in danger of extinction before that of Mohammed's desert followers. In face of common danger, others hastened to the support of Charles Martel, who, as king of the Franks, met and defeated the Saracens in the battle of Tours, in 732. Thus was Europe saved from Moslem rule, and the Christian civilization of the West perpetuated.

We have seen that the Franks under different kings tried to extend their sway in Europe. They attained greatest success under Charles the Great, or Charlemagne, as he has long been called. Belonging to the Carolingian house, Charlemagne gave early evidence of great ability. Opportunity offered to settle a quarrel which had arisen between the popes and the

Lombards in northern Italy. Conquering this people, he placed the iron crown of their king upon his own head, and annexed their territory to his own. He invaded Spain and delivered the northern portion of this country from the rule of the Saracens. On the east, he added Bavaria to his kingdom, and by his conquest of the Saxons along the Rhine he gained considerable land.

In the Eastern Empire, a woman, Irene, by crime had attained the throne. In the West it was felt that the authority of a woman should not be recognized. Charlemagne had defended the Christian religion and ably served the pope, who, as a reward, crowned him on Christmas day, in 800, and saluted him as "Charles Augustus, crowned of God, great and pacific emperor of the Romans." This was understood to mean a revival of the Western Empire of earlier times. To be sure, under weak successors of Charlemagne this great empire fell apart, but the conception of empire lived on and was later revived by men who called themselves successors of Charlemagne and the Caesars.

The age of Charlemagne marks the close of ancient history and the opening years of mediaeval history and civilization.

CHARLEMAGNE.

SOCIAL LIFE IN ROME

CHAPTER I.

THE ROMAN FAMILY.

In ancient Rome the family embraced a much larger, more comprehensive group of persons than it does with us today, and each member was submissive to one will. The *pater familias,* or father of the family, governed all members of the family. He controlled his wife and his children—not alone through their minority, but after they had attained maturity and had married and perhaps were parents themselves. The grandchildren might also be subject to his control. Release from his authority came only by emancipation—seldom practised—or by the death of the *pater familias,* upon which occasion new families were formed. Moreover, the family included various dependents and slaves. Over this numerous group the *pater familias* exercised absolute control, possessing even power of life and death over them. The state in no wise interfered with his authority nor sought to limit it until the period of the principate.

Possessing such unlimited sway, the father was nevertheless restricted by religious custom and by public opinion, and appears to have abused his power but seldom. Self-control and moderation characterized the Roman fathers in their domestic relationship. An old religious law declared a man accursed who sold his son into slavery. Hence it was unusual to find a father who went to any such extremes. In the eyes of the law, however, there was no limitation set upon the authority of the *pater familias*.

"He had absolute power over his children . He decided whether or not the newborn child should be reared; he punished what he regarded as misconduct with penalties as severe as banishment, slavery, and death; he alone could own and exchange property—all that his descendants earned or acquired in any way was his; according to the letter of the law they were little better than his chattels. If his right to one of them was disputed, he vindicated it by the same form of action that he used to maintain his right to a house or a horse; if one was stolen, he proceeded against the abductor by the ordinary action for theft; if for any reason he wished to transfer one of them to a third person, it was done by the same form of conveyance that he employed to transfer inanimate things. The jurists boasted that these powers were enjoyed by Roman citizens only."[1]

In early Rome, children were desired. As in all countries where ancestral worship is practised, it was deemed most desirable that families be perpetuated. The souls of ancestors were thought to return to those places they had frequented in life. Unless food and drink were provided for them, they missed these kindly attentions on the part of their descendants, and to provide for their future requirements was a sacred duty. The ancestral gods had their place on every hearth, with the gods of the state. The *pater familias* was the priest of the family and offered sacrifices and libations of wine upon all special family occasions. The parents of each generation, in their turn, expected to experience after death the same needs that they supposed their forefathers felt, and if any family was so unfortunate as to lose the children during their childhood, the parents usually adopted others in place of those they had lost. From regal times it was customary to rear the eldest son and daughter at least. It was the privilege of the father to determine at birth whether or not he would bring up the child as his own. Exposure of children was far less common among the Romans than the Greeks. The young state of Rome felt the need of fighting men and only in the decline of the country when luxury and license had done their worst, were children regarded as a burden.

Polygamy was not practised in Rome, and for more than five hundred years after the city's traditional founding, divorce was unknown. The position of woman was good, and nowhere was she more respected. Like most of the wholesome conditions of the early republic, this underwent a change in the later republic and principate, and a declining moral

[1] Johnston: Private Life of the Romans, 31.

tone of the country accompanied the loss of respect accorded Roman women.

Before the days of social equality, patrician married with patrician; plebeian with plebeian. Religious sentiment had much to do with this. It was not considered wise to leave the worship of national gods to persons who by birth were ignorant of them. The Roman deities were gods of the patricians. Plebeians might be foreigners, freed slaves or conquered people. Being non-citizens, not recognized by the law, they could not be trusted with the national gods. Yet in spite of laws, marriages did occur between citizen and non-citizen, and it came to pass in Rome that the status of the children in the eyes of the law followed that of the father. If the father were a citizen, his children were citizens; if he were a foreigner, then his children were also foreigners. In 445 B. C. a law was passed recognizing the validity of marriage between two classes.

At marriage, the wife passed from the authority of her father to the authority of her husband. She brought a dowry with her which in early times became the sole property of her husband. In later times, a portion of this was reserved for her personal use. Four requirements were to be met before a couple might be united in marriage. First, the consent of the contracting parties was necessary, but as a matter of fact, the consent of the bride's *pater familias* and of the father of the groom was sufficient. Marriages might be performed when both bride and groom were still mere children, according to present-day opinion. Probably in spite of numerous examples to the contrary, the bride was generally between fourteen and eighteen when married; the groom between twenty and thirty. Both must be Roman citizens if they would enjoy the ceremony peculiar to Rome. Both must be unmarried, for, as we have seen, polygamy was unknown in early Rome. Moreover, there must be no close blood relationship between the two.

Weddings were regarded as very auspicious occasions in Rome, and great care was taken to appease the Mighty Ones in every way. Special days were considered lucky for marriage, and whole months were regarded as unlucky. No special magistrates or class of people were given the right to perform a marriage ceremony. On the contrary, it consisted mainly of the consent of both parties given in the presence of assembled guests.

Upon the morning of her wedding, the bride's mother dressed her for this important occasion. The veil was always essential. Indeed, the verb "to veil" when used in connection with women had the significance of "to marry." The bride wore a wreath of flowers and herbs having certain religious connections or associations. The groom also wore a wreath. Accompanied by his friends, the groom went to the house of the bride, where guests had assembled early in the morning. All his friends were expected to do honor to a man by attending him upon this very important day of his life. The omens were taken before sunrise and as a rule they were found to be happy. In the presence of their friends, the bride and groom gave their consent to the union. A feast followed. Late in the afternoon the groom made a pretense of tearing his bride from the arms of her mother, perpetuating the ancient custom of stealing wives, as exemplified in the story of the Sabine women. A procession accompanied the wedded pair to the home of the groom, where the newly-made wife lighted the fire upon her husband's hearth by a torch brought from her own home. Merriment and festivity characterized the day. Shortly after the wedding, the wedded pair received their friends at a feast in their home and the ceremony ended.

The position of the wife in the Roman family was enviable, as compared with that of many early people. She superintended her husband's home, cared for his children and was a companion to her husband. In early times she mingled with his friends and was by no means secluded. This condition was somewhat modified in later times, under the influence of eastern civilization, but there was no parallel at any time to the seclusion which surrounded women of later Greek times.

Slave help was plentiful during the republic, and menial labor was never performed by the wife of the Roman citizen. She was nevertheless an industrious person, caring for her family, providing clothing, and fabrics for house adornment, which were woven by her own skillful hands and those of her slaves. The education of the children during their earliest years was her special trust, and her daughters remained with their mother to be trained in the various domestic duties which would fall to their lot as future wives. While the great majority of Roman women were educated merely in such accomplishments as household interests required, yet there were not lacking those who were accomplished in many of the higher branches. Nobility of soul was a Roman characteristic, and Portia, Cato's daughter, and, Cornelia, mother of the Gracchi, were but noted examples of a Roman type.

While there may not have been lacking feelings of romantic love between husband and wife in Rome, there is nothing to indicate that these were usual. As a nation the Romans were always practical. In the days of the early republic, men and women married in order to raise families—that the family line might be perpetuated and the state strengthened. In the later republic they married for the purpose of establishing settled homes and maintaining certain social positions. In the principate there was a marked falling off of marriage alliances. Men found married life burdensome. Divorces were common and the life of the women of the upper classes was less dignified and pure than it had earlier been. To be sure, the people of the lower and middle classes were less affected by this moral decline. Untouched by the rapid accumulation of wealth that had wrought great changes in the aristocracy, life went on as it had for generations. This was essentially true in country places and districts remote from the capital.

A surviving letter of Pliny's throws some light upon the Roman attitude toward suitable marriage alliances. Pliny had been asked to assist a friend in finding an acceptable husband for his niece. From all that we know of Roman life, his reply undoubtedly sets forth the usual sentiments of guardians concerning suitable matches. He replied to his friend:

"You desire me to look out a proper husband for your niece. I should be long in determining a choice were I not acquainted with Minucius Acilianus, who seems formed for our purpose. He is a native of Brixia, one of those provinces in Italy which still retain much of the old modesty, frugal simplicity, and even rusticity of manner.

He is the son of Minucius Macrinus, whose humble desires were satisfied with standing at the head of the equestrian order.

His grandmother on his mother's side is Serrana Procula, of Patavium; you are no stranger to the character of its citizens; yet Serrana is looked upon, even among those correct people, as an exemplary instance of strict virtue.

In short, you will find nothing in his family unworthy of yours. Minucius himself has plenty of vivacity, as well as application, together with a most amiable and becoming modesty. He has already, with considerable credit, passed through the offices of quaestor, tribune, and praetor; so that you will be spared the trouble of soliciting for him those honorable employments. He has a fine, well-bred countenance, with a ruddy, healthy complexion, while his whole person is elegant and comely, and his mien graceful and senatorian—advantages, I think, by no means to be slighted, and which I consider as the proper tribute to virgin innocence. I think I may add that his father is very rich. When I contemplate the character of those who require a husband of my choosing, I know it is unnecessary to mention wealth; but when I reflect upon the prevailing manners of the age, and even the laws of Rome, which rank a man according to his possessions, it certainly claims *some* regard; and, indeed, in establishments of this nature, where children and many other circumstances are to be duly weighed, it is an article that well deserves to be taken into the account."[2]

The letter contains no comment upon the temperament of those who were to be thus united for life—no thought of likes and dislikes, similarities and differences, temper or disposition. A man who, like this Minucius Acilianus, had come from a noble family of good standing, who had acquitted himself well in the service of the state, and who possessed ample means, was considered an acceptable match for a Roman maiden, and it is unnecessary to add that many were obliged to be satisfied with unions far less suitable. Marriages were almost wholly business concerns and were considered upon a purely business basis. Mutual respect allowed man and wife to take up their responsibilities of married life satisfactorily. The

[2] Quoted by Pellison: Roman Life in Pliny's Time, 39.

Roman matron was deeply respected and venerated, and her children seem to have regarded her with true affection. Examples are not lacking of men who loved their wives with more than dutiful feeling. Brutus loved Portia, and all his stoicism could not prevent him from deep grief at her death. Julia, daughter of Caesar, and wife of Pompey, was well beloved by her husband. However, any feeling of romantic love had of necessity to follow, not precede, marriage in Rome. It had no chance to develop prior to this union because the bride and groom had little or no opportunity to become acquainted with one another until their vows were plighted in the presence of the wedding guests. United upon this very practical business basis, for hundreds of years families flourished, reared children, and fulfilled their place in the Roman state.

After all, we have little actual information regarding the home life of Rome. Only in comparatively recent times has domestic life been considered a subject for investigation. The poets of antiquity now and then touched upon the sanctity of the home and human relationships, but only the life of the upper classes was ever treated. Of the lower classes we know little indeed. Nevertheless, the manner of life among the simple people changes but little in a country with the lapse of ages, and in Italy today families among the peasants follow a course not unlike that of the tiller of the soil in the Roman republic.

The purity of the Roman family, the high position of woman and the fidelity to the sanctity of the home until the late years of the republic are facts to be dwelt upon. With the corruption and laxity of the declining republic and dawning principate, and the moral decay of later years, we have less concern.

CHAPTER II.

Houses of the Ancient Romans.

It is a mistake to speak of the *Roman house* as though there had been but one type of Roman houses, and each householder constructed his dwelling upon one general plan. Nevertheless, it is much more possible to treat generally of the Roman than the American or English house, for a spirit of conservatism impelled the ancients to cling to forms with which they had been long accustomed. While some of their houses were small and simple, and some large and magnificent, an underlying plan was common to all.

Probably the earliest house built in Rome was not unlike straw huts seen today upon the Campania. Round in shape, the roof was thatched with straw and supported by young saplings, or the trunks of trees. A strong conservatism in religion led the people to perpetuate this earliest house, so far as its general form was concerned, in the temple of Vesta, goddess of the domestic hearth. However, before historical records begin, this primitive dwelling had given place to a more substantial abode, which was probably of Etruscan origin. Like the straw hut, it contained but one room, where the family lived. There was no chimney; a mere opening in the roof allowed the smoke rising from the hearth to escape, and together with the door, permitted air and light to enter. In the center of the room was the hearth where the housewife prepared the family meals and where the *pater familias* offered sacrifices upon all special occasions. Nearby were the primitive implements for spinning wool and linen for clothing. At night, mats were thrown down to serve as beds.

This one room, with its one door and opening in the roof, was called the *atrium*. The origin of the word has been disputed, but it is now believed to have been the Etruscan word for *house*. When other rooms were added, the name formerly applied to the entire house was limited to the principal room.

The first change in the general plan of the house was

wrought by building a sort of wing upon the side opposite the door. This at first may have had no inner connection with the atrium, but in course of time this wing or *tablinum* and the atrium were connected. Again, as the atrium was made wider and more spacious, it became necessary to supply pillars as supports for the roof. Gradually these pillars which marked off the atrium proper—leaving spaces like transepts on either side—were changed for partitions, and rooms were built on either side of the atrium, opening upon it and deriving thence light and air.

Contact with the Greeks brought another innovation to the Roman house. This was destined to admit of great possibilities and grew to be one of the pleasantest features of the dwelling. This was the court, or peristyle, so characteristic of the Grecian home. The peristyle was a court, open to the sky and outlined by columns. The room containing or surrounding this court, was itself in time surrounded on both sides with small apartments, used for sleeping chambers, storehouses, and the like.

Since the *atrium* depended not at all upon the street for its light, but received light and air from the aperture called the *impluvium,* in the roof, as the business district extended out into the residence portion of the city, it was a simple matter for the householder to construct shops and booths along the front and side of his house without in the least interfering with the privacy of his family. A somewhat parallel case might be drawn from many of our modern hotels, which rent rooms on the ground floor along the front,—or the side as well, if the building stands on a corner—for business uses, while the interior of the building and the upper floors are used for various needs of guests.

As stores were added to the front of the house—and even well-to-do families often dwelt in houses constructed in this way—opportunity was given for making an attractive approach to the atrium. This approach, or vestibule, was the only portion of the dwelling that extended to the street. Like the entrances to modern hotels, or apartments, the vestibule was paved and adorned to please the eye. Not infrequently a porter was stationed in a room off the vestibule to keep guard over those who entered and to serve them. A ferocious-looking dog, held by a chain, was often the design of the mosaic floor.

Generally speaking, simplicity characterized the houses antedating Sulla's time. The later republic and the principate saw whole fortunes expended in the construction and furnishment of homes. In the atrium where once a mere hollowed stone received the water that fell in rain through the impluvium, later years saw the substitution of an elaborate fountain. The columns in the peristyle, once simple wood, were later made of costly marble. Statues and works of art beautified the dwelling and intricate mosaic patterns in glazed tile covered the floors. The walls were also adorned as attractively as possible.

Rough stone and sun-dried brick supplied the material for the early Roman houses. Later, public buildings were built of smooth stone, covered with a marble stucco of dazzling whiteness. Houses were generally covered with some kind of stucco, for it was hard and preserved walls made of sun-dried brick, or, in case stone was used, gave a uniformity to the structure.

Floors in the dwellings of the poor were made by smoothing the earth and pounding bits of stone and tile firmly down. This was called a *pavimentum*, whence comes our word pavement. In houses of the wealthy, floors were constructed of slabs of stone, or of concrete. There were no windows on the first floor in the city dwellings. Light penetrated through the opening in the roof of the atrium and poured down through the court in the peristyle. It was necessary to have windows to light the rooms in the second story; these were small and were usually latticed. In the country it was possible to have more windows; adjoining buildings did not shut off the sun as they did in the city.

Artificial heat is necessary even in Italy, although for several months in the year the sun supplies sufficient warmth. Small portable stoves, in which charcoal was burned, were carried from room to room, to remove the chill. It is safe to say that this system of heating was not very satisfactory, and that it was as difficult to keep warm in ancient Italy as it is sometimes today.

Water was brought into Rome from some distance by means of aqueducts. Pure mountain water was thus available, being carried in mains through the streets of the city and piped into private houses, not unlike our modern systems.

The Romans, like the Greeks, had less furniture in their houses than we have in ours. In the first place, the walls were themselves decorative. Covered inside with stucco, the adornment depended upon the purse and the taste of the owner. Some walls were merely marked off into panels. Again, the panels might be painted in one solid color, or might each contain a picture, bordered with some conventional pattern. Cornices and relief work characterized the establishments of the wealthy in later times.

In rooms thus decorated, statuary and vases were often tastily arranged. Chairs, tables and lamps were found everywhere—simple and even crude in the homes of the common people; elaborate and costly among the wealthy. Couches were in general use, being used as beds and sofas. The most common chairs were mere seats, having no backs; these were used especially in early times. Tables were needed for various purposes; to support lamps, hold dishes or articles of the toilet. Made of various materials, some of the most costly were of citrus wood, valued for its beautiful grain. Fine workmanship is evinced by some of the old lamps which remain to us. They range in size from very slight vessels to hold oil, with a little hole for a wick, to tall candelabra, used for lighting banqueting rooms. The oil used in the lamps and the candles for the candelabra were both unsatisfactory and gave at best but a sorry light. Torches were used on the street in place of lanterns and modern street lights.

There was little about the exterior of these Roman houses to suggest the possible beauty within. Standing close to one another, plain in color, without any windows in the first story and few above, the outside view was bare indeed. The streets were narrow, the houses being built near one another for the purpose of excluding the hot sun. Little space was available for lawns or garden patches. Flowers usually adorned the court, and a tiny garden at the rear of the house allowed the cultivation of the "salad"—some green leaves, often lettuce—and a few table necessities.

In striking contrast to these unostentatious exteriors were the public buildings of the town and the country homes of the rich. The public buildings will be considered by themselves, but some comment may here be made upon the country villas of the Romans.

In the first place, a charming spot was usually selected for the great country home. It might be some pleasing mountain side, some bluff overlooking the sea, or some wooded height. Most desirable was the locality which united the mountains and the sea.

"When the Romans were resting, they liked to do so with a fine landscape before their eyes. In Italy there were, and are, two kinds of fine views obtainable. One may settle down inland, within view of the mountains, and, if possible, not far from forests and lakes; or one may take advantage of the admirable coast scenery, which is one of Italy's great attractions, and charms the traveler by the infinite variety of its effects. There the waves which lap upon its sands change with every hour, now lost in a golden halo, now flecked with silver spangles, the embodiment of liquid motion and sparkling radiance; that distant strip of blue sea which is the first thing that catches the eye after we have crossed the Alps, and which we never seem to weary of watching.

"The ancients fell under its charm as readily as we do; they knew and revelled in the delights of the Bay of Naples. But no matter where it was, no villa seemed quite satisfactory unless it enabled its inhabitants to obtain a glimpse of the sea."[1]

Seeking to escape from the heat, dust and noise of Rome, the wealthy fled to the seaside, often exchanging the crowds at home for the crowds of popular resorts, as do many people in our own generation. The comparatively few rich possessed several villas in different parts of the peninsula, and visited each according to the season. With talk of a simple life, so similar to that heard now that it sounds strangely familiar, they resorted to estates where simplicity alone was lacking. Just as it would be possible at the present time to find country homes which in their appointments exceeded any magnificence

[1] Roman Life under the Caesars: Emile Thomas, 191.

found in the city, so among the ancient Romans, many of these villas were extensive, having spacious grounds for the occupants, elaborate gardens, artificial lakes, and artificial groves.

"The Roman villas were much larger and more elaborately decorated than those of our own day. They abounded in statues, in mosaics, and in peristyles; they contained dining-rooms of every possible kind and for every season of the year; if there was no lake, its place was supplied by an euripus,[2] or a leafy grove of plane-trees; then there were porticoes and crytoporticos, whither the owner was carried in a litter to take the air, so that even the smallest villa covered a great deal of ground—so much so, that they presented the appearance of so many towns."[3]

Pliny left several descriptions of his numerous villas. One at Tibur, on the Anio, possessed many natural attractions, supplemented by artificial devices planned by an able architect of the time.

"The Anio, passing through the midst of marble porticoes whose pillars were reflected in its waters, gave forth coolness and verdure all around. A view of the neighboring woods gave promise of absolute quiet; countless works of art, statues, and mosaics, helped to rest the eye in whichever direction one looked."[4]

The palaces of the princes belong properly to the realm of private buildings, for they were not constructed for the adornment of Rome so much as for the glorification of the prince. The early princes, Augustus and Tiberius, were conspicuous for their simplicity of life, in no way distinguishing themselves in their dwellings from any other Roman noble. The Golden House of Nero was the first great palace, and it is safe to say that no one since has outdone Nero in the magnificence of his dwelling. There is probably no question but that descriptions given of it by Latin writers have been exaggerated, yet with allowance made for fulsome praise, it was nevertheless a stupendous undertaking.

"It was surrounded by parks, woods, and pools of great size, which seem to have been entirely within the walls. The

[2]Euripus—after the channel separating Euboea from Greece.
[3]Roman Life under the Caesars, 196.
[4]Ibid., 197.

colonnades of the house itself extended a Roman mile in length, and crossed some of the chief thoroughfares of the city. The cities of the East were ransacked for masterpieces of Greek art for the interior. The walls shone with gold and pearls, and the roof rested on marble columns of enormous size and beauty. If we put any faith in the accounts which have reached us, we must admit that the world saw then the crowning monument of the luxury of rulers and the servility of their subjects."[5]

Amid the luxury of villas and magnificent homes, men now and then cast longing glances at the simplicity of the common people, who, unblessed with material goods, were at the same time unburdened with heavy cares and responsibilities. Horace voiced this thought in several of his odes, particularly the following:

> "No walls, with ivory inlaid,
> Adorn my house; no colonnade
> Proudly supports my citron beams,
> Nor rich with gold my ceiling flames;
> Nor have I, like an heir unknown,
> Seized upon Atalus his throne;
> Nor dames, to happier fortunes bred,
> Draw down on me the purple thread;
> Yet with a firm and honest heart,
> Unknowing or of fraud or art,
> A liberal vein of genius blest,
> I'm by the rich and great carest.
> My patron's gift, my Sabine field
> Shall all its rural plenty yield,
> And, happy in that rural store,
> Of heaven and him I ask no more."

[5] Inge: Society in Rome under the Caesars.

CHAPTER III.

Wearing Apparel.

As is likely to be the case in mild climates, few garments were worn by the Romans. This was quite as true in later years as in the early republic. While considerable wealth might be expended in costly materials and jewelled accessories, nevertheless when compared with the elaborate wardrobe deemed necessary by devotees of modern society, the dress of ancient Rome appears simple indeed.

The tunic, a sort of short-sleeved, woolen skirt, extending from the neck to the middle of the leg, was worn by men in all periods. Its length could be controlled by drawing it up over a belt, which was ordinarily worn with the tunic. This garment was ample, and fell in folds over the girdle, hanging below it like a short skirt. Not interfering in any way with the movements of the body, this tunic was worn by workmen, and was the garment worn within the house by all classes of men. The tunic of the ordinary citizen was plain—white wool, unless one's calling or purse made it advisable to seek some dull color less quickly soiled. The wool, which was imported from various countries, differed in its natural color, some being brown, some grey. Thus in the undyed wool it was possible to find serviceable hues. The citizen whose time was not given to manual labor wore a white tunic. Knights and senators had a broad strip of purple running from the shoulder to the bottom of their tunics, this either being woven into the material or stitched upon it. In cold weather it was customary to wear a shorter tunic underneath this outer one.

The toga was the robe donned by the Roman citizen when he went abroad. It was also made of wool, being heavy and full. It was probably a strip of woolen goods, at least five yards long and three or four yards wide, and was thrown around the body in a peculiar way not quite known to us, completely covering the person, and falling in graceful folds. It was impossible to hasten in this robe, which was suitable only for men of leisure and dignity. We read of Romans hastily gathering up their togas when in the later republic there seemed to be danger of a riot in the streets. Encumbered with its long folds, reaching to his ankles, a man was ill prepared to make rapid movements. The toga was the garment of Roman citizenship. Clad in it, the citizen went forth to his duties as an officer of the city; senators appeared in togas in the senate; whenever men went forth from home, they were thus attired, save in late years alone, when a convenient cape threatened to replace the toga. It was one of Augustus' early efforts to restore the toga to its former popularity. This he found impossible to accomplish, for the freedom of the cloak was greatly enjoyed. Nevertheless, for social occasions and occasions of importance and dignity, the toga was the established dress. An exile from Rome, or one deprived of his rights as a citizen, was at the same time deprived of the privilege of wearing the toga—the distinctive Roman costume.

Even in the time of Nero, any attempt to dispense with this robe called forth criticism. We are told that Nero one day attired himself in a flowered tunic to receive guests who were attending one of his receptions, but he was sharply criticized for so doing. "He had even such a contempt for tradition that he would appear in public with his tunic flowing loose without a belt," Dion Cassius related.

"An emperor who gave audience without the *toga* shocked the Romans as much as we should be shocked to learn that an officer of state dressed in slippers and frock coat had formally received ambassadors."

It was no more the custom for a Roman citizen to appear in the streets without sandals or shoes than it is usual for us to do so today. Shoes were worn with the toga, and the senators had a special kind, as distinctive of their social position as their toga. Sandals were worn in the house, save during meals, when they were removed by slaves.

Men went about with no covering for the head. In stormy weather the toga was drawn up around the head, or if one went out prepared for rain, he wore a storm cloak supplied with a hood. Workmen whose employment kept them out of doors all day protected their heads by woolen caps. Even the better classes wore hats when traveling far in the hot sun.

Roman boys wore their hair long, allowing it to hang on their necks and over their shoulders. When the boy became a man and assumed the toga of the citizen, his hair was cut short. Beards were not seen during the republic, save in rare cases. They were, however, worn as a sign of mourning. In the later empire they were quite generally seen.

Each Roman citizen wore a signet ring. The ring itself was made of iron in early times, while the carving upon its stone might be most beautiful and costly. Gold rings were not permitted to any below the equestrians during the early republic, although later this prohibition was removed. An impression in soft wax was made by the owner when he wished to affix his seal to a document, in cases where we today sign our names. Aside from his signet ring, jewelry was not worn by citizens of good taste. This does not imply, of course, that there were not many devotees of fashion, who, like fops in modern times, adorned themselves with many jewels and expended much care and money upon their gems.

Woman's apparel was not radically different from man's. A woolen tunic, as a rule having sleeves, was worn by women. Over this was thrown the stola—a larger, more ample garment, open from the waist to the shoulders upon either side, and held in place on the shoulders by jeweled clasps. At the waist it was girded by a belt, the stola falling over the belt in loose folds. Below the waist it reached to the floor, finished at the bottom by a wide flounce. The flounce was the special privilege of the Roman matron, not being worn by women before their marriage.

When they went from home the Roman women donned a *palla,* comparable to our shawls. Slippers were worn at home; shoes upon the street. Hats were not in general use, but the hair was elaborately dressed, and ornamented with jewels. Parasols were carried by a matron's slave, as was also her fan.

The Roman women made up for any lack of jewelled splendor in their lords by their numerous ornaments. Pearls were always in favor. Diamonds were scarcely known and were not popular. Fabulous sums were paid then as now for rare gems. Caesar is said to have paid nearly $300,000 for a pearl, and the wife of Caligula was reputed to possess a set of pearls and emeralds worth nearly $2,000,000.

Wool was the material in greatest demand for clothing. Linen was sometimes used for under-tunics, and slaves were often dressed in linen garments. Cotton was known, as was silk in the later periods. However, because it was so filmy and transparent, silk was not serviceable for clothing, and it was forbidden for public wear.

Much is commonly made of the luxury of later Roman days, and in general there was conspicuous waste of wealth by the comparatively few who possessed it; nevertheless, it is possible to parallel many Roman excesses by those of the rich of our generation. Dress, like other elements of civilization, was affected by the riches which in the later republic poured into Italy.

"With the conquest of the world Roman commerce had become extended. From distant countries merchants imported rich and beautiful stuffs, precious stones, rare and curious jewels. Women then began to spend a great deal of time upon their dress. Though they were unacquainted with our extravagance in gloves, hats and coiffures, they delighted in the delicate textures from the East Indies or from China; though fur was used by them only in moderation, they indulged a fancy for garments of brilliant color—a rather expensive fancy, when you consider that the double-dyed purple wool which came from Tyre cost about $167 a pound. Pompey's triumph over Mithridates had introduced into Rome the Oriental luxury of precious stones. People went wild over them. The diamond seems to have been little employed for ornament, except to be set in rings. But people were passionately fond of the emerald, the aquamarine, the opal, the sardonyx, and especially of pearls. They trimmed the lacings and buckles of their shoes with pearls. They even covered their slippers with them. Luxury had become for women an absolute necessity."[1]

---
[1] Roman Life in Pliny's Time: Pellison, 51.

CHAPTER IV.

Food, Meals and Banquets.

Italy was fortunate in possessing a wealth of native food products. The earliest inhabitants found fruit, nuts and meat everywhere abundant, and when pastoral life gave way to settlements and agriculture, grain supplied meal, the olive tree, oil, and the grape, wine. Even today, these remain the staple articles of food for the peasants of the peninsula. Fruits grew in profusion from remote times; the grape, apple, pear, plum and quince were known in antiquity. The olive was introduced from Greece and developed better in Italy than in its native home. In the latter years of the republic Italy was a country of orchards. New fruits and nuts were imported with other Eastern products after Rome's campaigns in the East.

Vegetables were by no means few. Asparagus, beans, beets, cabbage, carrots, cucumbers, garlic, melons, onions, peas, and radishes were as well known to the ancient Romans as to the modern Italians. Especially they were fond of growing green stuff—lettuce and cress, for salads. No matter how tiny the plot of ground, room was generally found for these indispensable plants. The potato and tomato, so constantly in use today, were unknown.

Pork was the meat held in greatest favor by all classes. Beef was eaten only by the wealthy; goat meat was a food for the poor, who bought it only because it was cheap. Chickens, ducks and geese were grown for the market. The peacock was perhaps as popular a dish among the well-to-do as the turkey has become in America. Among wild game, cranes and partridges were greatly in demand.

In early times fish was not used to any extent, but later it came to be shared by rich and poor alike. Milk, cream and cheese were essential upon all tables; honey filled the place of modern sugar, and oil was used where today we use butter. Tea and coffee were unknown. Wine, well diluted with water, was the universal beverage.

Notwithstanding this wide diversity of foods, it is not to be supposed that all were commonly found on the tables of the masses. In the morning the peasant ate his porridge—not unlike some of our breakfast cereals. At noon, if his work took him some distance from home, he made a light lunch upon millet cakes, dried figs or raisins, olives and cheap wine. At night, he sometimes had pork or goat's meat, with vegetables and salad. Ordinarily, to be sure, the dinner was eaten in the middle of the day. In towns, however, the citizen enjoyed his substantial meal at night, sharing it as often as possible with friends, who prolonged the dinner into the late evening.

Eating for the mere pleasure it gave was characteristic of later Rome, it is true, but the early Romans cared little for eating for eating's sake. Simplicity of food, table appointment and service was apparent in the early republic. Members of the family sat around a table in the atrium—the only room in the house—frequently. Their receptacles were of the simplest nature, being made of crude pottery, or even wood. Knives and forks were unknown. Food was cut in small portions before being brought to the table; spoons were placed beside each plate. However humble the home, one dish was carefully chosen and gave evidence of some degree of taste and workmanship. This was the saltcellar, since salt was sacred to the gods. Together with meal, salt was offered to the Mighty Ones at each repast. This offering has been fittingly compared to the grace which it was once the custom to say before the partaking of food in Christian families.

With the influx of Eastern ideas and Eastern manners and customs that accompanied the return of the Roman army from conquests in the East, a decided change came about in Italy. Carrying things to excess, in accordance with their dispositions, the Romans took over the feasts of the Greeks, and, depriving them of their redeeming qualities, preserved all the objectionable ones. Cooks were imported to prepare sumptuous repasts. Palates were satiated with delicacies of the known world. Tables, dishes, and dining-rooms were given limitless care and attention that they might be faultless and might exceed the cost of those possessed by friends. The inborn moderation which had always prevented the Greeks from falling into mere crudity, was lacking in Roman temperament.

"The very rich, aping the luxury of the Greeks, but lacking their refinement, became gluttons instead of gourmands. They ransacked the world for articles of food, preferring the rare and the costly to what was really palatable and delicate. They measured the feast by the quantities they could consume, reviving the sated appetite by piquant sauces and resorting to emetics to prolong the pleasures of the table and prevent the effects of over-indulgence. The separate dining-room was introduced, the great houses having two or more. The dining-couch took the place of the bench or stool, slaves served the food to the reclining guests, a dinner dress was devised. Of course there were always wealthy men, Atticus, the friend of Cicero, for example, who clung to the simpler customs of the earlier days, but these could make little headway against the current of senseless dissipation and extravagance. Over against these must be set the fawning poor, who preferred the fleshpots of the rich patron to the bread of honest independence. Between the two extremes was a numerous middle class of the well-to-do."[1]

Even in later days, breakfast remained but a simple repast. Bread dipped in wine, raisins, olives and cheese were frequently eaten. Eggs were served sometimes, but as a rule the meal was very light and was taken upon rising. About eleven luncheon was ready. Cold foods were usually served. Bread, salad, fruits and nuts made up the midday meal, with some variations. Here again, only light foods were desired. The luncheon was followed by the siesta, during which the streets were practically deserted.

Dinner was an important feature of the day. Since there were no public functions, no theatres to attend, no parties, no entertainments of a various nature so constantly offered today, the dinner was made to serve several purposes. It was the occasion when hearty dishes were set before the man who had eaten lightly earlier in the day. But the mere satisfying of hunger was only one object of the dinner. It was the time when men exchanged ideas with their friends and acquaint-

[1] Private Life of the Romans, Johnston, p. 201.

ances. Guests were summoned. They came and reclined around a table. The wife of the host, and any other women who might make up the family, sat erect. With a reversed order of modern ideas, the places on either side of the host were assigned to the humbler guests, while the guest of honor was placed at the head of the table. The dining-room was suited to the season and the position of the sun. Wealthy men had several rooms adapted to the different hours of the day and different months. Costly tables stood in the dining-room. Until late times it was not customary to cover the table with a cloth. After the custom was introduced, still expensive and richly-carved tables were deemed necessary to a well-appointed dining-room.

At least three courses were served. Sometimes many more were added. The first course, as at the present time, was planned to sharpen the appetite. Oysters or some variety of seafish was served with appetizing sauces. The dinner proper consisted of fish, meat, vegetables, which were often served in several courses. Afterwards a dessert was brought in. Pastry, fruits, nuts were provided in abundance, while wine was freely used. The dinner lasted from two to four hours, and even more time might elapse if conversation waxed warm.

Much has come down to us regarding the extravagance of the Roman banquet, and without question many displays of wealth were made—less from desire for high living than from a hope of provoking comment. Riches were suddenly acquired with Rome's unparalleled expansion, and, intoxicated by rapid change of fortune, many Romans found the dinner a sure means of awaking the admiration and envy of their friends. When compared with dinners served occasionally in recent times, Roman meals no longer provoke the astonishment they did in ancient times, among a people unused to extravagant living. Yet, after all allowances have been made, the accounts which have come down to us are startling.

"Couches made of silver, wine instead of water for the hands, twenty-two courses to a single *cena,* seven thousand birds served at another, a dish of livers of fishes, tongues of flamingos, brains of peacocks and pheasants mixed up together, strike us as vulgarity run mad. The sums spent upon these feasts do not seem so fabulous now as they did then.

As signs of the times, however, as indications of changed ideals, of degeneracy and decay, they deserved the notice that the Roman historians and satirists gave them."[2]

The Roman who gave evidence of his riches by his splendid feasts, tried to surpass any effort of his friends. The spirit of rivalry entered into the competition of dinners as into other competitions. Skilled cooks were expected to produce new and original dishes, but the host must needs exercise his own wits to provide some striking feature for the evening.

"The dessert was composed of pastry and fruit. Since Priapus was the god of the gardens, it was natural that he should preside over this part of the meal; so the pastry cooks used to make out of their dough figures of Priapus gathering up his robe in front so that a deep pocket was formed in its folds; when these figures appeared as dessert the pockets would be filled with all kinds of fruit, which the god would seem to be offering to the guests. The final course, moreover, was the time for surprises. Sometimes the ceiling of the dining-room would open and flowers would rain down; sometimes a fountain of perfumed water would rise from a hidden pipe; sometimes even—and this was a less charming surprise—a skeleton would be brought into the dining-room. Petronius, in his romance, records such an occurrence as follows:

"'While we were drinking and admiring in detail the magnificence of the feast, a slave placed upon the table a silver skeleton, so well contrived that the vertebrae and the joints moved easily in all directions.' "[3]

In the midst of such lavish feasts, many Romans still clung to the simplicity of earlier days. In the humorous, kindly letter written by Pliny to his friend Septicius Clarus we learn how the well-bred gentleman of later Rome lived:

"How happened it, my friend, that you did not keep your engagement the other night to sup with me? But take notice, justice is to be had, and I expect you shall fully reimburse me the expense I was at to treat you; which, let me tell you, was no small sum. I had prepared, you must know, a lettuce

[1] Private Life of the Romans, Johnston, p. 214.
[3] Roman Life in Pliny's Time, Pellison, p. 173.

apiece, three snails, two eggs, and a barley cake, with some sweet wine and snow; the snow most certainly I shall charge to your account, as a rarity that will not keep. Besides all these curious dishes, there were olives of Andalusia, gourds, shalots and a hundred other dainties equally sumptuous. You should have likewise been entertained either with an interlude, the rehearsal of a poem, or a piece of music, as you like best; or, such was my liberality, with all three. But the luxurious delicacies and Spanish dancers of a certain—I know not who, were, it seems, more to your taste. However, I shall have my revenge of you, depend upon it—in what manner shall at present be a secret. In good truth, it was not kind thus to disappoint your friend. I had almost said yourself; and, upon second thought, I do say so. For how agreeably should we have spent the evening, in laughing, trifling, and deep speculation! You may sup, I confess, at many places more splendidly; but you can be treated nowhere, believe me, with more unconstrained cheerfulness, simplicity, and freedom; only make the experiment, and if you do not ever afterward prefer my table to any other, never favor me with your company again."

While inviting one to dine with him, Juvenal mentions various dishes with which he would serve his honored guest:

> "From Tibur's stock
> A kid shall come, the fattest of the flock,
> The tenderest too, and yet too young to browse
> The thistle's shoots, the willow's watery boughs,
> With more of milk than blood; and pullets dressed
> With new-laid eggs, yet tepid from the nest,
> And sperage wild, which, from the mountain's side,
> My housemaid left her spindle to provide;
> And grapes long kept, yet pulpy still, and fair,
> And the rich Signian and the Syrian pear;
> And apples, that in flavor and in smell
> The boasted Picene equal, or excel."

Baths of Caracalla.

CHAPTER V.

BIRTH AND CHILDHOOD.

As we have already seen, the *patria potestas* allowed the father to acknowledge his child or not, as he chose. Nevertheless, from earliest times it was customary to raise the eldest son and daughter, and need of fighting men in the Roman state led parents usually to bring up their children. In the late republic and early principate, to be sure, children were regarded as a burden, but this resulted in fewer marriages rather than in the exposure of babes. As a matter of fact, few Roman children were exposed, as compared with exposure among the Greeks.

The nurse placed the newly-born babe at the father's feet. If he desired to raise it, he took it up in his arms. Otherwise he turned away, indicating that he did not intend to care for it. In this latter case, the babe was left where it might be found by some one who would adopt it, as his own, or worse, by one who would bring it up to beg. Children were crippled and maimed by those who sought through them to obtain charity. Latin writers of the republic were outspoken against this wretched custom. Frequently the mother, unable to save her child, would leave trinkets with it, these possibly allowing the child to be later identified and received once more into the home from which in infancy it had been cast out. We must not dwell too much upon a habit which was possibly practised among the Romans no more than among certain classes in modern times.

Having been duly acknowledged by the father, the first few days were days for purification. The Romans, like the Greeks, felt that the mother and child needed to be purified, and this was accomplished by certain ceremonies in the home. On the eighth day after birth girls were named; boys were named upon the ninth day.

The name was an important matter. Boys were given three names: the first, a given name, corresponding to our so-called

Christian names. The second was the clan name, and the third, the name of his family. As compared with our numerous given names, the Romans had but few. Fifteen names include all those in common use among Roman citizens: Aulus, Decimus, Gaius, Gnaeus, Kaeso, Lucius, Manius, Marcus, Publius, Quintus, Servius, Sextus, Spurius, Tiberius and Titus comprised the list from which the father ordinarily chose a name for his son. The eldest son as a rule received the name of his father—a custom not infrequently followed today.

In the beginning these names had been given because of some special significance. Lucius once meant, "born by day"; Manius, "born in the morning"; Quintus, "the fifth"; Decimus, "the tenth"; Marcus was related to the name of the war-god, Mars, and Tiberius, to the river-god, Tiberis. Just as the original meaning of the vast number of given names among us has long since been forgotten, and names are now bestowed because they are liked for themselves alone or for some fond association, so the later Romans forgot entirely the early significance of their names, and the first or second born might receive the name of Quintus or Decimus.

The clan name, like the family name, was a matter of inheritance. *Ius* was the usual ending for the clan name, although this might be written *eius, aius,* or *eus.* Other endings as a rule indicated foreign origins. All members of the clan, whether men, women or freedmen, bore the clan name.

The family name indicated the particular family or branch of family to which the bearer belonged. The Roman aristocracy traced its history back long centuries, and the family name was prized because it gave evidence of long lineage. It was not infrequent for men to have more than three names: for example, if a youth were adopted into a new family, he adopted the name of his foster father; again, a general might be given a popular name by acclamation, as for example, Publius Cornelius Scipio was given the name Africanus, after his successful campaign in Africa. Nicknames were often given men, and these descended to their children, while the association was forgotten.

Less is known about the names given by Roman fathers to their daughters. *Paulla, Gaia,* and *Publia* were common names, and were no doubt but the feminine form of the father's name. When women married they frequently took their husband's name, but such was not the universal practice.

Slaves were merely given names by their owners, these not being transmitted to their children. Indeed, when slaves became the possessions of new masters, their names were generally changed.

The occasion of the naming was an important day in the child's life. Friends and relatives gathered to the festival, each bringing some little gift for the babe. These little tokens were usually of such a nature that they could be strung upon a cord and tied around the baby's neck. Superstition had much to do with the ceremony, and the tiny presents were chosen as preventives against the 'evil eye,' so greatly feared by the parents of the child. Each free-born child received on this occasion a *bulla* from its father—a sort of gold locket, containing an amulet which was supposed to bring good luck and ward off evil. This was worn by the maid until her wedding day and by the boy until he assumed the toga which signified citizenship. Then it was offered to the Lares of the family and was preserved with great care.

Roman writers did not deign to consider the simple details of domestic life among their customary topics, and our material for reconstructing family life is not very abundant. Nevertheless, we know that the Roman child had plenty of playthings, even though they were usually crude and unfinished, as compared with the wonderful toys of today. Dolls were popular then as now. They were made of clay or wax. Little wagons and carts were drawn around by small boys quite as they have been in all ages. Tops and hoops were known, and even more elaborate toys were provided for certain fortunate children.

"Children's toys and pocket knives with bone handles have been found, on which are engraved palms and whips, or the names of horses and charioteers, and their portraits. One small chariot made of lead, evidently intended as a toy for a child of two or three, is apparently a reproduction of some winning chariot, and is inscribed with the names of the horses and charioteers."[1]

[1] Life under the Caesars, 102.

Birds and animals were pets in antiquity, as to-day. Dogs were probably most favored, as they have always been. Cats as pets were not so generally known but monkeys were occasionally tamed. Doves, ducks, crows and geese amused the boys and girls of ancient Rome.

Until the age of seven, boys and girls were left to the care of their mothers. Slaves cared for the little ones under the mother's direction. In later times it was quite generally the case among the better classes that Greek nurses were employed, so that the children might learn to speak Greek from their infancy. It was quite usual for the young bride to take with her into her new home the nurse who had been her attendant since her childhood. By the time the boys were removed from their mother's care, at the age of seven years, they were expected to know how to speak correctly and to have been trained in obedience and orderly conduct.

The usual life of women determined the nature of the girl's education. During infancy, and girlhood as well, the maiden remained the special care of her mother.

"A girl has just been born. The anxiety of the mother is expressed by a thousand precautions, a thousand superstitious practices. Amulets are hung about the neck of the child, to preserve her from accidents and from suffering. Prayers are offered in the temples to the gods, that the child may be blessed with beauty. When intelligence begins to dawn in her young mind, her nurse or governess is at hand to narrate to her those marvelous stories which, from the earliest times, have fascinated and terrified children—stories about ghosts and specters, about the Lamiae, the Gorgon, hobgoblins, and about Gelo, the witch, the kidnapper of children, known at Lesbos from the time of Sappho.

"Soon it becomes necessary to arrange for the education of the little girl. The first thing is to teach her to perform the duties belonging to her sex—especially to weave and spin. These manual employments constituted an essential part of every good education, even in the most aristocratic families."[2]

[2] Life in Pliny's Time, 33.

CHAPTER VI.

SCHOOLS AND EDUCATION.

It is possible to discern four distinct stages in the development of Roman education: the so-called *National* stage, when the training that had sufficed for the father was deemed sufficient for the son, and foreign influences were yet unfelt in Rome; the *transition* stage, when Greek influence was permeating Italy, to be welcomed by some and descried by others; *the first period of Greek predominance in culture,* when the beauty of learning seemed enough to justify it; and lastly, the *later period of Greek learning,* when the ideas of the Greek savants were given a practical significance.

We know nothing whatever about education under the monarchy. It is safe to conclude that conditions were still more primitive than under the early republic, when the sons were instructed by the father in those duties which, as fathers of families and as citizens, they would be expected to perform. Religious obligations, glorification of the brave deeds and worthy qualities of ancestors, and a most elementary knowledge of reading, writing and calculation, made up the education of the Roman youth.

"If a boy grew up healthy and strong in mind and body, if he revered the gods, his parents and the laws and institutions of his country, if he was familiar with the traditional methods of agriculture, and had some knowledge of the way of conducting public business in times of peace and of serving in the field in time of war; if a girl learned from her mother to be modest, virtuous and industrious, skilled in the duties of the household, this was all that was needed, that children should grow up what their parents would have them to be. There was no conception of, still less any desire for, any system of progressive culture. The usage of their ancestors set the standard at which the Romans aimed. What had been good enough for the fathers was good enough for the sons. It was the severest censure to say of a man that he had acted as his fathers would not have done."[1]

It was not necessary to maintain schools to accomplish results such as these. The state made no requirements of parents, and each family instructed its young as the father saw fit. Under the care of their mother until they were seven years of age, the boys henceforth were instructed by the father, as time and opportunity permitted. The boy assisted his father in his function of priest, at the domestic hearth. Upon occasions of family sorrow or rejoicing, sacrifices were offered, and ceremonies were observed. Gradually the boy learned to understand what duties fell to the head of the family, if he would retain the favor of the gods, and prosper.

"There were certain things which must not be done, just as there were certain duties which must not be neglected, under pain of bringing down upon the offender their wrath and the ensuing punishment. But a faithful discharge of the traditional observances would secure their favour, and what these observances were it was the duty of each father to teach his son. The religion of early Rome had its good as well as its bad side. At least it kept a man face to face with his conscience. He knew that the conduct of his life was a matter to which the powers that ruled the world were not either blind or indifferent, and that they would be with him or against him according to his actions."

Virtue was engendered and bravery stimulated by exploiting the lives of one's ancestors. As sacrifices were offered to the gods of state, so they were made to the genius of departed relatives. Wax masks of the forefathers were preserved in aristocratic families, and these were occasionally brought out with great reverence. Stories of these departed ones were told and retold, and their heroism extolled at banquets and at family gatherings. From his infancy a youth heard such stories and through them learned to admire certain qualities and to despise others. Thus his own character was molded and his ideas were formed. At the age of sixteen or seventeen the boy was considered old enough to assume certain obligations for the state. He laid aside the toga hitherto worn and donned the white toga, indicative of Roman citizenship.

[1] Roman Education: Wilkins, p. 1.

As has been already stated, the girl continued under the direction of her mother until her marriage, which occurred when she was yet a mere child. It was her ambition to excel in spinning, weaving and in the various arts which as the matron of her husband's household she would be called upon to discharge.

In this way, without change from one generation to another, the childhood of Roman youth and maidens passed, unaffected by foreign influences. Yet we do not know how early the ideas of the Greeks crept into Roman thought. By the middle of the third century before Christ they had already wrought some changes, especially leading to the employment of Greek nurses for the children of the upper classes. Many Romans deplored the infusion of Greek ideas, but the transformation was bound to come, and now the training of earlier years no longer satisfied. Elementary schools sprang up. At first these were simple indeed. A busy father would acquire a Greek slave to teach his children. The children in the neighborhood would come in to profit by the same instruction. Ambitious slaves or freedmen would themselves secure a room or open space, with a roof overhead, but otherwise open to the air. Here with benches and no other equipment they would instruct their young charges in reading, writing and computation. For writing, tablets of wax were employed, a stilus being used to trace the letters. The Twelve Tables of Laws were learned as the children grew older. Since Latin literature was lacking, a freedman translated the Odyssey into Latin, this being the first literary production in Latin.

The teachers of these elementary schools, usually slaves or freedmen, sometimes received fees, and always received presents at the various yearly festivals. It is supposed that they were first compensated by these presents alone; later it became customary to pay also a stipulated fee, which was small. To any who were willing to pay this fee, the elementary school was open. Since the state made no requirement regarding the training of the young, it is probable that many children never attended schools at all.

In the better class of elementary schools, busts of famous men and national heroes were found. Tablets illustrating famous deeds and events were not unknown. Under the most favorable circumstances, however, the schools were but bare, unattractive places. The social position of the teacher was humble indeed. The state made no requirement of teachers, and he who would might teach.

School began early in the morning, and in the winter time the children came to school with lanterns, by which they studied until dawn. There was no long vacation, as in modern times, but frequent recesses occurred as state festivals were held. Some sixty of these festivals have been recorded, so quite a portion of the year was free from school duties. Moreover, although the schools were open in the summer months, the better classes took their children out of the city for the hot weather, and the requirements of those who remained were probably light. Discipline was always severe. While no uniformity of instruction in different schools was sought after, yet because all teachers were Greeks and had been trained according to Greek ideas, a certain similarity existed, after all.

For children whose parents desired them to advance beyond the elementary school training, there were higher schools which we may call Grammar schools, from the teacher, called *grammaticus*. Homer was studied in the Grammar school, and mythology, history, ethics and the interpretation of poetry were duly considered as the epic poems were studied. Verses were composed by boys in these schools, and the record has come down to us of one boy who before reaching his twelfth year took a prize for his verses. On the monument erected in memory of this youth, who died in early boyhood, it is related that in 94 A. D. Q. Sulpicius Maximus gained a prize for Greek verse in a contest that occurred during the festival of the Capitoline Games. "He had composed ex tempore 43 hexameters describing how Zeus rebuked Helios for entrusting his car to Phaethon." Music and geometry were sometimes taught in the Grammar school.

Only children of the noblest and wealthiest classes went beyond the Grammar school. These, however, found opportunity in schools of Rhetoric to continue their studies. In fact, grown men frequently attended lectures in the famous schools of Rhetoric, these being designed to fit men for a part in the political life of the day. All the work of these higher schools was carried on with the distinct object of preparing men to declaim. In order to be a successful public speaker, composition, dialectics—or debate—and oratory had to be mastered. The Romans never had the love of argument that was so inherent in the Greek mentality, and they found a very practical field for their rhetorical gifts and their oratory in the domain of law and jurisprudence.

As the old Roman religion declined, the greatest minds in Rome found a guide for conduct in philosophy. Large numbers of students flocked to the most distinguished teachers in this domain. Theophrastus and hundreds of pupils, and philosophers of less ability, were attended by men of mature years as well as by young men who found much that was satisfying in philosophical thought. Indeed, for the reflective man, philosophy supplied the only light obtainable upon problems of life in its broadest scope.

> "When first I laid the purple by, and free,
> Yet trembling at my new-felt liberty,
> Approached the hearth, and on the Lares hung
> The *bulla*, from my willing neck unstrung;
> When gay associates, sporting at my side,
> And the white boss, displayed with conscious pride,
> Gave me, unchecked, the haunts of vice to trace,
> And throw my wandering eyes on every face;
> When life's perplexing maze before me lay,
> And error, heedless of the better way,
> To straggling paths, far from the route of truth,
> Woo'd, with blind confidence, my timorous youth,
> I fled to you, Cornutus, pleased to rest
> My hopes and fears on your Socratic breast,
> Nor did you, gentle sage, the charge decline;
> Then, dextrous to beguile, your steady line
> Reclaimed, I know not by what winning force,
> My morals, warped from virtue's straighter course;
> While reason pressed incumbent on my soul,
> That struggled to receive the strong control,
> And took, like wax, tempered by plastic skill,
> The form your hand imposed, and bears it still!"[2]

---
[2] Persius. Trans. in Roman Life in Pliny's Time, 31.

Travel offered another means of attaining broad culture, and he who found himself possessed of sufficient means and leisure, betook him to Greece, to Rhodes and to Asia Minor, where were to be seen those spots which had witnessed critical events in the world's history, and where were to be also found collections of art and literature. For the student, no other place could offer such inducements as Athens, although Alexandria rose in importance as the venerated Attic center declined. Contact with other civilizations, other ideas and ideals, broadened the mind of the cosmopolitan Roman, and gave him a truer basis upon which to judge his own national achievements.

It is perhaps unnecessary to emphasize the fact that the wealthy and talented alone availed themselves of such opportunities as offered for higher study and culture. Failing to understand that which was beyond his reach, the average Roman looked with misgivings, to say the least, upon the higher learning.

"The fissure was always widening between the culture open to the mass of the people, and that enjoyed by the upper classes. The earlier education had been meager and narrow, but at least it had been the same for all; the newer culture was the privilege of a class. The plebeians suspected and disliked what they knew was not for them, and both the training and literature which resulted from it never wholly lost something of an exclusive and exotic character."[3]

Under the principate, steps were taken to bring a uniformity into the education of the young. Julius Caesar laid the foundation for state schools, but it was left for Vespasian to firmly establish higher schools by paying salaries to the teachers from the state treasury. Hadrian followed a policy of generosity regarding schools and the later princes gave special attention to the welfare of the children during those years when they should be given regular instruction. However, the conditions attending the late principate do not properly belong to this discussion.

[3] Roman Education, 29.

CHAPTER VII.

Sports and Pastimes.

The Romans had no such love for games as had the Greeks. To be sure, contests of an athletic character were held occasionally in Rome, but the enthusiasm so conspicuous in Hellas was lacking. The Roman could become enthusiastic only when actual danger was encountered by the one engaged to amuse him. For this reason his delight was in the struggles between wild animals in the arena, in the hunts, where men fought with these ferocious beasts, and in the gladiatorial shows, where man fought with man.

Because it was deemed necessary to preserve his health by physical exercise, the Roman practised during his youth with his companions in various feats of strength and skill. In the stadium, foot races, jumping contests, discus throwing, might be witnessed, and there was wholesome rivalry between the contestants. Nevertheless, all this was tolerated as necessary rather than enjoyable. Wrestling matches and boxing were perhaps more popular.

Several games of ball were played, but none so good as our own. Games of chance were so popular that they were forbidden by law save at the yearly festival of the Saturnalia. It was found impossible to enforce this law, however, because all kinds of lottery games were provided by gentlemen for the amusement of their private guests, and naturally, officers of the law were unable to detect them, or, again, prosecution of them would have been most unpopular. Dice, similar to those seen today, were thrown in ancient Rome. Sometimes dice were shaken for games not unlike our backgammon.

Public festivals were numerous during the republic and increased in the early empire. During the late republic, sixty-six days were appropriated by public games, and business was suspended for 135 days each year during the reign of Marcus Aurelius. Quite naturally it came about that so large a number of holidays, together with free distribution of bread, encouraged a constantly growing mob of idlers who found life agreeable enough if only they were fed and diverted.

Dramatic entertainments were never in great favor at Rome. Those who could so often witness real tragedy in the arena, found a mere make-believe tragedy in the theater much too tame to interest them. Yet there were large theaters where people flocked when nothing better offered. During the early republic there was some attempt at real dramatic art, but this shortly gave way to spectacular effects, produced by elaborate settings and the bringing of animals upon the stage. Soldiers in considerable numbers, mules laden with booty taken in war, and 3,000 bowls for the mixing of wine were produced in one dramatic representation for the pleasure of the audience. Less attention was given to what was sung and said than what was presented for the gratification of the eye. Naturally such conditions resulted in the extinction of the drama. From the standpoint of the dramatist, far better were the days of primitive equipment—when a temporary stage was erected at the foot of any hill, when having no scenery to represent a house, the incidents of the play had to occur upon the street, which highway the stage was made to represent. "An altar stood on the stage, we are told, to remind the people of the religious origin of the games. No better provision was made for the audience than for the actors. The people took their places on the slope before the stage, some reclining on the grass, some standing, some perhaps sitting on stools they had brought from home. There was always din and confusion to try the actor's voice, pushing and crowding, disputing and quarreling, wailing of children, and in the very midst of the play the report of something livelier to be seen elsewhere might draw the whole audience away."[1]

Beautiful theaters were not lacking in later times, but as we have just seen, lack of appreciation of dramatic art prevented the development of a national drama. Such plays as were shown were but imitations of the Greek; Greek characters were introduced in native costume. Lively comedies were better received. Mimes and pantomimes were always popular, but these catered to the crudest, coarsest and most sensual tastes of the people.

[1] Private Life of the Romans, 223.

Very exciting were the chariot races held frequently in the circuses. The word *circus* means *ring,* and the circus was used for many forms of entertainment, but chief always were the chariot races.

Strange to say, it was not the speed of the horses nor the skill of the charioteers that awakened wildest enthusiasm, but the danger which always attended the races in the circus. Two circuses were built within the city of Rome, and four more were within easy distance. Largest by far was the Circus Maximus, constructed between the Palatine and the Aventine. More than 2,000 feet long, it was about 400 feet broad. A wall, straight at one end, circular at the other, surrounded the whole. Seats were erected inside the wall, each row higher than the next, save on the straight end, which was left free. One hundred and fifty thousand people could find seats here in the time of Caesar, and the Circus Maximus was later enlarged to accommodate 100,000 more. The area enclosed by the seats in the interior of the structure, was divided lengthwise by a wall called the *spina*. Around this interior wall the race track lay. It was wide enough to allow four chariots to ride abreast, although as many as twelve occasionally entered. The straight end of the circus was furnished with twelve separate entrances, with a large one dividing six on either side. Through this middle entrance the procession wended its way on the day opening the games. Through the little cells on either side, each charioteer drove, having each his own entrance, wholly shut off from the rest. No advantage was given at the start, and the drivers drew for their positions.

At an early time, each Roman had exhibited his own horses in the contests of the circus, but in historic times, no man of repute and social standing drove his own teams. Indeed, so great was the expense connected with the races, and so costly were the horses that contended for first place that wealthy syndicates gained control of the entire matter. Each was known by its particular color, which was worn by the drivers and by the horses. There were syndicates of red, white, blue, green, purple and gold, and each had its local supporters who wagered large sums upon the horses of the blue or the green, as the case might be. Horses were imported at great cost and drivers were likewise eagerly sought after. All tricks known in modern times were understood in Rome, and it was considered perfectly legitimate to foul one another if possible. One driver would try to cross the track of another, or to crush his chariot at the turning. All means of winning were permitted, and charioteers were paid to lose, and were sometimes made way with by mysterious means when they proved to be beyond the reach of money. Plenty of chance was offered at the turnings to foul a rival, and a driver tried to do so if in that way he could improve his own position. The noise and confusion, with the blare of trumpets and cries of the drivers, the entangling of horses, chariots and charioteers, satisfied the Roman love of excitement, and we are told that not a seat was vacant when important races were given. Cheers and hisses of the multitudes, together with the tumult naturally attendant upon such an occasion, made the circus deafening. The charioteer who drove his team successfully was the idol of the hour. He was feted and lionized, received money and gifts from the society ladies of the day. The madness of the race might be compared perhaps to the intense excitement which still attends bull fights in Spain.

"Let us imagine ourselves among the spectators at one of the Roman chariot races. The procession forms on Capitoline Hill, passes down its sacred side, crosses the forum, the Vicus Tuscus, the Velabrum, the cattle market, and finally enters the circus, led by the presiding magistrate, standing in a chariot and wearing the dress of a triumphant general. His chariot is followed by musicians playing loudly upon their instruments and by a crowd of clients dressed in white togas. Then some statues of the gods, borne upon litters or carried in richly ornamented chariots and accompanied by the priests grouped in their religious corporations. This magnificent parade is welcomed by the cheers and acclamations of the crowd; but under the empire this demonstration lacks all enthusiasm. It has become an empty form like the procession itself; for the parade, splendid as it is, has grown monotonous, the religious sentiment connected with it has disappeared, and it no longer arouses curiosity. The spectators are in a hurry for the formality to end, they are impatient for the races to begin.

"At last the signal is given; the gates of the prisons are flung open and the contestants appear. They are standing in their two-wheeled chariots, which are usually very light and almost always drawn by four horses abreast. These charioteers are slaves or hirelings who drive for the owners of the horses. They are dressed in short, sleeveless tunics, with close-fitting caps upon their heads; the reins are wound around their waists, and each one has in his girdle a knife for cutting himself free from the reins in case of accident.

"Leaning over the necks of their horses, excited by the cries and the tumult of the crowd, who either hoot them or cheer them, they fling themselves into the contest. They must make the course seven times, seven times they must turn around the goals. As the contestants are usually numerous, as each round is eagerly disputed, they often come together in the narrow passage at the end of the spine—often they run into each other, and then there is, according to the expression of Sophocles, a shipwreck of men, horses and chariots. The one who has been able to avoid this danger arrives first at the chalk line in front of the balcony occupied by the presiding officer, and is proclaimed victor by the herald. Descending out of his chariot, he receives from the aedile a branch of Idumaean palm, or a wreath of gold and silver, wrought in imitation of laurel, or the more substantial but less brilliant prize of a sum of money."[3]

Hunts were sometimes held in the circus, and in earlier years gladiatorial contests were held here too, but for either use the plan of the circus, with its spine—its wall running lengthwise the greater part of the area—was not well adapted, so it grew to be the custom to hold such exhibitions in amphitheaters built for this purpose. Especially because the *spina* was decorated with works of art, altars in memory of the gods to whom games were first sacred, and even high obelisks, prevented the audience on one side the circus witnessing what might be transpiring upon the opposite side.

Most popular of all were the gladiatorial combats, introduced into Rome from Etruria. They had originated in Etruria in connection with funeral ceremonies, when human sacri-

[3] Roman Life in Pliny's Time, 192.

fices were offered as acceptable to the dead. In 264 B. C. the first exhibition of this kind was given in Rome, and for some time such combats were seen only at funeral games, upon which occasions captives in war were made to fight one another for the entertainment of the people and in honor of the dead. During the republic they remained private affairs, in that they were not held on any special holiday, that they were given ostensibly at least for some departed relative, and that the expense was borne by private purse. Under the principate, gladiatorial fights were still given as a free will offering to the people. One who desired popular favor for political advancement found it necessary to cater to the popular demand—for free bread and free shows. Even the highest minded of the emperors and the calmest philosophers regarded the custom as tolerable. Only occasionally did some humane spirit speak out against the incredible cruelty and demoralization attendant upon such exhibitions, and the voices of the few were lost amid the tumult of the multitudes.

The first gladiators were captives taken in war, who preferred death by the sword to slavery. As the demand for gladiators increased, the government established schools for training slaves and criminals to take part in these combats. Retired military officers were ordinarily set over them, and by severest training they were made indifferent to pain and suffering, and brutalized into mere beasts. Judges sentenced criminals of the worst type to death in the arena. They were sent for training in the gladiatorial schools, where the chance that they might become popular as gladiators, and, surviving many conflicts, ultimately win their freedom, encouraged many to enter into the work with zest. When gladiatorial shows sprang up in towns generally, and the people went mad over the struggles of desperate men fighting in the arena, many were unjustly sentenced to the gladiator's death—unjustly, be it said, even from the attitude of that day, which relegated only the most abandoned to this fate. It was the unceasing demand for victims that unquestionably caused many of the early Christians to meet death in the amphitheater. Not that the princes would have tolerated a faith which to them signified anarchy within the state, but a different punishment would otherwise have been meted out save for the demand for a large number of victims.

Because the circuses and stadiums were ill adapted to the gladiatorial fight, special amphitheaters were built to supply a suitable place in which to hold these combats. Greatest of these was the Coliseum, whose walls rose 160 feet in the air. Eighty entrances admitted men to the various parts of the building to which they might belong. Special reservations were made for the senators, knights, vestal virgins, and various officers of the state, to say nothing of the one who might be giving the show to appease the public. The arena could be instantly filled with water to represent a miniature lake, and could be as quickly emptied.

At first two or three pairs of gladiators fought for the edification of spectators, but this did not long satisfy the Roman appetite for blood. Caesar presented over 300 pairs of combatants, and more were exhibited later. Excavators at Pompeii found the following notice upon the walls of the fated city: "The gladiators of the aedile A. Suettius Curius will fight May 31st at Pompeii. There will be beast-fighting, and the spectators will be well sheltered by an awning." Awnings were quite essential in a land where the sun shone mercilessly in the hot months.

Soon the people wearied of single combats, and large numbers of victims were demanded. Moreover, novelties were introduced into the show. For example, some of the gladiators, attired as Samnites, would fight with the weapons and according to the method of that people; others would represent Thracians. After the conquest of Britain, gladiators were dressed after the manner of the newly won island, and many nationalities and styles of armour were thus brought before the people. Some fought blindfolded, the better to please the mob. Dwarfs were introduced, and not infrequently, women and children.

Beast hunts were another source of amusement for the Romans, and generals took pains to have strange animals collected and brought into the Roman arena to win popularity for them. Lions, panthers, elephants, wolves, hippopotami, bison, hyenas, giraffes and wild horses were all brought into the amphitheater to make Rome howl.

In enumerating the noteworthy events of his reign, Augustus wrote: "Three times in my own name and five times in that of my sons or grandsons, I have given gladiatorial exhibitions; in these exhibitions about 10,000 men have fought. Twenty-six times in my own name or in that of my sons and grandsons, I have given hunts of African wild beasts in the circus, the forum, the amphitheaters, and about 35,000 beasts have been killed." Titus exhibited 9,000 wild animals at the dedication of the Coliseum, and Trajan provided 11,000 in 106 A. D. Not only were these animals taught to fight one another, but many were trained to perform for the amusement of the spectators. Indeed, it has been said that in training animals, there has been little or no progress made since the days of the empire.

Probably the form of entertainment most enjoyed was that which included both animal and man struggles. Ordinarily the show opened with animal hunts and ended with gladiatorial combats. Wholesale numbers were provided at special occasions. It is curious to see how the more intelligent and cleverest of Romans approved of these exhibitions. A letter of Pliny to a friend sets forth his opinion of them:

"You did perfectly right in promising a gladiatorial combat to our good friends, the citizens of Verona, who have long loved, looked up to, and honored you; while it was from that city, too, you received that amiable object of your most tender affection, your late excellent wife. And since you owed some monument or public representation to her memory, what other spectacle could you have exhibited more appropriate to the occasion? I wish the African panthers, which you had largely provided for this purpose, had arrived on the day appointed, but though they were delayed by the stormy weather, the obligation to you is equally the same, since it was not your fault that they were not exhibited."

Probably the public baths of Rome properly belong to a consideration of Roman amusements, for they grew to include much that was conducive to the diversion of the people. The first of these public baths was provided in the third century before the present era. There were 170 in 33 B. C., and were as many as 800 in the later empire. Providing all sorts of baths, the buildings contained courts for games, libraries, conversation rooms, and adjoining were exercise grounds. Men resorted thither as much for the purpose of meeting their friends as for the pleasure of the bath. A small fee was required of those who frequented the baths, and this was the only restriction upon their use. Regarding the degeneracy and sensual indulgence that accompanied baths where people of all sorts and conditions in later times promiscuously resorted, it is unnecessary to speak, since Romans in the period of moral decay, seized upon every possible opportunity to indulge themselves in licentious practices, and these were no more connected with the nature of the bath than with the banquet, the amphitheater or the circus. Some of the most beautiful buildings of Rome were built to allow the people to have abundant means for bathing, and plentiful ruins allow us to reconstruct the general outlines and features of the *thermae,* as they were called.

A ROMAN HOUSE.

CHAPTER VIII.

Books, Letters and Libraries.

Because of the length of time involved in travel between one place and another, it was an expensive matter to send letters any considerable distance. On this account, it was customary for those about to take a journey to inform their friends and acquaintances of the fact, in order that letters to distant relatives and friends might be prepared and delivered by them in the course of their travels. Strangers might even request the deliverance of a letter of one embarking for foreign lands, or remote towns. It is safe to conclude that this was an unsatisfactory method of conducting correspondence, since letters might easily be lost, and change of plans might take the traveler away from the vicinity of him to whom letters had been addressed. The correspondence of the princes with officials in the provinces was managed quite differently, and probably not more time was involved in passage to and fro than until quite recent times was needed for letters to reach those in out-of-the-way districts.

That privacy in important matters might be insured, it was quite usual for men to have secret codes, unintelligible to any but the intended recipient. Writing letters was a somewhat laborious process and except for personal communications, or those relating to critical matters, slaves were employed to write them at the dictation of the master. Such slaves were called *librarii* or *amanuenses*.

For brief letters, wooden or ivory tablets were employed. These were hollowed slightly and filled with wax, upon which the words were inscribed with the point of a stilus. Longer communications were committed to papyrus with the reed pen and a sort of ink made of soot mixed with certain gums. Red ink was used for ornamental purposes and for headlines of books. Both these fluids were more like paint than modern ink. Parchment was not used until the fourth or fifth century after Christ.

Letters covering two tablets were held together by wire hinges and, face to face, these were bound around by a cord which was sealed at the knot. When the letter was opened, the cord was cut, but the knot preserved, to prove the authenticity of the communication.

The letters of two prominent Romans have come down to us: those of Cicero and Pliny the Younger. Both series were published during the life of the writers, but they are fundamentally different, in that Cicero wrote in the ordinary conversational way, while Pliny weighed each word, corrected and polished the whole, with a view to the publicity which he expected his writings to have. We are greatly indebted to the letters of these Romans for our intimate knowledge of their age.

Cicero's letters vary in length and importance. "Some are mere greetings or brief introductions, while others are carefully composed treatises; some are expressions of Cicero's inmost feelings to his intimate friends, while others are business notes or occasional letters to men with whom he was on a less familiar footing; some are addressed to the great leaders of the political parties, others to comparatively obscure persons; some are on literary subjects, others on private business, and still others on matters that pertain to the history of the world."

Pliny directed letters to people of no less importance and renown. Seventy-two were addressed to Trajan, under whose reign he was governor of an Eastern province. Fifty replies to these letters survive, and they lead us to infer that Trajan was possessed of great patience and forbearance to faithfully consider questions which the provincial governor ought himself to have settled rather than taxed the already overburdened prince. Other letters were written to Tacitus, Juvenal, Martial, to statesmen and men of affairs. To the revelations of these epistles we are indebted for an understanding of a typical gentleman of the empire—one of the most refined and cultivated, if not the keenest mind of the age.

Letters of other Romans have, of course, come down to us, but we lack the completeness of the correspondence in other cases.

Roman books, like those of Greece, took the form of rolls. Strips of papyrus were pasted together, side by side, and upon these strips, columns of writing were inscribed. Strips of wood were attached to the two ends, somewhat as maps are today mounted, and when not in use, the volumes were left rolled up. When it was desired to preserve the material indefinitely, the back of the papyrus was rubbed with cedar oil to preserve it from the moths. Each volume had a cover which fitted over it and protected it from dust. As a rule these rolls were kept in small closets, each section having the name of the author upon the door or top of the case. If several volumes were included in some one work, these several volumes were kept together. In early years rolls were often very long—long enough to contain the entire work of a writer. Later it was found far more convenient to divide the whole into two or more parts. Under these circumstances the history of Herodotus was allowed to fall into the nine books in which we know it, each being named for one of the Muses.

While the cost of books was considerable—each copy having to be made as accurately as the first, yet libraries of private persons were often of creditable size. Many private libraries contained as many as 1,500 or 2,000 volumes. Public libraries gradually came into existence and were liberally supplied with rolls of manuscript. We know more of the library at Alexandria than of any other containing Greek and Roman books. This is supposed to have owned at least 400,000 volumes.

In earlier times, when a man wanted a copy of a given work, he borrowed it from a friend and set his slaves to work to copy it. As the demand for books increased, men who corresponded in a measure to our publishers came into being. They employed slaves on a large scale, and if many copies of a given work were desired, they were able to save time in proof reading by having all the copies corrected at once. Collecting books became a fad in Rome, as it has been in modern times, and many who never wasted a moment in reading their contents, prided themselves upon the number they managed to accumulate.

It was regarded as prudent for an author to read portions of his production before a considerable number of people before he had it published. This was in order to protect him from the unscrupulous, who stood ready to appropriate the writings of another and claim them as their own. Writers of verse were sometimes imposed upon by members of their audiences, who, possessed of remarkable memories, were able to retain the lines and publish them as original. Indeed, the protection which is afforded modern writers was utterly unknown in antiquity, and authors were exposed to tricks and impositions of all sorts.

Libraries were often elaborately adorned with busts of famous authors, of the Muses and statues of the gods and heroes. As much care was expended upon the library of a Roman gentleman as upon the private libraries of modern times. As reading became more general, a demand for material was met by public libraries—twenty-eight of which were founded by one of the early princes, and by reading rooms, supplied in the great public baths.

ROMAN BOOKS.

CHAPTER IX.

Business Activities.

Roughly speaking, one might divide the society of ancient Rome into three classes: nobles, equestrians and plebeians. The nobles formed the aristocracy and constituted the senatorial class. They inherited certain ideas of the earlier patricians, among them the notion that it was beneath them to perform any remunerative labor. They filled the chief magistracies and the senate and received no salary for so doing. Since in the late republic and principate vast sums of money were required to keep up the display made by this social order, they took turns in filling the posts of provincial governor, which gave the honest man fine opportunities for investment and the unscrupulous, unparalleled chances for extortion.

The equestrian order had originally included those among the common people who were sufficiently well-to-do to equip themselves for cavalry service in the Roman army. After a regular army came into existence, made up of men regularly enlisted for a term of years, the equites, or knights, were no longer needed for military action, and, having become still wealthier, they comprised the moneyed class in Rome. They formed great syndicates, farmed out the taxes in the provinces, and performed duties similar to those of the great capitalists in modern times.

The large class of commoners might be subdivided into several factions: there was the class of poor farmers who lived upon the comparatively few remaining small farms; the mob, asking for nothing but free bread and amusement; and a numerous body of people who had drifted into the city as their property had disappeared, but who eagerly snatched at any opportunity to win back their old independence. These last were the ones who took advantage of all new lands thrown open for settlement in remote districts.

We shall consider first the careers open to the young noble when he had completed his education, or had gone as far as regular school training and the guidance of the philosophers could lead him—in other words, the possibilities open to one who did not intend to live the life of the scholar or recluse.

With all the stigma attached to labor, from the earliest times it remained perfectly honorable for a man to cling to agriculture. Many nobles constantly increased their estates and, through the industry of their slaves and freedmen, amassed goodly fortunes from the cultivation of the grape and the olive. Poets ceased not to sing of the beauties of the country and to extol the happy life of the farmer, who passed an existence remote from the sordid thoughts of the city, and in the days of extravagance and luxury, clung to the simple ways of his fathers. While the rich noble knew little of the joys of husbandry or the simple life, yet the associations of the farm, though it widened out to gigantic proportions, were always highly respectable, and the Roman gentleman, like the English gentleman of modern times, took pride in his landed possessions and reflected with satisfaction upon his yearly yield. Cato called attention to the worthy calling of the farmer:

"When our forefathers pronounced the eulogy of a worthy man, they praised him as a worthy farmer and a worthy landlord; one who was thus commended was thought to have received the highest praise. The merchant I deem energetic and diligent in the pursuit of gain; but his calling is too much exposed to perils and mischances. On the other hand, farmers furnish the bravest men and the ablest soldiers; no calling is so honorable, safe and inoffensive as theirs, and those who occupy themselves with it are least liable to evil thoughts."

Because of the favor in which agriculture was ever held among the Romans, many of the nobles invested a considerable amount of their wealth in country estates. While they spent much of the year in the city, or while they were absent acquiring property more rapidly in the provinces, their farms were tilled by their slaves under the supervision of a capable steward. When political responsibilties and aspirations permitted, it was the pleasure of these nobles to repair to their country homes, away from the cares and exacting life of their social order. Nevertheless, this was not the only door open to the aristocratic noble. Politics, the law, and the army offered inducements to men, according to their natural gifts and peculiar temperaments.

It was customary for a Roman to pass from the lower offices to the higher. There were no salaries attached to these positions, as has already been noted. However, when one had finished his term as praetor or consul, he was almost certain of a year in the provinces. One need not be unscrupulous to make the sojourn there a time of profit. The man who possessed a quick sense of fortunate investments found ample opportunity to increase his money several fold. It is unfortunate to find that many did not hesitate to resort to whatever means would insure personal gain, and while there were without question many conscientious provincial governors, there were many also who knew no limits to their cupidity.

The profession of the advocate, or lawyer, was a worthy one, although many imposed upon the patience of the judges and the people. There were no conditions restricting those who would enter the profession and plead in court. Since this offered a good opportunity to win publicity, many a young Roman first brought himself forward in the court room by pushing a charge against some well known man. Any one who would might enter charges against others. Advocates were not supposed to accept pay, and they were expected to be at the service of all who wished their professional advice. However, there could be no control exercised over presents made to advocates by grateful clients, and legacies were constantly left to them. It is not known that Cicero had any means of income save legacies received from those he had assisted. The men who pleaded cases in the Roman courts in later years were a motley throng—some able men of unquestioned familiarity with the Roman law and the decisions of gifted jurists; others were young men whose sole commendary power was their ability to use persuasive language and confuse those who heard them. Pliny complained bitterly of the habits of his day, which allowed these youthful aspirants for fame to bring hired bands into the courtroom to applaud for them at given signals.

"The youth of our days are so far from waiting to be introduced that they rudely rush in uninvited. The audience that follows them are fit attendants for such orators; a low rout of hired mercenaries, assembling themselves in the middle of the court, where the dole is dealt round to them as openly as if they were in a dining room; and at this noble price they run from court to court! The Greeks have a name in their language for this sort of people, importing that they are applauders by profession, and we stigmatize them with the appropriate title of table flatterers; yet the meanness alluded to in both languages increased every day. It was but yesterday two of my servants, mere striplings, were hired for this goodly office at the price of three denarii (about 50 cents); such is the easy purchase of eloquence! Upon these honorable terms we fill our benches and gather a circle; and thus it is those unmerciful shouts are raised when a man who stands in the middle of the ring gives the word. For you must know, these honest fellows, who understand nothing of what is said, or if they did, could not hear it, would be at a loss, without a signal, how to time their applause; for those who do not hear a syllable are as clamorous as any of the rest. If at any time you should happen to pass by while the court is sitting, and would know the merit of any of our advocates, you have no occasion to give yourself the trouble of listening to them; take it for a rule, he that has the loudest commendations deserves them the least.

"I am ashamed to say with what an unmanly elocution the orators deliver themselves, and with what a squeaking applause they are received; nothing seems wanting to complete this singsong oratory but the claps, or rather the music, of the stage. At present we choose to express our admiration by a kind of howling (for I can call it by no other term) which would be indecent even in the theater. Hitherto the interests of my friends and the consideration of my early time of life has retained me in this court; for it would be thought, I fear, rather to proceed from indolence than a just indignation at these indecencies were I yet to leave it; however, I come there less frequently than usual, and am thus making a gradual retreat."[1]

The career of the military officer will be considered in connection with the army in general.

---
[1] Trans. in Roman Life in Pliny's Time, p. 147.

Passing to the equestrians, or ancient knights, we find them expending their energies in the field of finance rather than in politics. They were the money-changers, in a land where the coins of the known world met. They were the money-loaners on a large scale, notwithstanding the fact that letting out money at interest was never regarded as honorable in Rome. Syndicates formed of the equestrians paid into the state treasury the sum of money deemed necessary to be collected from each province, and then proceeded to collect several times as much from the provinces as the senate had required. When damages for war, or when heavy penalties were demanded of a state by the victorious army, the Roman syndicates advanced to such states the sum of which they stood in immediate need, and assumed the responsibility of gathering much more than this from the masses of the people.

Nor were the concerns of the capitalists always on so great a scale. They supplied money necessary ofttimes to get crops upon the market; they furnished the means of working mines. They even loaned money to individuals at enormous rates of interest. In short, the knights ceased entirely to fulfill their earlier mission and became the financiers of the Roman state, even reaching out into other lands in course of their financial manipulations.

While commerce was not regarded as worthy the attention of a proud Roman noble, yet it was nevertheless carried on to a considerable extent, and the wares from all lands might be seen in the markets of the capital city.

"Into this city are brought, from all countries and from all seas, the fruits of all the seasons and the products of all lands, rivers and lakes; and whatever is created by the skill of the Greeks and of the barbarians. So that the man who wishes to view all these things must either travel over the whole world or visit this city, where there is always an abundance of whatever is grown or manufactured among all nations. In the course of a season so many freighted ships come into its port from all countries that a person there might almost think he was in a universal manufactory. So many cargoes from India and from Araby the Blessed are to be seen there that one might imagine that the trees of those countries are forever stripped of their fruits, and that the people who live in those countries will be forced to come to Rome to ask back again as much of the products of their own soil as their necessities require. The stuffs of Babylonia and the jewels from the barbarous region of interior Asia reach Rome in much larger quantities and far more easily than the products of Naxos and of Cythnus reach Athens. In fact, whatever commerce can lay hold of and ships can carry, whatever arts create, whatever exists in the earth, and whatever grows upon it, all this is gathered together in the market of Rome."[2]

It is to be noted, however, that goods were imported *into* Rome—not sent thence to other lands. There were plenty of producers on a small scale, but they merely supplied the home demand. Goldsmiths, shoemakers, sandalmakers, weavers, dyers, etc., carried on a considerable business, but their products were all needed by the inhabitants of Italy—even by the people of Rome.

The noble or the equestrian might hold heavy investments of a commercial order if only the scheme were large enough and his connection with it remote. The wholesale importer owned his ships that carried the goods from other lands to the Tiber; he owned many slaves and controlled the actions of many freedmen who attended to all the details of the business for him. The profits were his—the rest was but the investment of capital entrusted largely to another.

Of the small dealers we know less. Trades were multifarious, for the Romans shared the modern notion of division of labor. Even the venders of fruit and vegetables sometimes limited themselves to one variety. The booths of shopkeepers and retail dealers filled the busy streets. In light of ancient ideas regarding the humble walks of life, it is not strange that the Latin writers have given us so few accounts of those engaged in petty merchandise and in the trades. Regarding the latter, it is well established that at least a dozen guilds were of very ancient standing, but far from benefiting the conditions under which men labored or uniting for higher remuneration, they sought only to perfect the trades and to perpetuate them.

The business quarter of the capital varied in different eras.

[2]Trans. in Roman Life in Pliny's Time, p. 117.

In earliest times the people upon the three hills came down into the valleys which divided them to traffic with one another. The forum was located at the foot of the Palatine, and here were the different markets. One by one the markets were excluded from the forum. The objectionable ones left first— the fish market, for example. The cattle market gradually found other quarters. Places were sought a little away from the forum—the busy meeting ground for men. In the later empire, the finest shops were to be found on the Campus Martius.

"There was at Rome no quarter set apart by custom or by law especially for commerce. But the merchants themselves, according to the character of the goods in which they dealt, chose this or that part of the city for the establishment of their business. The handsomest shops in the time of Domitian were in the large enclosure caled the *Septa,* upon the Campus Martius. Here would come any one who wished to provide himself with the best slaves, elegant furniture, with any article made of choice wood, ivory, tortoise-shell, bronze, or Corinthian brass, with Greek statues, antique cups artistically carved, with crystal vases, with dishes and utensils of every kind, and with murrhine pottery. The *Via Sacra* was the headquarters for goldsmiths and jewelers. The great center for Egyptian and Arabian merchandise was in the Forum Pacis. Silks, perfumes and spices were sold in the Vicus Tuscus, and probably also in the Circus Maximus. Moreover, it frequently happened that those who were engaged in the same trade, or the same profession, would group themselves about a single point. We find that some of the streets were named from the traffic of those who lived upon them. There was the grain merchants' street, the belt-makers' street, the sandal-makers' street, the wood-dealers' street, the glaziers' street, etc."[3]

[3]Trans. in Roman Life in Pliny's Time, 130.

CHAPTER X.

Slavery in Rome.

The peculiar structure of society which prevailed in Rome would have been impossible without the system of slavery. The idle luxury of the late republic and the empire, the pampered whims and indulgences so common to the upper classes, were due wholly to a social life based upon human servitude. We know nothing about the beginnings of the institution and lack accurate data for conditions prevailing in historic times, yet nevertheless, details are not lacking for a sufficient understanding of the Roman slave.

In earliest times there probably were no slaves in Rome. In a rough settlement of shepherds and outlaws one would expect to find no evidences of leisure and wealth. No one knows how early slaves were introduced into the little village on the Tiber, but they were probably taken as captives in Rome's first wars. Because free men alone served in the army, and because these were frequently needed to fight for their little state, slaves were early employed to work the farms otherwise left idle by the absence of their masters. As more captives were secured, and as it was necessary for the Roman citizens to spend considerable time in the field, more slaves were employed to grow the crops and till the soil. Although they proved so useful in this capacity, the general ownership of slaves came only with extensive conquests, which threw great numbers of captives upon the market, thus reducing their money value.

While there is no means of estimating the number of slaves in Italy at any particular time, nor even estimating the number of slaves as compared with free men, we are able to judge somewhat of their strength in view of the many captives taken in the later wars. Pompey and Caesar threw more than 1,000,000 human chattels upon the slave market. Marius took 140,000 Cimbri as prisoners, and the destruction of Carthage at the close of the third Punic war plunged thousands upon thousands of people into captivity. Again, we know that insurrections of slaves were difficult to put down, one holding out in Sicily for two years and another in the same island lasting four years. Spartacus was able to defy Roman armies for two years, and was supported by large numbers of slaves.

While in early times two or three slaves sufficed for a noble, in the late republic and early empire, 400 might be employed in a single household. There are records of men who owned as many as 10,000 and 20,000 slaves, although, to be sure, these were employed on extensive estates, and performed many kinds of labor and business.

War constituted the greatest supply of these men in bondage. Even in times of comparative peace, wars were prosecuted on the frontiers for the purpose of taking captives to serve as laborers and as gladiators. Slave dealers ordinarily accompanied the army, bought up captives at once and hurried them on to the different markets. It was deemed advisable to get these men out of their native land as quickly as possible, for they were ordinarily soldiers who would snatch at the slightest opportunity to regain their liberty. Many took their own lives rather than fall into servitude, and some were likely to escape on the march. For this reason, the slave dealers bought them for small sums upon the battlefield.

While war supplied many slaves, it was in no way the only means of securing them. In later times, when many provinces paid tribute to the mistress of the world, slaves were sent, like other commodities. Again, they were supplied in the markets to meet constant demand, quite as articles for food, clothing, or any other use. Some were furnished by men who made a business of kidnapping the defenseless beings of uncivilized countries. While this trade was not regarded as honorable, it was not forbidden. Each country supplied bondsmen who were particularly valued for some especial labor.

"The slaves were brought from all the provinces of the empire; blacks from Egypt; swift runners from Numidia; grammarians from Alexandria; from Cyrene those who made the best house servants; from Greece handsome boys and girls, and well-trained scribes, accountants, amanuenses, and even teachers; from Epirus and Illyria experienced shepherds; from Cappadocia the most patient and enduring laborers."[1]

The price of a slave depended upon the condition of the market when one bought. Sometimes there was a temporary dearth even in Rome; sometimes the marts were overcrowded. Much depended again upon the qualities and accomplishments of the slave himself. Those whose sole commendation was physical strength brought least money. An ordinary man fitted to till the soil and work upon the farm, might bring approximately $100. Teachers sold for as much as $28,000. Those of medium gifts and attainments ranged somewhere between these prices. The Romans had a peculiar way of matching boys, as people today sometimes match their horses. A pair of boys, so to speak, alike in the color of hair and eyes and bearing strong resemblances in other respects, would bring much more than two who were unlike, for they were valued as household servants.

Those in bondage fell into two general classes: those who served the public and those who were the property of private owners. The lot of the public slave was considered the better of the two. Many public slaves were needed to care for public buildings, serve the magistrates in various capacities, assist the priests, and work upon public undertakings. These were less likely to be sold than were the private slaves; nor were they apt to be so harshly treated nor to be driven to their tasks so strenuously. However, the public slaves were always few in comparison with the many held by private masters.

The private servants again were divided into those who served in towns and those who worked in the country. The hardest lot fell to those who served in the stone quarries, cut timber in the country, or worked upon the great estates of landed proprietors. They were the cheapest, most brutal beings, who were never trusted by their overseers. By day they worked in fetters and at night they were housed in barracks not unlike prisons of mediaeval times. At the slightest lessening of authority they were watchful for a chance to retaliate upon those who made life wretched for them. Those who worked upon the country places of the nobles or who

[1] Private Life of the Romans, p. 90.

served in their city households had certain comforts and, except for being under the frequent eye of capricious masters, found existence more tolerable. It was to the interest of a thrifty manager to treat a slave, like every other animal valued for its service, decently. It is far from our purpose to enumerate various forms of torture to which slaves were not infrequently submitted. The weak and defenseless in all ages have been at the mercy of the strong and masterful, and this was especially true in Rome where, at best, a stern attitude prevailed and the quality of mercy certainly was strained. Men who possessed power of life and death over their own sons, who subjected their children to rigid discipline in school, and to even more vigorous treatment, accorded a slave—a mere chattel in their eyes and in the eyes of the law—small consideration. Yet, looking at the matter broadly, they were not likely to incur unnecessary loss by treating them cruelly. This by no means would imply that there was not plenty of heartless cruelty in Roman slavery; there was far too much.

These human beings, who were bought and sold in the market each day, performed all kinds of labor. They loaded and unloaded the ships in the harbors; they worked upon the highways and made excavations. Those a little higher in the scale of labor worked as artisans, mechanics and skilled workmen. They were employed as smiths, carpenters, masons—in short, every industry needed and secured them. Those who were educated copied books, kept accounts, treated the sick in the capacity of physicians. Some whose business capacity had been proved, were furnished with capital and established in business for their masters, who left all to their ingenuity and management. The hope of accumulating enough to purchase his freedom served as a great incentive to stimulate a slave to industry and faithfulness.

Sometimes men purchased slaves and let them out for hire. Because it was regarded as more worthy to employ them for their own concerns, this was usually done by Roman citizens. It was true that many who lived in servitude had received better training and were imbued with deeper culture than their masters, and more and more it came to pass that responsibilities were thrown upon them. It was not strange that having scores of servants at his call, the pampered noble turned over his responsibilities and cares. Nor this alone. As men have loved pomp and display in all ages, so the Romans were fond of it during their later life, and in no other way could a wealthy nobleman make a greater showing than by having a large retinue of servants accompany him as he went about from place to place. Servants carried his litter and the litters of the different members of his family when they went abroad. Some preceded him to clear the way; some followed to carry wraps, fans, and other articles which were necessary or unnecessary. Some amused him and some aided. Some wrote his letters and others kept his accounts. It was the pride of many to have one slave perform a certain task. If a nobleman took a journey, he might be accompanied by hundreds of servants to contribute to his comfort and idleness.

There were several methods of granting freedom to Roman slaves. Any slave might accumulate gradually, with a hope of purchasing his freedom. The more able he showed himself to be, the higher would be the price set upon him. While these men could accumulate as opportunity offered, they could not leave their savings to their families if they died in bondage. Public slaves were allowed to dispose of one-half their savings as they wished; the earnings of private slaves reverted to their masters. In the eyes of the law a slave had no rights; his marriage was not recognized as a binding relationship and he had no legal rights over his children. While this was theoretically the case, it was deemed desirable that household servants should marry, since they were then likely to be more contented and more attached to the family they served.

The majority of slaves who were set free, gained freedom through the gratitude or generosity of their masters. Some purchased their liberty, as has been noted. There were different ways of accomplishing this. "Manumission might be effected without formalities, but in case a regular form was observed, the slave was released in one of the three following ways: First—By *vindicta,* the Latin word for staff. This was a ceremony in which a third party, who must be a Roman citizen, touched a slave with a staff in the presence of a magistrate and of the master. The master, who was holding the slave, let him go, and the magistrate pronounced him free. Second—By census, when the master had the slave's name inscribed by the censor upon the list of citizens. Third—By will, or even by a wish expressed for the heir to carry out."[2]

Laws of the principate forbade a master turning away a slave who had grown old in his service, although this had been customary enough in earlier years. Finally masters were forbidden to put slaves to death without due process of law. Having touched upon the darkest side of slavery—the cruelty it involved, and hence the moral degeneracy attendant upon it—it is only fair to present the other side of the picture by quoting a letter written by Pliny the Younger, concerning one of his servants:

"As I know the humanity with which you treat your own servants, I do not scruple to confess to you the indulgence I show to mine. I have ever in my mind Homer's character of Ulysses: 'Who ruled his people with a father's love.' And the very expression in our language for the head of a family suggests the rule of one's conduct toward it. But were I naturally of a rough and hardened cast of temper, the ill state of health of my freedman Zosimus (who has the stronger claim of a humane treatment at my hands, as he now stands much in need of it) would be sufficient to soften me. He is a person of great worth, diligent in his services, and well skilled in literature; but his chief talent, and indeed his profession, is that of a comedian, wherein he highly excels. He speaks with great emphasis, judgment, propriety, and gracefulness; he has a very good hand, too, upon the lyre, which he understands better than is necessary for one of his profession. To this I must add, he reads history, oratory, and poetry as well as if he had singly applied himself to the art. I am thus particular in enumerating his qualifications that you may see how many agreeable services I receive from him. He is indeed endeared to me by the ties of a long affection, which seems to be heightened by the danger he is now in. Some years ago he strained himself so much by too vehement an exertion of his voice that he spit blood, upon which account I sent him to Egypt; from whence, after a long absence, he lately returned

[2] Quoted in Roman Life in Pliny's Time, 105.

with great benefit to his health. But having again exerted himself for several days together beyond his strength he was reminded of his former malady by a slight return of his cough and a spitting of blood. For this reason I intend to send him to your farm at Forum—Julii, which I have frequently heard you mention as having exceedingly fine air, and I remember your recommending the milk of that place as very good in disorders of this nature. I beg you would give direction to your people to receive him into your house and to supply him with what he shall have occasion for, which will not be much, for he is so temperate as not only to abstain from delicacies, but even to deny himself the necessaries his ill state of health requires. I shall furnish him toward his journey with what will be sufficient for one of his abstemious turn who is coming under your roof."[3]

[3] Quoted in Roman Life in Pliny's Time, 105.

A ROMAN SCHOOL.

Spring in Italy.

Fierce winter melts in vernal gales,
And grateful zephyrs fill the spreading sails;
No more the ploughman loves his fire,
No more the lowing herds their stalls desire,
While earth her richest verdure yields,
Nor hoary frosts now whiten o'er the fields.
Now joyous through the verdant meads,
Beneath the rising moon, fair Venus leads
Her various dance, and with her train
Of Nymphs and modest Graces shakes the plain,
While Vulcan's glowing breath inspires
The toilsome forge, and blows up all its fires.
Nor crowned with myrtle, or the flowers
Which the glad earth from her free bosom pours,
We'll offer, in the shady grove,
Or lamb, or kid, as Pan shall best approve.
With equal pace impartial Fate
Knocks at the palace as the cottage gate;
Nor should our sum of life extend
Our glowing hopes beyond their destined end.
When sunk to Pluto's shadowy coasts,
Oppressed with darkness and the fabled ghosts,
No more the dice shall there assign
To thee the jovial monarchy of wine.
No more shall you the fair admire,
The virgins' envy, and the youth's desire.
—Horace.

CHAPTER XI.

THE ARMY.

Military service offered opportunities to men of all classes. The general and the higher military officers, like the magistrates at Rome, received no stated compensation for their services. Spoils of war greatly exceeded any remuneration that the state would have been willing to award them. One desirous of acquiring wealth or attaining political ends in Rome, found the army a ready means for so doing. The career of Caesar is sufficiently familiar. While the spoils of war were supposed to go into the state treasury, the general first retained what he wished for himself, his staff, and the army, sending the rest to Rome. It was deemed perfectly legitimate to enrich one's self by booty taken and by ransom money, but the ways of the unscrupulous subordinate officer, who bettered his own lot by supplying the common soldier with food at inflated prices, or who kept for himself part of the army supplies, were condemned by public opinion of the day.

In the early republic, all able-bodied citizens were expected to serve the state in time of war. None but Roman citizens were admitted to the legion, but these must serve while of suitable age. Later, the army grew to be made up of regularly enlisted men, who entered upon military service as a profession. There were enough volunteers to fill the ranks, and the average citizen no longer found himself obliged to leave his usual duties and responsibilities to defend his native land. It naturally followed that it was possible to establish and maintain a far greater efficiency in this regular army than had been realized in the earlier forces which were composed of mere militia men.

In order to be accepted into the ranks, a man had to be between the years of 17 and 46, strong and healthy, and of a stipulated height and weight. As a matter of fact, the Romans tended to be somewhat under size. The large size of the Germans was always commented upon by the Romans.

All the soldiers dressed alike—in a woolen tunic, or shirt, a leather coat, protected with metal bands, and strips of cloth wound around the limbs. Sandals were sometimes worn, but usually shoes of stout leather were used instead. A kind of blanket took the place of a military cape.

The lot of the common soldier varied with the period under consideration. Caesar paid his soldiers about $45 a year, which was the amount earned by a day laborer in about 300 days. Slight deductions were made for clothing and food, but there was always the hope and expectation of booty. On occasions of taking plenty of spoils, the generals made presents to the soldiers, the centurions receiving twice as much as the privates; the tribunes and cavalry four times as much. After twenty years or less of service, the soldier hoped to receive a farm granted by the state to those who obtained their regular discharge.

Discipline was always strict. This was especially true when a regular army came into existence. Good commanders always understood that the easiest way to maintain good order was to keep the soldier too busy for aught save his duties. While punishments were brutal, daring and display of courage were likely to win gifts of money. Mutiny, desertion and cowardice were generally punishable by death, but slight offenses, as today, were met by lesser penalties.

The strength of the Roman army was in the infantry; the unit, the legion. It is not known just how many soldiers made up a legion, but it has been estimated to have been between three and four thousand. Six military tribunes originally commanded the legion. These were chosen from the equestrian order by the comitia and the consul. Political motives rather than military skill came to control these appointments, and Caesar greatly improved the discipline of the legion by placing over it a legatus, who first supervised and later commanded the legion, leaving the tribunes to assume other responsibilities and to conduct courts-martial.

The legion was composed of ten cohorts, each under the command of six centurions. Each cohort was divided again into three maniples, and each maniple into two centuries. Estimating the legion as comprising 3,600 men, each cohort would contain 360, and each maniple 120. It must be remembered that these are but estimates, and that, too, of the time of Julius Caesar. They cannot be far from right, and what was true at this particular time was generally the case in years shortly before and after this great general's leadership.

The centurions were taken from the ranks. Their rank depended upon their command. Those of first rank were invited to attend councils of war. They marched on foot and carried short staffs. Corresponding in a measure to non-commissioned officers in modern armies, they might rise to a place of first centurion, but rarely were promoted farther.

The armor of the Roman soldier included a helmet, greaves and a shield. The helmets were made of iron, leather or cork, and were protected with brass. Officers wore plumes of red or black in their helmets. The greaves were of bronze, and usually but one was worn by the soldier—on his right leg, since with that he advanced in battle. The shields were not far from four feet long, two feet wide. Made of wood, they were covered with leather, or with iron plates. On the outer side was the badge of the cohort; on the inside, the name of the soldier. During the march these were protected by leather cases.

Swords and spears were the distinctive weapons of the army. The swords, having blades two feet long, were double-edged and pointed. The spear was the special weapon of the legion.

In addition to his armor and arms, a soldier had to carry various tools, besides his utensils for cooking his food. On short marches he also carried his own food. This was impossible for a regular army while upon a campaign. The baggage train then came into play, and for a legion, perhaps 520 mules or pack animals were needed. Tents for the men, the centurions and the higher officers, food for the army, various tools and other material needed for the camp were carried by pack animals, each carrying perhaps two hundred pounds.

As each regiment today has its own standard, so the divisions of the Roman army had their own distinctive badge. The legions had an eagle of bronze or silver supported on a wooden staff. The cohorts usually had some animal, a cow, a horse, or a sheep, borne similarly. The cavalry and light-armed troops had small banners, attached to a pole at the top instead of at the side, as in the case of our modern flags. The general had his own flag—a banner usually white, with his name in letters of red, or some striking color. In camp this was posted near his tent.

In early times 300 cavalrymen accompanied each legion. This body, like the legion, had been composed entirely of Roman citizens. Caesar depended entirely upon his auxiliary forces to supply his cavalry. The auxiliary troops were supplied by subject nations, by allies or were raised among conquered tribes. They were never greatly depended upon, and were ordinarily placed on the wings. Horse, light armed infantry and slingers made up this part of the army. Just what armor and weapons should be used by the auxiliaries depended upon the customs of the nations furnishing them.

In the regular field action there was little which corresponded to the modern artillery. Several kinds of engines were used in sieges and were used to hurl missiles to demolish walls. Because it was not easy to construct such engines hastily, a siege train probably accompanied the army on its important campaigns.

There were fewer officers in the Roman army than are found in modern armies. The staff consisted of the general, the legates, chosen from the senatorial class and acting as lieutenants to the commanding general, and the quaestors, who had charge of the money of the province and attended to the army supplies. These corresponded somewhat to modern adjutant generals and quartermasters. In addition to these were the guards and engineers. These last superintended the construction of bridges and of the winter camps. They often repaired the weapons of the army.

During the period of the principate, the army was understood by the princes to embody the final authority of the land. Whatever strength belonged to any prince came because of his command over the military forces. Naturally it was to the interest of the general to keep his men under good discipline and control. In times of peace the soldiers were set to work upon roads and other public works, which benefited the country quite as much as the usual struggle for new territory.

CHAPTER XII.

Tombs and Funeral Customs.

The Romans, like the Greeks, attached great importance to the observance of burial ceremonies. It was popularly supposed that the soul could not enter upon its rest until the body had been covered with earth. Even after the habit of cremation supplanted the burying of the dead, some small bone—a bit of the finger, perhaps—was buried in order that the old custom might be perpetuated.

The earliest custom was that of burying the dead; cremation never wholly succeeded this, for the cost of it was beyond the reach of the poor, and many families of the upper classes did not adopt it, feeling a preference for the ancient method. It is known that in early times the head of the family was buried beneath his own hearth; somewhat later, in his garden. These customs had both passed away before history proper begins in Rome. The Twelve Tables forbade any one being interred within the city walls.

The poorest people, abandoned slaves, those who died in the arena, outlaws, etc., were buried in common burying grounds, corresponding to the potter's field. Even the humble took some precaution about the tomb in which they and their families should rest, however, and the wealthy expended vast sums of money and during their life prepared the tomb which should be their final abode. Being forbidden districts within the walls, they chose sites immediately without the gates; these being appropriated, the spaces upon either side of the great roads were deemed desirable, until the entire roadway would be lined on both sides by tombs for several miles outside the walls. Nor was this true of Rome alone—a similar custom prevailed throughout Italy.

"The Roman custom of extra-mural interment, wisely made compulsory by the city's earliest code of laws, resulted in giving the great roads a singular bordering of tombs. The countless majority of the dead—that is to say, the slaves and the lowest grade of Romans—were cast into the ground anywhere outside the walls. For all respectable families, however, there were separate tombs, and to the Roman mind no place was more suitable for these than the roadside, accessible, secure, and, above all things, conspicuous. The earliest monuments were nearest the gates, and as the space became filled, the line extended further, reaching to a distance of ten or twelve miles from town. Frontage on the roads was highly valued, and there was a distinct ownership of lots, their dimensions being frequently recorded at the end of the sepulchral inscription."[1]

The size and style of the tomb depended upon its purpose, whether it was designed for one individual or a family ; whether for the safe-keeping of the ashes merely, or for the bodies. Ordinarily, whatever the particular plan, the tomb contained a room, supplied with niches on either side. These were large enough to contain the coffin, or shaped to hold the funeral urns, according to the preference of the builder. An altar might be provided within this room, for the offering of sacrifices. Sometimes the grounds surrounding the tomb comprised several acres, and there might be ample provision made for the surviving members of the family, who would come thither upon festival occasions to offer sacrifices for the dead.

"If the grounds were small there would be at least a seat, perhaps a bench. On more extensive grounds there were places of shelter, arbors, or summer houses. Dining-rooms, too, in which were celebrated the anniversary feasts, and private *ustrinae* (places for the burning of bodies) are frequently mentioned. Often the grounds were laid out as gardens or parks, with trees and flowers, wells, cisterns or fountains, and even a house, with other buildings perhaps, for the accommodation of the slaves or freedmen who were in charge."[2]

Needless to say that such elaborate places were only in the possession of the rich. Far more numerous were those who had to be satisfied with meager tombs. In the country there was always space enough for the burial of the dead, but in the cities, whither people thronged in the later period of the republic

[1] Rome of Yesterday and Today, Dennie, p. 106.
[2] Private Life of the Romans, 319.

and during the principate, the situation was quite different. The cost of procuring even a tiny site for purposes of burial was far beyond the reach of the multitude. On this account, burial societies were formed, not unlike modern fraternal insurance societies. Instead of insuring the survivors a stipulated sum of money upon the death of a man, these societies of Rome were much more modest—they merely insured him decent burial and a place for the safe-keeping of his coffin or urn of ashes, as the case might be. Large buildings—underground for the most part, were constructed by these societies, and provision was made for all their members. A slight weekly or monthly payment entitled a member to all the privileges of the society. Sometimes those who wished to make good investments would provide a similar place, selling to any one desirous space for a coffin or an urn. The urns were usually sealed to the floor of the niche containing them.

It is not to be understood that conspicuous and costly tombs were the possession of the upper classes alone—it would be truer to say they were the privilege of the prosperous. The following account of the final resting-place of a Roman baker has its own interest.

"A third monument was also revealed by the destruction of parts of Aurelian's wall. This is the tomb of Eurysaces, the baker, than which nothing more grotesque ever served for so solemn a memorial. It is a huge structure of tufa and travertine, with an internal mass of concrete which appears where one side of the tomb is entirely torn away. It was in shape an irregular quadrilateral, standing in the fork of two roads, and widening to correspond with their radiation. The monument consists of a row of colossal cylinders, representing measures for grain, and upon them, in three tiers, huge circular kneading-troughs with their mouths outward. The cylinders and kneading-troughs surmount a high, plain basement, and above them is a frieze, with reliefs representing scenes connected with the baker's trade. An inscription, thrice repeated, indicates that this is the monument of Marcus Vergilius Eurysaces, baker, bread-contractor to the *apparctores* (the public servants of the Roman magistrates). So expensive a tomb demonstrates that contractors were a prosperous class in those days, as they have been since; but the difference of manners at different epochs appears in the readiness with which this rich contractor calls himself by the humble designation of his trade. This baker certainly was of a whimsical turn of mind, for even in ancient Rome men must have smiled to read the inscription to his wife, which seems to have made part of a similar tomb adjacent: 'Atistia was my wife; she was the best woman alive; of whose body the remains which are left are in this bread-basket.' Other bakers' tombs seem to have been in this neighborhood, for there are curious fragments of sculptured travertine, now set against the wall along the roadside, on which are representations in relief of flat round loaves, marked with a cross like the hot-cross buns of the English bake-shops."[3]

When a Roman of means was taken ill, he was naturally given whatever aid the physicians of his day could render. Sometimes he recovered, either because or in spite of them and sometimes he succumbed to his malady. Pliny, at least, thought none too well of those who practised medicine in his age.

"It is at our risk and peril that they learn their business, and it is in killing us that they acquire experience. No one but a physician can kill a man with impunity; moreover, the reproach does not rest upon the physician; people accuse the intemperance of the patient, and the dead are always to blame.

As avaricious as they are ignorant, the physicians will dispute about the price of their visits at the bed of the dying patient."[4]

We know nothing of the ceremonies connected with the burial of the simple people. At least they must have been very quiet. Slaves seem to have been accorded no ceremony whatever. Treated in life like useful animals, after death they were merely buried. In early times all burials took place at night. In the late republic and early principate, when they were celebrated during the day, torches were nevertheless carried in the procession—a relic of the night-interment.

When death occurred in a family, cypress was tied upon

[3] Rome of Yesterday and Today, 108.
[4] Pliny the Elder.

the door to give notice of the fact. There was no stipulated time allowed to elapse before the burial; as soon as the various duties and ceremonies had been observed, the dead was taken to his last resting-place. Friends and relatives were notified of the funeral. The body was dressed in the toga, the dress of the citizen. If he had held a curule office, a wax impression was made of his face. A procession was formed, headed by a band of musicians. These were followed by people hired to sing dirges. Bands of buffoons and jesters came next, these making sport and entertainment for the passersby in the street. The actors of the day donned the wax masks of the dead man's ancestors, and these they wore throughout the ceremony. If the dead had been a person of some importance, he was borne upon a couch to the forum, the couch rested upon the rostra while a son or near relative delivered an address, lauding his virtues and magnifying the honors he had received during life. It was often alleged that orators possessed of good imaginations ascribed to the dead glories that he had never experienced on earth, at least. After this address, with friends and family following, the procession took its way to the place of the interment. If the corpse was to be cremated, it was usual to throw tokens of esteem and regard upon the pile. After the burial, all save the near relatives withdrew, and the ground was purified by water. An animal—usually a pig—was sacrificed and the family partook of the meat of the sacrifice. Nine days later it was the custom to give a banquet in honor of the dead.

In later times the Etruscan habit of providing gladiatorial contests was brought into Rome. At first the gladiators fought by the very grave or funeral pile; this being inconvenient for everyone, it very soon became the habit to hold such contests, after the funeral rites had been celebrated, in the amphitheatre provided for these fights. It will be remembered that a letter of Pliny has been quoted in a previous chapter in which he assures a friend that it was only fitting that he provide a gladiatorial contest in memory of his dead wife.

From what has been said, it is plain that the Roman funeral, in so far as we know of it, was a strange mixture of customs, old and new, curious blendings of the natural and the weird, the grotesque and the pathetic.

LATIN LITERATURE

HISTORICAL REVIEW.

NE who is interested in tracing the world's progress from the beginnings of civilization in the far distant Orient, amid the twilight of history, can not pass over the influence of that mighty nation that has contributed so much to our own social order. The complex civilization of our twentieth century here in the United States has many sources, and not the least important one is imperial Rome. Our religion is Hebraic, greatly modified by Greek thought; our philosophy and laws of speech and methods of thinking come from Greece, but Rome has taught us to govern ourselves. It is to Rome that our social order, the protection of life and property, the maintenance of peace and with it prosperity, and the protection of every citizen in his personal and civil rights have mainly come, either directly or through the medium of Germany and England.

Now the life of a nation is recorded in many ways: in the material works of a people, such as cities, buildings, roads; in its institutions, social, political, or religious, which have come down to modern times; in its art, which is visible in statues, sculptures, coins, temples, frescoes; but its life and thought are found in the highest degree in its literature. As a man thinketh so is he, says holy writ, and the style is the man, said a great French savant. So if we want to know what the Romans really were in order that we may understand what we Americans owe to them, we shall find that it is in their literature especially that the national character is revealed. The written word remains and it is certainly wonderful that a thin leaf of paper or a crumbling sheet of parchment should be able to survive the wreck of time, and that although huge piles of masonry have perished and great dynasties of rulers have passed away, that the thin and fragile paper with its precious message has been able to survive. Truly the weak things of earth prevail, and in the many paradoxes of life the battle is not always to the strong.

Roman literature, then, is well worth studying by an American because it contains our own history. We are modern Romans just as we also are modern Greeks, and just as the Romans themselves were modern Greeks. When one surveys the history of the world's progress one finds that some one people has stood out prominently, from time to time, as the leader and pattern of all the rest, and the leading nation of any particular period in history has looked back on antiquity with mingled reverence and scorn; but it has, at the same time, been profoundly certain of one thing, namely, that it itself was and is modern. This modern note is characteristic of all the great literatures, and the reason is that all great literatures deal with the fundamental principles of human thought and conduct. When we look upon the beautiful Greek statues that have come down to our time we find that the human figure does not differ essentially from that of our own contemporaries; and in the same way the minds of the Greeks and Romans that are revealed to us in their literature are pretty much like our own. Men labored and suffered, rejoiced and sorrowed, did wrong and made mistakes just as we do, for human nature is always the same when exhibited in persons of the same race. The world was very evil then, as now, to some people: virtue seemed to languish and vice to be fortunate, government was often corrupt or incompetent; wealth was too often predatory; but, on the other hand, there were devoted patriots, liberal patrons of all that is good, stainless matrons, philanthropists, visionaries; the same kaleidoscopic mixture that we have today. So is Man; a bundle of contrarieties; good, bad, indifferent; variable, changeable. We follow a thread here and there, and take up first this clue and then that, set up this representative man over against another, this poet with this historian, and finally work out a conception of what we call the Roman; and this abstraction we can compare with what we may call the American and we shall find that the two have much in common and that the Roman's experience, as recorded in Roman literature, can help us and save us as a nation from some mistakes.

We Americans admire the Greeks, but we really have more in common with the Romans, for they were a practical and strenuous people who believed in doing things: literature to them, as to us, was not the first object in life; thus their literature was either practical or entertaining. And by practical I mean that their books were useful handbooks—manuals of land surveying, farming, engineering, law, cookery and the like; books that we usually do not class with literature, and which were ephemeral then as now, for who would keep a cook-book in his library? No traces of the books of the first five or six centuries have survived; they were probably books that were not books—account books, ledgers, legal documents and even laws; nursery rhymes and tribal legends; many, no doubt, were never committed to writing at all. Then there was much speech-making at Rome; at first every man prominent through social position was a lawyer, but one who gave his services free; and there were many orations or speeches delivered before legislative assemblies or courts, and some of these survived, either because they were delivered at some great crisis or because they dealt with some matter of great interest, or because they were delivered by some very prominent man or finally, were of attractive literary form. But this speech-making was practical like the political speeches of our own time.

Things went on in this way for centuries until the Romans were brought into contact with the Greeks through foreign wars, and for the first time as a people they began to see that there was something else in the world besides money and power. Captive Greece took captive her fierce conqueror, said Horace, and there is something almost grotesque, if not pathetic, in the conversion of Rome to what is ordinarily called culture. Rome strong, cruel, just, rich, found that the Greeks had something that she lacked, and that something in one word was beauty. The Greeks worshipped beauty, beauty in form, in color, in humanity, in thought, in expression, in literature, in religion. And the Roman said, come let us be cultured too, for the Greeks whom we have captured must not call us barbarians.

And so formal literature—what we call literature as the Greeks called it—began to be cultivated by the Romans. And it began with a Latin translation of Homer's Odyssey made by a Greek slave—a poor thing of little merit, but for a century or two a school book for Roman children. As time went on it became the fashion for rich young Romans to go to Athens and other Greek cities to complete their education;—it was like going to college with us,—and little by little there was established at Rome a company of liberally educated men who supported and encouraged a Roman literature that should resemble the Greek. And there was another strong reason, too, the love for amusement, particularly that of the theater, that has always distinguished the Italians. It was found an easy thing to adapt the Greek comedies and tragedies to Roman audiences—and there was money in it, too, to the thrifty Roman. The comedies held their own for centuries, but the tragedies did not last long: the circus and amphitheatre with its gladiators and real death and bloody contests gave those hard hearts, those cruel men of Rome greater pleasure than the imaginary woes of tragedy.

The note of utilitarianism is always found in Roman literature even where it is least expected. When a Roman wrote a book he intended to meet some definite need—sometimes it was avowedly commercial. Thus oratory is a considerable part of Roman literature, owing to the large number of speeches delivered by Cicero that have come down to us. But we have no orations that were written by stylists for the sake of style, like the great panegyric on Athens by Isocrates in Greek, even if a few rhetorical exercises have been handed down by the elder Seneca, a teacher of rhetoric in the time of the early empire when genuine oratory had ceased to find any outflow during the tyranny of the Empire. Virgil's great poem was written for the definte purpose of reconciling the minds of men to the new order of things introduced by the Emperor Augustus, and even Horace's Odes are quietistic, that is, they teach contentment with a little and the charm of a peaceful life.

Satire alone is the only original literary form discovered and developed by the Romans. We have this statement on the authority of Quintilian, a famous rhetorician who wrote a great book on the proper training of the future lawyer, and it is doubtless true, even if some who deny all originality to the Roman mind deny this also. Satire was not originally censorious as we understand it, but Lucilius, who lived before Cicero, gave it the sarcastic tendency that it has had, more or less, ever since. The greatest of all the satirists was Juvenal, who thundered away at the vices of his time and at evildoers who were already safely dead or exiled; his thunder is loud and perhaps he liked the thunder more than he hated the vices; but at any rate he is the greatest satirist that ever lived. About the same time there lived a clever epigrammatist, Martial, and he has no superior, either ancient or modern, in touching lightly on the foibles of men and of society also.

In history the Romans did not do very much. There were many reasons for this. In the first place they were satisfied with their notebooks of memoranda like our almanacs. Important facts were noted as in a diary and no attempt to trace cause and effect was made for many years. For History is the wisdom of events and the historian must have a philosophical mind, and the Romans cared little for philosophy. Here and there we hear of some ambitious man who had come into contact with Greek ideas and who tried his hand at the writing of history; but after all there is but one historian in Roman literature and he is Livy. This writer lived under the Emperor Augustus and died before he finished his great work that begins with Rome's birth and stops in Augustus' reign. Comparatively little of it has come down to us, but enough to show us that the Romans could have written history if they had cared to. There is another great writer that most people call a historian—Tacitus, who commenced on the history of the early empire. His writings are so pervaded by party spirit, so full of philosophic comment on Roman life that they are rather philosophical essays on historical subjects than histories. Some even have called him a writer of romance. Sallust, who lived almost a century earlier, was a writer of the same style as Tacitus, but most of his work is lost. The other historians were either dry annalists or servile compilers.

Philosophy seemed a waste of time to the practical Roman, and it is owing to his practical bent that today most people think of philosophy as ethics, that is the art of living righteously. The returning companies from Athens brought philosophic notions and sometimes philosophers, too, back with them to Rome, and the ethical principles of the Greek schools of philosophy influenced Roman thought deeply; but of strictly philosophical literature there is little. Cicero wrote a series of treatises planned to cover the whole field, regarding himself as a kind of missionary of Greek culture; and in the time of Nero

Seneca wrote much on ethical subjects. Epicureanism found in the sublime poem of Lucretius a worthy representative, but Lucretius was a man of one idea and his only object was to free humanity from the burden of superstition. The real influence of philosophic thought is to be found in the Roman, sometimes called the Civil Law, that is the common law of all civilized Europe except England, and of South America and many parts of Asia. The principles of justice and equity that were first defined by the acute Greek intellect were taken over and incorporated into the Roman law books. Indeed Roman genius is best seen in the ruins of buildings all over Europe and in the Roman law.

In poetry, pure and simple, that is lyric poetry in which the poet, like Tennyson, sings because he must, there is little in Roman literature. Catullus is almost alone, and he is a rare representative of the care-free, unattached singer; one who pours forth his liquid song with no thought of advantage or self-interest. But Catullus, after all, was not a Roman but a Gaul from the north of Italy. Next to Catullus is Propertius, a dark soul with an obscure style who was very much in love with a woman older than himself, and who wrote passionate appeals to win her.

After Christianity made its way into Rome there soon began to be written books on ecclesiastical subjects and from that time to this they have not ceased. The Bible was translated into Latin and of the many versions one finally emerged as superior to the rest and is known as the Vulgate. The accepted Latin Fathers of the Church are collected into some 260 stout quarto volumes in fine type. They deal almost wholly with ecclesiastical subjects but are a mine of information about manners and customs and historical facts; a mine that has only begun to be worked.

And so literature seems a mere episode in the life of the Roman people. For perhaps 500 years they did not have any in the strict sense of the term; then for 300 years or so they tried to imitate Greek literature with considerable success; and then the genius of the people turned back again to unliterary and practical subjects mostly. One must not think of Latin literature as something apart by itself; the torch of culture and the leadership of humanity passed from Greece to Rome and then on to the modern culture nations of Europe. Rome fell in 476 A.D. and the last Roman author is Boethius, a philosopher, mathematician and statesman. But that means only that the world was submerged for a few centuries in barbarism; the learning of Greece and Rome was faithfully preserved by the Church, mainly in the monasteries; and in the revival of the fourteenth century the aroused intellect of the emerging modern nations turned eagerly to ancient literature, for it was the literature of their intellectual ancestors, and it is of ours. Indeed French and Italian and Spanish are merely modern Latin. Greece and Rome have been the originators of modern thought. English literature is saturated with their influence; our whole life is Greek and Roman, but we do not know this until we read the literary works of the ancients. A knowledge of classical literature will be necessary for our comprehension of ourselves until our civilization becomes Asiatic or African, and may that never be!

LAOCOÖN GROUP

CHAPTER XIII.

Beginnings of Latin Literature.

For centuries the Romans were too busy fighting to maintain their little state and struggling among themselves for equal political privileges, to take thought for the more refining influences of civilization. Before a literature can arise, it is necessary to have a social class possessed of sufficient means and leisure to enjoy it. Not until the end of the first Punic war do we find such a class in Rome. Even then, it was too weak to make itself felt.

From a little hamlet of shepherds on Palatine Hill, Rome had expanded into a city, incorporating within her public lands the territories of her neighbors. Seeking an opportunity for trade to the west, she had come in conflict with the Carthaginians—the masters of the western Mediterranean. This was destined to be a fight to the death. Small chance appeared for the cultivation of the gentler arts during years filled with military deeds. When Greek slaves were finally provided to teach the children of the Roman republic, they found an utter dearth of literature in the Latin tongue.

To be sure, the Romans, like other primitive peoples, had their native hymns—their ballads, which glorified the deeds of heroes, their harvest songs, and wedding chants, but these existed alone in the hearts of the people. So far as we know, they were never committed to writing. The chant of the Arval Brothers may have been one of the old songs chanted by the "brothers of the ploughed fields," each year when they passed through the meadows, purifying the farms. If one wanders among the harvesters in rural districts of Italy today he may hear the peasants singing harvest songs, not unlike those, probably, which the earlier peasants sang, as they reaped the grain and gathered the grapes. Seldom, however, are such folk-songs preserved and almost none remain from early Roman days for the historical student who would gladly read through them the story of bygone ages.

From a literary standpoint, it is regretible that Italy lay so completely open to Greek influence during her early republican period. Otherwise a national literature might have developed in Rome—as it never did. The first productions rendered in Latin were translations from the Greek, and while later writers felt in no way bound to adhere to Greek forms and thought, nevertheless, literature among the Romans was hardly an end in itself, but served other ends. The very temperament of the Romans seemed to deprive them of any poetical conceptions. From the beginning they were a practical-minded people. While the early Greek productions seem born of the ages that produced them, while they breathe of the life, thought and feeling of the Hellenes, we find nothing in the early Latin worthy of comparison. Roman literature was too often made to serve political needs.

"Even those kinds of Roman literature which seem at first to have the least connection with political matters have nevertheless a political purpose. Plays were written to enhance the splendor of public festivals provided by office holders who were at the same time seekers and hoped to win the favor of the people by successful entertainments; history was written to teach the proper methods of action for future use or (sometimes) to add to the influence of living leaders of the state by calling to mind the great deeds of their ancestors; epic and lyric poems were composed to glorify important persons at Rome, or at least to prove the right of Rome to the foremost place among the nations by giving her a literature worthy of rank with that of the Greeks."[1]

Developing in this way, it was inevitable that the Latin literature should lack the completeness of the Greek. This does not imply that there were not brilliant writers in the Roman world, or that masterpieces were not therein produced. It is merely a criticism of Latin writings as a whole.

The first production in Latin was a translation of the "Odyssey," made by Andronicus, a Greek from Tarentum, taken to Italy as a prisoner of war. During the first Punic war he taught the children in the family of the Livii. Finding no available material in their native tongue, he translated this

[1] Fowler: Hist. of Roman Literature, p. 2.

masterpiece of Homeric ages, but from what we know of his work, it is supposed to have been but a crude effort. Nevertheless it marks the beginning of Latin literature.

Naevius was the first to use the Latin epic. He sang of the Punic war, a popular subject in his day, and he wove many mythological stories of Rome and Carthage into his tale. Virgil has been charged with borrowing frequently from his poem in the Aeneid. However, Naevius was succeeded by one far greater than himself—Quintus Ennius, the first genius in the realm of literature on Italian soil. In the Annals he wrote a long historical epic, unfolding the story of Rome from her mythological founding to his own time. For generations this poem embodied all that was greatest among Latin epics. It has come down to our time in numerous fragments.

Naevius and Ennius both wrote plays of which we know little. They were followed by two writers of comedy whose names stand with the gifted in the first period of Latin literature—the period of the republic. These were Plautus and Terence. Plautus was an Umbrian known to have been born in 254 B.C. He divided his time between writing plays and menial employments. Twenty of his comedies survive.

Terence was born in Carthage and came to Rome as a slave boy. Giving evidence of more than usual ability, he was educated and set free, becoming the companion of several public men of Rome who themselves belonged to the highest circles. Possessing far greater artistic qualities and a finer use of language, the plays of Terence lacked the originality and spontaneity so characteristic of Plautus. It is quite impossible to give a notion of either writer by brief quotations from their comedies, and it is safe to say that the plays of both today are read by few save students who value them both for their literary qualities and for the knowledge of early Latin to be gained from them.

Early Latin prose developed along the lines of history, law and oratory. From very early times it was no doubt customary to preserve annals pertaining to Rome's conquests and to her foreign relations. When the Gauls sacked Rome in 390 B. C., these were probably destroyed, and whatever official lists and records were accessible to the first writers of Roman history must have belonged to the years subsequent to this calamity.

Like the early tragedies and comedies, Roman histories were modeled after the Greek. Indeed, the first historian known to us, Quintus Fabius Pictor, wrote in Greek. He narrated the course of events from the arrival of Aeneas—thus including legendary lore, and closed with the second Punic war. This writing has not survived, but it is generally believed that Livy and Polybius gave considerable heed to it.

However closely the Romans might model their historical writings upon those of Hellas, in the realm of law and jurisprudence Rome stood alone. She soon advanced farther in this field than any other ancient nation and had nothing to gain by following outside examples. The famous Twelve Tables were accepted as early as 450 B. C. Comments upon them and decisions of jurists comprised Rome's legal lore.

In this age almost every man who sought political favor was an orator. Notable among public men at this time were the Gracchi. Not infrequently orations were committed to writing and thus preserved among Latin literary productions.

Poetry, the earliest form of literature among any people, soon proved inadequate for the conveyance of many kinds of thought, and prose gradually found a place in the writings of the Romans. Among those first to use this form of expression was Cato, who struggled long against the new learning, permeated so thoroughly with Greek influence. Of his writings, only his treatise on Agriculture survives.

The satires of Lucilius, while known only by fragments, deserve mention. Their loss is deplorable since they would have afforded many pictures of contemporary life.

"Lucilius is the first writer who gave to satire the definite character it has possessed ever since his time. He made his poems the vehicle for the expression of sharp and biting attacks upon persons, institutions, and customs of his day, for genial and humorous remarks about the failings of his neighbors, and for much information about himself. Ever since Lucilius, satire has been at once sharp and humorous, bitter and sweet."[2]

[2] Hist. of Roman Lit.: Fowler, 40.

Finally, the connecting link between the old literature and the new literature of Cicero's age, was Lucretius. His fame rests upon a long, didactic poem entitled: "On the Nature of Things." In this he sought to place the teachings of Epicurus before the Romans in their proper light. The theories of earlier philosophers were refuted. In the spirit of Epicurus, Lucretius tried to show how unnecessary was the superstitious fear of men respecting the gods—a fear that hampered free thought and made men slaves. Epicurus had taught that the gods were not concerned with the welfare of men, having interests of their own which precluded such a possibility.

Lucretius was not unaware that his subject was obscure and abstract, but he endeavored to set it forth with such power as belonged to him and to do justice to the sublimity of the theme. In this he was remarkably successful.

> " 'Tis sweet to go
> To fountains new and drink; and sweet it is
> To pluck new flowers and seek a garland thence
> For my own head, whence ne'er before a crown
> The Muses twined for any mortal's brow.
> 'Tis first because I teach of weighty things
> And guide my course to set the spirit free
> From superstition's closely knotted bonds;
> And next because concerning matters dark
> I write such lucid verses, touching all
> With th' Muses' grace. Then, too, because it seems
> Not without reason; but as when men try
> In curing boys to give them bitter herbs,
> They touch the edges round about the cups
> With yellow liquid of the honey sweet,
> That children's careless age may be deceived
> As far as to the lips, and meanwhile drink
> The juice of bitter herb, and though deceived
> May not be harmed, but rather in such wise
> Gain health and strength, so I now, since my theme
> Seems gloomy for the most part unto those
> To whom 'tis not familiar, and the crowd
> Shrinks back from it, have wished to treat for thee
> My theme with sweetly speaking poetry's verse
> And touch it with the Muses' honey sweet."

"Since the main purpose of the poem is to free men from religion and the fear of death by showing that all things, including the soul, came into being and are to pass away without any action of the gods, ethical doctrines are not systematically treated. Lucretius accepts, however, the Epicurean dogma that pleasure is the chief good, 'the guide of life,' but the pleasure he has in mind is not the common physical pleasure, but the calm repose of the philosopher:

> "Oh wretched minds of men, oh blinded hearts!
> Within what shades of life and dangers great
> Is passed whate'er of age we have! Dost thou
> Not see that nature makes demand for naught
> Save this, that pain be absent from our frame,
> That she, removed from care at once and fear,
> May have her pleasure in the joys of mind?"[3]

[3] Hist. of Roman Lit.: Fowler, 52.

THE PANTHEON OF AGRIPPA, ROME.

THE CHANT OF THE ARVAL BROTHERS.

This simple hymn is almost the only survival of indigenous Latin verse. The "Arval brothers,"—that is, "brethren of the ploughed field," were the tillers of the soil, who, led by the priests, marched in procession around the fields each spring. The only copy of the hymn was found on an inscription belonging to the reign of the Emperor Heliogabalus; the engraving shows the emperor in the dress of an Arval brother. The English version is by John Dunlop.

Ye Lares, aid us! Mars, thou
    God of might,
From murrain shield the flocks
    —the flowers from blight.
For thee, O Mars! a feast shall
    be prepared,
Salt, and a wether chosen from the herd:
Invite, by turns, each Demigod of spring.
Great Mars, assist us! Triumph! Triumph sing!

ENNIUS.

Quintus Ennius has been called "the Father of Latin poetry." His "Annals" versified Roman history in the Homeric hexameter. Though it was regarded with religious veneration by the ancients, hardly six hundred lines have been preserved. At its close he compared himself to a gallant horse, which, having often won the prize at the Olympic games, was entitled to rest in his old age. Yet he produced a tragedy just before his death in 169 B.C. His conscious hope of fame is witnessed in his Epitaph:—

    Ho, countrymen! old Ennius' form behold,
    Who sang your martial sires' achievements bold.
    No tears for me! no dirges at my grave!
    I live upon the lips of all the brave.

Reply of Pyrrhus to Fabricius.

Pyrrhus, King of Epirus, having defeated the Romans in his first encounter, in 280 B.C., sent an embassy, urging peace. The Romans sent Fabricius to redeem their soldiers taken captive, but the king replied with spirit :

> Your gold I seek not; take your ransoms home;
> Warriors, not traffickers in war, we come;
> Not gold, but steel, our strife should arbitrate,
> And valor prove which is the choice of fate.
> And hear me now proclaim this firm decree—
> "The brave whose lives the battle spared, with me
> Shall never mourn the loss of liberty."
> Unransom'd then your comrades hence remove,
> And may the mighty gods the boon approve.

The Lament of Andromache.

In this brief fragment from Ennius' tragedy Andromache, the widow of Hector laments the downfall of Troy. W. E. Aytoun has rendered it as follows:

Whither shall I flee for refuge? whither shall I look for aid?
Flight or exile, which is safer? Tower and town are both betrayed.
Whom shall I implore for succor? Our old altars are no more,
Broken, crushed they lie, and splintered, and the flames above them roar.
And our walls all blackened stand—O my father! fatherland!
O thou haughty house of Priam—temple with the gates surrounded,
I have seen thee—all thy splendor, all thy Eastern pomp unbounded—
All thy roofs and painted ceilings—all the treasures they contain,
I have seen them, seen them blazing—I have seen old Priam slain,
Foully murdered, and the altar of the Highest bears the stain.

FORTUNE-TELLERS.

(From a satire by Ennius, quoted by Cicero, and translated by Henry Thompson)

> I value not a rush your Marsian augurs,
> Your village seers, your market fortune-tellers,
> Egyptian sorcerers, dream-interpreters;
> No prophets they by knowledge or by skill,
> But superstitious quacks, shameless impostors,
> Lazy or crazy slaves of indigence,
> Who tell fine stories for their proper lucre:
> Teach others the highway, and cannot find
> A by-way for themselves; promise us riches,
> And beg of us a drachma; let them give
> Their riches first, then take their drachma out.

PLAUTUS.

PLAUTUS, the greatest comic poet in Latin literature, was born at Sarsina, in Umbria, about 225 B.C. His full name was Titus Maccius Plautus. In early life he was em- employed by actors at Rome; made some money, and then lost it in foreign trade, which, however, gave him a wide experience in cities of the Mediterranean. He returned to Rome to turn a hand-mill for a baker. He was probably forty years of age when he began to write comedies, which took the fancy of the people. His plays were based on the New Comedy of Athens, which dealt with recognized types of character—misers, parasites, hard-hearted masters, cheating slaves, gay courtesans and some worthy citizens. Plautus used his borrowed material with great freedom, making his Greeks speak and act like Romans. The scenes of his plays are in Greek cities, but there are frequent allusions to the laws, magistrates, streets and markets of Rome. He is more familiar with the trading classes than with the ruling aristocracy. Some of his plays are offensive by their grossness, while others are entirely free from this fault. In contrast with other great Latin writers, he refrains from moralizing.

The plays of Plautus continued to be acted more than three centuries after his death. His plots have served the turn of modern dramatists as eminent as Shakespeare and Moliere. "The Captives," one of his twenty surviving comedies, has been pronounced by Lessing the best constructed drama in existence.

The Captives.

The drama of the Captives, almost unique in the history of the stage as having no female character, is free from the usual buffoonery of Plautus. Its interest is pathetic, rather than comic. According to the story there was war between the Greek states of Elis and Ætolia. Hegio, a citizen of the latter, purchased captives brought thither, hoping, by means of them, to redeem his son, Philopolemus, now a prisoner of war in Elis. Among those purchased was a young noble, Philocrates, with his slave, Tyndarus; these two, however, secretly exchange clothes and deceive Hegio as to their previous condition. The new master is informed that his son is in the house of Philocrates's father, and to obtain his release is induced to send the supposed slave back to Elis. But another Elian captive, unaware of what has just happened to his friend Philocrates, seeks an interview with him. Finding only Tyndarus, he hastily reveals the imposture to Hegio. The master, enraged, forthwith orders the slave to be loaded with chains and sent to work in the quarries. But virtue triumphs. After an interval Philocrates returns, bringing not only the ransomed Philopolemus to his father, but also a slave, who, twenty years before, had run away from Hegio and carried off his younger son. On examination it appears that the fugitive had gone to Elis and sold the child to the father of Philocrates. This slave-child had been the playfellow of the young noble, and is now discovered to be the very Tyndarus who has been so severely punished by his father for fidelity to his master and friend.

The Generous Slave.

Hegio. Where are those captives,
I ordered to be brought before the house?
　Philocrates. Chain'd as we are, and wall'd in by our keepers,
You have provided that we shall not fail
To answer to your call.
　Heg. The greatest care
Is scarce enough to guard against deceit;
And the most cautious, even when he thinks
He's most upon his guard, is often trick'd.—
But have I not just cause to watch you well,
When I have bought you with so large a sum?
　Phil. 'Twould not be right in us to blame you for it;
Nor, should occasion offer to escape,
Would it be right in you to censure us,
That we make use of it.
　Heg. As you are here,
So in your country is my son confin'd.
　Phil. What! Is your son a captive?—
　Heg. Yes, he is.
　Phil. We are not then, it seems, the only cowards.
　Heg. (*to Philocrates, supposing him servant to Tyndarus*).
Come nearer this way—something I would know
In private of you,—and in this affair
You must adhere to truth.
　Phil. In what I know
I'll do it, sir; and, should you ask me aught
I do not know, I'll own my ignorance.
　Heg. Of what family
Is this Philocrates?
　Phil. The Polyphusian,
A potent and most honorable house!
　Heg. What honors held he in his country?
　Phil. High ones,
Such as the chief men can alone attain to.
　Heg. Seeing his rank's so noble, as you say,
What is his substance?
　Phil. As to that, the old one
Is very warm.

Heg. His father's living then?
Phil. We left him so, when we departed thence.
Heg. What's his name?
Phil. Thesaurochrysonicochrysides.*
Heg. A name bestowed upon him for his wealth?
Phil. Nay, rather for his avarice and extortion—
His real name was Theodoromedes.†
  Heg. How say you?—Is his father covetous?
  Phil. Very.—To let you more into his character,—
In sacrificing to his household genius
He uses nothing but vile Samian vessels,
For fear the god should steal them:—mark by this,
What trust he puts in others.
  Heg. Come you this way—
(*aside*) What further information I require,
I'll learn from him.
(*Addressing Tyndarus as Philocrates.*) Philocrates, your servant
Has acted as befits an honest fellow.—
I've learn'd from him your family:—he has owned it:—
Do you the same; 'twill turn to your advantage,
If you confess what, be assur'd, I know
From him already.
  Tynd. Sir, he did his duty,
When he confess'd the truth to you,—although
I would have fain conceal'd from you my state,
My family, and my means.—But now, alas!
Since I have lost my country and my freedom,
Can I suppose it right, that he should dread
Me before you? The power of war has sunk
My fortunes to a level with his own.—
  Heg. Speak on, and boldly.
  Tynd. I ere this was free
As your own son.—Him has the power of war
Depriv'd of liberty, as it has me.
He in my country is a slave,—as now
I am a slave in this.—There is indeed
A God that hears and sees whate'er we do:—
As you respect me, so will He respect

  * Son of the golden conqueror of the golden treasure.
  † Meditator on the gift of the god.

Your lost son.—To the well-deserving, good
Will happen, to the ill-deserving, ill. —
Think, that my father feels the want of me,
As much as you do of your son.

Heg. I know it.—
But say, will you subscribe to the account
Your servant gave?

Tynd. My father's rich, I own,
My family is noble;—but, I pray you,
Let not the thought of these my riches bend
Your mind to sordid avarice, lest my father,
Though I'm his only child, should deem it fitter
I were your slave, clothed, pamper'd at your cost,
Than beg my bread in my own country, where
It were a foul disgrace.

Heg. Thanks to the gods,
And to my ancestors, I'm rich enough.—
Nor do I hold that every kind of gain
Is always serviceable.—Gain, I know,
Has render'd many great.—But there are times,
When loss should be preferr'd to gain.—I hate it,
'Tis my aversion, money:—many a man
Has it enticed oft-times to wrong.—But now
Attend to me, that you may know my mind.
My son's a captive and a slave of Elis:—
If you restore him to me, I require
No other recompense;—I'll send you back,
You and your servant:—on no other terms
Can you go hence.

Tynd. You ask what's right and just,—
Thou best of men!—But is your son a servant
Of the public, or some private person?

Heg. A servant of Menarchus, a physician.

Phil, O 'tis his father's client;—and success
Pours down upon you, like a hasty shower.

Heg. Find means, then, to redeem my son.

Tynd. I'll find them.—
But I must ask you—

Heg. Ask me what you will,
I'll do't,—if to that purpose.

Tynd. Hear, and judge.—
I do not ask you, till your son's return

To grant me a dismission; but, I pray you,
Give me my slave, a price set on his head,
That I may send him forthwith to my father,
To work your son's redemption.

Heg. I'd despatch
Some other rather, when there is a truce,
Your father to confer with, who may bear
Any commands you shall intrust him with.

Tynd. 'Twould be in vain to send a stranger to him—
You'd lose your labor.—Send my servant: he'll
Complete the whole, as soon as he arrives.
A man more faithful you can never send,
Nor one my father sooner would rely on,
More to his mind, nor to whose care and confidence
He'd sooner trust your son.—Then never fear:
At my own peril will I prove his faith,
Relying on his nature, since he knows
I've borne me with benevolence towards him.

Heg. Well—I'll despatch him, if you will,—your word
Pawn'd for his valuation.

Tynd. Prithee do,
And let him be dismiss'd without delay.

Heg. Can you show reason, if he don't return,
Why you should not pay twenty minæ for him?

Tynd. No surely: I agree.

Heg. Take off his chains,—
And take them off from both.

Tynd. May all the gods
Grant all your wishes! Since that you have deign'd
To treat me with such favor, and releas'd me
From my vile bonds:—I scarce can think it irksome
To have my neck free from this galling collar.

Heg. The favors we confer on honest souls
Teem with returns of service to the giver.—
But now, if you'd despatch him hence, acquaint him,
Give him your orders, and forthwith instruct him
What you would have him say unto your father.—
Shall I then call him to you?

Tynd. Do, sir,—call him.
   (*Hegio calls Philocrates, who advances.*)
I thank you for the liberty you give me
To send this messenger to my relations,

That he may tell my father all about me,
And how I fare, and what I would have done.—
We have agreed betwixt us, Tyndarus,
To send you unto Elis to my father;
And, if thence you return not, I have bargain'd
To forfeit for your trespass twenty minæ.

Phil. Rightly agreed:—for the old gentleman
Expects me, or some other messenger,
To come to him from hence.

Tynd. Then mind me now,
What I would have you say unto my father.
First, to my dearest mother and my father
Bear my respects, and next to my relations,—
Then to whatever other friend you see,
Inform them of my health; and tell them likewise
That I am slave here to this best of men,
Who ever has, and still goes on to treat me
With honorable usage.—
Acquaint my father with th' agreement made
'Twixt me and Hegio, touching Hegio's son.—
'Tis to redeem the youth, and send him hither
Exchang'd for you and me.—

Phil. I shall remember.—

Heg. And soon too as he can, for both our sakes.

Phil. You long not more to see your son return'd,
Than he does his.

Heg. My son to me is dear;
Dear is his own to every one.

Phil. (to Tyndarus). Aught else
To bear unto your father?

Tynd. Say, I'm well;
And tell him, boldly tell him, that our souls
Were link'd in perfect harmony together;
That nothing you have ever done amiss,
Nor have I ever been your enemy;
That in our sore affliction you maintain'd
Your duty to your master, nor once swerv'd
From your fidelity, in no one deed
Deserted me in time of my distress.
For when my father is informed of this,
And learns how well your heart has been inclin'd
Both to his son and to himself, he'll never

Prove such a niggard, but in gratitude
He will reward you with your liberty;
And I, if I return, with all my power
Will urge him the more readily to do it.
For by your aid, your courtesy, your courage,
Wisdom and prudence, you have been the means
Of my return to Elis, since you own'd
To Hegio here my family and fortune,
By which you've freed your master from his chains.

Phil. True, I have acted as you say;—and much
It pleases me you bear it in remembrance.
What I have done was due to your deserts:
For were I in my count to tell the sum
Of all your friendly offices towards me,
Night would bear off the day ere I had done.
You've been obliging, been obsequious to me,
As though you were my servant.

Heg. O ye gods!—
Behold the honest nature of these men!—
They draw tears from me.—Mark, how cordially
They love each other! and what praise the servant
Heaps on his master!

Phil. He deserves from me
A hundred times more praise, than he was pleased
To lavish on me.

Heg. (to Philocrates). Then, since hitherto
You've acted worthily, occasion now
Presents itself to add to your good deeds,
That you may prove your faithfulness towards him
In this affair.

Phil. My wish to compass it
Cannot exceed th' endeavors I will use
To get it perfected.—And to convince you,
Here do I call high Jove to witness, Hegio,
I will not prove unfaithful to Philocrates.—

Heg. Thou art an honest fellow.—

Phil. Nor will I
Act otherwise to *him*, than I would act
To my own self.

Tynd. Would you might make your words
True by your actions!—Bear it in your mind,
That I have said less of you than I would,

And prithee be not angry with my words.
Think, I beseech you, that my honor's staked
For your dismission, and my life is here
A pledge for your return. When out of sight,
As shortly you will be, deny not then
All knowledge of me: when you shall have left me
Here as a pawn in slavery for you,
Yourself at liberty, desert not then
Your hostage, then neglect not to procure
His son's redemption in exchange for me.

THE IMPOSTOR EXPOSED.

THIS is another scene from "The Captives." The slave Tyndarus, on seeing his master's friend Aristophontes, now a captive, approach, tried to make Hegio believe that he was insane, but failed.

Hegio. If you would aught with me, I lend attention.
Aristophontes. Sir, you shall hear the real truth from me,
Which now you deem a falsehood.—But I first
Would wish to clear me from this charge of madness.—
Believe me, Hegio, I'm not mad, nor have I
Any complaint but this,—that I'm a slave.—
Oh, never may the King of gods and men
My native country suffer me to see,
If this is any more Philocrates
Than you or I.
Heg. Tell me, who is he then?
Arist. The same, I said he was from the beginning.
If you shall find it other, I can show
No cause, no reason, why I should not suffer
A lack of liberty, your slave forever.
Heg. (*to Tyndarus.*) And what do you say?
Tyndarus. That I am your slave,
And you my master.
Heg. I don't ask you that.—
Were you a free man?
Tynd. Yes, I was.
Arist. Indeed
He never was: he trifles with you, Hegio.
Tynd. How do you know? or were you peradventure
My mother's midwife, that you dare affirm
What you advance with so much confidence?

Arist. A boy I saw you when a boy.
Tynd. A man
I see you now a man.—So—there's an answer
If your behavior were as would become you,
You would not interfere in my concerns.—
Do I in yours?

Heg. (*to Arist.*) Say, was his father's name
Thesaurochrysonicochrysides?

Arist. 'Twas not,—nor did I ever hear the name
Before to-day.—Philocrates's father
Was called Theodoromedes.

Tynd. (*aside*). I'm ruin'd!
Be still, my heart!—prithee, go hang yourself—
Still, still will you be throbbing.—Woe is me!
I scarce can stand upon my legs for fear.

Heg. Can I be sure this fellow was a slave
In Elis, and is not Philocrates?

Arist. So certain, that you'll never find it other.
But where is he now?

Heg. Where I least could wish him,
And where he wishes most himself to be.
Ah me! I am disjointed, sawn asunder,
By the intrigues of this vile rascal, who
Has led me by the nose just at his pleasure.—
But have a care you err not.

Arist. What I say,
Is as a thing assur'd, a truth establish'd.

Heg. And is it certain?

Arist. Yes,—so very certain,
That you can never find anything that's more so.
I and Philocrates have been friends from boys.

Heg. What sort of person was Philocrates?

Arist. His hair inclin'd to red, frizzled and curl'd,
A lantern jaw, sharp nose, a fair complexion,
And black eyes.—

Heg. The description's very like him.

Tynd. Now by my troth it was a sore mischance,
My coming here:—woe to the hapless twigs,
Will die upon my back.

Heg. I plainly see,
I have been cheated.

Tynd. Why do ye delay?

Haste, haste, ye chains, come and embrace my legs,
That I may have you in my custody.—
  Heg. These villainous captives, how they have deceiv'd me!
He, that is gone off, feign'd himself a slave,
And this a free man.—I have lost the kernel,
And for security the shell is left me.—
Fool that I am! they have impos'd upon me
In ev'ry shape. But he shall never more
Make me his sport.—Ho, Colapho, Cordalio,
Corax, go in and bring me out the thongs.
  Slave. What, is he sending us to bind up fagots?
        (*The slaves go in and return with thongs.*)

  Heg. This instant manacle that rascal there.
                    (*To his slaves.*)
  Tynd. Ah! why is this? In what have I offended?
  Heg. See, with what assurance
He stands before me!
  Tynd. It becomes a slave,
That's innocent, unconscious of a crime,
To bear him with such confidence, especially
Before his master.—
  Heg. See you bind his hands,
And hard too.
  Tynd. I am yours, my hands are yours;
If 'tis your pleasure, bid them be cut off.—
But what's the matter?—why thus angry with me?

Heg. Because that by your knavish lying schemes
You have destroy'd, as far as in your power,
Me and my hopes, distracted my affairs,
And by your tricks have robbed me of Philocrates.
I thought he was a slave, and you a free man,
For so you said you were, and for that purpose
You chang'd your names.
　Tynd. I own that I have acted
E'en as you say,—that he has found the means
For his escaping, and through my assistance.—
Is it for this then you are angry with me?
　Heg. What you have done, you'll find will cost you dear!
　Tynd. Death I esteem a trifle, when not merited
By evil actions.—If I perish here,
And he return not, as he gave his word,
This act will be remember'd to my honor,
After I'm dead;—that I contriv'd to free
My master, when a captive, from his state
Of slavery and oppression with the foe;
Restor'd him to his country and his father,
Preferring rather to expose my life
To danger for him, than that he should suffer.
　Heg. Enjoy that fame then in the other world.
　Tynd. He dies to live, who dies in Virtue's cause.

THE PARASITE BRINGS GOOD NEWS.

THE parasite Ergasilus had been invited to sup with Hegio, and has in the meantime discovered the return of his host's captive son. Hegio, standing near his own house, wonders at the capers of Ergasilus.

　Ergasilus (knocking at Hegio's door.)
Ho there—where are ye? some one, ope the door.
　Heg. He's come to sup with me.
　Erg. Ope both the doors,
Ere piece-meal I demolish them with knocking.
　Heg. I have a mind to speak to him.—Ergasilus!
　Erg. Who calls Ergasilus?
　Heg. Turn your head—look on me.
　Erg. Look on you?—That's what Fortune never does,
Nor ever will.—Who is it?
　Heg Look.—I'm Hegio.

Erg. (*turning.*) Best of best men, most opportunely met.
Heg. You have found some one at the port to sup with,
And therefore do you treat me with this scorn.
Erg. Give me thy hand.
Heg. My hand?
Erg. Thy hand, I say.
Give it this instant.
Heg. There it is. (*Giving his hand.*)
Erg. Be joyful.
Heg. Joyful! for what?
Erg. Because it is my order.—
Come, come, be joyful.
Heg. Joy, alas! with me
By sorrow is prevented.
Erg. Do not grieve:
I'll wipe away, this instant, ev'ry stain
Of sorrow from your soul.—Pluck up,—be joyous.
Heg. Well,—though I see no reason to rejoice.
Erg. That's bravely done.—Now order—
Heg. Order what?
Erg. A monstrous fire.
Heg. A monstrous fire?
Erg. I say it:
A huge one let it be.
Heg. Why how now, Vulture?
Think you, that I will fire my house to please you?
Erg. Nay, prithee don't be angry.—Will you order,
Or will you not, the pots to be put on?
The dishes to be wash'd? the larded meats
And kickshaws to be set upon the stoves?
Won't you send some one to buy fish?
Heg. He dreams
With his eyes open!
Erg. Bid another go
For pork, lamb, pullets?
Heg. Yes, you understand
Good living, had you wherewithal to get it.
Erg. For hams, for turbot, salmon, mackerel, cod,
A fat cheese?
Heg. Easier 'tis for you to talk
Of all those dainties, than with me to eat them.
Erg. Think you, I speak this on my own account?

Heg. You will get nothing, don't deceive yourself,
Like what you talk of.—Prithee bring with you
A stomach suited to such common fare,
As you may meet with every day,—no nice one.
　Erg. But let me tell you, I shall be the author
Of your providing a most sumptuous treat,
E'en though I should forbid it.
　Heg. I?
　Erg. Yes, you.
　Heg. Hey! you are then my master.
　Erg. I'm your friend.—
Say, shall I make you happy?
　Heg. Certainly;
I'd rather so, than you should make me wretched.
　Erg. Give me your hand.
　Heg. There,—there's my hand.
　Erg. The gods,
The gods are all your friends.
　Heg. I feel it not.
　Erg. You are not in a thorn-bush, else you'd feel.—
But let your sacred vessels be prepar'd.
And bid them bring forthwith a fatted lamb.
　Heg. For what?
　Erg. To make a sacrifice.
　Heg. To whom?
Which of the gods?
　Erg. To me.—For I am now
Thy Jupiter supreme,—I thy Salvation,
Thy Life, thy Fortune, thy Delight, thy Joy.—
To make this god propitious, cram him well.
　Heg. May Jupiter and all the gods confound you.
　Erg. Nay, you should rather thank me for the news
I bring you from the port, such gladsome news.—
Your supper likes me now.
　Heg. Begone, you fool,—
You're come too late.
　Erg. Your words had been more true,
Had I come sooner.—Now receive from me
The transport that I bring you.—At the port
Just now I saw your son, your Philopolemus,
Alive and hearty,—in the packet-boat
I saw him,—with him too that other spark,

Your captive, him of Elis,—and besides,
Your slave Stalagmus, him that ran away,
And stole your little boy at four years old.
   Heg. Away,—you joke with me.
   Erg. Holy Gluttony
So help me,—as I wish for evermore
By her high title to be dignified,—
I saw—
   Heg. My son?
   Erg. Your son, my genius.
   Heg. O ye immortal gods!
If he speak truth, I shall seem born again.
   Erg. And can you doubt me, when I swore so solemnly?
If you have little faith then in my oaths,
Go to the port yourself.
   Heg. And so I will—
Take thou the necessary care within:
Use, and demand, broach any cask you like,
I make you cellar-man.
   Erg. And if you find me
Not a true prophet, curry me with your cudgel.
   Heg. If your intelligence should turn out true,
I will insure you everlasting eating.
   Erg. From whence?
   Heg. From me and from my son.
   Erg. You promise?
   Heg. I do.
   Erg. And I too, that your son is come.
   Heg. You'll manage for the best.
   Erg. All good attend you.
                    [*Exit* HEGIO.
He's gone,—and has intrusted to my care,
The high and grand concern of catering.—
Immortal gods! how I shall cut and quarter!
How I shall chop the necks from off the chines!
What devastation will befall the hams!
What a consumption rage among the bacon!
What massacre of fat sow's paps! of brawn
What havoc will arise!—Then what fatigue
Awaits the butchers! what the hog-killers!—
But to say more of what concerns good eating,
Is loss of time, and hindrance.

THE WALLET FISHED UP.

The play called in the original *Rudens*, "The Rope," might be called "The Shipwreck." The scene is laid near the city of Cyrene on the morning after a storm. Dæmones, an Athenian by birth, who lives in a cottage close by a temple of Venus, comes out to see what damage has been done. He sees a boat struggling through the waves; two girls who were in it escape to the rocks and seek refuge in the temple. One of them, Palæstra, tells her story; she had been stolen from Athens in childhood, and had passed into the hands of Labrax, a slave-dealer. Pleusidippus fell in love with her and endeavored to purchase her, but Labrax, hoping to secure a higher price for her and other slaves, set sail for Sicily. They were shipwrecked when going out of the harbor. Labrax, who had also escaped, hearing that the two girls were in the temple, sought to drag them out. Trachalio, a servant of Pleusidippus, meets him there, and runs to the cottage for aid. Dæmones, with two slaves, rescues Palæstra and her companion and leaves Labrax in custody. Pleusidippus, on being informed of what has happened, comes up and carries off the slave dealer to the nearest magistrate for sacrilege and other offences. Gripus, a fisherman and slave of Dæmones, now appears, dragging a long rope, having hauled up in his net a weighty wallet. But Trachalio, who has seen part of his proceedings, claims a share in the booty, and after wrangling, proposes to submit the case to the owner of the cottage, not knowing his relation to Gripus. The latter consents, and they meet Dæmones as he is leading the girls back to the temple.

  Dæmones. Now seriously, my girls, I wish to do
What you yourselves wish, but I fear, my wife
On your account would thrust me out of doors,
Pretending that I brought my misses home
Under her nose, before her eyes.—Do you, then,
Rather than I, take refuge at the altar.
  Palæstra and Ampelisca. We are undone!
  Dæm. Fear nothing: I'll protect you.
  (*To the servants.*) What brought you out of doors?
    Why do you follow me?
While I am present, no one shall molest them.
So, get ye in, I say, and there stand sentinel.
  Gripus (coming forward). Save you, good master.
  Dæm. How now, Gripus? Save you.
  Trachalio. Is this your servant?
  Grip. Yes, and no disgrace to him.

Trach. I've nothing to do with you.
Grip. Get you gone then.
Trach. I pray you, tell me, sir; is this your servant?
Dæm. He is.
Trach. So,—best of all then, if he is.
Dæm. What is the matter?
Trach. He's an arrant rascal.
Dæm. What has this arrant rascal done to you?
Grip. What! shall he speak the first?
Dæm. Attend, I say.
(*To Trach.*) Speak you.
Grip. And will you let a stranger speak
'Fore your own servant?
Trach. How impossible
To curb his tongue!—As I was going to say,
That curs'd procurer's wallet, whom you drove
Just now from Venus' temple,—lo! he has it.
Grip. I have it not.
Trach. And will you dare deny
What I beheld myself, with my own eyes?
Grip. Would you were blind, I say!—Suppose I have it
Or have it not, why d'ye concern yourself
With my affairs?
Trach. It does concern me, whether
You have possession justly or unjustly.
Grip. I caught it, or I'd give you leave to hang me.
Since in the sea I caught it with my net,
How is't more yours than mine?
Trach. He would deceive you:
He has it, as I told you.
Grip. What d'ye say?
Trach. If he's your servant, prithee keep him under,
That I, whose right it is, may speak the first.
Grip. How! would you have my master deal with me,
As yours with you? though he may keep you under,
Our master is not us'd to serve us so.
Dæm. Faith, he has match'd you there.—What would you?
tell me.
Trach. I ask no share, no portion of the wallet,
Nor did I say 'twas mine: but there is in it
A little casket of that damsel's, who
I told you was free-born.

11

Dæm. What? her you mean,
My countrywoman, as you said?
 Trach. The same.
And in that casket, which is in the wallet,
There are some toys of hers, which when a child
She had: to him they're of no use or service,
But if he give them her, may be the means
For her to find her parents.
 Dæm. Say no more,
I'll make him give them.
 Grip. Troth, I'll give her nothing.
 Trach. I ask but for the casket and those toys.
 Grip. But what if they be gold?
 Trach. Suppose they are,
You shall have gold for gold, of equal value,
Silver for silver.
 Grip. Let me see your gold,
And you shall see the casket.
 Dæm. Hold your tongue;
Beware you get a drubbing:—(*to Trach.*) You go on.
 Trach. I pray you have compassion on this damsel,
If it indeed be the slave-dealer's wallet.
 Grip. (*aside.*) See how the rascal tries to catch his favor!
 Trach. Let me proceed.—If 'tis the rascal's wallet,
These girls will surely know it:—order him
To show it them.
 Grip. How! show it them?
 Dæm. He asks
Nothing but what is reasonable, Gripus.
 Grip. If I produce it, they will cry out at once
They know it truly.
 Trach. Rascal! do you think
That everybody's like yourself?—false varlet!
 Grip. I bear all this with patience, while my master
Is on my side.
 Trach. But now he is against you,
And that the casket will bear testimony.
 Dæm. Gripus, be silent and attend! (*To Trach.*) Do you
Tell me briefly, what is it you would have?
 Trach. I've told you, and I'll tell it you again.
These damsels, I inform'd you, are free-born;
And one was stolen from Athens when a child.

Grip. But what is this, pray, to the wallet, whether
They're slaves or free?
Trach. You'd have me spend the day
In telling the whole o'er again, you villain!
Dæm. Spare your abuses, and inform me clearly
In what I ask.
Trach. There should be in the wallet
A wicker casket, that contains some tokens
Which the poor girl may find her parents by,
And which she had, when stol'n a little child
From Athens, as I told you.
Grip. Jupiter and all the gods confound you! Don't you see
The damsels are both dumb? Why cannot they
Speak for themselves?
Trach. Because it more becomes
A woman to be silent than to talk.
Pray, sir, command him to deliver up
That casket to the girls, and what reward
He asks for finding it, it shall be given:
What else is in the wallet, let him have.
Grip. Ah, so you say at last. Now you're convinc'd
I have a right to't, though just now you wanted
To go shares with me.
Trach. And I want it still.
Dæm. Give me the wallet, Gripus.
Grip. I'll trust it to you on condition you'll
Return it, if there's nothing in't of theirs.
Dæm. I will.
Grip. There—take it (*giving him the wallet*).
Dæm. Look now, Palæstra
And Ampelisca, attend to what I say.—
Is this the wallet, that contains your casket?
Pal. The same.
Grip. So,—I'm undone, I find.—Before
She could well see it, she cries out, "The same."
Pal. I'll make this matter plain, and clear up all.
There is a wicker casket in that wallet;
And each particular that it contains
I'll reckon one by one: you shall not show me:
If wrong, my word will serve me in no stead,
And all that's in the casket shall be yours;
If right, I pray you let me have my own.

Dæm. Agreed: she only asks for common justice,
In my opinion.
　Trach. And in mine.
　Dæm. Open then
The wallet; I would know the truth directly.
　Grip. (*opening it.*) The deed is done!—'tis opened.—Ah!
　　　　I'm ruin'd!
I see a casket.
　Dæm. Is this it?
　Pal. The same.
In this, my parents, are you lock'd; in this
My hopes and means of finding you are lodg'd.
　Grip. Verily you deserve the gods' displeasure,
To cram your parents in so close a compass.
　Dæm. Come hither, Gripus:—'tis your cause is trying.
(*To Pal.*) Now listen, girl; at distance where you are
Tell the contents, and give a just description
Of each particular within the casket.
If in the smallest tittle you mistake,
Though afterwards you'd wish to speak the truth,
I'll hold it nothing but egregious trifling.
Speak, girl.—Gripus, give ear, and hold your tongue.
　Pal. There are some toys.
　Dæm. I see them.
　Grip. (*aside*). I'm slain
At the first onset.—Hold, sir,—don't produce them.
　Dæm. Describe them,—and recount them all in order
　Pal. First, there's a little sword with an inscription.
　Dæm. What's the inscription?
　Pal. 'Tis my father's name.
Then, there's a little two-edg'd axe, of gold too,
Bearing the inscription of my mother's name.
　Dæm. Hold,—what's your father's name upon the sword?
　Pal. 'Tis Dæmones.
　Dæm. O ye immortal gods!
Where are my hopes?
　Grip. Nay truly, where are mine?
　Dæm. Proceed, I do beseech you, quickly.
　Grip. Gently.
(*Aside.*) Would you were hang'd!
　Dæm. Tell me your mother's name
Upon the axe.

Pal. 'Tis—Dædalis.

Dæm. The gods
Are anxious for my welfare.

Grip. And my ruin.

Dæm. Why, Gripus, she must surely be my daughter.

Grip. She may be so for me. (*To Trach.*) May all the gods
Confound you, that you chanc'd to spy me out;
And me too, that I did not look about me
A hundred times to watch if no one saw me,
Before I drew the net out of the water.

Pal. Then there's a small two-handed silver knife.
A little sow too.

Grip. Would that you were hang'd,
You and your sow too, pigs and all together!

Pal. There is besides a little heart of gold,
Given me by my father on my birth-day.

Dæm. 'Tis she, 'tis she!—I can refrain no longer,
I must embrace her. (*They embrace.*)
Save you, my dear daughter!
I, I am Dæmones, and Dædalis
Your mother is within here.

Pal. Blessings on you,
My unexpected, my unhop'd-for father!

Dæm. Heavens bless you!—With what joy do I embrace
you!

Trach. To me too 'tis a pleasure, since your piety
Has wrought this happy chance.

Dæm. Come, take the wallet,
And bear it in, Trachalio, if you can.

Trach. (*Taking the wallet.*) Behold the roguery of Gripus!
—Gripus,
I give you joy upon your ill success.

Dæm. Come, daughter, let us in now to your mother,
For she can question you of further proofs,
Who has been more accustom'd to you, more
Acquainted with your tokens.

Trach. We'll all go in,
Since we are all concerned in this event.

Pal. Follow me, Ampelisca.

Amp. I'm rejoic'd
To find the gods so favorable to you.

A Pitcher of Water.

This is an earlier scene of the same play. Ampelisca, the girl shipwrecked with Palæstra, was also cast ashore and rejoined her companion. They made their way to the temple of Venus, and were received hospitably by the priestess. The latter sent Ampelisca to the neighboring cottage to get water.

    Ampelisca. I'll now do what the priestess order'd me:
I'll beg some water here at the next house.
She told me if I ask'd it in her name,
They'd give it me forthwith. I never saw
A worthier old woman, more deserving
Favor from gods and men. How courteously,
And with what gentle breeding she receiv'd us
Trembling, in want, wet, cast away, half-dead,—
And treated us as though we were her children!
How readily herself did warm us water
For us to wash!—But I must mind her orders,
That I mayn't make her wait.
(*Knocking at Dæmones' door.*) Ho! who's within here?
Open the door.—Will nobody come forth?

    [*Enter* Sceparnio.
  Scep. Who's at the door there, banging so unmercifully?
  Amp. 'Tis I.
  Scep. What good d'ye bring us?—By Hercules,
A likely girl.
  Amp. Good day to you, young man.
  Scep. The same to you, young woman.
  Amp. I am come to you,—
  Scep. I'll entertain you, if you come anon,
As you could wish: at present I have nothing
To satisfy your wants.—Ah, ah, my pretty one!
My smirking, smiling rogue! (*Offering to embrace her.*)
  Amp. Let me alone:—
Hold, there. You're rude.
  Scep. By heavens, the very
Image of Venus! What a sparkling eye
The girl has!—what a shape!—what a complexion!—
A walnut,—a brunette I meant to say!—
What breasts!—what pretty pouting lips!—(*Lays hold of her.*)

Amp. (*Struggling.*) Be quiet!—
What!—can't you keep your hands off?—
   Scep. Prithee, sweet,
May I not toy a little?

   Amp. By-and-by,—
When I'm at leisure, I may trifle with you:—
Now let me have your answer, ay or no,
To that which I was sent to ask.
   Scep. What would you?
   Amp. Can you not guess by this?
                              (*Pointing to the pitcher.*)
   Scep. And can't you tell
What I would have of you?
   Amp. The priestess sent me
To beg some water.
   Scep. I am proud and lordly:
Unless you sue to me with low petition,
You will not get a drop.—Our well we dug,
At our own hazard, with our proper tools.—
Unless you woo me with much blandishment,
You will not get a drop.
   Amp. Why should you grudge

To give me water, which an enemy
Will give an enemy?
  Scep. Why should you grudge
To grant me that same favor, which a friend
Will give a friend?
  Amp. Well, well, my sweet, I'll do
All you desire.
  Scep. (*Aside.*) O charming!—I am blest!—
She calls me *sweet.*—(*To Amp.*) You shall have water:—No,
You shall not love in vain.—Give me the pitcher.
  Amp. Here,—take it.—Prithee, love, make haste, and bring
    it me.
  Scep. Stay:—I'll be here this instant, my sweet charmer.
            [*Exit* SCEPARNIO.
  Amp. What shall I tell the priestess in excuse
For tarrying here so long?—Oh, how I dread
Even now to look upon the deep!—
(*Looking towards the sea.*) Ah me!
What do I see there on the shore?—my master
And his Sicilian guest, whom I believed
Both drown'd!—More evil still survives to plague us
Than we imagin'd.—Now I must run
Into the temple to inform Palæstra,
That we may fly to the altar ere he come
And seize us.—I'll be off.--   [*Runs into the temple.*

        [*Enter* SCEPARNIO.

  Scep. Good heavens!
I ne'er believ'd such pleasure was in water:
I drew it with such heartiness!—The well
Methought too was less deep than heretofore,
With so much ease I drew it!—Verily
I am a fool, that I should fall in love now
For the first time.—Here, take your water, precious!
I would that you might carry it with that pleasure
Which I myself do; so shall I adore you.
Where are you, dainty dear?—Here, take your water.—
Where are you?—Verily, I think she loves me:
The wanton plays at bo-peep.—Ho! where are you?—
A pleasant joke i'faith:—but come, be serious.
Why won't you take it?—Where in the world are you?—
I see her nowhere:—she's making sport.—

I'll leave it on the ground.—But softly—what
If some one take the pitcher?—It belongs
To Venus; and 'twould bring me into trouble.
Now I'm afraid, the jilt has some design
To trap me by its being found upon me:
The magistrate would have a fair pretense
To clap me into chains, if any one
Should chance to see me with it:—for 'tis letter'd,—
Tells of itself whose property it is.
I'll call the priestess out, that she may take it.
I'll to the door then of the temple. (*Calling.*) Ho there,
Ptolemocratia!—Come, and take your pitcher.—
I'll carry it in.—Bless me, I've enough to do,
If I'm to fetch this water to all that ask for't.

[*Goes into the temple.*

The Braggart Captain.

Pyrgopolinices. See that the splendor of my shield outshine
The sun's bright radiance, when the heav'ns are fair:
That when we join in battle, it may dazzle
The enemies' eyes throughout their thickest ranks.
Fain would I comfort this good sword of mine,
Lest he despond in spirit, or lament,
Because I wear him unemploy'd, who longs
To make a carbonado of the foes.
But where is Artotrogus?
Artotrogus. He is here,
Close by a hero brave and fortunate,
And of a princely form,—a warrior! such
As Mars himself would not have dar'd to bring
His prowess in compare with yours.
Pyrg. Who was it
In the Gurgustidonian plains I spar'd,
Where Bombamachides Cluninstaridysarchides,
Great Neptune's grandson, bore the chief command?

Art. Oh, I remember—doubtless it is he
You mean to speak of, with the golden armor;—
Whole legions with your breath you puff'd away
Like the light leaves, or chaff before the wind.

Pyrg. Oh! that indeed? that on my faith was nothing.

Art. Nothing, 'tis true, compar'd with other feats
That I could mention, (*aside*) which you ne'er perform'd—
Show me, whoever can, a greater liar,
One fuller of vain boasting than this fellow
And he shall have me, I'll resign me up
To be his slave, though, when I'm mad with hunger,
He should allow me nothing else to eat
But whey and butter-milk.

Pyrg. Where art thou?

Art. Here —
How, in the name of wonder, was't you broke
In India with your fist an elephant's tusk?

Pyrg. How! tusk?

Art. His thigh, I meant.

Pyrg. I was but playing.

Art. Had you put forth your strength you would have driv'n
Your arm quite through his hide, bones, flesh, and all.

Pyrg, I would not talk of these things now.

Art. Indeed
You would but spend your breath in vain to tell
Your valorous feats to me, who know your prowess.
(*Aside*) My appetite creates me all this plague;
My ears must hear him, for my teeth want work;
And I must swear to every lie he utters.

Pyrg. Hold,—What was I about to say?

Art. I know
What you design'd to say—a gallant action!—
I well remember—

Pyrg. What?

Art. Whate'er it be.

Pyrg. Hast thou got tablets?

Art. Yes, I have—d'ye want them?—
A pencil too.

Pyrg. How rarely thou dost suit
Thy mind to mine!

Art. 'Tis fit that I should study

Your inclinations, and my care should be
Ev'n to forerun your wishes.,
    Pyrg. What remember'st?
    Art. I do remember—let me see—a hundred
Sycolatronidans—and thirty Sardians—
And threescore Macedonians,—that's the number
Of persons, whom you slaughter'd in one day.
    Pyrg. What's the sum-total of these men?
    Art. Seven thousand.
    Pyrg. So much it should be—thou'rt a right accountant.
    Art. I have it not in writing, but remember.
    Pyrg. Thou hast an admirable memory.
    Art. 'Tis sharpened by my stomach.
    Pyrg. Bear thyself
As thou hast hitherto, and thou shalt eat
Eternally,—forever shalt thou be
Partaker of my table.
    Art. Then again
What feats did you perform in Cappadocia!
Where at one single stroke you had cut off
Five hundred men together, if your sword
Had not been blunt, and these but the remains
Of th' infantry, which you before had routed,—
(*Aside*) If ever there were any such in being.
Why should I tell you, what all mortals know?
That Pyrgopolinices stands alone,
The only one on earth fam'd above men
For beauty, valor, and renown'd exploits.
The ladies are enamor'd of you all,
Nor without reason,—since you are so handsome;
Witness the gay young damsels yesterday,
That plucked me by the cloak.—
    Pyrg. (*smiling*). What said they to you?
    Art. They questioned me about you.—Is not that,
Says one of them, Achilles?—No, said I,
It is his brother.—Why, indeed, forsooth,
He's wondrous handsome, quoth another: how
His hair becomes him!—O what happiness
    Those ladies do enjoy, who share his favors!
        Pyrg. Did she indeed say so?
        Art. Two in particular
    Begged of me I would bring you by their way,

That they might see you march.

Pyrg. What plague it is
To be too handsome!

Art. They are so importunate,
They're ever begging for a sight of you?
They send for me so often to come to them,
I scarce have leisure to attend your business.

Pyrg. 'Tis time, methinks, to go unto the Forum,
And pay those soldiers I enlisted yesterday:
For King Seleucus pray'd me with much suit
To raise him some recruits.—I have resolv'd
To dedicate this day unto his service.

Art. Come, let's be going then.

Pyrg. Guards, follow me.

SCENE FROM A MANUSCRIPT OF PLAUTUS.

TERENCE.

THE second great comic poet of Rome was Publius Terentius Afer (the African). He lived probably between 186 and 160 B.C. Brought from Carthage as a captive, he came into the hands of the Roman senator, Terentius Lucanus, and received the best education of the age. Literary and artistic tastes combined with personal graces procured for him association with young patricians, and also the patronage of their elders, when he began to present translations of Greek plays. In Athens what was called the Old Comedy, treating of public and political affairs, had passed from the stage, and the New Comedy, dealing with the ordinary affairs of life had come to the front. Its leading spirit was Menander, and Terence became his Latin interpreter. He is not a creative genius; displays no inventive power; not one of his characters is original; but he gives faithful pictures of Greek life a hundred years before the Latin poet's time. Both Plautus and Terence were interpreters of the Attic wit of the New Comedy, but different tastes led them to follow different models. Hence the broad and boisterous humor of the one takes the form of pointed epigram and biting sarcasm in the other. Terence has gained the admiration of men of taste in all ages. His style is polished, his idiom pure. The better influences of the philosophy of Epicurus appear in his characters, and tend to mitigate the asperity of the old Roman virtue. He left to the world a refined picture of an interesting section of Greek society, and conferred on Roman literature its artistic elegance.

Of the six comedies written by Terence, the earliest was the "Andrian," or Maid of Andros, which was placed on the stage 166 B.C. The last was the "Adelphi," or The Brothers, which is generally considered the best, and was performed in 160 B.C. After seeing the Adelphi successfully performed, Terence visited Greece and never returned. The exact time and manner of his death are unknown.

The Andrian.

The story of Terence's first play reveals Athenian life. Chrysis had gone from the island of Andros to Athens, and after a hard struggle to make an honest living had become a hetæra. Among the visitors to her house was Pamphilus, whose father, Simo, wished him to marry Philumena, daughter of his friend Chremes. Though the father knows that Pamphilus frequents Chrysis' house, he is assured that his son has no attachment for her. But when Chrysis died, Simo saw his son at the funeral, and when her supposed sister Glycerium was nearly caught in the flames of the pile, Pamphilus rescued her in such a way as to reveal their mutual affection. Chremes hears of this, and learns that Pamphilus is privately married to the young foreigner. Such marriages, however, though commonly recognized, had no legal force in Athens. Simo, by false pretenses, gets Chremes to consent to marry his daughter to Pamphilus, and then orders his son to marry Philumena that very day. To complicate the affair, Glycerium bears a child the same day. The slave Davus, believing that Simo was not in earnest, persuaded Pamphilus to give his consent to the new marriage. But his friend Charinus, who is in love with Philumena, hearing of the proposed wedding, seeks Pamphilus, and is rejoiced to learn that no interference is really intended. Davus then gets the nurse to lay the baby at his master's door, just when Chremes is about to call. Finding out its parentage, Chremes is enraged, and again refuses his consent to the marriage.

But now a stranger has arrived at Athens with wonderful news. Glycerium, the supposed Andrian, is declared to be really a free-born Athenian. By law, therefore, Pamphilus is united to her. Davus, who carries this word to his master, is sent to prison as his reward. But further developments occur. Glycerium had been given into the care of Chrysis by a shipwrecked Athenian, who is found to be Chremes's brother, while she was Chremes's own child. Davus is now released amid general rejoicing, and the harmony of all parties is restored.

We give three scenes. In the first Simo tells the knavish slave Davus of the intended marriage; the second shows Pamphilus' embarrassment about it; in the last Simo thanks Davus for having secured the son's consent to it.

Davus. Ah! I was wondering where all this would end!
The master was so quiet, I suspected
He must mean mischief. When he heard that Chremes
Downright refused his girl, he never spoke
An angry word, nor stormed at any of us.

Simo. (behind, shaking his stick at Davus.) He will speak
   soon, and to your cost, you rascal!
Da. So, so! he thought to take us unprepared,
Lapping us up in this fools' Paradise,
To swoop upon us at the last, too late
To give us time to think, or opportunity
To hinder this cursed wedding. Clever man!
   Si. (trying to listen.) What is he muttering?
   Da. (discovering Simo.) Ha! my master there!
I had not seen him.
   Si. (coming forward.) Davus!
   Da. Hey? what is it?
   Si. Here, sirrah, come this way!
   Da. (aside.) What can he want?
   Si. What say you?
   Da. What about?
   Si. D'ye ask me, sirrah?—
They say my son has a love affair.
   Da. Good lack!
How folks will talk!
   Si. D'ye mind me, sir, or no?
   Da. I'm all attention.
   Si. Well—to inquire too closely
Into the past were harsh—let bygones rest.
But now he must begin a different life;
New duties lie before him from this day:
And you—I charge you—nay, indeed, good Davus,
I rather would entreat you, if I may,
Pray help to keep him straight.
   Da. Why—what's all this?
   Si. Young men, you know, with such whims, do not care
To have a wife assigned them.
   Da. So they say.
   Si. Then—if a young man have a knavish tutor
Who trains him in such courses, why, the evil
Will grow from bad to worse.
   Da. Hercules help me!
I can't tell what you mean.
Si. (ironically.) No—really?
   Da. No;
I'm only Davus—I'm no Œdipus.
   Si. You'd have me speak more plainly—is it so?

Da. Indeed I would.
Si. Then, if I catch you scheming
To disappoint this match of ours to-day,
By way of showing your own cursed cleverness,
I'll have you flogged within an inch of life,
And sent to the mill—on this condition, look you—
When I let you out I'll go and grind myself.
Now, sir, d'ye understand me? Is that plain?
 Da. Oh, perfectly! (*bowing.*) You state the case so clearly,
With such entire correctness of expression,
So free from ambiguity—it's quite charming!

THE DISTRACTED LOVER.

Pamphilus. Is this well done? or like a man?—Is this
The action of a father?
 Mysis (*behind.*) What's the matter?
 Pam. O all ye Pow'rs of heaven and earth, what's wrong
If this is not so?—If he was determin'd
That I to-day should marry, should I not
Have had some previous notice?—ought not he
To have inform'd me of it long ago?
 Mys. Alas! what's this I hear?
 Pam. And Chremes too,
Who had refus'd to trust me with his daughter,
Changes his mind, because I change not mine.
Can he then be so obstinately bent
To tear me from Glycerium? To lose her
Is losing life.—Was ever man so crossed,
So cursed as I?—O Pow'rs of heaven and earth!
Can I by no means fly from this alliance
With Chremes' family?—so oft contemn'd
And held in scorn!—All done, concluded all!—
Rejected, then recall'd.—And why?—unless,
For so I must suspect, they breed some monster:
Whom as they can obtrude on no one else,
They bring to me.
 Mys. Alas, alas! this speech
Has struck me almost dead with fear.
 Pam. And then
My father! what to say of him?—Oh, shame!

A thing of so much consequence to treat
So negligently!—For but even now
Passing me in the Forum, "Pamphilus!
To-day's your wedding-day," said he: "Prepare;
Go, get you home!"—This sounded in my ears
As if he said, Go, hang yourself!—I stood
Confounded. Think you I could speak one word?
Or offer an excuse, how weak soe'er?
No, I was dumb:—and had I been aware,
Should any ask what I'd have done, I would,
Rather than this, do any thing.—But now,
What to resolve upon?—So many cares
Entangle me at once, and rend my mind,
Pulling it diff'rent ways. My love, compassion,
This urgent match, my rev'rence for my father,
Who yet has ever been so gentle to me,
And held so slack a rein upon my pleasures.
—And I oppose him?—Racking thought!—Ah me
I know not what to do.

  Mys. Alas, I fear
Where this uncertainty will end. 'Twere best
He should confer with her; or I at least
Speak touching her to him. For while the mind
Hangs in suspense, a trifle turns the scale.

  Pam. Who's there? what, Mysis! save you!

  Mys. (*coming forward.*) Save you, sir.

  Pam. How does she?

  Mys. How! oppress'd with wretchedness;
To-day supremely wretched, as to-day
Was formerly appointed for your wedding.
And then she fears lest you desert her.

  Pam. I!
Desert her? Can I think on't? or deceive
A wretched maid, who trusted to my care
Her life and honor! Her, whom I have held
Near to my heart, and cherish'd as my wife?
Or leave her modest and well-nurtur'd mind
Through want to be corrupted? Never, never.

  Mys. No doubt, did it depend on you alone;
But if constrain'd—

  Pam. Do you think me so vile?
Or so ungrateful, so inhuman, savage,

That neither intercourse, nor love, nor shame,
Can make me keep my faith?
   Mys. I only know
That she deserves you should remember her.
   Pam. I should remember her? O Mysis, Mysis
The words of Chrysis touching my Glycerium
Are written in my heart. On her death-bed
She call'd me. I approach'd her. You retir'd.
We were alone; and Chrysis thus began:
"My Pamphilus, you see the youth and beauty
Of this unhappy maid: and well you know,
These are but feeble guardians to preserve
Her fortune or her fame. By this right hand
I do beseech you, by your better angel,
By your tried faith, by her forlorn condition,
I do conjure you, put her not away,
Nor leave her to distress. If I have ever,
As my own brother, lov'd you; or if she
Has ever held you dear 'bove all the world,
And ever shown obedience to your will—
I do bequeath you to her as a husband,
Friend, guardian, father: All our little wealth
To you I leave, and trust it to your care."—
She join'd our hands, and died.—I did receive her,
And, once receiv'd, will keep her.

The Clever Schemer.

   Simo. Davus, I do confess, I doubted:
I had my fears; slaves—common slaves, I mean—
Will do such things,—that you were cheating me
As to this matter of my son's.
   Davus. I, master! could you think it? cheat?—O dear!
   Si. (*soothingly.*) Well, well—I fancied so; and with that
        thought
I kept the secret which I tell you now.
   Da. What's that?
   Si. Well, you shall hear: for now at last
I almost think that I may trust you.—May I?
   Da. At last, sir, it seems, sir, you appreciate me.
   Si. This wedding was a mere pretense,
A scheme of mine, to test my son and you.

Da. Indeed!

Si. Yes, really.

Da. Look ye! what a wit
Our master has! I never could have guessed it.

Si. Listen; when I dismissed you, I met Chremes—

Da. (aside.) We're lost—I know it.

Si. Listen; straight I told him
What you told me, that Pamphilus was ready.
I begged and prayed that he would give his daughter;
At last I moved him.

Da. (aside.) Then I'm done for.

Si. Hey! did you speak?

Da. I only said, "well done," sir.

Si. And I beseech you, Davus, as you love me,
Since you alone have brought about this wedding—

Da. I! O dear, no! pray—

Si. For my son I ask you,
Still do your best to regulate his morals.

Da. I will, I will, sir—trust me.   [*Exit Chremes.*
I'm gone—a thing of nought. Why don't I go
Straight to the mill-prison of myself?—Forgiveness?
No hope of that from any one. I've played
The very mischief with the total household;
Cheated the master—got the son a wife—
This very night, much to the old gentleman's
Astonishment, and his son's disgust.—Ah! well!
This comes of cleverness. Had I held my tongue,
No harm had happened.

TARQUIN'S DREAM.

LUCIUS ATTIUS (170-86 B.C.) translated and imitated the Greek tragic poets. Though Cicero speaks highly of his plays, little of them survives. This fragment from the tragedy of Brutus, by Attius, is translated by W. E. Aytoun.

Tarquin. When repose had come upon me and I yielded to its power,
All my weary limbs composing, in the silent midnight hour;
It appeared to me in slumber, that a shepherd drove along
For my choice, it seemed, hish irsel; fair they were, and young, and strong.

Two I marked, that kindred seeming, most of all my fancy pleased,
And the comeliest and fairest of the twain, I straightway seized;
When behold, the other, turning, aimed at me his armed brow,
And so fiercely at me butted, that I fell beneath the blow.
There while lying, sorely wounded, to the heaven I cast my eyes,
And there saw I such an omen, as might well my soul surprise;
For the sun's resplendent body seemed towards the east to tend,
Leaving his accustomed orbit—what may such a sight portend?

 Soothsayers. Little need we wonder, monarch, if the thoughts our bosoms keep,
If the deeds we fashion waking, should return to us in sleep.
Yet not lightly may such visions in so great a thing be rated,
Therefore take thou heed lest any who thou thought'st was fitly mated
With the dull and senseless many, be not wise, and good, and brave,
Lest he drive thee from thy kingdom; for the sign that Phœbus gave,
Shows some swift and sudden changing—something which shall see the light,
Well-portending for the people; since that omen from the right
To the left its course pursuing, is a certain sign and sure,
That the Roman state shall flourish, and beyond all states endure.

Arch of Titus.

CHAPTER XIV.

The Age of Cicero.

During the forty years of Cicero's active life he was so pre-eminently the orator and man of letters in Rome that the period may well be called by his name.

The political situation was critical throughout. It had been already shown that the controlling power was the army—not the senate or the people. The city rabble had already reached large proportions and continued to increase. Slaves were seeking every opportunity to revolt against their intolerable condition. In the provinces the people were at the mercy of their governors. All depended upon the personal integrity of the man sent to them whether they would be shorn of their possessions, or whether their rights would be observed and protected. Pirates were openly carrying on their depredations on the high seas, endangering the commerce of the republic. Mithridates sought to drive the Romans from Asia and extend his boundaries at their expense. At home, the very government was threatened by the conspiracy of Catiline, while Pompey and Caesar soon after fought the battle which determined which should fill the place of dictator, earlier held by Sulla. All these happenings and circumstances fell within the period of Cicero's activity. In the social world, moreover, the pulse of life was quickened. Wide conquests had increased the material prosperity of Rome. The rapid accumulation of wealth made possible lavish displays of riches and vulgar parade of material goods. Yet, at the same time, a thorough culture permeated the more conservative of the upper class.

A group of lyric poets became prominent in this age, greatest among them being Catullus. Cinna and Calvus belonged also to this group, known as the Alexandrian group, but their fame was far outshadowed by that of Catullus.

REMORSE.

Why longer keep thy heart upon the rack?
  Give to thy soul a higher, nobler aim.
And tho' thou tear thy heart out, look not back
  In tears upon a love that was thy shame.

'Tis hard at once to fling a love away
  That has been cherished with the faith of years.
'Tis hard; but shrink not, flinch not. Come what may,
  Crush every record of its joys and fears.

O ye great gods, if ye can pity feel,
  If e'er to dying wretch your aid was given,
See me in agony before you kneel,
  To beg this plague from out my core be driven.

I only crave the health that once was mine,
  Some little respite from this sore disease.
If e'er I earned your mercy, powers divine,
  Grant me, O grant to a sick heart some ease!

—*Catullus: Trans. Sir Theo. Martin.*

Born of wealthy parents, all social doors lay open to Catullus, and he lived a gay life of excitement common to his circle. In a series of poems addressed to Lesbia, he has immortalized his love for a brilliant woman of the Clodian family. When she later proved unfaithful to him, Catullus traveled in Asia, writing beautiful poems associated with his journey. He is supposed to have died about 54 B. C., little over thirty years of age. His greatest fame rests upon his love lyrics, which give him place with Sappho and other of the most gifted lyrists the world has seen.

O best of all the scattered spots that lie
In sea or lake—apple of landscape's eye!
How gladly do I drop within thy nest,
With what a sigh of full, contented rest,
Scarce able to believe my journey's o'er
And that these eyes behold thee safe once more!
Oh where's the luxury like the smile at the heart,
When the mind breathing, lays its load apart:

> When we come home again, tired out, and spread
> The loosened limbs o'er the all wished-for bed!
> This, this alone is worth an age of toil—
> Hail, lovely Sirmio! Hail, parental soil!
> Joy, my bright waters, joy; your master's come!
> Laugh every dimple on the cheek of home!

—*Catullus, upon his return to his country home at Sirmio. Trans. by Leigh Hunt.*

The most radiant light of this period beyond all question, as has been already indicated, was Cicero. In his writings Latin prose reached its finest expression. "He found the Latin language the chief dialect of Italy, the speech of a great and mighty city; he made it the language of the world for centuries."

Cicero was born in a little town in Latium.

"On the steep side of one of the Volscian hills, below which the river Liris, now the Garigliano, flowed in a winding channel to the sea, and on the northern frontier of what has since been known as the Terra di Lavoro in the kingdom of Naples, lay the ancient town of Arpinum. The banks of the river were thickly wooded with lofty poplars, and a grove of oaks extended to the east, where, not far off, the little river Fibrenus, now the Fibreno, in the midst of one of the loveliest of Italian landscapes, mingled its ice cold waters with the waters of the Liris. Before its confluence with the larger stream it divided into two channels, and rushed rapidly past a small and beautiful island, now called the Isola di Carnello; and lower down at the point where the two rivers met, another island was formed, now known as the Isola Pan Paolo, or San Domenico, from a Dominican monastery, which in later times was erected there and still remains. In this pleasant spot, at the point where the Liris and the Fibrenus met, amidst hills and rocks and woods, on the 3d of January, 106 B. C., Cicero was born."

Cicero's father gave him all possible advantages for obtaining a liberal education. He was sent to Rome, where he studied under jurists, orators and philosophers. He travelled in Greece, Asia and Rhodes, studying in each of the centers of learning. In 77 B. C. he returned to Rome and soon after married Terentia, a lady of noble birth. While practising at the Roman courts he passed through the series of public magistracies usual for public men: quaestor, aedile, praetor and consul. It was during his consulship that he discovered the conspiracy of Catiline and made it famous among those who have read the Latin tongue in all subsequent ages by his four famous orations against the conspirator.

Cicero believed firmly in perpetuating the established forms of government, and when the final triumvirate was formed, as might have been expected, he was among those to oppose it. Realizing that he was no longer safe in Rome, he went into exile, from which he was recalled in 57 B. C. In 53 B. C. he was made augur, and in 51 B. C. proconsul of Cilicia. All his public duties were discharged with characteristic fidelity and painstaking. When the rupture occurred between Caesar and Pompey, and it was left for civil war to determine which should become the ruler of Rome, Cicero took the side of Pompey, as that which promised more liberty for the people. He later returned to Rome and denounced the selfish policy of Antony in a series of orations. When he found that personal motives prompted also the enemies of Antony, he became discouraged regarding the ultimate fate of Rome. Upon the formation of the second triumvirate, Antony demanded the death of Cicero, and it remains to the lasting disgrace of Octavius that he consented to this murder. In 43 B. C. Cicero was killed by soldiers of Antony, but as has often been noted, there was little left for him to live for.

Cicero's writings consist of fifty-seven orations, some philosophical treatises and some letters. Best known are his orations, read by students in every land when acquiring a familiarity with the Latin language. Among those to bring him renown aside from the Catiline orations, were those delivered against Verres, the unscrupulous governor of Sicily who plundered the people so wantonly that he is reputed to have said that were he required to deliver two-thirds of his gains, he would have still enough to allow him to live all his life in luxury. Cicero's letters, referred to in a previous chapter, help us to gain an insight into the personal life of the man. His greatest service probably was that he raised Latin to a place of first language among civilized people for centuries.

"Cicero's unique and imperishable glory is not, as he thought himself, that of having put down the revolutionary movement of Catiline, nor, as later ages thought, that of having rivalled Demosthenes in the *Second Philippic,* or confuted atheism in the *De Natura Deorum.* It is that he created a language which remained for sixteen centuries that of the civilized world, and used that language to create a style which nineteen centuries have not replaced, and in some respects have scarcely altered. Before his time Latin prose was, from a wide point of view, but one among many local dialects. As it left his hands it had become a universal language, one which had definitely superseded all others, Greek included, as the type of civilized expression."

Caesar alone deserved mention with Cicero. His writings on the Gallic and Civil Wars remain. Unlike Cicero's writings, they were prepared for mere temporary use, but their clear, simple language has given them a position which they well deserve.

LIVIA, WIFE OF AUGUSTUS.

The Age of Cicero.

The wars of the Italian allies, the insurrections of the slaves, the Civil wars of Marius and Sulla all brought an unrest that interrupted the progress of the arts of peace. The first period of Roman literature came to an end. After a half century barren of literary effort we note the outburst that characterized the age of Cicero. Lucretius, the philosophical poet, and Catullus, Rome's first great lyrist, belong to this period.

LUCRETIUS.

LUCRETIUS is the greatest philosophic poet of all time. Full of Greek learning, he was yet thoroughly Roman in spirit. In the development of Latin literature he forms a sort of connecting link between the ante-classical period of Ennius and Plautus and the classical period of Cicero and Virgil. His full name was Titus Lucretius Carus, and he lived probably between 97 and 53 B. C. But little is known of his personal history. The only surviving work of this great poet is the didactic poem, "De Rerum Natura," that was known to its orator Cicero. It was suggested by the "Nature" of the Sicilian Empedocles. There is internal evidence that it was written when Rome was in a state of civil commotion; but it is not decided whether this was owing to the disturbances caused by Marius and Sulla, or the disorders occasioned later by Clodius. It was written with the object of destroying belief in religion as the Romans understood it, and freeing men's minds from superstition. Scientific subjects are discussed with as much precision as the knowledge of the times permitted, and often with poetic grandeur and beauty. In his conservative style, Lucretius displays something of the spirit of Homer and other Greek poets, as well as the vigor of the Roman Ennius. The subject with which he deals is dry, but the discussion is often relieved by unexampled sublimity. Virgil, Ovid, Spenser, Tennyson and Swinburne have found in Lucretius poetic beauties worthy of imitation.

The "De Rerum Natura" is divided into six books. It begins with a magnificent invocation of Venus as the productive power; then follows a dedication of the work to Caius Memmius, who was prætor in 58 B.C. The whole work is a statement and defence of the philosophic system of Epicurus, and especially of the atomic theory. The great argument of the poet is, "Nothing can proceed from nothing." The universe is regarded as boundless, containing only matter and space. All matter is composed of atoms, or minute bodies, to the senses imperceptible, but conceivable in mind. These atoms are indivisible, infinite and eternal. The poet declares there is no centre of things to which bodies tend. He also asserts that the atoms, though having neither color, taste nor smell, produce substances having all these properties. Worlds grow, are diminished and dissolved, even as animals grow, decline and die. Even the mind and soul, diffused through the whole body, consist of minute atoms and act on the body. Finally the poet asserts that death is the end of man, and that there is nothing to be feared thereafter. The only consolation is in the reflection that the best of men have died as well as the worst. That an abstract philosophical poem, denying immortality and tending to atheism, should have been carefully preserved from the wreck of antiquity, is one of the strange facts of literary history.

INVOCATION TO VENUS.

In this grand opening of his work, the Roman philosopher, as Tennyson points out in his poem "Lucretius," regards Venus as the personification of the productive force of Nature. This translation, as well as the others following, is by W. H. Mallock.

> MOTHER and mistress of the Roman race,
>   Pleasure of gods and men, O fostering
> Venus, whose presence breathes in every place,
>   Peopling all soils whence fruits and grasses spring,
> And all the water's navigable ways,
>   Water and earth and air and everything,
> Since by thy power alone their life is given
> To all beneath the sliding signs of heaven;

Goddess, thou comest, and the clouds before thee
  Melt, and the ruffian blasts take flight and fly;
The dædal lands they know thee and adore thee,
  And clothe themselves with sweet flowers instantly;
Whilst pouring down its largest radiance o'er thee,
  In azure calm subsides the rounded sky,
To overarch thine advent; and for thee
A livelier sunlight laughs along the sea.

For lo, no sooner come the soft and glowing
  Days of the spring, and all the air is stirred
With amorous breaths of zephyr freshly blowing,
  Than the first prelude of thy power is heard
On all sides, in aerial music flowing
  Out of the bill of every pairing bird;
And every songster feels, on every tree,
Its small heart pulsing with the power of thee.

Next the herds feel thee; and the wild fleet races
  Bound o'er the fields, that smile in the bright weather,
And swim the streaming floods in fordless places,
  Led by thy chain, and captive in thy tether.
At last through seas and hills, thine influence passes,
  Through field and flood and all the world together,
And the birds' leafy homes; and thou dost fire
Each to renew his kind with sweet desire.

Wherefore since thou, O Lady, only thou
  Art she who guides the world upon its way;
Nor can aught rise without thee anyhow
  Up into the clear borders of the day,
Neither can aught without thee ever grow
  Lovely and sweet—to thee, to thee I pray—
Aid and be near thy suppliant as he sings
Of nature and the secret ways of things.

The Sacrifice of Iphigenia.

The story of Iphigenia (here called Iphianassa) has been given in connection with the plays of Euripides. Lucretius fixes upon this human sacrifice as a fatal argument against the religion which required it. He pays no attention to the modification of the legend by Euripides. Diana is called "the Trivian maid" because her temple was often placed where three ways met.

> YET fear I lest thou haply deem that thus
>   We sin, and enter wicked ways of reason.
> Whereas 'gainst all things good and beauteous
>   'Tis oft religion does the foulest treason.
> Has not the tale of Aulis come to us,
>   And those great chiefs who, in the windless season,
> Bade young Iphianassa's form be laid
> Upon the altar of the Trivian maid?
>
> Soon as the fillet round her virgin hair
>   Fell in its equal lengths down either cheek,—
> Soon as she saw her father standing there,
>   Sad, by the altar, without power to speak,
> And at his side the murderous minister,
>   Hiding the knife, and many a faithful Greek
> Weeping—her knees grew weak, and with no sound
> She sank, in speechless terror on the ground.
>
> But naught availed it in that hour accurst
>   To save the maid from such a doom as this,
> That her lips were the baby lips that first
>   Called the king father with their cries and kiss.
> For round her came the strong men, and none durst
>   Refuse to do what cruel part was his;
> So silently they raised her up and bore her,
> All quivering, to the deadly shrine before her.
>
> And as they bore her, ne'er a golden lyre
>   Rang round her coming with a bridal strain;
> But in the very season of desire,
>   A stainless maiden, amid bloody stain,
> She died—a victim felled by its own sire—
>   That so the ships the wished-for wind might gain,
> And air puff out their canvas. Learn thou, then,
> To what damned deeds religion urges men.

EPICURUS.

OF the writings of Epicurus but a few fragments have been preserved, yet his teaching has had a powerful influence on the world. He was born in Samos about 340 B.C., but lived chiefly at Athens where he died 270 B.C. His philosophic system is fully set forth by Lucretius, who pays him the following tribute.

> THOU who wert first in drowning depths of night
>   To lift aloft so clear a lamp, whose rays
> Strike along life, and put the shades to flight—
>   Thee, thee, chief glory of the Grecian race,
> I strive to follow, humbly and aright,
>   And my feet in thy very footprints place;
> Not that thy rival I would dare to be,
> But that I love, and loving follow thee.
>
> Thy rival? Nay; can swallows rival swans?
>   Or thunder-footed steeds competitors
> Find 'mongst the she-goat's gamb'ling little ones?
>   O first and best of all discoverers,
> We are but bees along the flowery lawns,
>   Who rifle for our food thy fields of verse,
> And on thy golden maxims pause and prey—
> All-gold, and worthy to endure for aye.
>
> For lo! no sooner does thy powerful line
>   Loud through the world the scheme of Nature sing,
> Than the mind hears, and at that note of thine
>   Its flocks of phantom terrors take to wing.
> The world's walls roll apart, and I divine
>   With opened eyes the ways of everything.
> And how through Nature's void immensity
> Things were not, were, and are, and cease to be.
>
> And lo! the gods appear, the immortal races,
>   Visible in the lucent windless air
> That fills their quiet blest abiding-places,
>   Which never noisy storm nor storm-clouds dare
> To trouble, where the frost's tooth leaves no traces,
>   And downwards no white falling snowflakes fare,
> But on their lips the laughters never cease,
> Nor want nor pain invades their ageless peace.
>
> But on the other hand we search in vain,
>   For those swart forms, the fearful deities
> Of Hell. Our vision roams the whole inane.
>   But aught like Acheron it nowhere sees.

And I, when I to this high view attain,
  Feel on my soul a maddening rapture seize,
And next a trembling, that thy hand should dare
Thus to the quick to lay all Nature bare.

CICERO.

This statesman, the great master of Roman eloquence, elegant essayist, delightful letter-writer and popularizer of philosophy, occupies the foremost place among Latin prose writers. He became the model of pure Latinity to all succeeding generations. Demosthenes was not so prominent among the orators of his age as was Cicero at Rome. Almost his only rival was Hortensius, for thirteen years the foremost barrister of the capital. Cicero owed less to fortuitous circumstances, and more to his own exertions and innate qualities, than any others with whom he may be compared. The orators who preceded him were usually, but not always men of high family.

Marcus Tullius Cicero was born of an ancient family of equestrian rank, 106 B.C. After a careful education, he traveled to Athens and Rhodes, and listened to the lectures of the most eminent teachers of philosophy and rhetoric. On his return to Rome his increased accomplishments helped him to become a public favorite. He was the first Roman who reached the highest honors of the state mainly by his eloquence and his general merits. At the age of thirty-one he was quæstor of Sicily, and became successively ædile, prætor and consul. His consulate is marked by the suppression of Catiline's conspiracy. His patriotic action in this case made him many enemies, among whom was Clodius, through whose measures he was driven into banishment, 58 B.C. In his exile Cicero did not exhibit the manliness which might have been expected from his philosophic education. After ten months he returned to Rome by a decree of the senate, was received by the Fathers at the city gate, and made his entry with all the pomp of a triumphal procession. Shortly after, as pro-consul for Cilicia, he was zealous in subduing marauding tribes, and returned to Rome to claim a triumph, which, however, was not granted.

Although the purest of all practical politicians, Cicero was not successful in this capacity. He was lacking in the firmness and calmness which should characterize a great statesman. On the outbreak of the Civil war, Cicero, though leaning to Pompey's party, gave cordial support neither to the senate, Cæsar nor Pompey, and received ill-treatment from all, which he had not disinterestedness enough to resent.

Cicero's real talent was that of oratory, and on this his fame is built. His remarkable faculty of reproducing anything he ever knew, his no less remarkable memory, his extraordinary command of words, both invective and laudatory, made him the creator of a new language, full and melodious, characterized by exactness, strength and beauty. With such power, aided by the physical advantages of a dignified presence and persuasive voice, it is not wonderful if in his hands a bad cause appeared worse, and a good cause better than it really was.

Cicero's chief fault was vanity. He was often weak, vacillating and inconsistent; but sometimes he showed unusual firmness, vigor and moral courage when others shrank from committing themselves. He was ever patriotic, unselfish in his aims to benefit the state. Vainglorious, restless, and exceedingly sensitive to public opinion, he made extraordinary efforts to outstrip all others in whatever he essayed.

Of the orations, numbering in all one hundred and seven, little more than half have been preserved entire. The first was delivered at the age of twenty-five. Of the later orations the most celebrated are the four against the conspirator, Catiline, and the seven against Verres, the plunderer of Sicily.

Only two of the latter were actually delivered, because the criminal went into voluntary exile. The orations against Mark Antony, commonly called the Philippics, from their resemblance to those of Demosthenes directed against Philip of Macedon, contain the strongest terms of invective ever written. They are fourteen in number, and were in the end fatal to Cicero as those of Demosthenes had been to him. When the First Triumvirate was formed, Antony demanded the death of Cicero. The orator was assassinated in 44 B.C.

Cicero's philosophical works are a most valuable legacy from antiquity. In them he summed up the ethics and metaphysics of the great Greek thinkers so that they became the common property of all who used the Latin language. The most important treatises are the Tusculan Disputations, the treatises on the Laws, The Nature of the Gods, Moral Duties, the Academics, Old Age and Friendship, The Orator, and Brutus. The De Senectute, although in the form of a dialogue, is really a charming essay on old age. Its companion treatise, "De Amicitia," is an animated and practical discussion on friendship. The best of his philosophical works is "De Finibus," which compares the Greek schools, the Epicureans, the Stoics, the Academy and the Lyceum, with regard to their different ideas of the greatest good and the greatest evil. Moral, natural and civil laws are discussed in the same manner in "De Legibus."

The "Republic" has been justly praised by ancient and modern writers. It contains a series of discussions on government, in which Scipio is the leading speaker, while Lælius, Manlius and others support the dialogue. Its best passage is the famous "Dream of Scipio," which teaches the immortality of the soul and enunciates the doctrine of rewards and punishments in a future world. The ideas of political science, persuasively set forth by Cicero in this and other treatises, had a profound influence on all subsequent European history. Other works of Cicero, historical and poetical, have been entirely lost, but a thousand of his letters have been preserved. Those addressed to Atticus, his school companion and life-long friend, are the most interesting, and throw much light on the writer's personality.

"I Am a Roman Citizen."

CAIUS VERRES was proprætor in Sicily for three years, 73-71 B.C., during which his extortions were so great that he afterwards boasted that if he were compelled to disgorge two-thirds of the plunder, he would still have enough for a life of luxury. At the close of his term the Sicilians employed Cicero to prosecute him on criminal charges. Verres was defended by Hortensius and supported by the full power of the aristocracy. Attempts were made to procure sham trials and to obstruct and delay the real prosecution. But such was the diligence of Cicero in procuring evidence, and such the danger of postponing the case, that after delivering two orations, he placed the testimony before the judges, trusting to its weight for success. Hortensius abandoned the case. Verres, leaving the city, was condemned in his absence and retired to Marseilles. Cicero had prepared five other orations which were published, though they had not been spoken. The following extract relates to one of Verres' most glaring offences.

How shall I speak of Publius Gavius, a citizen of Consa? With what powers of voice, with what force of language, with what sufficient indignation of soul, can I tell the tale? Indignation, at least, will not fail me: the more must I strive that in this my pleading the other requisites may be made to meet the gravity of the subject, the intensity of my feeling. For the accusation is such that, when it was first laid before me, I did not think to make use of it; though I knew it to be perfectly true, I did not think it would be credible.—How shall I now proceed?—when I have already been speaking for so many hours on one subject—his atrocious cruelty; when I have exhausted upon other points well-nigh all the powers of language such as alone is suited to that man's crimes;—when I have taken no precaution to secure your attention by any variety in my charges against him,—how can I now speak on a charge of this importance? I think there is one way—one course, and only one, left for me to take. I will place the facts before you; and they have in themselves such weight, that no eloquence—I will not say of mine, for I have none—but of any man's, is needed to excite your feelings.

This Gavius of Consa, of whom I speak, had been among the crowds of Roman citizens who had been thrown into prison under that man. Somehow he had made his escape out of the Quarries.* and had got to Messana; and when he saw Italy and the towers

---

* This was one of the state prisons at Syracuse.

of Rhegium now so close to him, and out of the horror and shadow of death felt himself breathe with a new life as he scented once more the fresh air of liberty and the laws, he began to talk at Messana, and to complain that he, a Roman citizen, had been put in irons—that he was going straight to Rome—that he would be ready there for Verres on his arrival.

The wretched man little knew that he might as well have talked in this fashion in the governor's palace before his very face, as at Messana. For Verres had selected this city as the accomplice in his crimes, the receiver of his stolen goods, the confidant of all his wickedness. So Gavius is brought at once before the city magistrates; and, as it so chanced, on that very day Verres himself came to Messana. The case is reported to him; that there is a certain Roman citizen who complained of having been put into the Quarries at Syracuse; that as he was just going on board ship, and was uttering threats—really too atrocious—against Verres, they had detained him, and kept him in custody, that the governor himself might decide about him as should seem to him good. Verres thanks the gentlemen, and extols their good-will and zeal for his interests. He himself, burning with rage and malice, comes down to the court. His eyes flashed fire; cruelty was written on every line of his face. All present watched anxiously to see to what lengths he meant to go, or what steps he would take; when suddenly he ordered the prisoner to be dragged forth, and to be stripped and bound in the open forum, and the rods to be got ready at once. The unhappy man cried out that he was a Roman citizen—that he had the municipal franchise of Consa—that he had served in a campaign with Lucius Pretius, a distinguished Roman knight, now engaged in business at Panormus, from whom Verres might ascertain the truth of his statement. Then that man replies that he has discovered that he, Gavius, has been sent into Sicily as a spy by the ringleaders of the runaway slaves; of which charge there was neither witness nor trace of any kind, nor even suspicion in any man's mind. Then he ordered the man to be scourged severely all over his body. Yes—a Roman citizen was slashed with rods in the open forum at Messana; and as the punishment went on, no word, no groan of the wretched man, in all his anguish, was heard amid the sound of the lashes, but this cry,—"I am a Roman citizen!" By such protest of citizenship he thought he could at least save himself from anything like blows—could escape the indignity of personal torture. But not only did he fail in thus deprecating the insult of the lash, but when he redoubled his entreaties and his appeal to the name of Rome, a cross—yes, I say, a cross—was ordered for that most unfortunate and ill-fated man, who had never yet beheld such an abuse of a governor's power.

O name of liberty, sweet to our ears! O rights of citizenship, in which we glory! O laws of Porcius and Sempronius! O privilege of the tribune, long and sorely regretted, and at last restored to the people of Rome! Has it all come to this, that a Roman citizen in a province of the Roman people—in a federal town—is to be bound and beaten with rods in the forum by a man who only holds those rods and axes—those awful emblems—by grace of that same people of Rome? What shall I say of the fact that fire, and red-hot plates, and other tortures were applied? Even if his agonized entreaties and pitiable cries did not check you, Verres, were you not moved by the tears and groans which burst from the Roman citizens who were present at the scene? Did you dare to drag to the cross one who claimed to be a citizen of Rome?—I did not intend, citizens, in my former pleading, to press this case so strongly—I did not indeed; for you saw yourselves how the public feeling was already imbittered against the defendant by indignation, and hate, and dread of a common peril.

But, Verres, you say you did not know who the man was; you suspected him of being a spy. I do not ask the grounds of your suspicion. I impeach you on your own evidence. He said he was a Roman citizen. Had you yourself, Verres, been seized and led out to execution, in Persia, say, or in the farthest Indies, what other cry or protest could you raise but that you were a Roman citizen? And if you, a stranger there among strangers, in the hands of barbarians, among men who dwell in the farthest and remotest regions of the earth, would have found protection in the name of your city, known and renowned in every nation under heaven, could the victim whom you were dragging to the cross, be he who he might—and you did not know who he was—when he declared he was a citizen of Rome, could he obtain from you, a Roman magistrate, by the mere mention and claim of citizenship, not only no reprieve, but not even a brief respite from death?

Men of neither rank nor wealth, of humble birth and station, sail the seas; they touch at some spot they never saw before, where they are neither personally known to those whom they visit, nor can always find any to vouch for their nationality. But in this single fact of their citizenship they feel they shall be safe; not only with our own governors, who are held in check by the terror of the laws and of public opinion—not only among those who share that citizenship of Rome, and who are united with them by community of language, of laws, and of many things besides—but go where they may, this, they think, will be their safeguard. Take away this confidence, destroy this safeguard for our Roman citizens—once establish the principle that there is no protection in the words, "I am a citizen of Rome"—that a prætor or other magistrate may with impunity sentence to what punishment he will a man who says he is a Roman citizen, merely because somebody does not know it for a fact; and at once, by admitting such a defense, you are shutting up against our Roman citizens all our provinces, all foreign states, despotic or independent—all the whole world, in short, which has ever lain open to our national enterprise beyond all.

[Cicero turns again to Verres.]

But why talk of Gavius? as though it were Gavius on whom you were wreaking a private vengeance instead of rather waging war against the very name and rights of Roman citizenship. You showed yourself an enemy, I say, not to the individual man, but to the common cause of liberty. For what meant it that, when the authorities of Messana, according to their usual custom, would have erected the cross behind their city on the Pompeian road, you ordered it to be set up on the side that looked toward the Strait? Nay, and added this—which you cannot deny, which you said openly in the hearing of all—that you chose that spot for this reason, that as he had called himself a Roman citizen, he might be able, from his cross of punishment, to see in the distance his country and his home! And so, Romans, that cross was the only one, since Messana was a city, that was ever erected on that spot. A point which commanded a view of Italy was chosen by the defendant for the express reason that the dying sufferer, in his last agony and torment, might see how the rights of the slave and the freeman were separated by that narrow streak of sea; that Italy might look upon a son of hers suffering the capital penalty reserved for slaves alone.

It is a crime to put a citizen of Rome in bonds; it is an atrocity to scourge him; to put him to death is well-nigh parricide; what shall I say it is to crucify him?—Language has no word by which I may designate such an enormity. Yet with all this yonder man was not content. "Let him look," said he, "towards his country; let him die in full sight of freedom and the laws." It was not Gavius; it was not a single victim unknown to fame, a mere individual Roman citizen; it was the common cause of liberty, the common rights of citizenship, which you there outraged and put to a shameful death.

CÆSAR DINES WITH CICERO.

A LETTER of Cicero to Atticus describes a visit which he received in his country house near Puteoli from Julius Cæsar, already Dictator.

To think that I should have had such a tremendous visitor! But never mind, for all went off very pleasantly. But when he arrived at Philippus' house on the evening of the second day of the Saturnalia, the place was so full of soldiers that they could hardly find a spare table for Cæsar himself to dine at. There were two thousand men. Really I was in a state of perplexity as to what was to be done next day: but Barba Cassius came to my aid,—he supplied me with a guard. They pitched their tents in the grounds, and the house was protected. He stayed with Philippus until one o'clock of the third day of the Saturnalia, and would see no one; going over accounts, I suppose, with Balbus. Then he walked on the seashore. After two he had a bath; then he listened to some verses on Mamurra, without moving a muscle of his countenance; then got himself oiled and sat down to dinner. He had taken a precautionary emetic, and therefore ate and drank heartily and unrestrainedly We had, I assure you, a very good dinner, and well served; and not only that, but "the feast of reason and the flow of soul" besides. His suite was abundantly supplied at three other tables; the freedmen of the lower rank, and even the slaves, were well taken care of. The higher class had really an elegant entertainment. Well, no need to make a long story; we found we were both "flesh and blood." Still, he is not the kind of guest to whom you would say—"Now do, pray, take us in your way on your return." Once is enough. We had no conversation on business, but a good deal of literary talk. In short, he seemed to be much pleased and to enjoy himself. He said he would stay one day at Puteoli, and another at Baiæ. So here you have an account of this visit, or, rather, quartering of troops upon me, which I disliked the thoughts of, but which really, as I have said, gave me no annoyance. I shall stay here a little longer, then go to my house at Tusculum. When Cæsar passed Dolabella's villa, all the troops formed up on the right and left of his horse, which they did no where else. I heard that from Nicias.

CICERO TO TIRO.

CICERO'S domestic affection extended to his faithful slave Tiro, who afterwards collected and published his master's letters. Tiro accompanied Cicero to Cilicia, but was taken ill on his return and left behind at Patræ. The following interesting letter was written soon afterwards.

I thought I could have borne the separation from you better, but it is plainly impossible; and although it is of great importance to the honors which I am expecting* that I should get to Rome as soon as possible, yet I feel I made a great mistake in leaving you behind. But as it seemed to be your wish not to make the voyage until your health was restored, I approved your decision. Nor do I think otherwise now, if you are still of the same opinion. But if hereafter, when you are able to eat as usual, you think you can follow me here, it is for you to decide. I sent Mario to you, telling him either to join me with you as soon as possible, or, if you are delayed, to come back here at once. But be assured of this, that if it can be so without risk to your health, there is nothing I wish so much as to have you with me. Still, if you feel it necessary for your recovery to stay a little longer at Patræ, there is nothing I wish so much as for you to get well. If you sail at once, you will catch us at Leucas. But if you want to get well first, take care to secure pleasant companions, fine weather, and a good ship. Mind this, my good Tiro, if you love me—let neither Mario's visit nor this letter hurry you. By doing what is best for your own health, you will be best obeying my directions. Consider these points with your usual good sense. I miss you very much; but then I love you, and my affection makes me wish to see you well, just as my want of you makes me long to see you as soon as possible. But the first point is the most important. Above all, therefore, take care to get well: of all your innumerable services to me, this will be the most acceptable.

*The triumph which he failed to get.

Scipio's Dream.

This remarkable vision is the end of Cicero's treatise on the Republic, which was written in emulation of Plato's dialogue, bearing the same name. The Scipio who here speaks was the destroyer of Carthage. He was the younger son of L. Æmilius Paulus, and had been adopted by the son of the Elder Scipio Africanus, who here appears to him in a dream.

On my arrival in Africa, whither I had been sent as military tribune in the fourth legion, my first step was to interview King Masinissa, who was linked by intimate bonds of friendship to our family. As soon as I approached him he embraced me, burst into tears, and raising his eyes heavenward, exclaimed:

"Thanks be to thee, O Sun, King of the planets, and to you all, gods of the Heavens! since I am permitted, before departing this life, to see in my kingdom and at my house, P. Cornelius Scipio, whose name alone cheers me! The remembrance of that excellent, that invincible hero, who has rendered this name famous, is never absent from my mind."

We then inquired of each other; I of his Kingdom, and he of our Republic, and after a long conversation, reached insensibly the close of the day. After a regal repast, we prolonged our conversation far into the night; the old king spoke of nothing save of Scipio Africanus, recalling not only his actions, but also his words.

Hardly had we lain our weary bodies down to rest, when the fatigue of the journey and the long vigil we had kept plunged us into a deeper sleep than usual. Then appeared before me (was it the effect of our conversation? I indeed believe it was) Scipio Africanus, whose features were so familiar to me; more from a long contemplation of his portrait, than from having seen him personally. I recognized him and shuddered, but he—

"Be calm," said he, "banish all fear, Scipio, and engrave in thy memory that which I am about to say to thee.

"Seest thou that city, which, forced by me to obey the Roman power, renews our old wars, and is unable to remain at peace (he pointed out to me Carthage, from an eminence studded with stars and resplendent), this city, which thou hast to-day come to besiege, as a mere soldier yet? In two years, as consul, thou shalt overthrow it, and have won for thyself the surname which thou hast from me as an heirloom. After having destroyed

Carthage, obtained triumphal honors, exercised the censorship, visited, as lieutenant of the Roman people, Egypt, Syria, Asia, and Greece, thou shalt be elected, during thy absence, consul a second time; finally thou shalt end this implacable war—thou shalt destroy Numantia. But after having ascended to the Capitol on thy victorious chariot, thou shalt find the Republic in a state of commotion, by the intrigues of my grandson. Then, O Scipio! for thy country's sake, cause to shine forth thy courage, thy genius, and thy prudence. But I see, in those times, a double road which opens, and destiny hesitates. Yes, when thy years shall have accomplished eight times seven of the revolutions of the sun, it is towards thee and to thy name only that Rome shall turn; to thee shall the senate, to thee shall all good citizens, to thee shall the allies, to thee shall the Latin people look. On thee alone shall rest the well-being of the State; in brief, become dictator, it must be. Strengthen the Republic, if thou escapest from the hands of thy near relatives.

"But, in order that thou may'st feel thine ardor redoubled to defend the State, Scipio, learn this: for all heroes who have saved, assisted, or enlarged the State, there is in Heaven a place reserved where they will enjoy a felicity without end. Because this supreme God, who governs the immense universe, finds nothing on earth so pleasing in his sight, and more agreeable to Him than these groupings of mortals associated by right, which are called cities. It is from hence that the genii emanate, by whom they are governed and defended, and it is here they return."

Hearing these words, although terror-stricken, not so much at the thought of death, as that of betrayal by my own immediate family, I nevertheless had the strength to ask him, "If he was still living, Paulus Æmilius, my father, and all those whom we here looked upon as being extinct?"

"Yes," said he, "they do really live, who have shaken off the bonds of the body, wherein they had been held captive; they have taken their flight, and that which you call life is really death. Behold, there is Paulus Æmilius, your father, coming towards you."

I saw him and burst into tears; he, embracing me, and lavishing caresses, forbade my weeping. As soon as I was able to restrain my sobs, I exclaimed:

"O my sainted father, best of men, since life is as you are, as I hear from Africanus, what keeps me on earth? Why should not I hasten myself to come to you?"

"Not thus," answered he, "before that God, of whom all that thou seest (the universe) is the Temple, has delivered thee from the prison of thy body, thou canst not obtain access to this abode. Because men are born to be the faithful guardians of this sphere, which thou seest in the midst of this Temple, and is called the Earth. They have been given a soul, a beam from these eternal lights, which are called the planets and stars, and which rounded in spheres, animated by divine intelligences, describe their periods and their orbits with a wonderful rapidity. It is then a duty for thee, Publius, and for all pious men, to retain their soul in the prison of the body, and thou canst not, without the order of Him who gave it, depart from this mortal life; it would seem like desertion from the human post assigned by God himself. But far better, Scipio, like thy grandfather, whom thou seest here, like me, the author of thy life, cherish justice and piety; that piety which is all love for thy parents and relatives, all devotion for thy country; this is the road which will lead thee to Heaven, in the company of men who have already lived, and who, liberated from the body, inhabit the abode which thou seest."

He then indicated the circle, which shines brilliantly by its dazzling whiteness, from among all the celestial bodies, and that which you, in imitation of the Greeks, call the Milky Way. Thence I surveyed the universe and saw nothing but grandeur and marvels. There were stars we have never perceived here below, and whose magnitude we have never dreamed of. The smallest of all was that one which, farthest from Heaven, and nearest to Earth, shone by a reflected light. In addition, the starry spheres far excel the earth in grandeur. Then the Earth itself appeared so small that our empire, visible only as a dot, looked insignificant.

"Since Earth seems so small to thee," said Africanus, "as it is in fact, raise continually thine eyes towards Heaven, and despise all earthly things. What renown, what glory worthy of thy ambition, canst thou acquire among men? Thou seest what small and narrow spaces are inhabited on the Earth, and what vast solitudes separate even these spots which form the inhabited dots. The inhabitants of this globe are so isolated from each other that they are unable to communicate with each other. Thou seest how far they live from you; some on the sides of the Earth, others on the face, others even under your feet. What glory can be expected from them?

"Thou seest the zones which seem to envelop and surround

the Earth; the two from among them which are at the extremities of the globe, covered with frost; and which from one point to the other lean against the poles of heaven; the centre zone, the greatest, is scorched by the sun's intense rays. Two of those are inhabitable: the Frigid Zone, where are found people, your antipodes, and which is a world wholly unknown to yours; and the one where blows the north wind, and which you inhabit. Look! you occupy but a very small portion thereof. All this region where you are, narrowed between the north and the south, more extended from the east to the west, forms a small island, bathed by this sea, which you designate the Great Sea and the Ocean, and notwithstanding all these great names, thou seest what a petty ocean it is. But in the midst of these known and inhabited lands, has thy name, or that of any of us, ever gone beyond this Caucasus which is beneath thine eyes, or crossed beyond the waves of the Ganges? At the extremities of the rising and setting of the sun, to the last confines of the north or the south, what man will hear the name of Scipio? Take away all these countries, and then judge of the narrow limits to which your glory aspires to extend. Those even who speak of you, will they continue to do so long?

"Even then, should the future races perpetuate to envy the inheritance of our glory, for each one of us, the deluges and conflagrations which are to change the face of the earth at stated periods, would prevent this glory from being eternal, or even durable. And of what consequence, then is it to thee of being celebrated in the centuries to come, when thou hast not been so in the past, and by these men, too, who are so numerous, who have lived before us?

"If thou wilt but cast thine eyes upwards, and gaze upon that eternal home, never allow vulgar influence to gain any mastery over thee; elevate thy heart above human recompense. May virtue, by its sole attractions, lead thee to real glory. It is for others to consider how they will speak of thee; that thou wilt be spoken of, no doubt exists; but all these speeches will never go beyond the narrow limits wherein your world is enclosed; they have never immortalized a single mortal; they perish with the men, and are extinguished in the forgetfulness of posterity."

When he had thus spoken: "O Scipio Africanus," I said, "if it is true that the services rendered to one's country open the gates of Heaven, I, who since my childhood have walked in the footprints of my father and yours, and who probably have not forfeited this glorious inheritance, I wish, to-day, in the sight of this sublime prize, to redouble my zeal and efforts."

"Take courage," said he, "and remember that if thy body must perish, thou thyself art not mortal; this apparent form is not thyself; that which constitutes the man is the soul, and not this form which can be pointed at with the finger. Know then that thou art a god; because he is a god who has the force of action, who feels, who remembers, who foresees, who governs, who rules and moves this body of which he is the master, even as the Supreme God governs this world. Similar to this Eternal God who moves this partly corruptible world, the immortal soul moves the perishable body.

"Exercise that soul to its most excellent purposes. Now, then, in the foremost rank are found the deeds for the welfare of one's country. Accustomed to this noble exercise the soul will fly more rapidly towards its celestial home; its journey will be the more accelerated, inasmuch as its flight will have been begun in its body prison, and, by sublime aspirations to detach itself, so far as it is in it, of its terrestrial envelope. But the souls of those, who, enslaved by sensual pleasures of which they have constituted themselves upholders, and submissive to the voice of passions, those vassals to pleasure, have violated all divine and human laws, when once disengaged from the body, wander in a woeful condition around the earth, and only return to this Heaven after an expiation of centuries."

The hero disappeared, and I awoke.

CATULLUS.

The first, and by far the most elegant, of the Latin lyric poets was Caius Valerius Catullus. Born near Verona in 84 B.C., he went in youth to Rome, where he squandered part of his fortune. Then to repair it, according to Roman practice, he went to Bithynia in the train of the prætor, Caius Memmius, to whom Lucretius dedicated his great poem. But Catullus quarreled with Memmius, and returned to Italy. Thenceforth he divided his time between the dissipations of the capital and the seclusion of his villa at Sirmio, a promontory on Lake Benacus (now Lago di Garda). His accomplishments obtained for him intimacy with some of the most distinguished men of his time, including Cicero and Cæsar. His favorite mistress, whom he has immortalized under the name of Lesbia, is supposed to have been Clodia, the daughter of Q. Metellus Celer. He died about 54 B.C. His works comprise more than a hundred poems in a great variety of styles. The longest is an heroic poem on "The Nuptials of Peleus and Thetis" Others are translations or imitations from the Greek. The shorter poems are characterized by originality and felicity of expression.

TO LESBIA.

LET us, my Lesbia, live and love,
And, though sour Cynics disapprove,
　Heed not their frowns a stiver;
Suns set, and suns again may rise,
But we, when once our daylight dies,
　Must sleep, sleep on, forever.
Give me then a thousand kisses,
Then a hundred of like blisses,
Hundreds then to thousands add,
And, when thousands more we've had,
We'll blend, confuse them all, that so
Nor you, nor I their sum may know,—
No; nor e'en Envy's self e'er guess
Our half amount of happiness.

THE DEATH OF LESBIA'S SPARROW.

MOURN, all ye Loves and Graces! mourn,
　Ye wits, ye gallants, and ye gay!
Death from my fair her bird has torn,
　Her much-loved sparrow snatched away.

Her very eyes she priz'd not so,
　For he was fond and knew my fair
Well as young girls their mothers know,
　And sought her breast and nestled there.

Once fluttering round, from place to place,
　He gaily chirp'd to her alone;
But now that gloomy path must trace,
　Whence Fate permits return to none.

Accursed Shades, o'er hell that lower,
　Oh, be my curses on you heard!
Ye, that all pretty things devour,
　Have torn from me my pretty bird.

O evil deed! O sparrow dead!
　　O wretched bird, if thou canst see
My fair one's eyes with weeping red,
　　And know how much she grieves for thee!

LESBIA'S LOVER.

This ode, imitated from Sappho, is translated by W. E. Gladstone.

Him rival to the gods I place,
　　Him loftier yet, if loftier be,
Who, Lesbia, sits before thy face,
　　Who listens and who looks on thee,
Thee smiling soft. Yet this delight
　　Doth all my sense consign to death;
For when thou dawnest on my sight,
　　Ah, wretched! flits my laboring breath.
My tongue is palsied. Subtly hid
　　Fire creeps me through from limb to limb:
My loud ears tingle all unbid:
　　Twin clouds of night mine eyes bedim.

ON MAMURRA.*

(Addressed to Cæsar.)

Who can behold, or who endure,
　　Save rakes devoid of truth and shame,
　　Or gambling cheats, or gluttons tame,
That base Mamurra should procure
And squander free the spoil and products all
Of farthest Britain's isle, and rich Transalpine Gaul?

Miscreant Romulus! canst thou see
　　And suffer this? Then thine the shame,
　　The rake's, the cheat's, the glutton's name.
Some proud and all-abounding he
Through all our marriage beds shall rove
Gay as Adonis, soft as Venus' dove.

Canst thou still see and bear this thing,
　　Miscreant Romulus? Thine the shame,
　　The rake's, the cheat's, the glutton's name.

* A profligate Roman knight, who, by the favor of Cæsar, amassed an immense fortune in the Gallic wars.

And for this name, unrivall'd king,
Proud didst thou bear afar thy conquering crest
E'en to the farthest isle that gems the distant West?

   That he, thy lustful friend, should prey
     On all the spoil, thy valor's prize!
     "What matters it?" thy bounty cries,
   "A little wealth he throws away."
And has he then but little wealth devour'd?
First he his father's hoards on low companions shower'd;

   Then by the spoil of Pontus fed,
     And then by all Iberia gave,
     And Tagus from its golden wave;
   Him justly Gaul and Britain dread;
Justly his grasping sway may cause alarms,
More than his emperor's name and all-victorious arms.

   Oh! why so base a favorite choose,
     Who has not wit, nor use, nor power,
     Save all thy riches to devour?
   Didst thou, O son-in-law!* then lose,
Didst thou, O conquering father! then obtain
The empire of the world to be this minion's gain?

ACME AND SEPTIMIUS.

SEPTIMIUS said, and fondly pressed
The doating Acme to his breast:
"My Acme, if I prize not thee
With love as warm as love can be,
With passion spurning any fears
Of growing faint in length of years,
Alone may I defenceless stand
To meet, on Libya's desert sand,
Or under India's torrid sky,
The tawny lion's glaring eye!"

   Love, before who utter'd still
   On the left-hand omens ill,
   As he ceased his faith to plight,
   Laugh'd propitious on the right.

* Pompey, who married Cæsar's daughter, Julia

Then Acme gently bent her head,
Kiss'd with those lips of cherry red
The eyes of the delighted boy,
That swam with glistening floods of joy;
And whisper'd as she closely pressed—
" Septimius, soul of Acme's breast,
Let all our lives and feelings own
One lord, one sovereign, Love alone!
I yield to love, and yield to thee,
For thou and love art one to me.
Though fond thy fervent heart may beat,
My feelings glow with greater heat,
And madder flames my bosom melt
Than all that thou hast ever felt."

   Love, before who utter'd still
   On the left-hand omens ill,
   As she ceased her faith to plight,
   Laugh'd propitious on the right.

Since favoring omens thus approved,
They mutual love and are beloved;
Septimius prizes Acme more
Than Syria's realm and Britain's shore;
And from Septimius only flows
The bliss that faithful Acme knows.
Then search the world, and search in vain
For fonder maid or happier swain.
Ask men below and gods above,
Ask Venus kind and potent Love,
If e'er they with propitious care,
Heap'd equal bliss on any pair.

A Morning Call.

This little sketch of the life of gay idlers in Rome has been paraphrased by W. S. Landor.

   Varus would take me t'other day
     To see a little girl he knew,—
   Pretty and witty in her way,
     With impudence enough for two.

   Scarce are we seated, ere she chatters
     (As pretty girls are wont to do)

About all persons, places, matters :—
   "And pray, what has been done for *you*?"

"Bithynia, lady!" I replied,
   "Is a fine province for a prætor;
For none (I promise you) beside,
   And least of all am I her debtor."

"Sorry for that!" said she. "However,
   You have brought with you, I dare say,
Some litter-bearers; none so clever
   In any other part as they.

"Bithynia is the very place
   For all that's steady, tall and straight;
It is the nature of the race.
   Could you not lend me six or eight?"

"Why six or eight of them or so,"
   Said I, determined to be grand;
"My fortune is not quite so low
   But these are still at my command."

"You'll send them?" "Willingly!" I told her,
   Although I had not here or there
One who could carry on his shoulder
   The leg of an old broken chair.

"Catullus! what a charming hap is
   Our meeting in this sort of way!
I would be carried to Serapis
   To-morrow!"—"Stay, fair lady, stay!

"You overvalue my intention.
   Yes, there *are* eight . . . there may be nine;
I merely had forgot to mention
   That they are Cinna's, and not mine."

FAREWELL TO LESBIA.

THOU told'st me in our days of love,
   That I had all that heart of thine;
That e'en to share the couch of Jove,
   Thou wouldst not, Lesbia, part from mine.

How purely wert thou worshipp'd then!
　Not with the vague and vulgar fires
Which beauty wakes in soulless men,
　But loved as children by their sires.

That flattering dream, alas, is o'er;
　I know thee now—and, though these eyes
Dote on thee wildly as before,
　Yet, e'en in doting, I despise.

Yes, sorceress—mad as it may seem—
　With all thy craft, such spells adorn thee,
That passion e'en outlives esteem,
　And I, at once, adore—and scorn thee.

THE PENINSULA OF SIRMIO.

(Written upon his return to his villa there.)

SIRMIO, of all the shores the gem,
　The isles where circling Neptune strays,
　Whether the vast and boisterous main
Or lake's more limpid waves they stem;
　How gladly on thy lands I gaze!
　How blessed to visit thee again!

I scarce believe, while rapt I stand,
　That I have left the Thynian fields
　And all Bithynia far behind,
And safely view my favorite land.
　O bliss, when care dispersing yields
　To full repose the placid mind!

Then when the mind its load lays down;
　When we regain, all hazards past,
　And with long ceaseless travel tired,
Our household god again our own;
　And press in tranquil sleep at last
　The well-known bed so oft desired—

This can alone atonement make
　For every toil. Hail, Sirmio sweet!
　Be gay, thy lord hath ceased to roam!
Ye laughing waves of Lydia's Lake,
　Smile all around! Thy master greet
　With all thy smiles, my pleasant home!

ATYS.

CATULLUS in his sojourn in Bithynia came in contact with the worship of Cybele on its native soil. The mingled attraction and repulsion of this Oriental cult for educated Romans is exhibited in this unique poem.

BORNE swiftly o'er the seas to Phrygia's woody strand,
Atys with rapid haste infuriate leap'd to land;
Where high-inwoven groves in solemn darkness meet,
Rushed to the mighty Deity's remote and awful seat;
And wildered in his brain, fierce inspirations prey,
There with a broken flint he struck his sex away.
Soon as he then beheld his comely form unmann'd,
While yet the purple blood flowed reeking on the land;
Seized in his snowy grasp the drum, the timbrel light,
That still is heard, dread Cybele, at thine initiate rite,
And struck the quivering skin, whence hollow echoes flew,
And raised this panting song to his infuriate crew.
"Ye priests of Cybele, or rather let me say,
For ye are men no longer, ye priestesses, away!
Together pierce the forest, great Cybele's domains,
Ye vagrant flocks of her on Dindymus who reigns.
Ye, like devoted exiles, who seeking foreign lands,
Have followed me, your leader, have bow'd to my commands;
Have crossed the salt-sea wave, have dar'd the raging storms,
And, loathing woman's love, unmann'd your lusty forms;
The sense of error past let laughing frenzy blind;
Let doubt, let thought itself, be driven from the mind.
Haste, haste, together haste to Cybele divine!
Seek we her Phrygian grove, and dark sequestered shrine,

Where cymbals clash, where drums resound their deepening tone,
Where Phrygia's crooked pipe breathes out its solemn drone;
Where votaresses toss their ivy-circled brows,
And urge with piercing yells their consecrated vows;
Where the delirious train disport as chance may lead:
Thither our vows command in mystic dance to speed."

Thus Atys, female now, to female comrades sung.
The frantic chorus rose from many a panting tongue;
Re-echoed the deep timbrel, the hollow cymbals rang,
And all to verdant Ida ran madly at the clang.
Though breathless, still impetuous with inspiration's force;
Raving and bewildered, scarce conscious of her course;
As the unbroken heifer will fly the threaten'd yoke,
Atys through gloomy woods, where never sunbeam broke,
Loud striking the light timbrel, rush'd on with bounding stride,
And all the frantic priestesses pursue their rapid guide.
The fearful fane at length their panting ardor stops;
Each, faint and unrefreshed, in leaden slumber drops,
In languor most profound their eyelids are depress'd,
And all ecstatic rage is lull'd in torpid rest.

But when again the sun, returning to the skies,
Put forth his golden brow: when now his radiant eyes
Throughout wide heaven, and earth, and ocean pour'd their light;
And with thunder-pacing steeds, he chased the shades of night;
When slumber's reign serene had frenzy's flame subdued,
When Atys her fell deed in clearer reason view'd,
Beheld in what abode her future lot was placed,
And, ah! how low she stood in Nature's rank, disgraced;
Then, hurried to despair by passion's rising tide,
Again she wildly sought the country's sea-girt side;
And casting her full eyes o'er boundless ocean's flow,
Address'd her native land in these plaintive strains of woe.

"My country, O my country, creatress, parent earth!
My country, my dear country, that sustained me from my birth!
Must I for dreary woods forsake thy smiling shore,
And see my friends, my home, my parents nevermore?
No more the Forum seek, or the gay Palæstra's court,
Or urge, as wont of old, each fam'd gymnastic sport?

O wretched, wretched man ! while years shall slowly roll,
Forever, o'er and o'er again, forever grieve, my soul !
What grace, what beauty's there, that I did not enjoy?
I, when in manhood's prime, a youth, or yet a boy,
The flower of all who trod the firm gymnastic floor,
The victor 'mid the crowd who the wrestler's prizes bore.
My gates were ever throng'd, and full my threshold swarm'd,
With blooming garlands hung that love-sick maidens form'd;
My mansion gaily glitter'd each morning as I sped,
At earliest blush of sunrise, with lightness from my bed.

And must I ever now a maniac votaress rave,
Heaven's devoted handmaid, to Cybele a slave?
Her frantic orgies ply, disgrac'd in Nature's plan,
A part of what I was, a maim'd, a barren man;
And dwell in Ida's caves, which snow forever chills,
And pass my savage life on Phrygia's rugged hills;
Placed with the sylvan stag, the forest-raging boar?
Oh ! now how soon I rue the deed, how bitterly deplore ! "

As from her rosy lips these wandering murmurings broke,
They rose to heav'n and bore th' unwonted words she spoke:
Indignantly unyoking her lions on the plain,
And rousing the grim beast that bore the left-hand rein
Great Cybele, enrag'd, her dread injunction told,
And thus to fury wak'd the tyrant of the fold.

" Haste, fierce one, haste away ! rush on with glaring ire,
With inspiration's rage, with frenzy's goad of fire,
Drive the too daring youth, who would my service fly,
Again to seek the gloom of yonder forest high.
Haste; lash thyself to rage till all thy flank be sore;
Let all around re-echo to thine appalling roar:
Toss with thy sinewy neck on high thy glossy mane."
So spake terrific Cybele, and loos'd her lion's rein.
Gladly the beast awakes his ruthlessness of mind ;
Bounds, rages, reckless leaves the thicket crush'd behind;
Then swiftly gained the beach wash'd by the foamy flood,
Where Atys, in despair, amid the breakers stood ;
And springing fiercely forth—the wretch, no longer brave,
Into the forest plung'd, and in a living grave,
There pass'd her long, devoted life, a priestess and a slave.

O great, O fearful goddess! O Cybele divine!
O goddess, who hast placed on Dindymus a shrine!
Far be from my abode thy sacred frenzy's fire;
Madden more willing votaries, more daring minds inspire.

LABERIUS.

THIS Prologue was recited by the Roman knight Laberius, whom Julius Cæsar, to inflict on him a public disgrace, required to appear on the stage and act those mimes which he had written. The translation is by W. E. Aytoun.

Whither hath Destiny (whose current strong
Hath spared so few, so many swept along)
Flung me, her victim, in my latter days,
Whom not ambition, nor the meed of praise,
Nor fear, nor power, nor frowns, nor aught beside,
Could move, when youthful, from my place of pride?
Lo! in mine age how easily I fall!
One horrid speech from Cæsar's tongue was all.
For how might I refuse his sovereign will,
Whose every wish the gods themselves fulfill?

Twice thirty years passed by without a scorn—
A Roman knight I left my home this morn,
And thither I return—as what? a Mime!
Oh! I have lived one day beyond my time—
Fortune, unequal both in good and ill,
If thou hadst power, by this unhappy skill,
To tear the wreath of honor from my brow,
Why was I not far earlier taught to bow,
When with such aid as youth and strength afford,
I might have won the crowd and pleased their lord?
Now, why thus humbled? Where's the form and face
The mien majestic, and the gallant grace—
The fire of soul, the harmony of tone,
That can adorn the mimic scene alone?
As the slow ivy kills the stately tree,
So age in its embrace is stifling me;
And nothing's left of all my former fame
Save the poor legend of a tomb—my name.

Like the first mortals blest is he,
    From debts, and usury and business free,
With his own team who ploughs the soil,
    Which grateful once confesst his father's toil.
The sound of war nor break his sleep,
    Nor the rough storm, that harrows up the deep:
He shuns the courtier's haughty doors,
    And the loud science of the bar abjures.
Sometimes his marriageable vines
    Around the lofty bridegroom elm he twines;
Or lops the fragrant boughs away,
    Ingrafting better as the old decay;
Or in the vale with joy surveys
    His lowing herds safe-wandering as they graze;
Or careful stores the flowing gold
    Prest from the hive, or sheers his tender fold;
Or when, with various fruits o'erspread,
    The mellow autumn lifts his beauteous head,
His grafted pears or grapes, that vie
    With the rich purple of the Tyrian dye,
Grateful he gathers, and repays
    His guardian gods upon their festal days;
Sometimes beneath an ancient shade,
    Or on the matted grass supinely laid,
Where pours the mountain stream along,
    And feather'd warblers chant the soothing song;
Or where the lucid fountain flows,
    And with its murmurs courts him to repose.
But when the rain and snow appear,
    And wintry Jove loud thunders o'er the year,
With hounds he drives into the toils
    The foaming boar, and triumphs in his spoils;
Or for the greedy thrush he lays
    His nets, and with delusive baits betrays;
Artful he sets the springing snare,
    To catch the stranger crane, or timorous hare.
            —*Horace: Epode. Philip Francis' trans.*

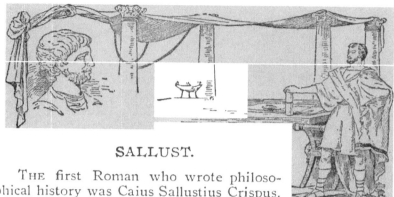

SALLUST.

The first Roman who wrote philosophical history was Caius Sallustius Crispus. He was a plebeian born in 86 B.C. in the country of the Sabines. He was engaged in the civil wars on the popular side, and held many offices. In 50 B.C. he was expelled from the senate on a charge of flagrant immorality, though the true reason was that he belonged to Cæsar's party. He remained faithful to that leader, and was in a few years restored to his rank. For a time he was governor of Numidia, in which capacity he oppressed the people, but, though charged with maladministration, he was not brought to trial. Retiring to private life on his return from Africa, he entered on his historical works, and passed quietly through the turbulent period after Cæsar's death. His immense wealth was attested by the expensive gardens which he formed on the Quirinal hill. He died in 34 B.C. In his writings Sallust took Thucydides as his model, but he did not possess the same philosophic spirit. His language is concise and usually clear, except where his love of brevity renders it ambiguous. His graphic account of the conspiracy of Catiline is valuable, since he was a spectator of the scenes he describes and was unfriendly to Cicero. His other work relates in rhetorical style the history of Jugurtha, King of Numidia, but is not as exact in its statements as the former. Though notorious for immorality, Sallust, in his writings, poses as a moralist, and rebukes the degeneracy of the Romans.

JUGURTHA AT ROME.

The tribune Caius Memmius persuaded the Roman people to send Lucius Cassius, who was then prætor, to Jugurtha, and bring him from Africa to Rome on the public faith: that, by his evidence, Scaurus and others who were charged with betraying their trust might be clearly convicted.

The prætor Cassius, in consequence of this ordinance of the people, procured by Memmius, to the great surprise of the nobility, went to Jugurtha, who, from a consciousness of his guilt, was doubtful of his cause, and persuaded him "that since he had already delivered himself up to the Roman people, he should trust to their mercy rather than provoke their vengeance." He likewise pledged to him his own faith, which Jugurtha reckoned as strong a security as that of the republic; such at that time was the reputation of Cassius.

Jugurtha accordingly went to Rome with Cassius, yet divested of regal pomp, and dressed in such a manner as to excite compassion. But though he was himself of an intrepid spirit, and was moreover encouraged by assurances from those in reliance on whose power and criminal practices he had hitherto been supported, yet, by an immense sum of money, he secured the assistance of Caius Bæbius, tribune of the people, one who trusted to his invincible impudence for protection against all law and all manner of injuries.

When an assembly of the people was called by Memmius, though they were so highly exasperated against Jugurtha that some of them were for putting him in chains, others for putting him to death as a public enemy, according to the ancient usage, unless he discovered his associates, yet Memmius, more concerned for their dignity than the gratification of their fury, endeavored to calm the tumult and soften their minds, and declared that he would take care that the public faith should not be violated.

Having obtained silence and ordered Jugurtha to be brought before the assembly, he proceeded in his speech; recounted all his wicked actions, both in Rome and Numidia; exposed his unnatural behavior to his father and brothers, adding, that the Roman people, though they were not ignorant by whom he had been aided and supported, still desired full information of the whole from himself. If he declared the truth, he had much to hope from the faith and clemency of the Roman people; but if he concealed it, he would not save his friends by such means, but ruin his own fortune and his prospects forever.

When Memmius had concluded and Jugurtha was ordered to reply, the tribune Bæbius, who had been secured by a sum of money, as already mentioned, ordered him to be silent; and though the people there assembled were highly incensed, and endeavored to terrify him with their cries, with angry looks, with acts of violence, and every other method which indignation inspires, yet his impudence triumphed over it all. The people departed after being thus mocked; Jugurtha, Bestia and the rest, who were at first fearful of this prosecution, now assumed greater courage.

There was at this juncture a certain Numidian at Rome called Massiva, the son of Gulussa, and grandson of Masinissa, who, having taken part against Jugurtha in the war between the three kings, had fled from Africa on the surrender of Cirta and the murder of Adherbal. Spurius Albinus, who with Quintus Minucius Rufus, succeeded Bestia in the consulship, persuaded this man to apply to the senate for the kingdom of Numidia, as he was descended from Masinissa, and Jugurtha was now the object of public abhorrence on account of his crimes, and alarmed with daily fears of the punishment he merited. The consul, who was fond of having the management of the war, was more desirous that the public disturbances should be continued than composed. The province of Numidia had fallen to him, and Macedonia to his colleague.

When Massiva began to prosecute his claim, Jugurtha, finding that he could not rely on the assistance of his friends, some of whom were seized with remorse, others restrained by the bad opinion the public had of them and by their fears, ordered Bomilcar, who was his faithful friend and confidant, "to engage persons to murder Massiva for money, by which he had accomplished many things, and to do it by private means, if possible; but if these were ineffectual, by any means whatever."

Bomilcar quickly executed the king's orders, and, by employing proper instruments, discovered his places of resort, his set times and all his movements, and when matters were ripe laid a scheme for the assassination. One of those who were to put the murder into execution attacked Massiva and slew him, but, so imprudently, that he was himself apprehended, and being urged by many, especially by the consul Albinus, confessed all. Bomilcar was arraigned, more agreeably to reason and justice than to the law of nations, for he had accompanied Jugurtha, who came to Rome on the public faith.

Jugurtha, though clearly guilty of so foul a crime, repeated his endeavors to bear down the force of truth, till he perceived that the horror of his guilt was such as to baffle all the power of interest or bribery, on which, though he had been compelled in the commencement of the prosecution of Bomilcar to give up fifty of his friends as sureties for his standing his trial, he sent him privately to Numidia, being more concerned for his kingdom than the safety of his friends; for he was fearful, should this favorite be punished, that the rest of his subjects would be discouraged from obeying him. In a few days he himself followed, being ordered by the senate to depart out of Italy. When he left Rome, it is reported that, having frequently looked back to it with fixed attention, he at last broke out into these words: "O venal city, and ripe for destruction when a purchaser can be found."

Caius Marius Seeks the Consulship.

About the same time Marius happened to be at Utica, and as he was sacrificing to the gods the augur announced to him, "that great and wonderful things were presaged to him; he should therefore pursue whatever designs he had formed, and trust to the gods; he might push his fortune to the utmost, regardless of difficulty and confident of success."

Marius had been long seized with an ardent desire of the consulship, and possessed every qualification for obtaining it, except that of noble descent; he had industry, probity, consummate skill in war, and an intrepid spirit in battle; he displayed a model of temperance, and, completely master of his passions, looked with indifference on wealth and pleasure, but was covetous of renown, and possessed an insatiable thirst of glory. He was born at Arpinum, where he passed his childhood, and from the time that he was capable of bearing arms took no delight in the study of Grecian eloquence, nor in the luxurious manners of Rome, but entered with ardor on the military life, and thus in a short time, by a proper course of discipline, acquired a masterly knowledge in the art of war; so that when he first solicited from the people the military tribuneship, although his person was unknown, his character obtained it by the unanimous suffrages of all the tribes. From this time he rose still higher in public favor, and in every office which he filled still rendered himself worthy of greater dignity. Yet Marius, with all his merit, till this time (for ambition afterward fatally urged him to the wildest excesses) had not ventured to offer himself for the consulship; for though the people at that time conferred all the other offices, that of consul was reserved for the nobility, and the most renowned or distinguished by merit, unsupported by birth, were reckoned by them unworthy of the supreme magistracy.

Marius, perceiving that the prediction of the augur was agreeable to his own inclinations, petitioned Metellus for leave to visit Rome as a candidate for the consulship. Metellus, though distinguished for his virtue and honor, and other desirable qualities, yet possessed a haughty and disdainful spirit, the common vice of the nobility: struck with so extraordinary a request, he therefore expressed surprise at his designs, and cautioned him, as in friendship, not to entertain such unreasonable views, nor suffer his mind to be exalted above his station. To all men, he observed, the same objects could not be the aim of reasonable ambition, adding that Marius ought to be contented with his present fortune; and, in a word, that he should take care not to demand from the Roman people what they might justly refuse. After these and the like remonstrances, the consul still found Marius steady to his purpose, and promised to comply with his request as soon as it was consistent with the public service; and as he still continued to urge his petition, Metellus is reported to have told him, "that it was needless to be in such a hurry, as it would be time enough for him to think of standing for the consulship when his son should be of age to join with him." This youth was then about twenty years of age, and serving under his father without any command.

This fired Marius with a more ardent desire of obtaining the consulship, and highly incensed him against Metellus; so that he blindly followed the dictates of ambition and resentment, the most pernicious of counsellors. He did and said every thing that could promote his views; gave greater liberty to the soldiers under his command than formerly; inveighed severely to our merchants, then in great numbers at Utica, against Metellus's manner of conducting the war; and boasted of himself, "that were but half the army under his own command he would in a few days have Jugurtha in chains; that the consul prolonged the war on purpose, being a vain man, possessed of kingly pride, and intoxicated with the love of command." This was the more readily believed by the merchants, as they had suffered in their fortunes by the long continuance of the war; and to an impatient spirit no measures appear sufficiently expeditious.

CAIUS JULIUS CÆSAR.

GREATEST among the ancient Romans, Caius Julius Cæsar changed the course of the world's history. He turned an aristocratic republic into a democratic empire. Though he was removed by assassination in the very hour of his triumph, his work remained and his spirit dominated the civilized world for centuries. One of his names has become the title of the autocratic sovereigns of Europe; another is imbedded in the calendar of all Christian countries. It is impossible in a work of this kind to set forth in detail the successive audacities and glories of his career. Born of noble family on the 12th day of the month Quintilis (afterwards called in his honor July), in the year 100 B.C., he early engaged in party strife, contracted enormous debts, but won the favor of the people, and was raised in quick succession to the highest offices of state. He was nearly forty years of age when he began his series of foreign conquests by a war in Spain. He reconciled Pompey to Crassus, the wealthiest man in Rome, and with them formed the first triumvirate, to accomplish their respective designs. For himself he obtained command of Gaul for five years, and there, in wars with various tribes, trained an army by which he hoped to terminate the party struggles at Rome. He crossed the Rhine into Germany and the Channel into Britain, but effected no permanent conquests in either country. When Pompey saw that his own prestige was eclipsed by that of his younger rival, he became estranged. Cæsar was ordered by the Senate to disband his army, but in defiance crossed the Rubicon, the boundary of his province, towards Rome. Pompey saw his troops deserting him, and fled from Rome to

Capua, and thence to Greece, where he collected a formidable army. Cæsar was made dictator, but did not cross to Greece until some months later. At Pharsalia the decisive battle took place on the 9th of August, 48 B.C. Pompey fled and was slain on the coast of Egypt. Cæsar was now master of the Roman world and, though careless of human life in time of war, used his power with marked clemency. His victories in Gaul, Egypt, Pontus and Africa were celebrated with magnificent triumphs; but there was none for his victory in the Civil War. Although he inaugurated numerous schemes for the benefit of the Roman people, the patricians could not witness his success without envy. He was already dictator, and was made imperator (emperor) for life, but after a movement was begun to bestow on him the hated title of king, he was assassinated in the Senate house on the 15th of March, 44 B.C.

This great statesman and general was gifted by nature with the most varied talents, and excelled in the most diverse pursuits. He was an accomplished orator and a profound jurist. He holds high rank in literature by brief and perspicuous narratives of the Gallic and Civil wars in which he was engaged. These "Commentaries," as he chose to call them rather than histories, are models of historical composition. His style is noted for its purity and elegance. In youth he wrote some poems, which were suppressed by Augustus; in later life he did not disdain to compose some grammatical treatises, of which a few fragments remain. But the world has especially cherished and admired his modest narrative of his astonishing career in Gaul.

CÆSAR'S FIRST INVASION OF BRITAIN.

Though but a small part of the summer now remained, Cæsar resolved to pass over into Britain, having certain intelligence that in all his wars with the Gauls, the enemies of the commonwealth had ever received assistance from thence. He indeed foresaw that the season of the year would not permit him to finish the war; yet he thought it would be of no small advantage if he should but take a view of the island, learn the nature of the inhabitants, and acquaint himself with the coast, harbors and landing places, to all which the Gauls were perfect strangers, for almost none but merchants resort to that island, nor have even they any knowledge of the country, except the sea coast and the parts opposite to Gaul. Before he embarked himself, he thought proper to send C. Volusenus with a galley to get some knowledge of these things, commanding him, as soon as he had informed himself in what he wanted to know, to return with all expedition. He himself marched with his whole army into the territory of the Morini, because thence was the nearest passage into Britain. Here he ordered a great many ships from the neighboring ports to attend him, and the fleet he had made use of the year before in the Venetian war.

Meanwhile, the Britons having notice of his design by the merchants that resorted to their island, ambassadors from many of their states came to Cæsar with an offer of hostages and submission to the authority of the people of Rome. To these he gave a favorable audience, and, exhorting them to continue in the same mind, sent them back into their own country. Along with them he dispatched Commius, whom he had appointed king of the Atrebatians, a man in whose virtue, wisdom and fidelity he greatly confided, and whose authority in the island was very considerable. To him he gave it in charge to visit as many states as he could and persuade them to enter into an alliance with the Romans, letting them know at the same time that Cæsar designed as soon as possible to come over in person to their island. Volusenus, having taken a view of the country, as far as was possible for one who had resolved not to quit his ship or trust himself in the hands of the barbarians, returned on the fifth day and acquainted Cæsar with his discoveries.

Cæsar, having got together about eighty transports, which he thought would be sufficient for carrying over two legions, distributed the galleys he had over and above to the questor, lieutenants and officers of the cavalry. There were, besides, eighteen transports detained by contrary winds at a port about eight miles off, which he appointed to carry over the cavalry.

Temple of Vesta.—Restored.

The wind springing up fair, he weighed anchor about one in the morning, ordering the cavalry to embark at the other port and follow him. But as these orders were executed but slowly, he himself about ten in the morning reached the coast of Britain, where he saw all the cliffs covered with the enemy's forces. The nature of the place was such that the sea being bounded by steep mountains, the enemy might easily launch their javelins upon us from above. Not thinking this, therefore, a convenient landing place, he resolved to lie by till three in the afternoon and wait the arrival of the rest of his fleet. Meanwhile, having called the lieutenants and military tribunes together, he informed them of what he had learned from Volusenus, instructed them in the part they were to act, and particularly exhorted them to do everything with readiness and at a signal given, agreeably to the rules of military discipline, since sea affairs especially require expedition and dispatch, because the most changeable and uncertain of all. Having dismissed them, and finding both the wind and tide favorable, he made the signal for weighing anchor, and after sailing about eight miles farther, stopped over against a plain and open shore.

But the barbarians, perceiving our design, sent forward their cavalry and chariots, which they frequently make use of in battle, and following with the rest of their forces, endeavored to oppose our landing; and indeed we found the difficulty very great on many accounts; for our ships being large, required a great depth of water; and the soldiers, who were wholly unacquainted with the places, and had their hands embarrassed and loaded with a weight of armor, were at the same time to leap from the ships, stand breast high amidst the waves, and encounter the enemy, while they, fighting upon dry ground, or advancing only a little way into the water, having the free use of all their limbs, and in places which they perfectly knew, could boldly cast their darts, and spur on their horses, well inured to that kind of service. All these circumstances serving to spread a terror among our men, who were wholly strangers to this way of fighting, they did not push the enemy with the same vigor and spirit as was usual for them in combats upon dry ground.

Cæsar, observing this, ordered some galleys, a kind of vessels less common with the barbarians, and more easily governed and put in motion, to advance a little from the transports towards the shore, in order to set upon the enemy in flank, and by means of their engines, slings, and arrows, drive them to some distance. This proved of considerable service to our men, for what with the surprise occasioned by the shape of our galleys, the motion of the oars, and the playing of the engines, the enemy were forced to halt, and in a little time began to give back. But when our men still delayed to leap into the sea, chiefly because of the depth of the water in those places, the standard-bearer of the tenth legion, having first invoked the gods for success, cried out aloud: "Follow me, fellow-soldiers, unless you will betray the Roman eagle into the hands of the enemy; for my part, I am resolved to discharge my duty to Cæsar and the commonwealth." Upon this he jumped into the sea, and advanced with the eagle against the enemy; whereat, our men exhorting one another to prevent so signal a disgrace, all that were in the ship followed him. When this was perceived by those in the nearest vessels, they did likewise, and boldly approached the enemy.

The battle was obstinate on both sides; but our men, as being neither able to keep their ranks, nor get firm footing, nor followed their respective standards, because leaping promiscuously from their ships, every one joined the first ensign he met, were thereby thrown into great confusion. The enemy, on the other hand, being well acquainted with the shallows, when they saw our men advancing singly from the ships, spurred on their horses, and attacked them in that perplexity. In one place great numbers would gather round an handful of the Romans; others falling upon them in flank, galled them mightily with their darts, which Cæsar observing, ordered some small boats to be manned, and ply about with recruits. By this means the foremost ranks of our men having got firm footing, were followed by all the rest, when falling upon the enemy briskly, they were soon put to rout. But as the cavalry were not yet arrived, we could not pursue or advance far into the island, which was the only thing wanting to render the victory complete.

The enemy being thus vanquished in battle, no sooner got together after their defeat, than they dispatched ambassadors to Cæsar to sue for peace, offering hostages, and an entire submission to his commands. Along with these ambassadors came Commius the Atrebatian, whom Cæsar, as we have related above, had sent before him into Britain. The natives seized him as soon as he landed, and though he was charged with a commission from Cæsar, threw him into irons. But upon their late defeat, they thought proper to send him back, throwing the blame of what had happened upon the multitude, and begged of Cæsar to excuse a fault proceeding from ignorance. Cæsar, after some complaints of their behavior, in that having of their own accord sent ambassadors to the Continent to sue for peace, they had yet without any reason begun a war against him, told them at last he would forgive their fault, and ordered them to send a certain number of hostages. Part were sent immediately, and the rest, as living at some distance, they promised to deliver in a few days. Meantime they disbanded their troops, and the several chiefs came to Cæsar's camp to manage their own concerns and those of the states to which they belonged.

A peace being thus concluded four days after Cæsar's arrival in Britain, the eighteen transports appointed to carry the cavalry, of whom we have spoken above, put to sea with a gentle gale. But when they had so near approached the coast as to be even within view of the camp, so violent a storm suddenly arose, that being unable to hold on their course, some were obliged to return to the port whence they set out, and others were driven to the lower end of the island, westward, not without great danger; there they cast anchor, but the waves rising very high, so as to fill the ships with water, they were again in the night obliged to stand out to sea, and make for the Continent of Gaul. That very night it happened to be full moon, when the tides upon the sea coast always rise highest, a thing at that time wholly unknown to the Romans. Thus at one and the same time, the galleys which Cæsar made use of to transport his men, and which he had ordered to be drawn up on the strand, were filled with the tide, and the tempest fell furiously upon the transports that lay at anchor in the road; nor was it possible for our men to attempt anything for their preservation. Many of the ships being dashed to pieces, and the rest having lost their anchors, tackle, and rigging, which rendered them altogether unfit for sailing, a general consternation spread itself through the camp; for there were no other ships to carry back the troops, nor any materials to repair those that had been disabled by the tempest. And as it had been all along Cæsar's design to winter in Gaul, he was wholly without grain to subsist the troops in those parts.

All this being known to the British chiefs, who after the battle had repaired to Cæsar's camp, to perform the conditions of the treaty, they began to hold conferences among themselves; and as they plainly saw that the Romans were destitute both of cavalry, shipping, and grain, and easily judged from the smallness of the camp, that the number of their troops was but inconsiderable; in which notion they were the more confirmed, because Cæsar having brought over the legions without baggage, had occasion to inclose but a small spot of ground; they thought this a convenient opportunity for taking up arms, and by intercepting the Roman convoys, to protract the affair till winter; being confidently persuaded, that by defeating these troops, or cutting off their return, they should effectually put a stop to all future attempts upon Britain. Having, therefore, entered into a joint confederacy, they by degrees left the camp, and began to draw the islanders together; but Cæsar, though he was not yet apprized of their design, yet guessing in part at their intentions, by the disaster which had befallen his fleet, and their delays in relation to the hostages, determined to provide against all chances. He, therefore, had grain daily brought in to his camp, and ordered the timber of the ships that had been most damaged to be made use of in repairing the rest, sending to Gaul for what other materials he wanted. As the soldiers were indefatigable in this service, his fleet was soon in a condition to sail, having lost only twelve ships.

During these transactions, the seventh legion being sent out to forage, according to custom, as part were employed in cutting down the grain, and part in carrying it to the camp, without suspicion of attack, news was brought to Cæsar, that a greater cloud of dust than ordinary was seen on that side where the legion was. Cæsar, suspecting how matters went, marched with the cohorts that were upon guard, ordering two others to take their places, and all the soldiers in the camp to arm and follow him as soon as possible. When he was advanced a little way from the camp, he saw his men overpowered by the enemy, and with great difficulty able to sustain the fight, being driven into a small compass, and exposed on every side to the darts of their adversaries. For as the harvest had been gathered in everywhere else, and only one field left, the enemy suspecting that our men would come thither to forage, had hid themselves during the night in the woods, and waiting till our men had quitted their arms, and ispersed themselves for reaping, they suddenly attacked them, killed some, put the rest into disorder, and began to surround them with their horses and chariots.

Their way of fighting with their chariots is this: first they drive their chariots on all sides, and throw their darts, insomuch, that by the very terror of the horses, and noise of the wheels, they often break the ranks of the enemy. When they have forced their way into the midst of the cavalry, they quit their chariots, and fight on foot; meantime the drivers retire a little from the combat, and place themselves in such a manner as to favor the retreat of their countrymen, should they be overpowered by the enemy. Thus in action they perform the part both of nimble horsemen and stable infantry; and by continual exercise and use have arrived at such expertness, that in the most steep and difficult places they can stop their horses upon a full stretch, turn them which way they please, run along the pole, rest on the harness, and throw themselves back into their chariots with incredible dexterity.

Our men being astonished and confounded with this new way of fighting, Cæsar came very timely to their relief; for upon his approach the enemy made a stand, and the Romans began to recover from their fear. This satisfied Cæsar for the present, who not thinking it a proper season to provoke the enemy, and bring on a general engagement, stood facing them for some time, and then led back the legions to the camp. The continual rains that followed for some days after, both kept the Romans within their intrenchments, and withheld the enemy from attacking us. Meantime the Britons dispatched messengers into all parts, to make known to their countrymen the small number of the Roman troops and the favorable opportunity they had of making immense spoils and freeing their country for ever from all future invasions by storming the enemy's camp. Having by this means got together a great body of infantry and cavalry, they drew towards our intrenchments.

Cæsar, though he foresaw that the enemy, if beaten, would in the same manner as before escape the danger by flight; yet having got about thirty horse, whom Commius the Atrebatian had brought over with him from Gaul, he drew up the legions in order of battle before the camp; and falling upon the Britons, who were not able to sustain the shock of our men, soon put them to flight. The Romans, pursuing them as long as their strength would permit, made a terrible slaughter, and setting fire to their houses and villages a great way round, returned to the camp.

The same day ambassadors came from the enemy to Cæsar, to sue for peace. Cæsar doubled the number of hostages he had before imposed upon them, and ordered them to be sent over to him into Gaul, because the equinox coming on, and his ships being leaky, he thought it not prudent to put off his return till winter. A fair wind offering, he set sail a little after midnight, and arrived safe in Gaul.

The Battle of Pharsalia.

There was as much space left between the two lines as sufficed for the onset of the hostile armies; but Pompey had ordered his soldiers to await Cæsar's attack, and not to advance from their positions, or suffer their line to be put into disorder. And he is said to have done this by advice of Caius Triarius, that the impetuosity of the charge of Cæsar's soldiers might be checked and their line broken, and that Pompey's troops, remaining in their ranks, might attack them when in disorder; and he thought that the javelins would fall with less force if the soldiers were kept on their ground than if they met them in full course; at the same time he trusted that Cæsar's soldiers, after running over double the usual ground, would become exhausted by the fatigue. But to me Pompey seems to have acted without sufficient reason; for there is a certain impetuosity of spirit and an alacrity implanted by nature in the hearts of all men, which is inflamed by a desire to meet the foe. This a general should endeavor not to repress, but to increase; nor was it a vain institution of our ancestors that the trumpets should sound on all sides and a general shout be raised; by which they imagined that the enemy were struck with terror, and their own army inspired with courage.

But our men, when the signal was given, rushed forward with their javelins ready to be launched, but perceiving that Pompey's men did not run to meet the charge, having acquired experience by custom, and being practiced in former battles, they of their own accord repressed their speed and halted almost midway, that they might not come up with the enemy when their strength was exhausted; and after a short respite they again renewed their course and threw their javelins, and instantly drew their swords, as Cæsar had ordered them. Nor did Pompey's men fail in this crisis, for they received our javelins, stood our charge, and maintained their ranks; and having launched their javelins, had recourse to their swords. At the same time Pompey's horsemen, according to their orders, rushed out at once from his left wing, and his whole host of archers poured after them. Our cavalry did not withstand their charge, but gave ground a little, upon which Pompey's troops pressed them more vigorously, and began to file off in troops and flank our army.

When Cæsar perceived this he gave the signal to his fourth line, which he had formed of the six cohorts. They instantly rushed forward and charged Pompey's cavalry with such fury that not a man of them stood; but all wheeling about, not only quitted their posts, but galloped forward to seek refuge in the highest mountains. By their retreat the archers and slingers, being left destitute and defenseless, were all cut to pieces. The cohorts, pursuing their success, wheeled about upon Pompey's left wing, while his infantry still continued to make battle, and taking them in the rear at the same time Cæsar ordered the third line to advance, which till then had not been engaged, but had kept their post. These new and fresh troops having come to the assistance of the fatigued, and others having made an attack upon their rear, Pompey's men were not able to maintain their ground, but all fled; nor was Cæsar mistaken in his opinion, that the victory, as he had declared in his speech to the soldiers, must have its beginning from these six cohorts, which he had placed as the fourth line to oppose the horse. For by them the cavalry were routed, by them the archers and slingers were cut to pieces, by them the left wing of Pompey's army was surrounded and obliged to be the first to fly. . . .

In Pompey's camp you might see arbors, in which tables laid; a large quantity of plate set out; the floors of the tents covered with fresh sods; the tents of Lucius Lentulus and others shaded with ivy; and many other things which were proofs of excessive luxury and a confidence of victory; so that it might readily be inferred that they had no premonitions of the issue of the day, as they indulged themselves in unnecessary pleasures, and yet upbraided with luxury Cæsar's army, distressed and suffering troops, who had always been in want of common necessaries.

Pompey, as soon as our men had forced the trenches, mounting his horse and stripping off his general's habit, went hastily out of the back gate of the camp, and galloped with all speed to Larissa. Nor did he stop there, but with the same dispatch, collecting a few of his flying troops, and halting neither day nor night, he arrived at the sea-shore attended by only thirty horsemen, and went on board a victualling bark, often complaining, as we have been told, that he had been so deceived in his expectation, that he was almost persuaded that he had been betrayed by those from whom he had expected victory, when they began the fight.

CHAPTER XV.

The Age of Augustus.

Virgil, the greatest poet of Italy, was born in the Cisalpine town of Mantua in 70 B. C. He was educated in Rome and became an earnest student. While comparatively young he came under the influence of one of Augustus' ministers, who encouraged men of letters, and sought to create a literary spirit in Rome.

The Eclogues—a series of short, pastoral poems, were the first of his writings to be published. They marked a new epoch in literature, but whether it was the dawn of a golden age, or a period of decadence in Roman literature, men have not always been agreed. These poems were unquestionably modeled after poems of Theocritus.

"The mood of the Eclogues is one most natural to man's spirit in the beautiful lands of Southern Europe. The freshness and softness of Italian scenes are present in the Eclogues, in the rich music of the Italian language, while it still retained the strength, fulness and majesty of its tones. These poems are truly representative of Italy, not as a land of old civilization, or historic renown, of great cities, of corn-crops and vineyards—'the mighty mother of fruits and men'; but as a land of a soft and genial air, beautiful with the tender foliage and fresh flowers and blossoms of spring, and with the rich coloring of autumn; a land which has most attuned man's nature to the influences of music and of pictorial art. As a true and exquisite symbol of this vein of sentiment associated with Italy the Eclogues hold a not unworthy place beside the greater work—the 'temple of solid marble'—which the matured art of Virgil dedicated to the genius of his country, and beside the more composite but stately and massive monument which perpetuates the national glory of Rome."

The Georgics, Virgil's next effort, were undertaken with a distinct purpose: that of leading people back to rural Italy, which in the later republic had been depopulated, while the idle of the cities constantly increased. In following the development of events in Rome, we have seen that the death blow was dealt the small farmer when the state agreed to supply grain to the populace for less than its market price. Farming could no longer be carried on profitably, and the small farmers got rid of their lands and flocked to the capital in hope of finding employment. When to win their favor politicians secured the passage of the free grain law, and when to retain this favor ambitious aspirants for office provided free shows, the tendency became strong to abandon honest labor and drift with the idle mobs. With free bread and occasional entertainment the crowds in the city sold their votes to the highest bidder, and sank lower and lower in virtue and morality.

Such being the condition of society during the late republic and principate, Virgil produced a work which in many respects may be compared with Hesiod's Works and Days—a didactic poem giving instruction in the simple laws of husbandry. The quiet beauty of modest farm houses and fields of grain, of cattle, of reaping and sowing and gathering into barns—all this is reflected in the Georgics. Virgil's boyhood and his residence in the country during his later life well fitted him for this theme.

Falling into four books, the first treats of the tilling of the soil; the signs of the weather, which must be regarded by him who would prosper; of implements needed for earth's cultivation, etc. The second book offers instruction in the culture of trees and the vine. The third deals with the care of horses and the fourth of bee culture. Mythology and legendary lore were closely interwoven with the precepts offered. 'The glorification of Italy' in its widest scope was Virgil's theme. To this end, the rustic beauty of the peninsula was pictured, the productive possibilities of the land dwelt upon and the whole work savors of freshly-turned soil, heavy-laden trees, fragrant vines, contented cattle, and humming bees. Such a production forthcoming at this time was bound to draw men's attention away from the sordid interests of the town to the broader, freer air of country life.

Virgil's epic, the Aeneid, was published after his death and against his wishes. Having contracted a fever while travelling in Sicily, he returned to Italy and died in 19 B. C. He was buried at Naples. Through some misinterpretation of his writings he was believed to have foretold the coming of Christ, and during the Middle Ages his tomb was regarded as a shrine.

Realizing his precarious condition, Virgil desired his last work—the Aeneid—to be burned, because he felt that it needed additional labor which he could not give. However, the wishes of others persuaded him to allow it to stand, and from the first it was very popular.

This epic—perhaps the greatest of Latin writings, tells the story of the coming of Aeneas from burning Troy and his arrival in Italy, where he founded the Latin kingdom. The greatness of Rome was magnified and confidence of the Romans of the empire strengthened in the destiny of the city which had come so auspiciously into being. Rome then encompassed the ancient world; the wonders of the Orient, the riches of many kingdoms had fallen to her share. Rome, *Rome,* her strength, her vastness, her supremacy, all were extolled in this mighty epic.

"The first great epic poem of the ancient world is buoyant with the promise of the mighty life which was to be; the last great epic is weighty with the accumulated experience of all that had been. The stream of epic poetry shows no longer the jubilant force and purity of waters which rise in the high mountain-land separating barbarism from civilization; it moves more slowly and less clearly through more level and cultivated districts; its volume is swollen and its weight increased by tributaries which have never known the 'bright speed' of its nobler sources."

Second only to Virgil was another poet who made brilliant this age of Augustus, prince of the Roman people. Horace was born in 65 B. C., the son of a freedman. However humble his own origin, this man was determined to give his son the best possible education. He went to Rome in order that Horace might study there, and later sent the boy to Athens. Horace referred to his father's care in giving him good educational opportunities:

> "If pure and innocent I live, and dear
> To those I love (self-praise is venial here),
> All this I owe my father, who, though poor,
> Lord of some few lean acres, and no more,
> Was loath to send me to the village school,
> Whereto the sons of men of mark and rule—
> Centurions and the like—were wont to swarm,
> With slate and satchel on sinister arm,
> And the poor dole of scanty pence to pay
> The starveling teacher monthly to the day;
> But boldly took me when a boy to Rome,
> There to be taught all arts, that grace the home
> Of knight and senator."

Later, when Brutus and Octavius waged war with one another, Horace took the side of Brutus. After the war he returned to Rome and received his pardon. His later years were passed rather quietly, at the capital and at his Sabine farm.

Although Virgil sang of loftier themes, Horace has been at least as popular in modern times. Best-loved are his odes, which far from being the spontaneous outpourings of a passionate soul, are the studied result of painstaking effort. His epodes, satires and epistles have also found an abiding place in Latin literature.

Of Propertius, a contemporary and friend of Virgil, little is known. His fame rests upon four books of elegies. Love was the theme of many of his poems. The poet seems to have been given to introspections of a gloomy nature, although we possess too little data regarding him to understand his temperament and character.

Ovid has sometimes been called the society poet. He belonged to the equestrian order. Born in 43 B. C., he was given ample opportunities for studying in Rome, Athens and Syria, as were the sons of wealthy families at this time. Although it was at first expected that he would take his place as a public man in Rome, Ovid soon withdrew from political life, the better to enjoy a life of ease and social pleasure. He shortly became a popular leader among those who made up the idle, pleasure-seeking element of the upper classes.

Against the lavish expenditure of wealth, the display, the indulgences, laxity and moral degeneracy of these classes, Augustus spared no effort. He sought to limit the reckless waste of money, to restore the moral tone and bring back the sense of social responsibility which had prevailed in earlier times. To this end he issued his sumptuary laws, imposing penalties upon those who failed to comply with the new social regulations. Teaching by example as well as by precept, this prince of the Roman people lived in simplicity, preferring garments woven by his own family to the most luxurious imported fabric. In every respect his family was conducted after the wholesome manner of the early republic. Meantime his only daughter, Julia, was a leader of Rome's most shameless and sensual circles, far surpassing any of her companions in the extremes to which she was willing to go. At last, obliged to take notice of her conduct, which had long been the wonder of the capital, Augustus caused her to be exiled and imprisoned. Her daughter and namesake followed in her mother's footsteps, and became involved in many intrigues.

In circles where life passed in this way, Ovid moved easily, and for the diversion of his friends wrote lightly of the weakness of society around him. In the *Art of Love* he touched, with light, jesting air, upon all that pertained to the winning of purely sensual love. Young men desirous of winning hearts were advised to go to the gladiatorial shows, where, under excitement of the fight, women would be found more susceptible to the blandishments of lovers. Having explained how their favor might be won, Ovid showed how it might be retained. The whole poem is wholly immoral, but was written with such apparent lack of earnestness that it probably made little impression upon its Roman readers, to whom such doings were too common to excite comment.

Far greater than this was the series of mythological stories known as the Metamorphoses. Before this latter work was completed, an imperial edict commanded Ovid to leave Rome and go into exile to a small settlement on the Black Sea, where the remainder of his days were spent. The cause of the action on the part of Augustus will never be known, but it was possibly due to the implication of the poet in some scandal connected with the granddaughter of the prince. The immorality of the *Art of Love* was assigned as the reason by many, but this is nonsense, since the poem had already been published ten years.

The Metamorphoses was considered by Ovid to be his strongest production. He concluded with the lines:

> "And now my work is done; which not Jove's wrath,
> Nor fire, nor sword, nor all-consuming age
> Can e'er destroy. Let when it will that day,
> Which only o'er this body's frame has power,
> Make ending of my life's uncertain space;
> Yet shall the better part of me be borne
> Above the lofty stars through countless years,
> And ever undestroyed shall be my name.
> Where'er the Roman power o'er conquered lands
> Extends, shall I be read by many tongues,
> And through all ages, if there's aught of truth
> In prophecies of bards, my fame shall live."

In exile Ovid addressed many conciliatory lines to the prince, but no official notice was taken of them. After the death of Augustus friends of Ovid still hoped for his release, but Tiberius soon showed that nothing could be expected from him by way of favor. Under such conditions Ovid's ability lessened, and his writings became little else than complaints against the fate that held him in exile from the capital.

Livy: Greatest Roman Historian.

The most distinguished prose writer of the Augustan age was Livy. Of his personal experiences we know little. Born in the town of Padua in 69 B. C., he removed to Rome when still a young man, spending the greater portion of his later life in the capital. However, he never seems to have broken away from his earlier associations and he died in Padua in 17 A. D.

Livy's gigantic work was a history of Rome: *Libri ab Urbe Condita*, or Books from the Foundations of the City. The whole treatise comprised one hundred and forty-two books, and covered the development of Rome from its beginning to

9 A. D. Livy had intended nothing so comprehensive, but after fame and renown had long been accorded him, he says that he continued his history from force of habit. He found himself restless and unhappy when not prosecuting a task that had become the predominating interest of his life.

At the time Livy lived and wrote there was much in Roman life to call forth the disapproval of the discerning, and serious men found satisfaction in reverting to the earlier periods of Roman development, when patriotism had been wellnigh universal and when the moral tone of the country had been pure. Livy was a conservative; he always avoided extremes. When it was plain that the days of popular governments were passed he adapted himself easily to a one-man rule, although without doubt he was gratified to find the forms of the republic preserved. He made few enemies and was highly regarded by men of his own day. We are told that one who deeply revered his writings traveled from Spain to see Livy, and having seen him, returned home without staying to see the wonders of the great capital. It was enough to look upon the man who had recorded the deeds of his country for future ages.

Of the original one hundred and forty-two books, only thirty-five remain to us. Both in mediaeval and modern times these have been highly prized. However, in the light of modern investigation no great dependence can be placed upon the historical data these books supply. It is the task of the modern historian to carefully separate fact from fiction, exaggerated statements from accurate truth, and to weigh authority. Livy had access to a vast deal of material which has not survived. When he understood the truth, he faithfully recorded it with clearness and directness. When his authorities differed, however, he appears to have chosen among them quite at random, with little effort to ascertain the facts in the case. Even with the destruction of the ages, had Livy compiled his history after the fashion of Thucydides we might yet have hoped to come to an understanding of early Rome. As it is, in spite of Livy's surviving books, any detailed account of the Romans before the time of the Gracchi can never be hoped for.

The language of the history is wellnigh perfect, and it is

for its merits as a literary masterpiece that it is particularly valued today. As has been noted, the age of Cicero marked the most perfect prose expression of Roman literature, and after that age the tendency was toward a gradual decline. Poetical and flowery language drifted into prose to a damaging extent. Nevertheless, Livy's writings show little of this fault and even where such criticism has been drawn forth, investigation reveals a mere reflection of contemporary usage rather than any studied attempt to produce effects of sound at the expense of clearness and meaning.

FAUN OR SATYR OF PRAXITELES.

Rules of Husbandry.

Many the precepts of the men of old,
I can recount thee, so thou start not back,
And such slight cares to learn not weary thee.
And this among the first: Your threshing-floor
With ponderous roller must be levelled smooth,
And wrought by hand, and fixed with binding chalk,
Lest weeds arise, or dust a passage win
Splitting the surface, then a thousand plagues
Make sport of it; oft builds the tiny mouse
Her home, and plants her granary, underground,
Or burrow for their bed the purblind moles,
Or toad is found in hollows, and all the swarm
Of earth's unsightly creatures; or a huge
Corn-heap the weevil plunders, and the ant,
Fearful of coming age and penury.
Mark, too, what time the walnut in the woods
With ample bloom shall clothe her, and bow down
Her odorous branches: if the fruit prevail,
Like store of grain will follow, and there shall come
A mighty winnowing-time with mighty heat;
But if the shade with wealth of leaves abound,
Vainly your threshing-floor will bruise the stalks
Swoln but with chaff. Many myself have seen
Steep, as they sow, their pulse-seeds, drenching them
With lees of oil and natron, that the fruit
Might swell within the treacherous pods, and they
Make speed to boil at howso' small a fire.
Yet, culled with caution, proved with patient toil,
These have I seen degenerate, did not man
Put forth his hand with power, and year by year
Choose out the largest. So, by fate impelled,
Speed all things to the worse, and backward borne
Glide from us; even as who with struggling oars
Up stream scarce pulls a shallop, if his arms
Relax but for one moment, and the boat
Is headlong swept adown the hurrying tide.

—*Georgics I. Rhoades' trans.*

The Golden Mean.

Licinius, wouldst thou steer life's wiser voyage,
Neither launch always into deep mid-waters,
Nor hug the shores, and, shrinking from the tempest,
    Hazard the quicksand.

He who elects the golden mean of fortune,
Nor where dull squalor rots the time-worn hovel,
Nor where fierce envy storms the new-built palace,
    Makes his safe dwelling.

The wildest winds rock most the loftiest pine-trees,
The heaviest crash is that of falling towers,
The spots on earth most stricken by the lightning
    Are its high places.

The mind well-trained to cope with either fortune,
Take hope in adverse things and fear in prosperous;
Deforming winters are restored or banished
    By the same Father.

If today frown, not therefore frowns tomorrow;
His deadly bow not always bends Apollo,
His hand at times the silent muse awakens
    With the sweet harpstring.

In life's sore straits brace and display thy courage;
Boldness is wisdom then; as wisely timid
When thy sails swell with winds too strongly fav'ring,
    Heed, and contract them.
    —*Horace: Odes, II, 10. Trans. Lord Lytton.*

SIMPLICITY.

Off with the Persian gear, I hate it,
   Hate the wreaths with limebark bound,
Care not where the latest roses
   Linger on the ground.

Bring me myrtle, naught but myrtle!
   Myrtle, boy, will well combine
Thee attending, me carousing,
   'Neath the trellised vine.
       —*Horace: Odes 1. 38. Gladstone's trans.*

Dear girl, what boots it thus to dress thy hair,
Or flaunt in silken garments rich and rare,
To reek of perfume from a foreign mart,
And pass thyself for other than thou art—
Thus Nature's gift of beauty to deface
And rob thy own fair form of half its grace?
Trust me, no skill can greater charms impart;
Love is a naked boy and scorns all art.
Bears not the sod unbidden blossoms rare?
The untrained ivy, is it not most fair?
Greenest the shrub on rocks untended grows,
Brightest the rill in unhewn channel flows.
The beach is with unpolished pebbles gay,
The birds untutored trill the sweetest lay.
Not thus the damsels of the golden age
Were wont the hearts of heroes to engage:
Their loveliness was to no jewels due,
But to such tints as once Apelles drew.
From vain coquettish arts they all were free,
Content to charm with simple modesty.
By thee despite to me will ne'er be done;
The woman pleases well who pleases one.
       —*Propertius. Trans. Goldwin Smith.*

Tityrus and Meliboeus.

In this First Eclogue, under a transparent disguise, are set forth the sufferings of Virgil (Tityrus) and his neighbors near Mantua, when their lands were distributed to the victorious soldiers of Augustus, and also the special favor which Virgil received from the emperor in having his farm restored.

Meliboeus. Beneath the shade which beechen boughs
 diffuse,
You, Tityrus, entertain your sylvan muse.
Round the wide world in banishment we roam,
Forc'd from our pleasing fields and native home;
While, stretch'd at ease, you sing your happy loves,
And "Amaryllis" fills the shady groves.
 Tityrus. These blessings, friend, a deity bestow'd;
For never can I deem him less than God.
The tender firstlings of my woolly breed
Shall on his holy altar often bleed.
He gave my kine to graze the flow'ry plain,
And to my pipe renew'd the rural strain.
 Mel. I envy not your fortune, but admire,
That, while the raging sword and wasteful fire
Destroy the wretched neighborhood around,
No hostile arms approach your happy ground.
Far diff'rent is my fate: my feeble goats
With pains I drive from their forsaken cotes.
This one, you see, I scarcely drag along,
Who, yearning, on the rocks has left her young;
The hope and promise of my falling fold.
My loss, by dire portents the gods foretold;
For, had I not been blind, I might have seen—
Yon riven oak, the fairest of the green,
And the hoarse raven, on the blasted bough,
By croaking from the left, presaged the coming blow.
But tell me, Tityrus, what heavenly power
Preserved your fortune in that fatal hour?
 Tit. Fool that I was, I thought imperial Rome
Like Mantua, where on market days we come,
And thither drive our tender lambs from home.
So kids and whelps their sires and dams express;

And so the great I measur'd by the less.
But country towns, compar'd with her, appear
Like shrubs, when lofty cypresses are near.
> *Mel.* What great occasion called you hence to Rome?
> *Tit.* Freedom, which came at length, though slow to come.

Nor did my search of liberty begin
Till my black hairs were changed upon my chin;
Nor Amaryllis would vouchsafe a look,
Till Galatea's meaner bonds I broke.
Till then, a hapless, hopeless, homely swain,
I sought not freedom, nor aspired to gain:
Though many a victim from my folds was bought
And many a cheese to country markets brought,
Yet all the little that I got, I spent,
And still returned as empty as I went.
> *Mel.* We stood amazed to see your mistress mourn,

Unknowing that she pined for your return;
We wondered why she kept her fruit so long,
For whom so late the ungathered apples hung.
But now the wonder ceases, since I see
She kept them, only, Tityrus, for thee.
For thee the bubbling springs appeared to mourn,
And whisp'ring pines made vows for thy return.
> *Tit.* What should I do?—While here I was enchain'd.

No glimpse of god-like liberty remained;
Nor could I hope in any place but there,
To find a god so present to my prayer.
There first the youth of heavenly birth I viewed,
For whom our monthly victims are renewed.
He heard my vows, and graciously decreed
My grounds to be restored, my former flocks to feed.
> *Mel.* O fortunate old man! whose farm remains—

For you sufficient—and requites your pains;
Though rushes overspread the neighb'ring plains,
Though here the marshy grounds approach your fields,
And there the soil a stony harvest yields.
Your teeming ewes shall no strange meadows try,
Nor fear a rot from tainted company,
Behold! yon bord'ring fence of sallow trees
Is fraught with flow'rs, the flow'rs are fraught with bees—
The busy bees, with a soft murmuring strain,

Invite to gentle sleep the lab'ring swain,
While, from the neighb'ring rock, with rural songs,
The pruner's voice the pleasing dream prolongs,
Stock-doves and turtles tell their am'rous pain,
And from the lofty elms, of love complain.

Tit. Th' inhabitants of seas and skies shall change,
And fish on shore, and stags in air shall range,
The banish'd Parthian dwell on Arar's brink,
And the fair German shall the Tigris drink,
Ere I, forsaking gratitude and truth,
Forget the figure of that godlike youth.

Mel. But we must beg our bread in climes unknown,
Beneath the scorching or the freezing zone:
And some to far Oaxis shall be sold,
Or try the Libyan heat or Scythian cold;
The rest among the Britons be confin'd,
A race of men from all the world disjoin'd.
Oh! must the wretched exiles ever mourn,
Nor, after length of rolling years, return?
Are we condemn'd by fate's unjust decree,
No more our houses and our homes to see?
Or shall we mount again the rural throne,
And rule the country kingdoms once our own;
Did we for these barbarians plant and sow?
On these—on these—our happy fields bestow?
Good heaven! what dire effects from civil discord flow!
Now let me graft my pears, and prune the vine;
The fruit is theirs, the labor only mine.
Farewell, my pastures, my paternal stock,
My fruitful fields, and my more fruitful flock!
No more, my goats, shall I behold you climb
The steepy cliffs, or crop the flow'ry thyme!
No more, extended in the grot below,
Shall see you browsing on the mountain's brow
The prickly shrubs; and after on the bare,
Leap down the deep abyss, and hang in air.
No more my sheep shall sip the morning dew;
No more my song shall please the rural crew:
Adieu, my tuneful pipe! and all the world, adieu!

Tit. This night, at least, with me forget your care,
Chestnuts and curds and cream shall be your fare:
The carpet-ground shall be with leaves o'erspread;

And boughs shall weave a cov'ring for your head,
For see, yon sunny hill the shade extends,
And curling smoke from cottages ascends.

POLLIO.

The Fourth Eclogue, addressed to Virgil's friend, the consul Pollio, probably on the birth of his son, is a remarkable prophecy of a speedy return of the Golden Age. The Muse is called Sicilian because Theocritus, the Greek pastoral poet, was a native of Sicily.

Sicilian Muse, begin a loftier strain!
Though lowly shrubs and trees, that shade the plain,
Delight not all; Sicilian Muse, prepare
To make the vocal woods deserve a consul's care.
The last great age, foretold by sacred rhymes,
Renews its finish'd course: Saturnian times
Roll round again; and mighty years begun
From their first orb, in radiant circles run.
The base degenerate iron offspring ends,
A golden progeny from heaven descends.
O chaste Lucina! speed the mother's pains,
And haste the glorious birth! thine own Apollo reigns!
The lovely boy, with his auspicious face,
Shall Pollio's consulship and triumph grace:
Majestic months set out with him to their appointed race.
The father banished virtue shall restore;
And crimes shall threat the guilty world no more.
The son shall lead the life of gods, and be
By gods and heroes seen, and gods and heroes see.
The jarring nations he in peace shall bind,
And with paternal virtues rule mankind.
Unbidden, earth shall wreathing ivy bring,
And fragrant herbs, the promises of spring,
As her first offerings to her infant king.
The goats, with strutting dugs, shall homeward speed,
And lowing herds, secure from lions, feed.
His cradle shall with rising flowers be crown'd;
The serpent's brood shall die; the sacred ground
Shall weeds and poisonous plants refuse to bear;
Each common bush shall Syrian roses wear.
But when heroic verse his youth shall raise,
And form it to hereditary praise,

Unlabored harvests shall the fields adorn,
And clustered grapes shall blush on every thorn;
The knotted oaks shall showers of honey weep,
And through the matted grass the liquid gold shall creep.
Yet, of old fraud some vestige shall remain:
The merchant still shall plough the deep for gain;
Great cities shall with walls be compassed round,
And sharpened shares shall vex the fruitful ground;
Another Tiphys shall new seas explore,
Another Argo land her chiefs upon th' Iberian shore;
Another Helen other wars create,
And great Achilles urge the Trojan fate.
And when to ripen'd manhood he shall grow,
The greedy sailor shall the seas forego:
No keel shall cut the waves for foreign ware,
For every soil shall every product bear.
The laboring hind his oxen shall disjoin:
No plough shall hurt the glebe, no pruning-hook the vine;
Nor wool shall in dissembled colors shine;
But the luxurious father of the fold,
With native purple and unborrowed gold,
Beneath his pompous fleece shall proudly sweat;
And under Tyrian robes the lamb shall bleat.
The Fates, when they this happy web have spun,
Shall bless the sacred clue and bid it smoothly run.
Mature in years, to ready honors move,
Son of celestial seed! O foster son of Jove!
See, laboring Nature calls thee to sustain
The nodding frame of heaven, and earth and main!
See, to their base restored, earth, seas, and air;
And joyful ages, from behind, in crowding ranks appear.
To sing thy praise, would heaven my breath prolong,
Infusing spirits worthy such a song,
Not Thracian Orpheus should transcend my lays,
Nor Linus, crowned with never-fading bays;
Though each his heavenly parent should inspire,
The Muse instruct the voice, and Phœbus tune the lyre.
Should Pan contend in verse, and thou my theme,
Arcadian judges should their god condemn.
Begin, auspicious boy! to cast about
Thy infant eye, and, with a smile, thy mother single out.
Thy mother well deserves that short delight,

The nauseous qualms of ten long months and travail to requite.
Then smile! the frowning infant's doom is read:
No god shall crown the board, nor goddess bless the bed.

Orpheus and Eurydice.

The well-known myth of Orpheus and his descent into Hades to recover his lost Eurydice is related incidentally in the Fourth Book of the Georgics.

> Sad Orpheus, doom'd, without a crime, to mourn
> His ravish'd bride that never shall return;
> Wild for her loss, calls down th' inflicted woes,
> And deadlier threatens, if no fate oppose.
> When urged by thee along the marshy bed,
> Th' unhappy nymph in frantic terror fled;
> She saw not, doom'd to die, across her way,
> Where, couch'd beneath the grass, the serpent lay.
> But every Dryad, their companion dead,
> O'er the high rocks their echo'd clamor spread,
> The Rhodopeian mounts with sorrow rung,
> Deep wailings burst Pangæa's cliffs among
> Sad Orithyia, and the Getæ wept,
> And loud lament down plaintive Hebrus swept.
> He, lonely, on his harp, 'mid wilds unknown,
> Sooth'd his sad love with melancholy tone:
> On thee, sweet bride! still dwelt th' undying lay,
> Thee first at dawn deplor'd, thee last at close of day.
> For thee he dar'd to pass the jaws of hell,
> And gates where death and darkness ever dwell,
> Trod with firm foot in horror's gloomy grove,
> Approach'd the throne of subterraneous Jove,
> Nor fear'd the Manes * and stern host below,
> And hearts that never felt for human woe.
> Drawn by his song from Erebus profound
> Shades and unbodied phantoms flock around,
> Countless as birds that fill the leafy bow'r
> Beneath pale eve, or winter's driving show'r.
> Matrons and sires, and unaffianc'd maids,
> Forms of bold warriors and heroic shades,
> Youths and pale infants laid upon the pyre,
> While their fond parents saw th' ascending fire:

* The Manes were the spirits of the dead.

All whom the squalid reeds and sable mud
Of slow Cocytus' unrejoicing flood,
All whom the Stygian lake's dark confine bounds,
And with nine circles, maze in maze, surrounds.
On him astonish'd Death and Tartarus gazed,
Their viper hair the wond'ring Furies raised:
Grim Cerberus stood, his triple jaws half closed,
And fixed in air Ixion's wheel reposed.
  Now ev'ry peril o'er, when Orpheus led
His rescu'd prize in triumph from the dead,
And the fair bride (so Proserpine enjoin'd)
Press'd on his path, and followed close behind,
In sweet oblivious trance of amorous thought,
The lover err'd, to sudden frenzy wrought:
Ah! venial fault! if hell had ever known
Mercy, or sense of suffering not its own.
He stopp'd, and, ah! forgetful, weak of mind,
Cast, as she reached the light, one look behind.
There die his hopes, by love alone betray'd,
He broke the law that hell's stern tyrant made;
Thrice o'er the Stygian lake a hollow sound
Portentous murmur'd from its depth profound.
"Alas! what fates our hapless love divide,
What frenzy, Orpheus, tears thee from thy bride?
Again I sink! A voice resistless calls.
Lo! on my swimming eye cold slumber falls.
Now, now farewell! involv'd in thickest night,
Borne far away, I vanish from thy sight,
And stretch towards thee, all hope forever o'er,
These unavailing arms, ah! thine no more."
She spoke, and from his gaze forever fled,
Swift as dissolving smoke through æther spread,
Nor more beheld him, while he fondly strove
To catch her shade, and pour the plaints of love.
Deaf to his pray'r no more stern Charon gave
To cross the Stygian lake's forbidden wave.
  Ah! many a month he wept in lofty caves
By frozen Strymon's solitary waves;
With melting melodies the beasts subdu'd,
And drew around his harp the list'ning wood.
Thus Philomel.* beneath the poplar spray,

*The nightingale.

Mourns her lost brood untimely snatch'd away,
Whom some rough hind, that watch'd her fost'ring nest,
Tore yet unfledg'd from the maternal breast:
She on the bough all night her plaint pursues,
Fills the far woods with woe, and each sad note renews.
No earthly charms had power his soul to move,
No second hymeneal lured to love.
'Mid climes where Tanais freezes as it flows,
'Mid deserts hoary with Rhipæan snows,
Lone roam'd the bard, his ravish'd bride deplored,
And the vain gift of hell's relenting lord.

Scorned by the youth, whom grief alone could charm,
Rage and revenge the Thracian matrons arm;
'Mid the dark orgies of their god, they tore
His mangled limbs, and toss'd along the shore.
Ah! at that time while roll'd the floating head,
Torn from his neck, down Hebrus' craggy bed,
His last, last voice, his tongue now cold in death,
Still nam'd Eurydice with parting breath;
"Ah! dear Eurydice!" his spirit sigh'd,
And all the rocks "Eurydice" replied.

Laocoön and His Sons.

Æneas tells the story of Laocoön, who alone of the Trojan leaders resisted the bringing of the wooden horse within the walls of the doomed city. By striking it with his spear he was said to have offended the deities to whom it was consecrated. He was therefore punished by being crushed, with his sons, in the folds of two enormous serpents.

Laocoön, named as Neptune's priest,
Was offering up the victim beast,
When lo! from Tenedos—I quail,
E'en now, at telling of the tale—
Two monstrous serpents stem the tide,
And shoreward through the stillness glide.
Amid the waves they rear their breasts,
And toss on high their sanguine crests;
The hind part coils along the deep,
And undulates with sinuous sweep.
The lashed spray echoes: now they reach
The inland belted by the beach,
And rolling bloodshot eyes of fire,

Dart their forked tongue, and hiss for ire.
We fly distraught; unswerving they
Toward Laocoön hold their way;
First round his two young sons they wreathe,
And grind their limbs with savage teeth:
Then, as with arms he comes to aid,
The wretched father they invade
And twine in giant folds; twice round
His stalwart waist their spires are wound,
Twice round his neck, while over all
Their heads and crests tower high and tall.
He strains his strength their knots to tear,
While gore and slime fillets smear,
And to the unregardful skies
Sends up his agonizing cries:
A wounded bull such moaning makes,
When from his neck the axe he shakes,
Ill-aimed, and from the altar breaks.
The twin destroyers take their flight
To Pallas' temple on the height;
There by the goddess' feet concealed
They lie and nestle 'neath her shield.

The Death of Priam.

Perhaps you may of Priam's fate inquire?
He—when he saw his regal town on fire,
His ruined palace, and his ent'ring foes,
On every side inevitable woes—
In arms disused invests his limbs, decayed,
Like them, with age; a late and useless aid.
His feeble shoulders scarce the weight sustain:
Loaded, not armed, he creeps along with pain,
Despairing of success, ambitious to be slain.
Uncovered but by heaven, there stood in view
An altar: near the hearth a laurel grew,
Doddered with age, whose boughs encompass round
The household gods, and shade the holy ground.
Here Hecuba, with all her helpless train
Of dames, for shelter sought, but sought in vain,
Driv'n like a flock of doves along the sky,
Their images they hug, and to their altars fly.
The queen when she beheld her trembling lord,
And hanging by his side a heavy sword,
"What rage," she cried, "has seized my husband's mind?
What arms are these, and to what use design'd?
These times want other aid! Were Hector here,
E'en Hector now in vain, like Priam, would appear.
With us one common shelter thou shalt find,
Or in one common fate with us be joined."
She said, and with a last salute embraced
The poor old man, and by the laurel placed.

Behold! Polites, one of Priam's sons,
Pursued by Pyrrhus,* there for safety runs.
Through swords and foes, amaz'd and hurt, he flies
Through empty courts and open galleries.
Him Pyrrhus, urging with his lance, pursues,
And often reaches, and his thrusts renews.
The youth transfix'd, with lamentable cries,
Expires before his wretched parents' eyes:
Whom gasping at his feet when Priam saw,
The fear of death gave place to nature's law;

* Pyrrhus, called also Neoptolemus, was the son of Achilles.

And, shaking more with anger than with age,
"The gods," said he, "requite thy brutal rage!
As sure they will, barbarian, sure they must,
If there be gods in heaven, and gods be just—
Who tak'st in wrongs an insolent delight;
With a son's death t' infect a father's sight.
Not he, whom thou and lying fame conspire
To call thee his—not he, thy vaunted sire,
Thus us'd my wretched age: the gods he feared,
The laws of nature and of nations heard.
He cheer'd my sorrows, and, for sums of gold,
The bloodless carcass of my Hector sold;
Pitied the woes a parent underwent,
And sent me back in safety from his tent."

This said, his feeble hand a javelin threw,
Which flutt'ring, seemed to loiter as it flew;
Just, and but barely, to the mark it held,
And faintly tinkled on the brazen shield.
  Then Pyrrhus thus: "Hence, dotard; meet thy fate,
And to my father my foul deeds relate.
Now die!"—With that he dragg'd the trembling sire,
Slidd'ring through clottered blood and holy mire
(The mingled mire his murder'd son had made),
Haled from beneath the violated shade,
And on the sacred pile the royal victim laid,
His right hand held his bloody falchion bare;

His left he twisted in his hoary hair:
Then, with a speeding thrust, his heart he found:
The lukewarm blood came rushing through the wound,
And sanguine streams distained the sacred ground.
Thus Priam fell, and shar'd one common fate
With Troy in ashes, and his ruin'd state—
He, who the sceptre of all Asia sway'd,
Whom monarchs like domestic slaves obeyed.
On the bleak shores now lies th' abandoned king,
A headless carcass, and a nameless thing.

The Lament of Dido.

The following translation is from William Morris' "Æneids of Virgil."

And now Aurora left alone Tithonus' saffron bed,
And first light of another day across the world she shed.
But when the Queen from tower aloft beheld the dawn grow white,
And saw the ships upon their way with fair sails trimmed aright,
And all the haven shipless left, and reach of empty strand,
Then thrice and o'er again she smote her fair breast with her hand,
And rent her yellow hair and cried, "Ah, Jove! and is he gone?
And shall a very stranger mock the lordship I have won?
Why arm they not? Why gather not from all the town in chase?
Ho ye! why run ye not the ships down from their standing place?
Quick, bring the fire! shake out the sails! hard on the oars to sea!
What words are these, or where am I? What madness changeth
    me?
Unhappy Dido! now at last thine evil deed strikes home.
Ah, better when thou mad'st him lord—lo, whereunto are come—
His faith and troth, who erst, they say, his country's house-gods
    held
The while he took upon his back his father spent with eld!
Why might I not have shred him up, and scattered him piecemeal
About the sea, and slain his friends, his very son, with steel,
Ascanius on his father's board for dainty meat to lay?
But doubtful, say ye, were the fate of battle. Yea, O yea!
What might I fear, who was to die?—if I had borne the fire
Among their camp, and filled his decks with flame, and son and
    sire
Quenched with their whole folk, and myself had cast upon it all!
—O Sun, whose flames on every deed earth doeth ever fall,

O Juno, setter-forth and seer of these our many woes,
Hecate, whose name howled out a-nights o'er city crossway goes,
Avenging Dread Ones, Gods that guard Elissa* perishing,
O hearken, turn your might most meet against the evil thing!
O hearken these our prayers! and if the doom must surely stand,
And he, the wicked head, must gain the port and swim a-land,
If Jove demand such fixèd fate and every change doth bar,
Yet let him faint mid weapon-strife and hardy folk of war!
And let him, exiled from his house, torn from Iulus,† wend,
Beseeching help mid wretched death of many and many a friend.
And when at last he yieldeth him to pact of grinding peace,
Then short-lived let his lordship be, and lovèd life's increase.
And let him fall before his day, unburied on the shore:
Lo, this I pray, this last of words forth with my blood I pour.
And ye, O Tyrians, 'gainst his race that is, and is to be,
Feed full your hate! When I am dead, send down this gift to me:
No love betwixt the peoples twain, no troth for anything!
And thou, Avenger of my wrongs, from my dead bones outspring,
To bear the fire and the sword o'er Dardan-peopled earth
Now or hereafter—whensoe'er the day brings might to birth.
I pray the shore against the shore, the sea against the sea,
The sword 'gainst sword—fight ye that are, and ye that are to be!"

So sayeth she, and everywise she turns about her mind
How ending of the loathèd light she speediest now may find.
And few words unto Barce spake, Sychæus' nurse of yore;‡
For the black ashes held her own upon the ancient shore:
"Dear nurse, my sister Anna now bring hither to my need,
And bid her for my sprinkling-tide the running water speed;
And bid her have the hosts§ with her, and due atoning things;
So let her come; but thou, thine head bind with the holy strings;
For I am minded now to end what I have set afoot,
And worship duly Stygian Jove and all my cares uproot;
Setting the flame beneath the bale‖ of that Dardanian head."

She spake; with hurrying of eld the nurse her footsteps sped.
But Dido, trembling, wild at heart with her most dread intent,
Rolling her blood-shot eyes about, her quivering cheeks besprent

---

* Another name of Dido.

† Iulus, called also Ascanius, was the son of Æneas, from whom the Julian family of Rome claimed descent.

‡ Sychæus was Dido's first husband, and Barce, who had been his nurse, remained in Dido's household.

§ **Victims** for sacrifice. ‖ Funeral pile.

With burning flecks, and otherwhere dead-white with death
    drawn nigh,
Burst through the inner doorways there and clomb the bale on
    high,
Fulfilled with utter madness now, and bared the Dardan blade,
Gift given not for such a work, for no such ending made.
There when upon the Ilian gear her eyen had been set,
And bed well known, 'twixt tears and thoughts a while she
    lingered yet;
Then brooding low upon the bed her latest word she spake:
    "O raiment dear to me while Gods and fate allowed, now take
This soul of mine and let me loose from all my woes at last!
I, I have lived, and down the way fate showed to me have passed;

And now a mighty shade of me shall go beneath the earth!
A glorious city have I raised, and brought my walls to birth,
Avenged my husband, made my foe, my brother, pay the pain:
Happy, ah, happy overmuch were all my life-days' gain,
If never those Dardanian keels had drawn our shores anigh."
    She spake—her lips lay on the bed: "Ah, unavenged to die!
But let me die! Thus, thus 'tis good to go into the night!
Now let the cruel Dardan eyes drink in the bale-fire's light,
And bear for sign across the sea this token of my death."
    Her speech had end; but on the steel, amid the last word's
    breath,
They see her fallen; along the blade they see her blood foam out,
And all her hands besprent therewith; wild fly the shrieks
    about
The lofty halls, and Rumor runs mad through the smitten town.

The houses sound with women's wails and lamentable groan;
The mighty clamor of their grief rings through the upper skies,
'Twas e'en as if all Carthage fell mid flood of enemies,
Or mighty Tyre of ancient days,—as if the wildfire ran
Rolling about the roof of God and dwelling-place of man.
    Half dead her sister heard, and rushed distraught and trembling there,
With nail and fist befouling all her face and bosom fair:
She thrust amidst them, and by name called on the dying Queen:
"O was it this, my sister, then! guile in thy word hath been!
And this was what the bale, the fire, the altars wrought for me!
Where shall I turn, so left alone? Ah, scorned was I to be
For death-fellow! Thou shouldst have called me too thy way to wend.
One sword pang should have been for both, one hour to make an end.
Built I with hands, on Father-Gods with crying did I cry,
To be away, a cruel heart, from thee laid down to die?
O sister, me and thee, thy folk, the fathers of the land,
Thy city hast thou slain——O give, give water to my hand,
And let me wash the wound, and if some last breath linger there,
Let my mouth catch it!"
    Saying so she reached the topmost stair,
And to her breast the dying one she fondled, groaning sore,
And with her raiment strove to staunch the black and flowing gore.
Then Dido strove her heavy lids to lift, but back again
They sank, and deep within her breast whispered the deadly bane:
Three times on elbow struggling up a little did she rise,
And thrice fell back upon the bed, and sought with wandering eyes
The light of heaven aloft, and moaned when it was found at last.
    Then on her long-drawn agony did Juno pity cast,
Her hard departing; Iris then she sent from heaven on high,
And bade her from the knitted limbs the struggling soul untie.
For since by fate she perished not, nor waited death-doom given,
But hapless died before her day, by sudden fury driven,
Not yet the tress of yellow hair had Proserpine off-shred,
Nor unto Stygian Orcus yet had doomed her wandering head.
So Iris ran adown the sky on wings of saffron dew,
And colors shifting thousand-fold against the sun she drew
And overhead she hung: "So bid, from off thee this I bear,
Hallowed to Dis, and charge thee now from out thy body fare."

She spake and sheared the tress away; then failed the life-heat spent,
And forth away upon the wind the spirit of her went.

THE YOUNG MARCELLUS.

VIRGIL, in the Sixth Book, represents Æneas descending into the under world, and there meeting his father, who prophesies the greatness of Rome and shows him the spirits of her future heroes. Among the rest pointed out was the young Marcellus, the nephew of Augustus, who died in his twentieth year. The following lines were read by Virgil to the Emperor, in the presence of Octavia, the mother of Marcellus, soon after her loss. She fainted at the recital, but afterwards ordered the poet to be paid a magnificent sum of money for his tribute to her son's memory.

Æneas here beheld, of form divine,
A godlike youth in glittering armor shine,
With great Marcellus keeping equal pace;
But gloomy were his eyes, dejected was his face.
He saw, and wond'ring, asked his airy guide,
"What and from whence was he, who press'd the hero's side,
His son, or one of his illustrious name?
How like the former, and almost the same!
Observe the crowds that compass him around;
All gaze, and all admire, and raise a shouting sound;
But hov'ring mists around his brows are spread,
And night, with sable shades, involve his head."
"Seek not to know," the ghost replied with tears,
"The sorrows of thy sons in future years.
This youth (the blissful vision of a day)
Shall just be shown on earth, then snatched away.
The gods too high had raised the Roman state,
Were but their gifts as permanent as great.
What groans of men shall fill the Martian field! *
How fierce a blaze his flaming pile shall yield!
What funeral pomp shall floating Tiber see,
When, rising from his bed, he views the sad solemnity!
No youth shall equal hopes of glory give,
No youth afford so great a cause to grieve.
The Trojan honor, and the Roman boast,
Admired when living, and adored when lost!

* The Campus Martius at Rome.

Mirror of ancient faith in early youth!
Undaunted worth, inviolable truth!
No foe, unpunish'd, in the fighting-field
Shall dare thee, foot to foot, with sword and shield;
Much less in arms oppose thy matchless force,
When thy sharp spurs shall urge thy foaming horse.
Ah! couldst thou break through Fate's severe decree,
A new Marcellus shall arise in thee!
Full canisters of fragrant lilies bring,
Mix'd with the purple roses of the spring;
Let me with funeral flowers his body strow;
This gift which parents to their children owe,
This unavailing gift, at least, I may bestow!"

VIRGIL READING TO AUGUSTUS AND OCTAVIA.

THE DESCENT OF AVERNUS.

In one of the most famous passages of the Æneid Virgil contrasts in a few lines the easy descent of Avernus with the difficulty of return. It has thus been translated by Prof. J. Conington.

> The journey down to the abyss
>   Is prosperous and light;
> The palace-gates of gloomy Dis [Pluto]
>   Stand open day and night;
> But upward to retrace the way
> And pass into the light of day,
> Then comes the stress of labor; this
>   May task a hero's might.

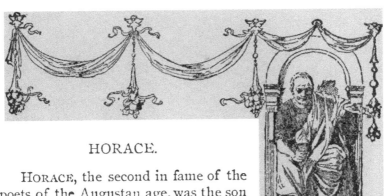

HORACE.

HORACE, the second in fame of the poets of the Augustan age, was the son of a freedman who had acquired a modest competence. His full name was Quintus Horatius Flaccus. He was born in 65 B.C., at Venusium, on the border of Apulia. His father, not satisfied with the educational resources of the Venusian school, took him to Rome and placed him with Orbilius, whom Horace has immortalized for his propensity to flog the boys. From Rome he proceeded to Athens for further study, and, after the assassination of Julius Cæsar, joined the army of Brutus in Macedonia. He was present at the battle of Philippi, where he sportively says he threw down his shield and sought safety in flight. The fortunes of war deprived him of his home, and, his father being dead, audacious poverty drove him to write verses. Through Varius and Virgil he was introduced to Mæcenas at the age of twenty-seven, and henceforth his position as a court poet was assured. Not a few of Horace's best traits are due to the influence of his patron Mæcenas, a polished man of the world, possessed of much tact and discretion. The compositions written by Horace after his introduction to court are quite different from those written before. Coarse personality gave place to urbanity and candor. Henceforward the poet places before himself higher ideals and nobler aims, and a more genial and kindly spirit pervades his work. The Satires are the product of the first decade of Horace's literary career, the Epistles belong to the second. Together they may be considered specimens of the poet's critical capacity, while the Odes exemplify his power as a lyric artist. The Satires are didactic, practical, somewhat prosaic, and deal with every-day life in familiar language. They teach the Stoic doctrine of self-mastery and consistency of conduct. They condemn the inordinate love of pleasure and craving for luxuries. The Epistles, with their musical ring and clear presentation of ideas, may be considered an innovation in poetic forms. The poet, in giving an honest estimate of himself, his critics and imitators, establishes a confidential relation with his readers. The longer epistles are almost purely didactic, the shorter resemble in tone the lighter odes.

Scarcely anything in literature has become so widely known and so popular among men of literary bent as the Odes of Horace. It is from them that he derives his immortality. They have produced a great variety of impressions among his admirers, and this itself is a token of the poet's flexibility of mind and talent. The Odes still hold a high position as models and educational elements in regard to literary taste and delicacy of language. They furnish specimens of the epigrammatic, the grave and the gay, the purely didactic and the simple Greek imitation. As a lyric poet Horace reaches his zenith in the Third Book. Here he stands forth, like Virgil, the poet of Roman national and religious sentiment. In the First Book he prays to Apollo for a life free from everything degrading, and yet not without gaiety; in the Second he predicts his survival after death; in the Third he throws down his implements, so to speak, and exclaims with confidence, "I have raised a monument more lasting than bronze." As poet laureate, Horace wrote the ode for the celebration of the Secular Games in 17 B. C. He died 8 B. C.

To the Roman People.

This is one of the earliest odes, and Horace never surpassed it in patriotic inspiration.

Another age in civil wars will soon be spent and worn,
And by her native strength our Rome be wrecked and overborne,—
That Rome the Marsians could not crush, who border on the lands,
Nor the shock of threatening Porsena with his Etruscan bands,
Nor Capua's strength that rivalled ours, nor Spartacus the stern,

Nor the faithless Allobrogian, who still for change doth yearn.
Aye, what Germania's blue-eyed youth quelled not with ruthless sword,
Nor Hannibal, by our great sires detested and abhorred,
We shall destroy with ruthless hands imbrued in brothers' gore,
And wild beasts of the wood shall range our native land once more.
A foreign foe, alas! shall tread the City's ashes down,
And his horse's ringing hoofs shall smite her places of renown;
And the bones of great Quirinus,* now religiously enshrined,
Shall be flung by sacrilegious hands to the sunshine and the wind
And if ye all from ills so dire ask how yourselves to free,
Or such at least as would not hold your lives unworthily—
No better counsel I can urge than that which erst inspired
The stout Phocæans when from their doomed city they retired,
Their fields, their household gods, their shrines surrendering as a prey
To the wild boar and ravening wolf: so we in our dismay,
Where'er our wandering steps may chance to carry us should go,
Or where'er across the sea the fitful winds may blow.
How think ye then? If better course none offer, why should we
Not seize the happy auspices, and boldly put to sea?
The circling ocean waits us: then away, where Nature smiles,
To those fair lands, those blissful lands, the rich and happly isles,
Where Ceres year by year crowns all the untilled land with sheaves,
And the vine with purple clusters droops, unpruned of all her leaves;
Where the olive buds and burgeons, to its promise ne'er untrue,
And the russet fig adorns the trees that graff-shoot never knew;
Where honey from the hollow oaks doth ooze, and crystal rills
Come dancing down with tinkling feet from the sky-dividing hills?
There to the pails the she-goats come, without a master's word,
And home with udders brimming broad returns the friendly herd;
There round the fold no surly bear its midnight prowl doth make,
Nor teems the rank and heaving soil with the adder and the snake;
There no contagion smites the flocks, nor blight of any star,
With fury of remorseless heat, the sweltering herds doth mar.

* Quirinus was the name under which Romulus was deified and worshiped.

Nor are the swelling seeds burnt up within the thirsty clods—
So kindly blends the seasons there the King of all the gods.
That shore the Argonautic bark's stout rowers never gained,
Nor the wily She of Colchis with step unchaste profaned;
The sails of Sidon's galleys ne'er were wafted to that strand,
Nor ever rested on its slopes Ulysses's toil-worn band:
For Jupiter, when he with brass the Golden Age alloyed,
That region set apart by the good to be enjoyed;
With brass and then with iron he the ages seared; but ye,
Good men and true, to that bright home arise, arise and follow me.

MÆCENAS, PATRON AND FRIEND.

LUCKY I will not call myself, as though
Thy friendship I to mere good fortune owe.
No chance it was secured me thy regards,
But Virgil first—that best of men and bards,
And then kind Varius mentioned what I was.
Before you brought, with many a faltering pause,
Dropping some few brief words (for bashfulness
Robbed me of utterance) I did not profess
That I was sprung of lineage old and great,
Or used to canter round my own estate
On a Satureian barb; but what and who
I was, as plainly told. As usual, you
Brief answer make me. I retire, and then—
Some nine months after—summoning me again,
You bid me 'mongst your friends assume a place;
And proud I feel that thus I won your grace;
Not by an ancestry long known to fame,
But by my life and heart, devoid of blame.

HIS DAILY LIFE IN ROME.

I WALK alone, by mine own fancy led,
Inquire the price of pot-herbs and of bread,
The circus cross, to see its tricks and fun,
The forum too, at times near set of sun;
With other fools there do I stand and gape
Round fortune-tellers' stalls; thence home escape
To a plain meal of pancakes, pulse, and peas;
Three young boy-slaves attend on me with these.

Upon a slab of snow-white marble stand
A goblet and two beakers; near at hand
A common ewer, patera, and bowl:
Campania's potteries produced the whole.
To sleep then I. . . .
   I keep my couch till ten, then walk a while,
Or having read or writ what may beguile
A quiet after-hour, anoint my limbs
With oil—not such as filthy Natta skims
From lamps defrauded of their unctuous fare.
And when the sunbeams, grown too hot to bear,
Warn me to quit the field and hand-ball play,
The bath takes all my weariness away.
Then having lightly dined just to appease
The sense of emptiness—I take mine ease,
Enjoying all home's simple luxury.
This is the life of bard unclogged, like me,
By stern ambition's miserable weight.
So placed, I own with gratitude, my state
Is sweeter, aye, than though a quæstor's power
From sire and grandsires had been my dower.

INVITATION TO PHYLLIS.

I HAVE laid in a cask of Albanian wine,
   Which nine mellow summers have ripened and more.
In my gardens, dear Phyllis, thy brows to entwine,
   Grows the brightest of yellow parsley in plentiful store:
There's ivy to gleam on thy dark glossy hair:
   My plate, newly burnished, enlivens my rooms,
And the altar, athirst for its victim, is there,
   Enwreathed with chaste vervain and choicest of blooms.

Every hand in the household is busily toiling,
   And hither and thither boys bustle and girls;
Whilst, up from the hearth-fires careering and coiling,
   The smoke round the rafter-beams languidly curls.
Let the joys of the revel be parted between us!
   'Tis the Ides of young April, the day which divides
The month, dearest Phyllis, of ocean-sprung Venus—
   A day to me dearer than any besides.

And well may I prize it, and hail its returning—
  My own natal day not more hallowed or dear;
For Mæcenas, my friend, dates from this happy morning
  The life which has swelled to a lustrous career.
So come, my own Phyllis, my heart's latest treasure—
  For ne'er for another this bosom shall long—
And I'll teach, while your loved voice re-echoes the measure,
  How to charm away care with the magic of song.

The Literary Bore.

It chanced that I, the other day
Was sauntering up the Sacred Way,
And musing, as my habit is,
Some trivial random fantasies,
When there comes rushing up a wight
Whom only by his name I knew.
"Ha! my dear fellow, how d'ye do?"
Grasping my hand, he shouted. "Why,
As times go, pretty well," said I;
"And you, I trust, can say the same."
But after me as still he came,
"Sir, is there anything," I cried,
"You want of me?" "Oh," he replied.
"I'm just the man you ought to know:
A scholar, author!" "Is it so?
For this I'll like you all the more!"
  Then, writhing to escape the bore,
I quicken now my pace, now stop,
And in my servant's ear let drop
Some words; and all the while I feel
Bathed in cold sweat from head to heel.
"Oh, for a touch," I moaned in pain,
"Bolanus, of thy madcap vein,
To put this incubus to rout!"
As he went chattering on about
Whatever he descries or meets—
The city's growth, its splendor, size.
"You're dying to be off," he cries:
(For all the while I'd been stock dumb);
"I've seen it this half-hour. But come,
Let's clearly understand each other;

It's no use making all this pother.
My mind's made up to stick by you;
So where you go, there I go too."
"Don't put yourself," I answered, "pray,
So very far out of your way.
I'm on the road to see a friend
Whom you don't know, that's near his end,
Away beyond the Tiber far,
Close by where Cæsar's gardens are."
"I've nothing in the world to do,
And what's a paltry mile or two?
I like it; so I'll follow you!"
   Down dropped my ears on hearing this
Just like a vicious jackass's,
That's loaded heavier than he likes;
But off anew my torment strikes:
   "If well I know myself, you'll end
With making of me more a friend
Than Viscus, aye, or Varius; for
Of verses who can run off more,
Or run them off at such a pace?
Who dance with such distinguished grace?
And as for singing, zounds!" says he,
"Hermogenes might envy me!"
   Here was an opening to break in:
"Have you a mother, father, kin,
To whom your life is precious?" "None;
I've closed the eyes of every one."
O happy they, I inly groan;
Now I am left, and I alone.
Quick, quick dispatch me where I stand;
Now is the direful doom at hand,
Which erst the Sabine beldam old,
Shaking her magic urn, foretold
In days when I was yet a boy:
"Him shall no poison fell destroy,
Nor hostile sword in shock of war,
Nor gout, nor colic, nor catarrh.
In fulness of time his thread
Shall by a prate-apace be shred;
So let him, when he's twenty-one,
If he be wise, all babblers shun."

HORACE'S MONUMENT.

I'VE reared a monument—my own—
   More durable than brass;
Yea, kingly pyramids of stone
   In height it doth surpass.

Rain shall not sap, nor driving blast
   Disturb its settled base,
Nor countless ages rolling past
   Its symmetry deface.

I shall not wholly die. Some part,
   Nor that a little, shall
Escape the dark Destroyer's dart,
   And his grim festival.

For long as, with his Vestals mute,
   Rome's Pontifex shall climb
The Capitol, my fame shall shoot
   Fresh buds through future time.

Where brawls loud Aufidus and came
   Parched Daunus erst, a horde
Of mystic boors to sway, my name
   Shall be a household word,

As one who rose from mean estate,
   The first, with poet's fire,
Æolic song to modulate
   To the Italian lyre.

Then grant, Melpomene, thy son
   Thy guerdon proud to wear.
And Delphic laurels, duly won,
   Bind thou upon my hair.

CHAPTER XVI.

Later Writers.

After the passing of the Augustan age, we find a gradual decline in letters. Periods of peace and prosperity brought intermittent periods of literary excellence, but these were too frequently divided by years of such insecurity and unrest—especially among the leisure and wealthy class to which men of letters generally belonged—that all cultured arts and interests suffered. The Julian princes in several instances surrounded themselves with men of brilliant minds and attempted to give encouragement to writing; but their fickleness and caprice made the very existence of such men insecure and rendered the independent expression of thought and opinion impossible. It was during these trying times that Stoicism gained a tremendous hold upon the intelligent classes. The theory that mind was supreme, that even the bondsman might be free in the world of mind—over which no tyrant could gain control—brought comfort and sustaining power.

One of the most tragic figures during these years was Seneca—a man of undoubted scholarship and literary ability. His life was filled with changing fortunes. As a young man he was exiled from Rome, only to be recalled later to become the teacher of Nero. Such ascendancy did he gain over the mind of his young pupil that the peace and moderation of Nero's earlier administration can largely be ascribed to Seneca's influence. To maintain his position he found it necessary to indulge Nero's wild whims, to such an extent finally that he became silently tolerant of cold-blooded crimes. This apparently broke the bond of reverence on the part of Nero, and his fantastic passion soon turned against his former friend and tutor. Seneca, as a result of Nero's favoritism and his own prudent investments, had become very wealthy, and the emperor's greed reached out for his possessions. The imperial command to commit suicide was not unwelcome to the man who had looked for it hourly for some time.

Seneca's writings consist of tragedies, moral letters, studies in natural philosophy and at least one satire. The tragedies were based upon the time-worn hero stories of the Greeks. Indeed, for the most part they are in close imitation of the Greek masters—chiefly Euripides. They would have been long since forgotten but for one circumstance: during the Middle Ages Greek was, generally speaking, unknown. Latin lived on and these Latin tragedies were read by scholars and deeply influenced the early French dramatists.

Seneca's letters upon varied subjects filled a place not unlike that held in modern times by Bacon's Essays and some of the miscellaneous contributions of Emerson. As a matter of fact, Seneca's influence upon some of Emerson's writings is quite apparent. Seneca was one of the most distinguished Stoics among the Romans, and the mental calm and poise inculcated by this philosophy are reflected in Emerson's Essays. The studies in natural philosophy were widely read during the Middle Ages, but have no particular value today; modern science has rendered them of no account from a scientific standpoint, and their literary merit is not great.

Seneca wrote a satire upon the death of Claudius—designed for the entertainment of Nero's court. It in no way contributes to the writer's literary fame, but even to-day it is somewhat amusing as preserving an exaggerated picture of Claudius' vanity and shallow mental attainments.

Martial, like Seneca, was born in Spain and through Seneca's favor he received some attentions upon removal to Rome. He differed from many of the Roman writers of later years, in that he would be himself. In an age when the majority of aspirants to literary fame sought it by clever imitation of past writers, Martial was, generally speaking, true to his natural style and his original thought. He gave the *epigram* a permanent form; heretofore it had been a couplet, or a stanza, written frequently to accompany a gift or give a happy turn to some special occasion. Martial gave the epigram a *point*—a salient shaft of fun, wit, or malice, that has continued to be its chief merit.

The Julian house was followed by the Flavian princes. They ruled with moderation and good judgment; in comparison with the period just passed their age was a fortunate time for Rome.

There were quite a number of noted writers who belonged to this period, but they were learned rather than gifted, familiar with past writings, imitating these, rather than producing original ones.

One of the most painstaking men of the Flavian Age was Pliny the Elder—so-called to distinguish him from his nephew, Pliny the Younger. The elder Pliny was a naturalist, and he wrote a Natural History—comprising thirty-seven books. These treated of the geography of the earth, the plant life, animal life, and every subject that could be embraced by science in antiquity. Unlike his predecessors and contemporaries, Pliny gave heed to his authorities and was discriminating in his use of material at hand. During the Middle Ages his history was supposed to contain all available knowledge of the natural world, and was the basis of several works drawn from it.

Pliny's spirit of investigation was the means of his death. In 79 A. D., while Vesuvius was pouring forth its fire and molten lava that laid waste Pompeii, the Elder Pliny stayed near too long and was overcome with smoke and cinders.

Unquestionably the greatest writer of later Roman times was Tacitus. Born in 55 A. D., he died in 117 A. D. The exact place of his birth is uncertain, but he came early to Rome and entered upon an official life that extended over many years. From one responsibility he was promoted to another, until he became praetor and then proconsul of Asia. He married the daughter of Agricola, the famous general who completed the conquest of Britain. Probably his Germania is best known today of all his writings, but it was by no means the most able. His treatise upon the Germans was interesting to the men of his day, and for centuries after it included most that was known of the Teutonic peoples who finally overcame the Romans and appropriated their wide territory. Tacitus found his material for the German history in the writings of many of his countrymen—for he probably had no personal acquaintance with the Germans. From the writings of Caesar,

272   THE WORLD'S PROGRESS.

the History of the Germans by the Elder Pliny, from the reports of those in military service who came in contact with the Teutons, and other means he found abundant data for his Germania.

The Agricola, written in memory of his wife's father, possesses greater literary merits. For this redoubtable general Tacitus felt a deep affection and, although there were certain qualities lacking in Agricola—such as independence of spirit in public matters, etc., that might have appealed to the popular mind, yet these were largely lost sight of because of his success in Britain.

Tacitus also wrote concerning his own country. His descriptions, like those preserved in Juvenal's Satires, present a sorry spectacle of the Rome of this period. Society was diseased to the core and the city was ill-kept and untidy. As we read the descriptions of Tacitus or the scathing satires of Juvenal, we can almost see the short-sighted social body of Rome moving on to its ruin, while we feel the silent approach of the Teutonic hordes, biding the time when the show of force shall melt away and the corruption within the empire yield to the fresh vigor of a new race.

TOMB OF HADRIAN, ROME.

Poverty the Handmaid of Philosophy.

He has even gone so far as to reproach me with my poverty,—a charge truly acceptable to a philosopher, and one to which I readily plead guilty. For Poverty has long been the handmaid of Philosophy; frugal, temperate, contented with little, eager for praise, averse from the things sought by wealth, safe in her ways, simple in her requirements, in her counsels a promoter of what is right. No one has she ever puffed up with pride, no one has she corrupted by the enjoyment of power, no one has she maddened with tyrannical ambition; for no pampering of the appetite or of the passions does she sigh, nor can she indulge it. But it is your fosterlings of wealth who are in the habit of perpetrating these disgraceful excesses, and others of a kindred nature. If you review all the greatest enormities that have been committed in the memory of mankind, you will not find a single poor man among the perpetrators; whilst, on the other hand in the number of illustrious men hardly any of the rich are to be found. Poverty has nurtured from his very cradle every individual in whom we find anything to admire and commend,—Poverty, I say,—she who in former ages was the foundress of all cities, the inventress of all arts, she who is guiltless of all offence, who is lavish of all glory, who has been honored with every praise among all nations. For this same Poverty it was that, among the Greeks, showed herself just in Aristides, humane in Phocion, resolute in Epaminondas, wise in Socrates, and eloquent in Homer. It was this same Poverty, too, that for the Roman people laid the very earliest foundations of their sway, and that offers sacrifice to the immortal gods in their behalf, with the ladle and the dish of clay, even to this day.

If there were now sitting as judges at this trial C. Fabricius, Cneius Scipio, and Manius Curius, whose daughters, by reason of their poverty, went home to their husbands portioned at the public expense, carrying with them the glories of their family and the money of the public; if Publicola,* the expeller of the kings, and Agrippa,† the reconciler of the people, the expense of whose funeral was, in consequence of their limited fortunes, defrayed by the Roman people, by contributions of the smallest coins; if Atilius Regulus,‡ whose little field was, in consequence of a like poverty, cultivated at the public expense; if, in fine, all those ancient families, ennobled by consulships, censorships, and triumphs, could obtain a short respite, and return to light, and take part in this trial, would you then have dared to reproach a philosopher for his poverty, in the presence of so many consuls distinguished for theirs? . . .

I could, indeed, raise an argument with you about the very name itself, and I could show that none of us are poor who do not wish for superfluities, and who possess the things which are necessary, which, by nature, are but few indeed. For he has the most who desires the least; he who wants but little is most likely to have as much as he wants. It is with the mind just as it is with the body: in a healthy state it is lightly clad, but in sickness it is wrapped in cumbrous clothing; and it is a sure sign of infirmity to have many wants. It is with life just as with swimming: the man is the most expert who is the most disengaged from all encumbrances. For my part, I have learned that in this especially the gods surpass mankind, that they have to satisfy no necessities. Hence it is that I consider him among us who has the fewest possible necessities most strongly to resemble a god.

---

* On the death of L. Junius Brutus in the year 508 B.C., after the expulsion of the kings, C. Valerius was appointed consul in his stead. He introduced a special decree by which royal rule was forever interdicted at Rome. For his patriotism he was awarded the surname Publicola or Poplicola, "server of the people."

† Menenius Agrippa, after the withdrawal of the plebeians to the Sacred Mount, in 494 B.C., induced them to return by reciting the fable of "The Belly and the Members."

‡ Atilius Regulus was the leader of an unsuccessful expedition against Carthage in 256 B.C. He was captured by the Carthaginians, and is said to have been put to death by them for refusing to persuade his countryman to make peace.

OVID.

Ovid is more truly the representative poet of Roman imperialism than even Virgil. The latter constantly looks back to the national traditions and shows how the Roman republic rose and grew to greatness. Ovid began his career at a time of national prosperity when peace was firmly established and amid the reaction of public feeling after the turmoil and carnage of civil war. The regard for history had declined and the severer studies which involved intellectual exertion had given way to love of pleasure and literature of a lighter kind. The smooth-flowing, gaily-tripping, harmonious metres of Horace and Ovid were suited to the luxurious sentiments and mental debauchery of the age. Virgil had endeavored, by appealing to the higher motives of the governing classes, to create loyalty and enthusiasm towards the newly-established Empire; but now the people sought pleasure, and Rome was the seat of pleasure as well as the seat of government. The old Roman virtue and force of character which had once been the mainstay of the people's power, were now sapped by the encroaching tide of Italian effeminacy, which portended the notorious corruption of the later Empire.

Publius Ovidius Naso was born at Sulmo, B.C. 48. He was trained for the bar, but never practiced in courts, being indolent and of weak constitution. His equestrian origin, his culture, and his independent fortune gave him easy access to the fashionable and cultivated society of Rome. His poetical talent was early developed. He knew what pleased and interested his audience and sang accordingly. Ovid is presented to us in two phases of life, which stand in violent contrast to each other. In the former we see him as the gay-hearted gallant, reckless and amatory, devoting his highest art to the service of sensuous pleasure; in the latter, we see the broken-hearted exile wearing out a burdensome life on the inhospitable shores of the Black Sea, seeking in vain for sympathy, and striving by fulsome adulation to move the clemency and obtain the forgiveness of the emperor. The exact cause of Ovid's banishment, in 9 A.D., can only be surmised. He himself mentions two charges, a "song" and an "error." The "song" may refer to the "Art of Love," to which Augustus may have traced evil influences in the imperial family. But this work had been published ten years before the banishment. The "error" might have reference to some compromising act in the royal family which Ovid may have witnessed or abetted. It is significant that Julia, the emperor's granddaughter, was banished in the same year as the poet, and Silanus, her paramour, being disgraced, went into voluntary exile. Ovid died in Tomi on the Euxine Sea, A.D. 17.

Ovid's literary career may be divided into three periods corresponding to the vicissitudes of his life. The first period is that of the amatory poems, the lascivious and wanton tones of which are once interrupted by the plaintive note of the death of his fellow-poet Tibullus. To this period belong also the "Amores" suggested by a series of trifling incidents in the love adventures of the poet. His mistress, he tells us, was a "lady" (ingenua), yet he likens her to Lais, the ideal queen of Corinthian courtesans. The broad freedom, and yet refinement, with which such subjects were treated proved very attractive to the fashionable pleasure-seeking class in which the wanton Julia was the shining light. The "Heroïdes," called also "Epistles," are also assignable to the first period. They are a series of imaginary letters artificial and monotonous, supposed to be written by such noted characters as Briseis, Penelope and others. Then follows the "Art of Love," a poem more powerful and startling than anything Ovid had yet attempted. In it the poet plays the role of teacher, and professedly gives a recital of his own experiences. Notwithstanding the didactic and indelicate tendency of the poem, there is frequently a streak of genuine poetry and artistic refinement interwoven with the expression of lewd conceptions.

The "Metamorphoses" belongs to the second period of Ovid's literary life, and disputes with the "Art of Love" the claim to be the poet's masterpiece. This poem traverses the whole area of Greek mythology from chaos and the creation of man down to the transformation of Julius Cæsar into a star and the deification of Augustus. The "Fasti" also mostly belongs to the second period. It is simply a sort of calendar giving an account, partly historical, partly mythical, of the Roman festivals. The "Tristia" (Lamentations) mark the last period of the poet's work and life. In these, like Cicero, he broods over and bewails his sad fate, and prays that if release is not granted, another place of banishment may be assigned to him. His prayer was never answered.

NIOBE.

FAIR Niobe, who, when a virgin dwelt
In Lydian Sipylus, now queen of Thebes,
Proudly refused before the gods to bend,
And spoke in haughty boasting. Much her pride
By favoring gifts was swollen. Not the fine skill
Amphion practiced; not the lofty birth
Each claimed; not all their mighty kingdom's power,
So raised her soul (of all though justly proud)
As her bright offspring. Justly was she called
Most blest of mothers; but her bliss too great
Seemed to herself, and caused a dread reverse.
 Now Manto, sprung from old Tiresias, skilled
In future fate, impelled by power divine,
In every street with wild prophetic tongue
Exclaimed: "Ye Theban matrons, haste in crowds,
Your incense offer, and your pious prayers,
To great Latona and the heavenly Twins,
Latona's offspring; all your temples bind
With laurel garlands. This the goddess bids;
Through me commands it." All of Thebes obey,
And gird their foreheads with the ordered leaves,
The incense burn, and with the sacred flames
Their pious prayers ascend. Lo! 'midst a crowd
Of nymphs attendant, far conspicuous seen,
Comes Niobe, in gorgeous Phrygian robe,
Inwrought with gold, attired. Beauteous her form,
Beauteous, as rage permitted. Angry shook
Her graceful head; and angry shook the locks
That o'er each shoulder waved. Proudly she towered

Her haughty eyes round from her lofty stand
Wide darting, cried: "What madness this to place
Reported gods above the gods you see!
Why to Latona's altars bend ye low,
Nor incense burn before my power divine?
My sire was Tantalus: of mortals sole,
Celestial feasts he shared. A Pleiad nymph
Me bore. My grandsire is the mighty king,
Whose shoulders all the load of heaven sustain.
Jove is my father's parent: him I boast
As sire-in-law too. All the Phrygian towns
Bend to my sway. The hall of Cadmus owns
Me sovereign mistress. Thebes' high towering walls,
Raised by my consort's lute, and all the crowd
Who dwell inclosed, his rule and mine obey.
Where'er within my palace turn mine eyes,
Treasures immense I view. Brightness divine
I boast: to all seven blooming daughters add,
And seven fair sons; through whom I soon expect,
If Hymen favors, seven more sons to see,
And seven more daughters. Need ye further seek
Whence I have cause for boasting? Dare ye still
Latona, from Titanian Cæus sprung,—
The unknown Cæus,—she to whom all earth
In bearing pangs the smallest space denied:—
This wretch to my divinity prefer?
Not heaven your goddess would receive; not earth;
Not ocean: exiled from the world, she wept,
Till Delos sorrowing,—wanderer like herself,
Exclaimed: 'Thou dreary wanderest over the earth,
I o'er the main;'—and sympathizing thus,
A resting spot afforded. There become
Only of two the mother—can she vie
With one whose womb has sevenfold hers surpassed?
Blest am I. Who can slightly e'er arraign
To happiness my claim? Blest will I still
Continue. Who my bliss can ever doubt?
Abundance guards its surety. Far beyond
The power of fortune is my lot upraised:
Snatch them in numbers from me, crowds more great
Must still remain. My happy state contemns
Even now the threats of danger. Grant the power

Of fate this nation of my womb to thine,—
Of part deprived, impossible I shrink
To poor Latona's two—how scant removed
From mothers childless! Quit your rites;—quick haste
And tear those garlands from your flowing hair."

    Aside the garlands thrown, and incomplete
The rites relinquished, what the Thebans could
They gave: their whispering prayers the matron dame
Addressed. With ire the angry goddess flamed,
And thus on Cynthus' lofty top bespoke
Her double offspring: "O my children! see
Your parent, proud your parent to be called,—
To no celestial yielding, save the queen
Of Jove supreme. Lo! doubted is my claim
To rites divine; and from the altars, burnt
To me from endless ages, driven, I go,
Save by my children succored. Nor this grief
Alone me irks, for Niobe me mocks!
Her daring crime increasing, proud she sets
Her offspring far above you. Me too she spurns,—
To her in number yielding; childless calls
My bed, and proves the impious stock which gave
Her tongue first utterance." More Latona felt
Prepared to utter; more beseechings bland
For her young offspring, when Apollo cried:
"Enough, desist to plain;—delay is long
Till vengeance." Diana joined him in his ire.

    Swift gliding down the sky, and veiled in clouds,
On Cadmus' roof they lighted. Wide was spread
A level plain, by constant hoofs well beat,
The city's walls adjoining; crowding wheels
And coursers' feet the rolling dust upturned.
Here of Amphion's offspring daily some
Mount their fleet steeds; their trappings gaily press
Of Tyrian dye: heavy with gold, the reins
They guide. 'Mid these Ismenos, primal born
Of Niobe, as round the circling course
His well-trained steed he sped, and strenuous curbed
His foaming mouth,—loudly "Ah me!" exclaimed,
As through his bosom deep the dart was driven:
Dropped from his dying hands the slackened reins;
Slowly and sidelong from his courser's back

He tumbled.   Sipylus gave unchecked scope
To his, when through the empty air he heard
The rattling quiver sound: thus speeding clouds
Beheld, the guider of the ruling helm,
A threatening tempest fearing, looses wide
His every sail to catch the lightest breeze.
Loose flowed his reins.   The inevitable dart
The flowing reins quick followed.   Quivering shook,
Fixed in his upper neck, the naked steel,
Far through his throat protruding.   Prone he fell
O'er his high courser's head; his smoking gore,
The ground defiling.   Hapless Phœdimas,
And Tantalus, his grandsire's name who bore,
Their accustomed sport laborious ended, strove
With youthful vigor in the wrestling toil.
Now breast to breast they strained with nervous grasp,
When the swift arrow from the bended bow
Both bodies pierced, as close both bodies joined;
At once they groaned; at once their limbs they threw,
With agonies convulsed, prone on the earth;
At once their rolling eyes the light forsook;
At once their souls were yielded forth to air.

Alphenor saw, and smote his grieving breast;
Flew to their pallid limbs, and as he raised
Their bodies, in the pious office fell:
For Phœbus drove his fate-winged arrow deep
Through what his heart inclosed.   Sudden withdrawn,
On the barbed head the mangled lungs were stuck;
And high in air his soul gushed forth in blood.
But beardless Damasichthon by a wound
Not single fell, as those; struck where the leg
To form begins, and where the nervous ham
A yielding joint supplies.   The deadly dart
To draw essaying, in his throat, full driven
Up to the feathered head, another came:
The sanguine flood expelled it, gushing high,
Cutting the distant air.   With outstretched arms
Ilioneus, the last, besought in vain;
Exclaiming,—"Spare me, spare me, all ye gods!"
Witless that all not joined to cause his woe.
The god was touched with pity, touched too late,—
Already shot the irrevocable dart:

Yet light the blow was given, and mild the wound
That pierced his heart, and sent his soul aloft.

The rumored ill; the mourning people's groans;
The servants' tears, soon made the mother know
The sudden ruin: wondering first she stands,
To see so great Heaven's power, then angry flames
Indignant, that such power they dare to use.
The sire Amphion in his bosom plunged
His sword, and ended life at once and woe.
Heavens! how removed this Niobe from her
Who drove so lately from Latona's fane
The pious crowds; who marched in lofty state,
Through every street of Thebes, an envied sight!
Now to be wept by even her bitterest foes.
Prostrate upon their gelid limbs she lies;
Now this, now that, her trembling kisses press;
Her livid arms high-stretching unto heaven,
Exclaims,—"Enjoy, Latona, cruel dame,
My sorrows; feed on all my wretched woes;
Glut with my load of grief thy savage soul;
Feast thy fell heart with seven funereal scenes;
Triumph, victorious foe! conqueror, exult!
Victorious! said I?—How? To wretched me
Still more are left, than joyful thou canst boast:
Superior I midst all this loss remain."

She spoke;—the twanging bowstring sounded loud!
Terrific noise—to all, save Niobe:
She stood audacious, callous in her crime.
In mourning vesture clad, with tresses loose,
Around the funeral couches of the slain,
The weeping sisters stood. One strives to pluck
The deep-stuck arrow from her bowels,—falls,
And fainting dies, her brother's clay-cold corpse
Pressed with her lips. Another's soothing words

Her hapless parent strive to cheer,—struck dumb,
She bends beneath an unseen wound; her words
Reach not her parent till her life is fled.
This, vainly flying, falls: that drops in death
Upon her sister's body. One to hide
Attempts: another pale and trembling dies.
Six now lie breathless, each by varied wounds;
One sole remaining, whom the mother shields,
Wrapt in her vest; her body o'er her flung,
Exclaiming,—"Leave me this, my youngest,—last,
Least of my mighty numbers,—one alone!"
But while she prays, the damsel prayed for dies.

Of all deprived, the solitary dame,
Amid the lifeless bodies of her sons,
Her daughters, and her spouse, by sorrows steeled,
Sits hardened: no light gale her tresses moves;
No blood her reddened cheeks contain; her eyes
Motionless glare upon her mournful face;
Life quits the statue: even her tongue congeals
Within her stony palate; vital floods
Cease in her veins to flow; her neck to bow
Resists; her arms to move in graceful guise;
Her feet to step; and even to stone are turned
Her inmost bowels. Still to weep she seems.
Rapt in a furious whirlwind, distant far
Her natal soil receives her. There fixed high
On a hill's utmost summit, still she melts;
Still does the rigid marble flow in tears.

Pyramus and Thisbe.

Thisbe, the brightest of the eastern maids;
And Pyramus, the pride of all the youths,
Contiguous dwellings held, in that famed town,
Where lofty walls of stone we learn were raised
By bold Semiramis. Their neighboring site
Acquaintance first encouraged,—primal step
To further intimacy: love, in time,
Grew from this chance connection; and they longed
To join by lawful rites: but harsh forbade
Their rigid sires the union fate had doomed.
With equal ardor both their minds inflamed
Burnt fierce; and absent every watchful spy,
By nods and signs they spoke; for close their love
Concealed they kept;—concealed, it burned more fierce.
The severing wall a narrow chink contained,
Formed when first reared;—what will not love espy?
This chink, by all for ages past unseen,
The lovers first espied.—This opening gave
A passage for their voices; safely through
Their tender words were breathed in whisperings soft.
Oft punctual at their posts,—on this side she,
And Pyramus on that;—each breathing sighs,
By turns inhaling, have they mutual cried;
"Invidious wall! why lovers thus divide?
Much were it, did thy parts more wide recede,
And suffer us to join? were that too much
A little opening more, and we might meet
With lips at least. Yet grateful still we own
Thy kind indulgence, which a passage gives,
And amorous words conveys to loving ears."
Thus they loquacious, though on sides diverse,
Till night their converse stayed:—then cried "Adieu!"
And each imprinted kisses, which the stones
Forbade to taste. Soon as Aurora's fires
Removed the shades of night, and Phœbus' rays
From the moist earth the dew exhaled, they meet
As 'customed at the wall: lamenting deep,
As wont in murmuring whispers: bold they plan,

Their guards evading in the silent night,
To pass the outer gates. Then, when escaped
From home, to leave the city's dangerous shade;
But lest, in wandering o'er the spacious plains
They miss to meet, at Ninus' sacred tomb
They fix their assignation,—hid concealed
Beneath the umbrageous leaves. There grew a tree,
Close bordering on a cooling fountain's brink;
A stately mulberry;—snow-white fruit hung thick
On every branch. The plot pleased well the pair.

And now slow seems the car of Sol to sink;
Slow from the ocean seems the night to rise;
Till Thisbe, cautious, by the darkness veiled,
Soft turns the hinges, and her guards beguiles.
Her features veiled, the tomb she reaches,—sits
Beneath the appointed tree: love makes her bold.
Lo! comes a lioness,—her jaws besmeared
With gory foam, fresh from the slaughtered herd,
Deep in the adjoining fount her thirst to slake.
Far off the Babylonian maid beheld
By Luna's rays the horrid foe,—quick fled
With trembling feet, and gained a darksome cave:
Flying, she dropped and left her robe behind.
Now had the savage beast her thirst allayed,
And backward to the forest roaming, found
The veiling robe, its tender texture rent,
And smeared the spoil with bloody jaws. The youth
(With later fortune his strict watch escaped)
Saw the plain footsteps of a monster huge
Deep in the sand indented!—O'er his face
Pale terror spread: but when the robe he saw,
With blood besmeared and mangled; loud he cried,—
"One night shall close two lovers' eyes in death!
She most deserving of a longer date;
Mine is the fault alone. Dear luckless maid!
I have destroyed thee;—I, who bade thee keep
Nocturnal meetings in this dangerous place,
And came not first to shield thy steps from harm.
Ye lions, wheresoe'er within those caves
Ye lurk! haste hither,—tear me limb from limb!
Fierce ravaging devour, and make my tomb
Your horrid entrails." But for death to wish

A coward's turn may serve. The robe he takes,
Once Thisbe's, and beneath the appointed tree
Bearing it, bathed in tears; with ardent lips
Oft fondly kissing, thus he desperate cries;—
"Now with my blood be also bathed!—drink deep!"
And in his body plunged the sword, that round
His loins hung ready girt: then as he died,
Hasty withdrew, hot reeking from the wound,
The steel; and backwards falling, pressed the earth.
High spouts the sanguine flood! thus forth a pipe
(The lead decayed, or damaged) sends a stream
Contracted from the breach; upspringing high
And loudly hissing, as the air it breaks
With jets repeated. Sprinkled with the blood,
The tree's white fruit a purple tinge received;
Deep soaked with blood the roots convey the stain
Inly, and tinge each bough with Tyrian dye.

  Now Thisbe comes, with terror trembling still,
Fearful she Pyramus expecting waits:
Him seek her beating bosom and her eyes;
Anxious the peril she escaped to tell.
Well marked her eyes the place,—and well the tree;
The berries changed in color, long she doubts
The same or no. While hesitating thus,
The panting members quivering she beholds,
Upon the sanguined turf; and back recoils!
Paler than box her features grow; her limbs
More tremble than when ocean fretful sounds,
Its surface briskly by the breezes swept.
Nor long the pause, her lover soon is known;
And now her harmless breast with furious blows
She punishes: her tresses wild she rends;
Clasps the loved body; and the gaping wound
Fills with her tears,—their droppings with the blood
Immingling. On his clay-cold face she pressed
Her kisses, crying: "Pyramus! what chance
Has torn thee from me thus? My Pyramus!
Answer me,—'tis thy dearest Thisbe speaks!
She calls thee,—hear me,—raise that dying face!"
At Thisbe's name, his lids, with death hard weighed,
He raised—beheld her,—and forever closed.

  Him dying thus,—her lacerated veil,

The ivory scabbard emptied of its sword,
She saw,—at once the truth upon her mind
Flashed quick. "Alas! thy hand, by love impelled,
Has wrought thy ruin: but to me the hand,
In this, at least, shall equal force display,
For equal was my love; and love will grant
Sufficient strength the deadly wound to give.
In death I'll follow thee; with justice called
Thy ruin's wretched cause,—but comrade too.
Thou, whom but death seemed capable to part
From me, shalt find even death too weak will prove.
Ye wretched mourning parents, his and mine!
The dying prayers respect of him,—of me:
Grant that, entombed together, both may rest;
A pair by faithful love conjoined,—by death
United close. And thou, fair tree, which shad'st
Of one the miserable corpse; and two
Soon with thy boughs wilt cover,—bear the mark
Of the sad deed eternal;—tinged be thy fruit
With mournful coloring—monumental type
Of double slaughter." Speaking thus, she placed
The steely point, while yet with blood it smoked,
Beneath her swelling breast; and forward fell.
Her final prayer reached heaven; her parents reached:
Purple the berries blush, when ripened full;
And in one urn the lovers' ashes rest.

BAUCIS AND PHILEMON.

Two neighboring trees, with walls encompass'd round,
Stand on a moderate rise, with wonder shown;
One a hard oak, a softer linden one:
I saw the place and them, by Pittheus sent
To Phrygian realms, my grandsire's government.
Not far from thence is seen a lake, the haunt
Of coots and of the fishing cormorant:
Here Jove with Hermes came; but in disguise
Of mortal men concealed their deities;
One laid aside his thunder, one his rod,
And many toilsome steps together trod:
For harbor at a thousand doors they knocked;
Not one of all the thousand but was locked.

At last a hospitable house they found,
A homely shed; the roof, not far from ground,
Was thatched, with reeds and straw together bound.
There Baucis and Philemon lived, and there
Had lived long married, and a happy pair:
Now old in love, though little was their store,
Inured to want, their poverty they bore,
Nor aimed at wealth, professing to be poor.
For master or for servant here to call
Were all alike, where only two were all.
Command was none, where equal love was paid,
Or rather both commanded, both obeyed.

   From lofty roofs the gods repulsed before,
Now stooping, entered through the little door:
The man (their hearty welcome first expressed)
A common settle drew for either guest,
Inviting each his weary limbs to rest.
But ere they sat, officious Baucis lays
Two cushions stuffed with straw, the seat to raise;
Coarse, but the best she had; then rakes the load
Of ashes from the hearth, and spreads abroad
The living coals; and, lest they should expire,
With leaves and bark she feeds her infant fire.
It smokes; and then with trembling breath she blows,
Till in a cheerful blaze the flames arose.
With brushwood and with chips she strengthens these,
And adds at last the boughs of rotten trees.
The fire thus formed, she sets the kettle on
(Like burnished gold the little seether shone;)
Next took the coleworts which her husband got
From his own ground (a small, well-watered spot;)
She stripped the stalks of all their leaves; the best
She culled, and them with handy care she dressed.
High o'er the hearth a chine of bacon hung;
Good old Philemon seized it with a prong,
And from the sooty rafter drew it down,
Then cut a slice, but scarce enough for one;
Yet a large portion of a little store,
Which for their sakes alone he wished were more.
This in the pot he plunged without delay,
To tame the flesh and drain the salt away.
The time between, before the fire they sat,

And shortened the delay by pleasing chat
A beam there was, on which a beechen pail
Hung by the handle on a driven nail:
This filled with water, gently warmed, they set
Before their guests; in this they bathed their feet,
And after with clean towels dried their sweat.
This done, the host produced the genial bed,
Sallow the feet, the borders, and the stead,
Which with no costly coverlet they spread,
But coarse old garments; yet such robes as these
They lay alone at feasts on holydays.
The good old housewife, tucking up her gown,
The table sets; the invited gods lie down.
The trivet-table of a foot was lame,
A blot which prudent Baucis overcame,
Who thrust beneath the limping leg a sherd;
So was the mended board exactly reared;
Then rubbed it o'er with newly-gathered mint,
A wholesome herb, that breathed a grateful scent.
Pallas began the feast, where first was seen
The party-colored olive, black and green;
Autumnal cornels next in order served,
In lees of wine well pickled and preserved.
A garden salad was the third supply,
Of endives, radishes, and succory:
Then curds and cream, the flower of country fare,
And new-laid eggs, which Baucis' busy care
Turned by a gentle fire, and roasted rare.
All these in earthenware were served to board,
And, next in place, an earthen pitcher stored
With liquor of the best the cottage could afford.
This was the table's ornament and pride,
With figures wrought: like pages at his side
Stood beechen bowls; and these were shining clean,
Varnished with wax without, and lined within.
By this the boiling kettle had prepared
And to the table sent the smoking lard;
On which with eager appetite they dine,
A savory bit, that served to relish wine;
The wine itself was suiting to the rest,
Still working in the must, and lately pressed.
The second course succeeds like that before.

Plums, apples, nuts; and of their wintry store
Dry figs, and grapes, and wrinkled dates were set
In canisters, to enlarge the little treat:
All these a milkwhite honey-comb surround,
Which in the midst a country banquet crowned:
But the kind hosts their entertainment grace
With hearty welcome and an open face:
In all they did, you might discern with ease
A willing mind and a desire to please.

 Meanwhile the beechen bowls went round and still,
Though often emptied, were observed to fill:
Filled without hands, and, of their own accord,
Ran without feet, and danced about the board.
Devotion seized the pair, to see the feast
With wine, and of no common grape, increased;
And up they held their hands, and fell to prayer,
Excusing, as they could, their country fare.

 One goose they had ('twas all they could allow),
A wakeful sentry, and on duty now,
Whom to the gods for sacrifice they vow:
Her with malicious zeal the couple viewed;
She ran for life, and limping they pursued;
Full well the fowl perceived their bad intent,
And would not make her master's compliment;
But persecuted, to the powers she flies,
And close between the legs of Jove she lies:
He with a gracious ear the suppliant heard,
And saved her life; then what he was declared,
And owned the god, "The neighborhood," said he,
"Shall justly perish for impiety;
You stand alone exempted: but obey
With speed, and follow where we lead the way:
Leave these accursed, and to the mountain's height
Ascend, nor once look backward in your flight."

 They haste, and what their tardy feet denied,
The trusty staff (their better leg) supplied.
An arrow's flight they wanted to the top,
And there secure, but spent with travel; stop;
They turn their now no more forbidden eyes;
Lost in a lake the floated level lies:
A watery desert covers all the plains,
Their cot alone, as in an isle, remains.

Wondering, with weeping eyes, while they deplore
Their neighbors' fate and country now no more;
Their little shed, scarce large enough for two,
Seems, from the ground increased, in height and bulk to grow.
A stately temple shoots within the skies,
The crotches of their cot in columns rise;
The pavement polished marble they behold,
The gates with sculpture graced, the spires and tiles of gold.
Then thus the sire of gods, with looks serene:
"Speak thy desire, thou only just of men;
And thou, O woman, only worthy found
To be with such a man in marriage bound."
A while they whisper; then, to Jove addressed,
Philemon thus prefers their joint request:
"We crave to serve before your sacred shrine,
And offer at your altar rites divine:
And since not any action of our life
Has been polluted with domestic strife,
We beg one hour of death, that neither she
With widow's tears may live to bury me,
Nor weeping I, with withered arms, may bear
My breathless Baucis to the sepulchre."
The godheads sign their suit. They run their race,
In the same tenor, all the appointed space:
Then, when their hour was come, while they relate
These past adventures at the temple gate,
Old Baucis is by old Philemon seen
Sprouting with sudden leaves of sprightly green:
Old Baucis looked where old Philemon stood,
And saw his lengthen'd arms a sprouting wood:
New roots their fastened feet begin to bind,
Their bodies stiffen in a rising rind:
Then, ere the bark above their shoulders grew,
They give and take at once their last adieu.
At once "Farewell, O faithful spouse," they said;
At once the encroaching rinds their closing lips invade.
Even yet, an ancient Tyanæan shows
A spreading oak, that near a linden grows;
The neighborhood confirm the prodigy,
Grave men, not vain of tongue, or like to lie;

I saw myself the garlands on their boughs,
And tablets hung for gifts of granted vows;
And offering fresher up, with pious prayer,
"The good," said I, "are God's peculiar care,
And such as honor Heaven shall heavenly honor share."

TIBULLUS.

THROUGH the patronage of the Emperor Augustus, amatory or erotic poetry received a powerful impulse and rose to a high position. The Roman names that overshadow all others in this variety of lyric, are those of Tibullus, Propertius and Ovid, who excelled their Greek models.

Albius Tibullus came of an equestrian family whose estate was near Tibur. Here he passed most of his brief life. The inspiration for the first of his three books of elegies arose out of his attachment to Delia, a real personage. When Delia proved faithless, the poet's love was transferred to Nemesis, the subject of the second book. Later he turned to Glycera, probably the Glycera mentioned by Horace, and to her the third book is devoted. The fourth book is a sort of supplement, containing pieces by Tibullus and some of his friends, one of whom was a lady.

Tibullus is a poet of refined taste; his verses are smooth and polished; his metres are varied, and always skillfully handled. He was much esteemed by Horace, and still occupies the first place in Roman elegy, which, like the Greek, permitted a wide range of personal feeling.

ELEGY TO DELIA.

OH! I was harsh to say that I could part
 From thee; but, Delia, I am bold no more!
Driven like a top, which boys with ready art
 Keep spinning round upon a level floor.

Burn, lash me, love, if ever after this
 By me one cruel, blustering word is said;
Yet spare, I pray thee by our stolen bliss,
 By mighty Venus and thy comely head.

When thou didst lie by fell disease o'erpowered,
  I rescued thee, by prayers, from death's domain;
Pure sulphur's cleansing fumes I round thee showered,
  While an enchantress sung a magic strain.

Yes—and another now enjoys the prize,
  And reaps the fruit of all my vows for thee;
Foolish, I dreamed of life 'neath golden skies,
  Wert thou but saved—not such great Heaven's decree.

I said—I'll till my fields, she'll guard my store
  When crops are threshed in autumn's burning heat;
She'll keep my grapes in baskets brimming o'er,
  And my rich must* expressed by nimble feet.

She'll count my flock; some home-born slave of mine
  Will prattle in my darling's lap and play:
To rural god ripe clusters for the vine,
  Sheaves for my crops, cates for my fold, she'll pay.

Slaves—all shall own her undisputed rule;
  Myself a cypher—how the thought would please;
Here will Messala come, for whom she'll pull
  The sweetest apples from the choicest trees;

And, honoring one so great, for him prepare
  And serve the banquet with her own white hands.
Fond dream! which now the east and south winds bear
  Away to far Armenia's spicy lands.

Sulpicia on Cerinthus Going to the Chase.

Whether, fierce boars, in flowery meads ye stray,
Or haunt the shady mountain's devious way,
Whet not your teeth against my dear one's charms,
But oh, let faithful Love restore him to my arms.
  What madness 'tis the trackless wilds to beat,
And wound with pointed thorns thy tender feet:
Oh! why to savage beast thy charms oppose?
With toils and bloodhounds why their haunts enclose?
  Yet, yet with thee, Cerinthus, might I rove,
Thy nets I'd trail through every mountain grove,

---

* The unfermented juice of the grape.

Would track the bounding stags through tainted grounds,
Beat up their covers and unchain thy hounds.
But most to spread our artful toils I'd joy,
For, while we watched them, I could clasp my boy!
   Oh, without me, ne'er taste the joys of love,
But a chaste hunter in my absence prove;
And oh, may boars the wanton fair destroy,
Who would Cerinthus to her arms decoy!
Yet, yet I dread!—Be sports thy father's care;
But thou, all love! to these fond arms repair!

Cerinthus to Sulpicia.

"Never shall woman's smile have power
    To win me from those gentle charms!"—
Thus swore I in that happy hour
    When Love first gave them to my arms.

And still alone thou charm'st my sight—
    Still, though our city proudly shine
With forms and faces fair and bright,
    I see none fair or bright but thine.

Would thou wert fair for only me
    And couldst no heart but mine allure!—
To all men else unpleasing be,
    So shall I feel my prize secure.

Oh, love like mine ne'er wants the zest
    Of others' envy, others' praise;
But, in its silence safely blest,
    Broods over a bliss it ne'er betrays.

Charm of my life! by whose sweet power
    All cares are hushed, all ills subdued—
My light in even the darkest hour,
    My crowd in deepest solitude!

No; not though Heaven itself sent down
    Some maid of more than heavenly charms,
With bliss undreamt thy bard to crown,
    Would I for her forsake those charms.

PROPERTIUS.

The social and domestic relations of Propertius bear a striking resemblance to those of Tibullus. Both were of good parentage; both suffered from the public distribution of land occasioned by the civil war; both derived their poetical inspiration from the objects of their love, and both were removed by death before reaching the prime of life.

Sextus Aurelius Propertius, born about 50 B.C., died at the age of thirty-five. He formed one of the brilliant coterie of Mæcenas, and was on intimate terms with Ovid and Virgil, but his literary tastes differed somewhat from those of his colleagues. He was still more attracted by the complete mastery of form shown by the Alexandrian school. Besides the erotic elegies addressed to his mistress Cynthia, Propertius wrote various pieces relating to the early history of Rome. He was a man of extensive learning, thoroughly versed in Greek mythology, the repeated allusions to which frequently interrupt the course of his theme, and destroy sequence and coherency of thought. He makes a display of his learning in the use of Greek idioms, by which his style is rendered cramped, forced, and often inharmonious. The poetry of Propertius is passionate, sometimes licentious, but it does not approach that of Ovid in flagrant indelicacy.

The Image of Love.

Had he not hands of rare device, whoe'er
  First painted Love in figure of a boy?
He saw what thoughtless beings lovers were,
  Who blessings lose, whilst lightest cares employ,
Nor added he those airy wings in vain,
  And bade through human hearts the godhead fly;
For we are tossed upon a wavering main;
  Our gale, inconstant, veers around the sky.
Nor, without cause, he grasps those barbéd darts,
  The Cretan quiver o'er his shoulder cast;
Ere we suspect a foe, he strikes our hearts;
  And those inflicted wounds forever last.

In me are fixed those arrows—in my breast;
    But, sure, his wings are shorn, the boy remains;
For never takes he flight, nor knows he rest;
    Still, still I feel him warring through my veins.
In these scorched vitals dost thou joy to dwell?
    Oh, shame! to others let thine arrows flee;
Let veins, untouched, with all thy venom swell;
    Not me thou torturest, but the shade of me.
Destroy me,—who shall then describe the fair?
    This my light Muse to thee high glory brings;
When the nymphs' tapering fingers, flowing hair,
    And eyes of jet, and gliding feet, she sings.

Love's Dream Realized.

Not in his Dardan triumph so rejoiced the great Atrides,
    When fell the mighty kingdom of Laomedon of yore,
Not so Ulysses, when he moored his wave-worn raft beside his
    Beloved Dulichian island home—his weary wanderings o'er.

As I, when last eve's rosy joys I ruminated over:
    To me another eve like that were immortality!
A while before with downcast head I walked a pining lover—
    More useless I had grown, 'twas said, than water-tank run dry.

No more my darling passes me with silent recognition,
    Nor can she sit unmoved while I outpour my tender vow.
I wish that I had sooner realized this blest condition;
    'Tis pouring living water on a dead man's ashes now.

In vain did others seek my love, in vain they called upon her,
    She leaned her head upon my breast, was kind as girl could be.
Of conquered Parthians talk no more, I've gained a nobler honor,
    For she'll be spoils, and leaders, and triumphal car to me.

Light of my life! say, shall my bark reach shore with gear befitting,
    Or, dashed amid the breakers, with her cargo run aground?
With thee it lies; but if, perchance, through fault of my committing,
    Thou giv'st me o'er, before thy door let my cold corpse be found.

LIVY.

In the Augustan period the one great historian is Titus Livius, born of illustrious parentage at Padua, B.C. 69. On his removal to Rome he came under the favorable notice of Augustus. The great work by which he is known to posterity is the "History of Rome" from the time of Æneas to the death of Drusus, in 9 A.D. The whole history consisted originally of 142 Books, of which only thirty-five have been transmitted to us—the first ten and Books XXI. to XLV. inclusive.

Livy charms us by his romantic narrative, his lucid style, and his matchless descriptions. He desires to be truthful, and never falsifies intentionally, but he shrinks from telling the whole truth. Patriotism, or pride of race, prompts him to make more of a Roman victory than a Roman defeat. And this desire to celebrate the triumphs and the military glory of Rome occasions some strange inconsistencies.

Livy's ideal of social and political life is in the past, and he loves to call up the glories of the republic, and bring them back to life. He sometimes laments the loss of modesty, simplicity, loftiness of mind, and especially the piety of bygone days. The Rome of Cincinnatus and Fabius Cunctator is his ideal, and in his unhesitating patriotism he crowns the "Eternal City" with glory, and overwhelms her foes with ignominy. Livy accepts the narratives of his predecessors, and contents himself with improving upon their style. This he accomplishes with eminent success, and never loses his charm as a narrator. No one could have been better fitted than Livy to be the favorite historian of the Augustan period. It was a time of peace and self-complacency, luxurious ease, and

Panorama of Rome from St. Peter's.

the refined pleasures of advanced civilization, when praise was more acceptable than criticism. He was eminently a rhetorician, and he finds an outlet for his rhetorical learning in the speeches which he puts into the mouths of his chief characters. Yet thus he often gives a faithful picture of the person under review, but he is not careful to avoid sameness in the style of his speeches, nor to adapt them to the speakers. Livy believed in the republic and government by the "optimates," or "best men,"—the aristocracy.

Livy died the same year as Ovid, 17 A.D., and was buried in his native city, where a mausoleum was raised to him in the middle of the sixteenth century.

Brutus and his Sons.

Lucius Junius Brutus, who had freed Rome from the tyranny of the Tarquins in 510 B.C., was made one of the first consuls. His administration was embarrassed by attempts to restore the kings. The chief attempt is here reported.

Though nobody doubted that a war was impending from the Tarquins, yet it broke out later than was universally expected; but liberty was well nigh lost by treachery and fraud, a thing they had never apprehended. There were, among the Roman youth, several young men of noble families, who, during the regal government, had pursued their pleasures without any restraint; being of the same age with, and companions of, the young Tarquins, and accustomed to live in princely style. Longing for that licentiousness, now that the privileges of all were equalized, they complained that the liberty of others had been converted to their slavery: "that a king was a human being, from whom you could obtain what may be necessary; that there was room for favor and for kindness; that he could be angry, and could forgive; that he knew the difference between a friend and an enemy; that laws were a deaf, inexorable thing, more beneficial and advantageous for the poor than the rich; that they allowed of no relaxation or indulgence, if you transgress bounds; that it was perilous, amid so many human errors, to live solely by one's integrity." Whilst their minds were already thus discontented, ambassadors from the royal family came unexpectedly, demanding restitution of their effects merely, without any mention of return. After their application was heard in the senate, the deliberation on it lasted for several days, fearing lest the non-restitution might be a pretext for war, and the restitution a fund and assistance for war. In the meantime the ambassadors were planning different schemes; openly demanding the property, they secretly concerted measures for recovering the throne, and soliciting persons as if for the object which appeared to be under consideration, they sound their feelings; to those by whom their proposals were favorably received they give letters from the Tarquins, and confer with them about admitting the royal family into the city secretly by night.

The matter was first intrusted to brothers named Vitellii and those named Aquilii. A sister of the Vitellii had been married to Brutus the consul, and the issue of that marriage were young men, Titus and Tiberius; these their uncles admitted into a participation of the plot: several young noblemen also were taken in as associates, the memory of whose names has been lost from distance of time. In the meantime, when that opinion had prevailed in the senate, which recommended the giving back of the property, and the ambassadors made use of this as a pretext for delay in the city, because they had obtained from the consuls time to procure modes of conveyance, by which they might convey away the effects of the royal family; all this time they spend in consulting with the conspirators, and by pressing they succeed in having letters given to them for the Tarquins. For otherwise how were they to believe that the accounts brought by the ambassadors on matters of such importance were not idle? The letters, given to be a pledge of their sincerity, disclosed the plot; for when, the day before the ambassadors set out to the Tarquins, they had supped by chance at the house of the Vitellii, and the conspirators there in private discoursed much together concerning their new design, one of the slaves, who had already perceived what was going on, overheard their conversation; but waited for the occasion when the letters should be given to the ambassadors, the detection of which would prove the transaction; when he perceived that they were given, he laid the whole affair before the consuls. The consuls, having left their home to seize the ambassadors and conspirators, crushed the whole affair without any tumult; particular care being taken of the letters, lest they should escape them. The traitors being immediately thrown into chains, but doubt arose respecting the ambassadors, and though they deserved to be considered as enemies, the law of nations prevailed.

The question concerning the restitution of the tyrants' effects, which the senate had formerly voted, came again under consideration. The Fathers, fired with indignation, expressly forbade them either to be restored or confiscated. They were given to be rifled by the people, that after being made participators in the royal plunder, they might lose forever all hopes of a reconciliation with the Tarquins. A field belonging to them, which lay between the city and the Tiber, having been consecrated to Mars, has been called the Campus Martius. It happened that there was a crop of corn upon it ready to be cut down, which produce of the field, as they thought it unlawful to use, after it was reaped, a great number of men carried the corn and straw in baskets, and threw them into the Tiber, which then flowed with shallow water, as is usual in the heat of summer; that thus the heaps of corn as it stuck in the shallows became settled when covered over with mud; by these and the afflux of other things, which the river happened to bring thither, an island was formed by degrees. Afterwards mounds were added, and aid was afforded by art, that a surface so well raised might be firm enough for sustaining temples and porticoes.

After plundering the tyrants' effects, the traitors were condemned and capital punishment inflicted. Their punishment was the more remarkable, because the consulship imposed on the father the office of punishing his own children, and the one who should have been removed as a spectator, Fortune assigned as the person to exact the punishment. Young men of the highest quality stood tied to a stake; but the consul's sons attracted the eyes of all the spectators from the rest of the criminals, as from persons unknown; nor did the people pity them more on account of the severity of the punishment, than the horrid crime by which they had deserved it. "That they, in that year particularly, should have brought themselves to betray into the hands of Tarquin, formerly a proud tyrant, and now an exasperated exile, their country just delivered, their father its deliverer, the consulate which took its rise from the family of the Junii, the Fathers, the people, and whatever belonged either to the gods or the citizens of Rome." The consuls seated themselves in their tribunal, and the lictors, being despatched to inflict punishment, strip them naked, beat them with rods, and strike off their heads. During all this time, the father's looks and countenance presented a touching spectacle, his natural feelings bursting forth occasionally during the office of superintending the public execution. Next after the punishment of the guilty, that there might be a striking example in either way for the prevention of crime, a sum of money was granted out of the treasury as a reward to the informer; liberty also and the rights of citizenship were granted him.

THE GAULS ENTER ROME

IN the year 387 B.C., the Gauls under Brennus invaded Italy. At the river Allia, a branch of the Tiber, they defeated the Romans with great slaughter, and might at once have entered the city, but delayed, being amazed at their own success.

AT the enemy's first approach, it was supposed that they would begin the attack, as soon as they should arrive at the city, since, if this were not their intention, they would probably have remained at the Allia. The fears of the citizens were various; first, they imagined that the place would be instantly stormed, because there was not much of the day remaining; then that the design was put off until night, in order to strike the greater terror. At last, the approach of light sunk them in dismay, and the evil itself which they dreaded, closed this scene of unremitted apprehension, the enemy marching through the gates in hostile array. During that night, however, and also the following day, the state preserved a character, very different from that which such a dastardly flight at the Allia had indicated: for there being no room to hope, that the city could possibly be defended by the small number of troops remaining, a resolution was taken, that the young men who were fit to bear arms, and the abler part of the senate, with their wives and children, should go up into the citadel and the Capitol; and having collected stores of arms and corn, should, in that strong post, maintain the defence of the deities, of the inhabitants, and of the honor of Rome. That the Flamen Quirinalis, and the vestal priestesses, should carry away, far from slaughter and conflagration, all that appertained to the gods of the state; and that their worship should not be intermitted until there should be no one left to perform it. That such of this deserted multitude as consisted of plebeians, might bear their doom with the greater resignation, the aged nobles, formerly dignified with triumphal honors and consulships, openly declared, that "they would meet death along with them, and would not burthen the scanty stores of the fighting men, with bodies incapable of carrying arms, and of protecting their country."

Such were the consolations addressed to each other by the aged who were destined to death.

Their exhortations were then turned to the band of young men, whom they escorted to the Capitol and citadel, commending to their valor and youthful vigor the remaining fortune of their city, which, through the course of three hundred and sixty years, had ever been victorious in all its wars. When those who carried with them every hope and every resource, parted with the others, who had determined not to survive the capture and destruction of the city, the view which it exhibited was sufficient to call forth the liveliest feelings, the women at the same time running up and down in distraction, now following one party, then the other, asking their husbands and their sons, to what fate they would consign them? All together formed such a picture of human woe as could admit of no aggravation. A great part, however, of the women followed their relatives into the citadel, no one either hindering or inviting them; because, though the measure of lessening the number of useless persons, in a siege, might doubtless be advisable in one point of view, yet it was a measure of extreme inhumanity. The rest of the multitude, consisting chiefly of plebeians, for whom there was neither room on so small a hill, nor a possibility of support in so great a scarcity of corn, pouring out of the city in one continued train, repaired to the Janiculum.

Meanwhile at Rome, when every disposition for the defence of the citadel had been completed, as far as was possible, the aged crowd withdrew to their houses, and there, with a firmness of mind not to be shaken by the approach of death, waited the coming of the enemy: such of them as had held curule offices, choosing to die in that garb which displayed the emblems of their former fortune, of their honors, or of their merit, put on the most splendid robes worn, when they drew the chariots of the gods in procession, or rode in triumph. Thus habited, they seated themselves in their ivory chairs at the fronts of their houses. Some say that they devoted themselves for the safety of their country and their fellow-citizens; and that they sung a hymn upon the occasion, Marcus Fabius, the chief pontiff, dictating the form of words to them. On the side of the Gauls, as the keenness of their rage, excited by the fight, had abated during the night; and, as they had neither met any dangerous opposition in the field, nor were now taking the city by storm or force; they marched next day, without any anger or any heat of passion, into the city, through the Colline gate, which stood open, and advanced to the Forum, casting round their eyes on the temples of the gods, and on the citadel, the only place which had the appearance of making resistance. From thence, leaving a small guard to prevent any attack from the citadel or Capitol, they ran about in quest of plunder. Not meeting a human being in the streets, part of them rushed in a body to the houses that stood nearest; part sought the most distant, as expecting to find them untouched and abounding with spoil. Afterwards, being frightened from thence by the very solitude, and fearing lest some secret design of the enemy might be put in execution against them, while they were thus dispersed; they formed themselves into bodies, and returned again to the Forum and places adjoining to it. Finding the houses of the plebeians shut up, and the palaces of the nobles standing open, they showed rather greater backwardness to attack these that were open, than such as were shut; with such a degree of veneration did they behold men sitting in the porches of those palaces, who, beside their ornaments and apparel, more splendid than became mortals, bore the nearest resemblances to gods, in the majesty displayed in their looks, and the gravity of their countenances. It is said, that while they stood gazing as on statues, one of them, Marcus Papirius, provoked the anger of a Gaul, by striking him on the head with his ivory sceptre, while he was stroking his beard, which at that time was universally worn long; that the slaughter began with him, and that the rest were slain in their seats. The nobles being put to death, the remainder of the people met the same fate. The houses were plundered and then set on fire.

Scipio and Allucius.

[WHILE Publius Scipio had charge of Roman affairs in Spain], a captive was brought before him by his soldiers—a grown-up maiden of such remarkable beauty, that wherever she moved she attracted the eyes of all. Scipio inquired her country and her parentage, and ascertained, among other things, that she was affianced to a young chief of the Celtiberi, whose name was Allucius. He at once sent for her lover and her parents from their homes, and heard in the meanwhile that the youth was passionately attached to her.

As soon as they arrived, he addressed himself to the lover more particularly than to the parents: "I address myself," said he, "as one young man to another, that there may be less embarrassment between us in this interview. When your betrothed bride was brought to me by our soldiers, I heard that you were very much in love with her—a fact which indeed her beauty makes me readily believe, inasmuch as, were I at liberty to indulge the passions natural to my age, especially in a honorable and lawful way, and if public duty did not engross all my thoughts, I might have claimed indulgence, had I become desperately enamored of some lady myself. Your passion, at least, I can favor, and I do. Your betrothed has been treated with the same respect while in my charge as she would have been under the roof of her own parents and your future connections. She has been kept safe for you, that I might present her to you untarnished, a gift worthy alike of myself and you. This one return I bargain for in repayment for this gift of mine. Become the friend of the Roman people. And if you believe me to be a man of honor, as these tribes know my father and my uncle to have been, I would have you learn that there are many like us in the state of Rome, and that no nation can be named at this day upon earth whom you ought less to wish to have for enemies to you and yours, or should prefer as friends."

The young chief, overwhelmed with embarrassment and joy, grasped Scipio's hand, and called upon all the gods to repay his benefactor an obligation which it would never be in his own power to discharge in any way correspondent to his own feelings and Scipio's claims upon his gratitude. Then the maiden's parents and relatives were summoned. Finding that she was to be restored to them gratuitously, whereas they had come prepared with a considerable weight of gold for her ransom, they began to entreat Scipio to receive it from them as a present, protesting that in so doing he would confer upon them an obligation not less than this free and honorable restoration of their daughter. Seeing them so earnest in their request, Scipio promised that he would accept the gold, and ordered it to be laid at his feet. Then, calling Allucius to him, he said: "As an addition to the dowry which you will receive from your father-in-law, take this as my wedding present;" and he desired him to take the gold for himself.

The bridegroom took his leave, delighted alike at the gift and the compliment, and went home to fill the ears of his countrymen with the praises of Scipio: "There had come upon earth a hero like unto the gods, conquering all men not only by his valor, but by his kindness and munificence." And he straightway made a levy of his retainers, and, with fifteen hundred picked horsemen, returned in a few days to Scipio.

THE ROMAN DEBATE ON WOMEN'S RIGHTS.

THE Oppian law, enacted during the heat of the Punic War, required that "no woman should possess more than half an ounce of gold, or wear a garment of various colors, or ride in a carriage drawn by horses, in a city, or any town, or any place nearer thereto than one mile; except on occasion of some public religious solemnity." In the year 196 B.C. two tribunes of the people proposed to repeal this law, while two other tribunes opposed the movement. Many of the nobility argued for and against the motion proposed. Livy's account of the agitation in Rome and the debate in the Senate has many features of modern aspect.

THE Capitol was filled with crowds, who favored or opposed the law; nor could the matrons be kept at home, either by advice or shame, nor even by the commands of their husbands; but beset every street and passage in the city, beseeching the men as they went down to the forum, that in the present flourishing state of the commonwealth, when the private fortune of all was daily increasing, they would suffer the women to have their former ornaments of dress restored. This throng of women increased daily, for they arrived even from the country towns and villages; and they had at length the boldness to approach the consuls, prætors, and magistrates, to urge their request. One of the consuls, however, they found especially inexorable—Marcus Porcius Cato—who, in support of the existing law, spoke to this effect:

"If, Romans, every man among us had made it a rule to maintain the husband's prerogative and authority with respect to his own wife, we should have less trouble with the whole sex. But now, our rights, being overpowered at home by female contumacy, are, even here in the forum, spurned and trodden under foot; and because we are unable to withstand each woman separately, we now dread their collective body. I was accustomed to think it a fabulous and fictitious tale, that, in a certain island the whole race of males was utterly extirpated by a conspiracy of the women. But the utmost danger may be apprehended equally from either sex, if you suffer cabals, assemblies, and secret consultations to be held: scarcely, indeed, can I determine, in my own mind, whether the act itself, or the precedent that it affords, is of more pernicious tendency. The latter of these more particularly concerns us consuls and the other magistrates: the former concerns you all. It was not without painful emotions of shame, that I just now made my way into the forum through the midst of a band of women. Had I not been restrained by respect for the modesty and dignity of some individuals among them, rather than of the whole number, and been unwilling that they should be seen rebuked by a consul, I should have said to them, 'What sort of practice is this, of running out into public, crowding the streets, and addressing other women's husbands? Could not each have made the same request to her husband at home? Are your blandishments more seducing in public than in private; and with other women's husbands than with your own? Although if the modesty of matrons confined them within the limits of their own rights, it did not become you, even at home, to concern yourselves about what laws might be passed or repealed here.'

"Our ancestors thought it not proper that women should perform any, even private business, without a director; but that they should be ever under the control of parents, brothers, or husbands. We, it seems, suffer them now to interfere in the management of state affairs, and to introduce themselves into the forum, into general assemblies, and into assemblies of election. For, what are they doing at this moment in your streets and lanes? What but arguing, some in support of the motion of the plebeian tribunes; others for the repeal of the law? Will you give the reins to their intractable nature, and their uncontrolled passions, and then expect that themselves should set bounds to their licentiousness, when you have failed to do so? This is the smallest of the injunctions laid on them by usage or the laws, all which women bear with impatience: they long for liberty; or rather, to speak the truth, for unbounded freedom in every particular. What will they not attempt if they now come off victorious?

"Recollect all the institutions respecting the sex, by which our forefathers restrained their undue freedom, and by which they subjected them to their husbands; and yet, even with the help of all these restrictions, you can scarcely keep them within bounds. If, then, you suffer them to throw these off one by one, to tear them all asunder, and, at last, to be set on an equal footing with yourselves, can you imagine that they will be any longer endurable by you? The moment they have arrived at an equality with you, they will have become your superiors.

"I should like, however, to hear what this important affair is which has induced the matrons thus to run out into public in this excited manner, scarcely refraining from pushing into the forum and the assembly of the people. Is it to solicit that their parents, their husbands, children, and brothers may be ransomed from captivity under Hannibal? By no means: and far be ever from the commonwealth so unfortunate a situation. Yet, even when such was the case, you refused this to their prayers. But it is not duty, nor solicitude for their friends; it is religion that has collected them together. They are about to receive the new goddess, the Idæan mother (Cybele) coming out of Phrygia! What motive, that even common decency will allow to be mentioned, is pretended for this female insurrection? Why, say they, that we may shine in gold and purple; that, both on festal and common days, we may ride through the city in our chariots, triumphing over vanquished and abrogated·law, after having captured and wrested from you your suffrages; and that there may be no bounds to our expenses and our luxury.

"Often have you heard me complain of the profuse expenses of the women—often of those of the men; and that not only of men in private stations, but of the magistrates: and that the state was endangered by two opposite vices, luxury and avarice; those pests, which have been the ruin of all great empires. These I dread the more, as the circumstances of the commonwealth grow daily more prosperous and happy; as the empire increases; as we have now passed over into Greece and Asia, places abounding with every kind of temptation that can inflame the passions; and as we have begun to handle even royal treasures, so much the more do I fear that these matters will bring us into captivity, rather than we them.

"Do not suppose that the matter will hereafter be in the same state in which it was before the law was made on the subject. It is safer that a wicked man should even never be accused, than that he should be acquitted; and luxury, if it had never been meddled with, would be more tolerable than it will be now, like a wild beast, irritated by having been chained, and then let loose. My opinion is that the Oppian law ought, on no account, to be repealed. Whatever determination you may come to, I pray all the gods to prosper it."

After him the plebeian tribunes, who had declared their intention of protesting, added a few words to the same purport. Then Lucius Valerius spoke thus in support of the measure which he himself had introduced:—"If private persons only had stood forth to argue for and against the proposition which we have submitted to your consideration, I for my part, thinking enough to have been said on both sides, would have waited in silence for your determination. But since a person of most respectable judgment, the consul, Marcus Porcius Cato, has reprobated our motion, not only by the influence of his opinion, which, had he said nothing, would carry very great weight, but also in a long and careful discourse, it becomes necessary to say a few words in answer. He has spent more words in rebuking the matrons than in arguing against the measure proposed; and even went so far as to mention a doubt, whether the matrons had committed the conduct which he censured in them spontaneously or at our instigation. I shall defend the measure, not ourselves: for the consul threw out those insinuations against us, rather for argument's sake, than as a serious charge. He has made use of the terms 'cabal and sedition,' and, again, 'secession of the women:' because the matrons had requested of you, in the public streets, that, in this time of peace, when the commonwealth is flourishing and happy, you would repeal a law that was made against them during a war, and in times of distress. I know that these and other similar strong expressions are easily invented for the purpose of exaggeration; and, mild as Marcus Cato is in his disposition, yet in his speeches he is not only vehement, but sometimes even austere. What new thing, let me ask, have the matrons done in coming out into public in a body on an occasion which nearly concerns themselves? Have they never before appeared in public? I will turn over your own Antiquities,* and quote them against you.

* Cato's "Origines," or Early History of Rome, which has been lost.

Hear, now, how often they have done the same, and always to the advantage of the public, In the earliest period of our history, even in the reign of Romulus, when the Capitol had been taken by the Sabines, and a pitched battle was fought in the Forum, was not the fight stopped by the intervention of the matrons between the two armies? When, after the expulsion of the kings, the legions of the Volscians, under the command of Marcius Coriolanus, were encamped at the fifth milestone, did not the matrons turn away that army, which would have overwhelmed this city? Again, when Rome was taken by the Gauls, whence was the city ransomed? Did not the matrons, by unanimous agreement, bring their gold into the public treasury? In the late war [against Hannibal], not to go back to remote antiquity, when there was a want of money, did not the funds of the widows supply the treasury? And when even new gods were invited hither to the relief of our distressed affairs, did not the matrons go out in a body to the seashore to receive the Idæan Mother?

"I come now to the question in debate, with respect to which the consul's argument is two-fold: for, first, he is displeased at the thought of any law whatever being repealed; and then, particularly, of that law which was made to restrain female luxury. His former argument, in support of the laws in general, appeared highly becoming of a consul; and that on the latter, against luxury, was quite conformable to the rigid strictness of his morals. . . .

"Now, is there a man among you who does not know that this is a new law, passed not more than twenty years ago, in the consulate of Quintus Fabius and Tiberius Sempronius? And as, without it, our matrons sustained, for such a number of years, the most virtuous characters, what danger is there of their abandoning themselves to luxury on its being repealed? For, if that law had been passed for the purpose of setting a limit to the passions of the sex, there would be reason to fear lest the repeal of it might operate as an incitement to them. But the real reason of its being passed, the time itself will show. Hannibal was then in Italy, victorious at Cannæ: he already held possession of Tarentum, of Arpi, of Capua, and seemed ready to bring up his army to the city of Rome. Our allies had deserted us. We had neither soldiers to fill up the legions, nor seamen to man the fleet, nor money in the treasury. Under these circumstances, who does not clearly see that the poverty and distress of the state, requiring that every private person's money should be converted to the use of the public, brought into being that law, with intent that it should remain in force so long only as the cause of enacting the law should remain?

"Shall, then, every other class of people, every individual, feel the improvement in the condition of the state; and shall our wives alone reap none of the fruits of the public peace and tranquillity? Shall we men have the use of purple, wearing the purple-bordered gown in magistracies and priests' offices? Shall our children wear purple-bordered gowns? Shall we allow the privilege of wearing such gowns to the magistrates of the colonies and borough towns, and to the lowest of them here at Rome, the superintendents of the streets; and not only of wearing such an ornament of distinction while alive, but of being buried with it when dead; and shall we interdict the use of purple to women alone? And when you, the husband, may wear purple in your great coat, will you not suffer your wife to have a purple mantle? Shall your horse be more splendidly caparisoned than your wife is clothed? But with respect to purple, which will be worn out and consumed, I can see an unjust, indeed, but still a sort of reason, for parsimony; but with respect to gold, in which, excepting the price of the workmanship, there is no waste, what objection can there be? It rather serves as a reserve fund for both public and private exigencies, as you have already experienced. Cato says there will be no emulation between individuals, when no one is possessed of it. But, in truth, it will be a source of indignation to all, when they see those ornaments allowed to the wives of the Latin confederates of which they themselves have been deprived; when they see those women riding through the city in their carriages, and decorated with gold and purple, while they are obliged to follow on foot, as if the seat of empire were in the country of the others, not in their own. This would hurt the feelings even of men, and what do you think must be its effect on those of weak women, whom even trifles can disturb? Neither offices of state, nor of the priesthood, nor triumphs, nor badges of distinction, nor military presents, nor spoils, can fall to their share. Elegance of appearance, and ornaments, and dress, these are the women's badges of distinction; in these they delight and glory; these our ancestors called the women's world. What else do they lay aside when in mourning, except their gold and purple? And what else do they resume when the mourning is over? How do they distinguish themselves on occasion of public thanksgivings and supplications, but by adding unusual splendor of dress? But then (it may be said) if you repeal the Oppian law, should you choose to prohibit any of those particulars which the law at present prohibits, you will not have it in your power; your daughters, wives, and even the sisters of some, will be less under control. The bondage of women is never shaken off without the loss of their friends; and they themselves look with horror on that freedom which is purchased with the condition of the widow or the orphan. Their wish is, that their dress should be under your individual regulation, as husbands and fathers, not under that of the law; and it ought to be your wish to hold the women in control and guardianship, not in bondage; and to prefer the title of father or husband to that of master. The consul just now made use of some invidious terms, calling it a female sedition and secession; because, I suppose, there is danger of their seizing the Sacred Mount, as formerly the angry plebeians did, or the Aventine. Their feeble nature must submit to whatever you think proper to enjoin; and, the greater power you possess, the more moderate ought you to be in the exercise of your authority."

Although all these considerations had been urged against the motion and in its favor, the women next day poured out into public in much greater numbers, and in a body beset the doors of the tribunes who had protested against the measure of their colleagues; nor did they retire until this intervention was withdrawn. There was then no further doubt that every one of the tribes would vote for the repeal of the law. Thus was this law annulled, in the twentieth year after it had been made.

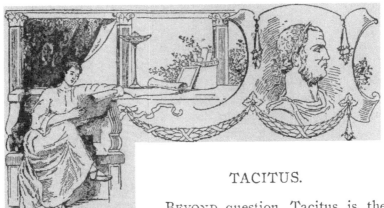

TACITUS.

BEYOND question, Tacitus is the greatest of Roman historians, as Thucydides is of the Greek. Like the latter, Tacitus chose for his theme a period with which he was practically familiar, having himself been engaged in public life. His field was vaster than that of the Athenian historian, and the events were of more consequence to the world in general, yet in philosophic insight into the causes and tendencies of events he does not equal his great predecessor. Tacitus related the history of the early Roman empire from 14 to 97 A.D., but only parts of his works have been preserved, which do not bring the narrative later than 70 A.D. His moral purpose is revealed in his statement of the historian's duty, "to rescue merit from oblivion, and to expose evil words and actions to the reprobation of posterity." This purpose he faithfully executed with regard to some of the best and some of the worst Roman emperors, as well as other prominent men and women of the time. His chief excellence, indeed, lies in the delineation of characters; to each of those described he imparts a distinctive individuality, such as is seldom seen except in the works of the greatest dramatists and novelists, yet the portraits drawn by Tacitus are felt to have inherent fidelity to facts.

The dates of the birth and death of this eminent historian are matters of inference from scanty data. Caius Cornelius Tacitus was born about 52 A.D., and seems to have lived beyond 117. In spite of this uncertainty about dates, he was a man of noble family and connections, and early attained eminence as a pleader at the bar. According to his own statement, his promotion was begun by Vespasian, augmented by Titus, and further advanced by Domitian. In 88 he was prætor, afterwards was in the Senate, and in 97 was made consul. He confesses that while he was in the Senate he was an unwilling participant in deeds of blood and persecution carried out by the imperial will under forms of law. In the quiet reign of Trajan, when personal freedom was restored, Tacitus appears to have retired from public life to devote himself entirely to literary work, in which he had already won some distinction. Throughout his career he enjoyed the friendship of Pliny the Younger, and much of their correspondence has been preserved to shed grateful light on their times and characters.

Besides his two historical works, the "Histories" and the "Annals," which form in fact a continuous narrative, Tacitus wrote an admirable, though highly eulogistic, biography of his father-in-law, Julius Agricola. As this man was the Roman conqueror of Britain, Tacitus gives considerable in formation about the inhabitants of that island. Another work which has proved of great value in recent researches in race-history, is his description of Germany and its tribes. Tacitus had never visited that country, but he was deeply impressed with the reports brought by those who had come into close contact with the fair-haired, blue-eyed Teutons. In their barbarian freedom and simplicity he recognized something akin to ancestral Roman virtue, and he warned his countrymen of the danger of sinking to inferiority to the hardy warriors beyond the Rhine. Perhaps the earliest of the writings of Tacitus was the "Dialogue on Orators," in which he discusses the cause of the decay of Roman eloquence. In all his works he displays a conservative spirit. He sees the demoralization prevailing and increasing under the Empire, and he looks back regretfully and wistfully to the old senatorial rule, under which the glory of Rome had steadily advanced. Examples of virtue, public and private, could still be found in his own degenerate days, but he feared that the excess of wealth, and consequent luxury, and the influx of a heterogeneous multitude had destroyed the vitality of the commonwealth. The style of Tacitus is marked by brevity and epigrammatic conciseness. While usually brief and rapid in his sketches, he sometimes goes into minute detail in dramatic passages. His extreme condensation often renders his meaning obscure, as the precise meaning of a single word gives effect to a whole sentence, and if that be missed, the significance of all is blurred. Hence he is one of the most difficult authors to translate. Frequent reading is necessary to bring out the full meaning of his pregnant sentences.

The Death of Tiberius.

(From the Annals, Book VI.)

The bodily powers of Tiberius were now leaving him, but not his skill in dissembling. There was the same stern spirit; he had his words and his looks under strict control; and occasionally would try to hide his weakness, evident as it was, by a forced politeness. After frequent changes of place, he at last settled down on the promontory of Misenum, in a country-house once owned by Lucius Lucullus. It was there discovered that he was drawing near his end; and thus there was a physician of the name of Charicles usually employed, not indeed to have the direction of the Emperor's varying health, but to put his advice at his immediate disposal. This man, as if he were leaving on business of his own, clasped his hand with a show of homage, and touched his pulse. Tiberius noticed it. Whether he was displeased, and strove the more to hide his anger, is a question. At any rate, he ordered the banquet to be resumed, and sat at the table longer than usual, apparently by way of showing honor to his departing friend. Charicles, however, assured Macro that his breath was failing, and that he would not last more than two days. All was at once hurry; there were conferences among those on the spot, and dispatches to the generals and armies. On the 15th of March [37 A.D.] his breath failing, he was believed to have expired; and Caius Cæsar [Caligula] was going forth, with a throng of congratulating followers, to take first possession of the empire, when suddenly news came that Tiberius was recovering his voice and sight, and calling for persons to bring him food to restore him from his faintness. Then ensued a universal panic; and while the rest fled hither and thither, every one feigning grief or ignorance, Caius Cæsar, in silent stupor, passed from the highest hopes to the extremity of apprehension. Macro, nothing daunted, ordered the old emperor to be smothered under a huge heap of clothes, and all to quit the entrance-hall.

Thus died Tiberius, in the seventy-eighth year of his age. His father was Nero, and he was on both sides descended from the Claudian house, though his mother passed, by adoption, first into the Livian, then into the Julian family. From earliest infancy perilous vicissitudes were his lot. Himself an exile, he was the companion of a proscribed father; and on being admitted as a step-son into the house of Augustus, he had to struggle with many rivals so long as Marcellus and Agrippa, and subsequently Caius and Lucius Cæsar, were in their glory. Again, his brother Drusus enjoyed in a greater degree the affection of the citizens. But he was more than ever on dangerous ground after his marriage with Julia, whether he tolerated or escaped from his wife's profligacy. On his return from Rhodes he ruled the Emperor's now heirless house for twelve years, and the Roman world, with absolute sway, for twenty-three. His character, too, had its distinct periods. It was a bright time in his life and reputation when, under Augustus, he was a private citizen or held high offices; a time of reserve and crafty assumption of virtue as long as Germanicus and Drusus were alive. Again, while his mother lived he was a compound of good and evil. He was infamous for his cruelty, though he veiled his debaucheries while he loved or feared Sejanus. Finally he plunged into every wickedness and disgrace when, fear and shame being cast off, he simply indulged his own inclinations.

His Mention of Christ.

This brief reference to Jesus Christ, inserted as a trifling circumstance in the life of Nero, Carlyle pronounces "the most earnest, sad and sternly significant passage that we know to exist in writing."

So, for the quieting of this rumor [of his having set fire to Rome], Nero judicially charged with the crime, and punished with most studied severities, that class, hated for their general wickedness, whom the vulgar called *Christians*. The originator of that name was one CHRIST, who, in the reign of Tiberius, suffered death by sentence of the Procurator, Pontius Pilate. The baneful superstition, thereby repressed for the time, again broke out, not only over Judea, the native soil of that mischief, but in the city [Rome] also, where from every side all atrocious and abominable things collect and flourish.

NERO SLAYS HIS MOTHER.

NERO at length feeling his mother [Agrippina] as an oppression to him wherever she resided, resolved to kill her, and was in suspense only about the mode; by poison, the sword, or any other violent means. Anicetus, an enfranchised slave, tutor to Nero in his infancy, but now commander of the fleet at Misenum, hated by and hating Agrippina, here proffered the aid of his ingenuity. Accordingly he explained, "how a vessel might be so constructed that a portion of it might by a contrivance fall to pieces and plunge her unawares into the water. Nothing," he said, " was so prolific in accidents as the sea; and if she were thus cut off by shipwreck, who could be so injurious as to ascribe the offence of wind and waves to the malice of men? The prince should also erect a temple and altars to the deceased, and adopt every other means of parading his filial reverence."

Nero was pleased with the device, which was also favored by the particular juncture, for he was then keeping the holidays at Baiæ. Thither he enticed his mother, frequently declaring "that the hasty humor of parents should be borne with, and her spirit should be soothed," in order to raise a rumor of his being reconciled to her, which Agrippina might believe with the credulous facility with which women acquiesce in whatever gratifies their wishes. When she approached he met her upon the shore—for she came from Antium—gave her his hand, embraced her, and conducted her to Bauli; so the villa is called, which, lying between the cape of Misenum and the gulf of Baiæ, is washed by the winding sea. Here, among other vessels, lay one more ornamental than the rest, as if in this too he sought to honor his mother; for she had been always wont to make her excursions in a galley with three banks of oars, rowed by mariners from the fleet. She was then invited to a banquet, that the shades of night might assist in shrouding the horrid deed. It was, however, apparent that somebody had betrayed the design, since Agrippina, upon hearing of the plot, though doubtful whether to believe it, was conveyed to Baiæ in a litter; but, upon her arrival, his caresses assuaged her fear. He received her graciously, and placed her at table above him; entertained and amused her with a variety of conversation; at one time with the frankness natural to youth, at another with an air of gravity, pretending to communicate with her upon serious topics: and after he had drawn out the banquet to a late hour, he escorted her on her departure, fixing his eyes upon her, and clinging to her bosom, whether it was to complete the hollow part he had assumed, or that the last sight of a mother on the point of perishing, had power to fix the attention of his mind, though brutalized.

The gods, as if to bear damning testimony against the impious deed, granted a night lit up with stars; while not a breath disturbed the unruffled deep. Agrippina was attended by two only of all her train, of whom Crepereius Gallus stood by the steerage, and Aceronia, who, as Agrippina reposed, lay at her feet, was again setting before her, with joy, the remorse of her son, and her recovered influence with him: the vessel had not yet made much way, when suddenly, upon a given signal, the roof of the cabin fell in, being loaded with a quantity of lead, and instantly crushed Crepereius to death. Agrippina and Aceronia were protected by the sides of the couch, which rose above them, and happened to be too strong to yield to the weight: neither did the vessel at once fall to pieces; for the sailors were all in confusion, and the greater part of them, not being privy to the plot, embarrassed even such as were. The sailors then proposed to bear the vessel down on one side, and so sink her: but neither did all the accomplices themselves fall in with a project thus startling; and others resisting it, diminished the violence with which they were thrown into the sea. Now Aceronia, little thinking of the consequence, while she cried out that she was

Agrippina, and bade them succor the prince's mother, was pursued with poles and oars, and whatever other naval weapons came first to hand, and so slain. Agrippina kept silence, and being therefore the less known, escaped, with one wound, however, upon her shoulder. By swimming, and then meeting with some small barks, she reached the lake Lucrinus, and was thence conducted to her own villa.

There, reflecting that for this very end she had been summoned by the fraudulent letters of her son, and treated with especial honor: that the vessel, close to the shore, not from the violence of winds, or from striking upon rocks, had given way in its upper works, and fallen to pieces like a frail structure for land purposes; taking into her consideration also the fate of Aceronia, and looking upon her own wound, she inferred that her only resource against these treacherous machinations was to act as if she saw them not. With this view she dispatched Agerinus, her freedman, to notify to her son, "that through the mercy of the gods, and the auspicious influence of his fortune, she had escaped a grievous casualty; but besought him, however terrified at the danger which had threatened his mother, to postpone the attention of visiting her; for what she needed at present was rest."

As for Nero, while he was waiting for messengers to apprise him that the deed was done, tidings arrived "that she had escaped with a slight hurt; having been so far imperilled as to leave no doubt who was the author." Overpowered with terror and dismay at this intelligence, he summoned Burrus and Seneca; it is not clear whether they were previously informed of the conspiracy: they both kept silence for a long time, either lest they should fail in dissuading him from his purpose, or else convinced that matters had gone so far that either Agrippina must be cut off or Nero perish. At length Seneca, heretofore the more forward, fixed his eyes on Burrus, and asked, "whether orders for this execution might be given to the soldiery?" he answered, that "the pretorian guards were so attached to the whole family of the Cæsars, and so revered the memory of Germanicus, that they would shrink from executing severity on one of his descendants: Anicetus should carry out his engagement." Anicetus paused not a moment, but even demanded the task of completing the murder. Nero at these words declared himself to be that day presented with the empire, and that his freedman was the author of the costly present. He bade him hasten, and take with him such as would most promptly execute his orders. The freedman, however, having heard that Agerinus had arrived as a messenger from Agrippina, contrived a plot to turn the treason upon her: as he was delivering his message, Anicetus dropped a dagger between his feet; and then, as if he had caught him in treason, ordered him to be put in chains. This he did to give consistency to a fiction, that the mother of the emperor had concerted his destruction, and then from shame, on the detection of the treason, had put herself to death.

Meanwhile the circumstance of Agrippina's peril had been made known among the people, and as it was represented as the effect of pure accident, each, as soon as he heard it, hastened down to the beach. Some climbed up the piers which jut out into the sea; some got into the barks that were at hand; others entered the sea, and waded as far as their height would permit; some stretched out their arms; so that the whole coast resounded with lamentations, with vows, and with the shouts of the multitude, asking various questions, or returning unsatisfactory answers. A great number crowded to the spot with torches in their hands; and, as soon as it was confirmed that Agrippina was out of danger, they were preparing to offer her their congratulations, when an armed band appearing and threatening them, they were dispersed. Anicetus beset the villa with a guard, and bursting open the gates, seized such of her slaves as he met on his way to the door of her chamber, which he found guarded by very few, the rest being scared away by the terror of the irruption. In her chamber was a small light, and only one of her maids. Agrippina was more and more agitated with anxious thoughts that no one had yet arrived from her son, not even Agerinus: she observed the alteration in the general aspect of the shore, the solitude that reigned, startling noises, and symptoms of some dire catastrophe. Her maid then leaving her, she said, "You too are deserting me;" when, looking round, she saw Anicetus, accompanied by Herculeus, captain of a galley, and Oloaritus, a centurion of the navy: she told him, "if he came from the emperor to be informed of her health, to say she was revived; if for any sanguinary purpose, she would never believe it of her son; he had never given orders for parricide." The assassins placed themselves round her bed, the captain first struck her violently upon the head with a club: but to the centurion, as he was drawing his sword to dispatch her, she presented her womb, crying with a loud voice, "Strike your sword into my belly." She was instantly dispatched with a number of wounds.

In these particulars authors are unanimous: but as to whether Nero surveyed the breathless body of his mother, and applauded its beauty, there are those who have affirmed it, and those who deny it. Her body was committed to the funeral pile the same night on a common couch; and her obsequies performed in a mean manner: neither, during the reign of Nero, was any tomb raised, nor her grave enclosed. Agrippina had been taught to expect many years before that she would end her life thus, but cared not for it: for the Chaldeans, whom she consulted on the fortune of Nero, answered, that "he would certainly reign, and kill his mother;" when she replied, "Let him kill me, provided he reign."

AGRIPPINA, THE MOTHER OF NERO.

PHÆDRUS.

As Æsop was recognized as the Greek fabulist, his imitator, Phædrus, was the acknowledged Roman writer of this kind. According to his own account, he was a Thracian by birth, had been brought to Rome as a slave, and was made a freedman by Augustus. During the reign of Tiberius his literary skill was employed in putting into Latin verse such stories as had already been collected and versified in Greek by Babrius. Though most of the matter was not original, he used freedom in handling it, and had such grace of style as to give him an assured position among the writers of the Silver Age. His satire was lively, and his brevity and ingenuity admirable. For the cultivated Romans, satiated with pretentious mediocrity, his simple apologues had the attraction of novelty. He is said to have been persecuted by Sejanus, who discovered personal attacks in some of his fables.

The Frogs and the Sun.

When Æsop saw, with inward grief,
The nuptials of a neighboring thief,
He thus his narrative begun:
Of old 'twas rumored that the Sun
Would take a wife: with hideous cries
The querulous Frogs alarmed the skies.
Moved at their murmurs, Jove inquired,
What was the thing that they desired?
When thus a tenant of the lake
In terror for his brethren spake:
"Even now one Sun too much is found,
And dries up all the pools around,
Till we thy creatures perish here;
But oh, how dreadfully severe,
Should he at length be made a sire,
And propagate a race of fire!"

The Lion and the Mouse.

This fable is a moral song,
To bid us not inferiors wrong.

As fast asleep a Lion lay,
The sylvan Mice began to play,
Till one, by rash misconduct, leapt
Upon his body as he slept.
The Lion, rousing from his nap,
Seized instant on the little chap.—
But he begs pardon for the offence,
The fault of mere improvidence.
The king of beasts, who wisely knew
No glory could to him accrue
By taking vengeance for the deed,
At once the Mouse forgave and freed.
The Lion, in a little space,
As late at night he urged the chase,
Fell down into a pit, and there
Found himself tangled with a snare.
Then making all the roar he could,
The listening Mouse came from the wood,
And drawing near, " Be not afraid,
For I'll requite your love," he said.
Then he his nibbling skill applies,
And all the knots and joints he tries.
At last he loosens every thread,
With which his net the artist spread,
And leaving nothing unexplored,
The Lion to the woods restored.

PERSIUS.

ROMAN satire is representative of three distinct, though not very remote, periods of national history. Horace represents the palmy days of the empire; Persius, the rise of tyranny and the decline of literature; Juvenal, the period of imperial degeneracy and moral depravity. Nothing is more striking than the rapidity with which the literary tastes of the empire changed. Virgil's example and success caused an epidemic of epic-writing. Horace in like manner gave occasion for a tribe of satirists. Fifty years had scarcely passed from the publication of the Æneid, when Persius appeared to satirize the heroic verses written by the "scribbling schoolboys and unlettered dunces" of his times.

Aulus Persius Flaccus was born at Volaterræ, in Etruria, in 34 A.D. Removing to Rome, he studied with the Stoic philosopher Cornutus. Between the teacher and his pupil there sprang up a paternal and filial affection which was interrupted only by the death of the latter in his twenty-eighth year. The young man acted up to his principles, and practised the discipline and self-restraint inculcated by his excellent tutor.

The satires of Persius—there are but six in all—are censured for obscurity, but that was a justifiable fault in the times, when to speak plainly would have led to death. The first satire, aimed at false taste in poetry and eloquence, is bitter in the extreme; those addressed to his teacher Cornutus and his friend Bassus, show amiability, affection and all the tenderness of true friendship.

The Stoic Instructor.

(From Satire V.—To Annæus Cornutus.)

Yes, best of friends! 'tis now my pride to own,
How much that "breast" is fill'd with you alone!
Ring then—for, to your practised ear, the sound
Will show the solid, and where guile is found
Beneath the varnished tongue. For this, in fine,
I dared to wish an hundred voices mine;
Proud to declare, how closely twined you dwell—
How deeply fixed in my heart's inmost cell,
And paint, in words—ah, could they paint the whole!—
The ineffable sensations of my soul.

When first I laid the purple by—and free,
Yet trembling at my new-felt liberty,
Approached the hearth, and on the Lares hung
The bulla, from my willing neck unstrung;*
When gay associates, sporting at my side,
And the white boss, displayed with conscious pride,
Gave me, unchecked, the haunts of vice to trace,
And throw my wandering eyes on every face;

---

* Roman boys of noble birth wore a purple-bordered gown and a golden ball, or bulla, hung from the neck. About the age of twelve these marks of childhood were laid aside, the bulla being given to the Lares or household gods.

When life's perplexing maze before me lay,
And error, heedless of the better way,
To straggling paths, far from the route of truth,
Wooed, with blind confidence, my timorous youth,
I fled to you, Cornutus, pleased to rest
My hopes and fears on your Socratic breast;
Nor did you, gentle sage, the charge decline:
Then, dexterous to beguile, your steady line
Reclaimed, I know not by what winning force,
My morals, warped from virtue's straighter course,
While reason pressed incumbent on my soul,
That struggled to receive the strong control,
And took, like wax, subdued by plastic skill,
The form your hand imposed—and bears it still!

 Can I forget, how many a summer's day,
Spent in your converse, stole unmarked away?
Or how, while listening with increased delight,
I snatched from feasts the earlier hours of night?
—One time (for to your bosom still I grew)
One time of study, and of rest, we knew;
One frugal board, where, every care resigned,
An hour of blameless mirth relaxed the mind.

 And sure our lives, which thus accordant move,
(Indulge me here, Cornutus,) clearly prove,
That both are subject to the self-same law,
And from one horoscope their fortunes draw:
And whether destiny's unerring doom
In equal Libra poised our days to come;
Or friendship's holy hour our fates combined,
And to the Twins a sacred charge assigned;
Or Jove, benignant, broke the gloomy spell
By angry Saturn wove;—I know not well—
But sure some star there is, whose bland control
Subdues to yours the temper of my soul!

 Countless the various species of mankind,
Countless the shades which separate mind from mind;
No general object of desire is known;
Each has his will, and each pursues his own.
With Latian wares, one roams the Eastern main,
To purchase spice, and cumin's blanching grain;
Another, gorged with dainties, swilled with wine,
Fattens in sloth, and snores out life supine;

This loves the Campus; that destructive play;
And those, in wanton dalliance, melt away:—
But when the knotty gout their strength has broke,
And their dry joints crack like some withered oak,
Then they look back, confounded and aghast
On the gross days in fogs and darkness past,
With late regret the waste of life deplore:
No purpose gained, and time, alas! no more.

But you, my friend, whom nobler views delight,
To pallid vigils give the studious night,
Cleanse youthful breasts from every noxious weed,
And sow the tilth with Cleanthean seed—
There seek, ye young, ye old (secure to find),
That certain end, which stays the wavering mind;—
Stores which endure when other means decay,
Through life's last stage, a sad and cheerless way!

"Right: and to-morrow this shall be our care."
Alas! to-morrow, like to-day, will fare.
"What! is one day, forsooth, so great a boon?"
But when it comes (and come it will too soon),
Reflect that yesterday's to-morrow's o'er.—
Thus one "to-morrow!" one "to-morrow!" more,
Have seen long years before them fade away;
And still appear no nearer than to-day!—

So while the wheels on different axles roll,
In vain (though governed by the self-same pole),
The hindmost to o'ertake the foremost tries;
Fast as the one pursues, the other flies!

The Slothful Pupil.

"What? is it ever thus? Noon's entering ray
Broadens the shutter's chinks with glare of day;
But still you snoring lie; a spell of rest
That might the surfeit-fumes of wine digest.
The shadowed dial points eleven; arise!
The dog-star heat is raging in the skies;
The sun already burns the parching wheat,
And the faint flocks to spreading elms retreat!"
Thus to his hopeful charge some tutor cries:
"Indeed? and is it so?" the youth replies:

"Come quick, my slave!" Is none at hand? how green
 His color instant changes with the spleen!
 He splits his throat with rage: a man would say,
 He heard a hundred asses deafening bray.
 At length he's dressed; his book he handles then,
 Fumbles his papers o'er, and dips his pen.
 But now the ink in globules clots the quill;
 Now, too diluted, pale weak drops distill
 From the pen's point, and blot the paper o'er;
 O wretched wight! and wretched more and more,
 As every day grows old! and is it come
 To this at last? are these the youth of Rome?
 But why not rather then be cockered up
 At home, and pap and tender spoon-meat sup,
 Like royal infants, or pet doves, and cry
 In peevish passion at the lullaby?
"How can I write with such a wretched pen?"
 Are these excuses for the ears of men?
 For ever whining is this shuffling tone?
 Yours is the loss and ridicule alone.
 Your life, poor silly one! is flowing by;
 Contempt be sure will glance from every eye.
 The jar ill-baked, when rung, will shrill betray,
 With its cracked sound, the raw, unhardened clay.
 You now are moist and ductile loam; begin,
 Let the lathe turn, the wheel swift-circling spin,
 And fashion you to shape. "But I've enough
 Of victuals, and bright plate, and household stuff
 And platters, safely stored, of ample size
 To feed the fire with bits of sacrifice;
 Then what have I to fear?" And is this all?
 And do you puff and swell, if you can call
 Some kinsman censor, wear a robe of state,
 Or trace your pedigree to ancient date,
 The thousandth from a Tuscan sire?—away!
 Dazzle the crown with trappings, as you may;
 My glance can pierce thee deeper than thy skin,
 Can look thee through, and know thee from within.

SENECA.

Seneca is regarded as the foremost philosopher of the Roman empire, yet he was a rhetorical moralist rather than a genuine philosopher. Lucius Annæus Seneca was born at Corduba (now Cordova), in Spain, about 3 B. C. That country had accepted Roman civilization and the arts were flourishing there. But Seneca's father, who was an eminent rhetorician, took his son to Rome for his education, which was afterwards supplemented by travel in Greece and Egypt. Admitted to the bar, he soon won distinction as a pleader of causes. In due time he obtained a quæstorship, and seemed to have fairly entered on a political career, when an unproved charge of intimacy with Julia, the daughter of Germanicus, led her uncle, the Emperor Claudius, to banish him to Corsica. Here Seneca remained eight years, meantime writing letters to his mother, which form his treatise on "Consolation." Like the banished poet Ovid, he also tried to regain the emperor's favor by flattery in letters to a courtier. When Claudius married Agrippina, she induced him to recall Seneca that he might be the tutor of her son Domitius, known in history as the Emperor Nero. Seneca was also raised to the dignity of prætor, and when in 54 A.D. his pupil became emperor, he used his influence to check Nero's vicious propensities. Yet at the same time he profited by his position to become immensely wealthy, the possessor of villas and gardens in the country and a palatial residence in Rome. He supported Nero in his contests with his imperious mother, and was a party to her death in 60 A. D. He probably wrote the letter Nero addressed to the Senate in justification of her murder. This is the greatest blot on his reputation as a moralist. But the reaction from this subserviency proved fatal to himself. The very presence of Seneca became irksome to Nero, who had abandoned himself to his vicious propensities, while the teacher's wealth excited the emperor's cupidity. Nero, ambitious of fame as an artist, was also offended at the philosopher's reported disparagement of his skill in driving and music. Seneca, apprehending the course of events, asked permission to retire from court, and offered to surrender his estate. Nero affected to be grateful and declined the gift. Seneca, on the plea of ill health, altered his mode of life and kept himself secluded. But the emperor's favorites were urgent for his death, and a pretext was found for involving him in Piso's conspiracy in 65 A.D. When Seneca received the imperial mandate to terminate his own life, he cheered his weeping wife and friends with the lessons of philosophy. He opened veins in his legs, and when the blood would not flow freely, entered a warm bath and was finally suffocated.

It was Seneca's misfortune to have been connected with Nero. There is diversity of opinion as to his real character, and as to his influence on his pupil, but it is probable that his professions of virtue were sincere, and that he did the best for his pupil that could be done. He is accused of pandering to vice, and he certainly palliated it. His reputation was injured in his lifetime by his immense wealth. Yet he was an admirer and supporter of the old Roman faith and devotion to duty. He may fairly be regarded as "a good man in the direful grasp of ills." As he was a victim of Nero's cruelty, and also an advocate, in his writings, of a high morality, he came to be regarded among the Christians of the fourth century as a secret disciple of the new faith. St. Jerome was tempted to ascribe to Seneca a correspondence with St. Paul, consisting of fourteen letters. His genuine "Epistles to Lucilius" are serious and meditative, and rebuke the follies of his time. They probably belong to the latter part of his life. His other treatises, on Anger, on Tranquillity of Mind, on Clemency, on Providence, on the Happy Life, on Kindness, show that he had embraced the doctrines of the Stoics. They were formerly more read and admired than they are at present. His ten tragedies are examples of the dramatic literature which arose during the temporary revival of culture under Nero. These frigid imitations of the tragedies of Euripides show less of true dramatic genius than of skilful rhetoric. They became the models of French tragedy when brought forward by Corneille and Racine. Showy declamation, epigram and antithesis are their striking characteristics.

Anger and its Remedies.

This quaint translation is by Thomas Lodge (1556-1625), a dramatist, novelist and poet of Elizabeth's reign.

A good man rejoiceth when he is admonished; a wicked man cannot brook a reprover. At a banquet some men's bitter jests and intemperate words have touched thee to the quick: remember to avoid the vulgar company: after wine men's words are too lavish, and they that are most sober in their discourses are scarce modest. Thou sawest thy friends displeased with the porter of a counselor's chamber, or some rich man, because he would not suffer him to enter; and thou thyself, being angry for this cause, growest in choler with the cullion. Wilt thou therefore be angry with a chained dog, who when he hath barked much will be satisfied with a piece of bread?—get farther off him, and laugh. He that keepeth his master's door, and seeth the threshold besieged by a troop of solicitors, thinketh himself no small bug; and he that is the client thinketh himself happy in his own opinion, and believeth that so hard an access into the chamber is an evident testimony that the master of the same is a man of great quality and a favorite of fortune. But he remembereth not himself that the entry of a prison is as difficult likewise. Presume with thyself that thou art to endure much. If a man be cold in winter, if he vomit at sea, if he be shaken in a coach, shall he marvel hereat? The mind is strong, and many endure all that whereunto he is prepared. If thou hast been seated in a place scarce answerable to thine honor, thou hast been angry with him that stood next thee, or with him that invited thee, or with him that was preferred before thee. Fool as thou art, what matter is it in what place thou art set at the table?—a cushion cannot make thee more or less honorable. Thou wert displeased to see such a one, because he spake ill of thy behavior. By this reckoning, then, Ennius, in whose poetry thou art noways delighted, should hate thee, and Hortensius should denounce war against thee, and Cicero, if thou shouldst mock his verses, should be at odds with thee. When thou suest for an office, dost thou not peaceably entertain those that give their voices to the election, although they nominate not thyself?

Some man hath disgraced thee: what more than Diogenes the Stoic was, who, discoursing one day very effectually upon the subject of anger, was scornfully spat upon by a froward young man? This injury entertained he both mildly and wisely: "Truly (saith he), I am not angry, yet doubt I whether I ought to be angry." But our friend Cato demeaned himself better, whom, as he pleaded a cause, Lentulus, that factious and seditious fellow in the time of our forefathers, similarly insulted. For in wiping his face he said no other thing but this: "Truly, Lentulus, I will now maintain it against all men that they are deceived who say thou hast no mouth."

Now, my Novatus, we are already instructed how to govern our minds, either to feel not wrath, or be superiors over it. Let us now see how we may temper other men's ire; for not only desire we to be healthful ourselves, but to heal others. We dare not attempt to moderate and pacify the first anger by persuasion, for she is deaf and mad; we will give her some time: remedies are best in the declination of fevers. Neither will we attempt her when she is inflamed and in fury, for fear lest in striving to quench we enkindle the same. . . . To check him that is angry, and to oppose thyself against him, is to cast oil on the fire. Thou shalt attempt him divers ways, and after a friendly manner, except haply it be so great a personage that thou mayest diminish his wrath as Augustus Cæsar did when he supped with Vedius Pollio. One of the servants had broken a crystal glass, whom Vedius commanded to be carried away and to be punished by no ordinary death; for he commanded him to be thrown amongst his lampreys, which were kept in a great fish-pond. The boy escaped out of their hands, and fled to Cæsar's feet, desiring nothing else but that he might die otherwise, and not be made meat for fishes. Cæsar was moved with the novelty of the cruelty, and commanded him to be carried away, yet gave orders that all the crystal vessels should be broken in his presence, and that the fish-pond should be filled up. So thought Cæsar good to chastise his friend, and well did he use his power.

Commandest thou men to be dragged from the banquet and to be tortured by new kinds of punishment? If thy cup be broken, shall men's bowels be rent in pieces? Wilt thou please thyself so much as to command any man to death where Cæsar is present?

Let us give repose unto our minds, which we shall do if we dilate continually upon the precepts of wisdom and the acts of virtue, and likewise whilst our thoughts desire nothing but that which is honest. Let us satisfy our conscience; let us do nothing for vainglory's sake; let thy fortune be evil, so thine actions be good. But (sayest thou) the world admireth those that attempt mighty matters, and audacious men are reported honorable, and peaceable are esteemed sluggards. It may be, upon the first sight; but as soon as a well-governed mind showeth that it proceedeth not from the weakness, but the moderation, of the mind, the people regard and reverence it. So, then, this cruel and blood passion is not profitable in any sort, but contrariwise; all evils, fire and blood, feed her; she treadeth all modesty under foot, embrueth her hands with infinite murders; she it is that teareth children in sunder and scattereth their limbs here and there. She hath left no place void of heinous villanies, neither respecting glory nor fearing infamy; incurable, when of wrath she is hardened and converted into hatred.

JASON AND MEDEA.

SENECA'S tragedy of "Medea" follows the story as set forth in the "Medea" of Euripides. The following soliloquy and dialogue occurs after Creon, having accepted Jason as a son-in-law, has ordered Medea to depart from Corinth.

Jason [*alone*]. Still cruel fates! Fortune severe alike!
Equally bad, or if she spare or strike!
So often Heaven hath for our desp'rate woes
Found remedies more desperate than those.
If we the faith, to our wife's merits due,
Had kept, we must have died. Death to eschew,
We must be faithless; not to this inclined
By abject fear, but a paternal mind.
For in their parents' ruin our poor race

Would be involved. O justice! if a place
In Heaven thou hast, by thy white throne I swear
The children overcame their sire. Nor e'er
Shall I think other, but that she (though fierce
Of heart, and beyond all reclaim perverse),
Her children's lives would 'fore my bed desire.
With prayers we were resolved to accost her ire.
But see! she hath spied us; ill the sight she brooks,
Disdain and passion printed in her looks.

  Medea. We fly! Jason, we fly! for us to change
Seats is not new; the cause is new and strange.
To whom dost send us? shall we Phasis flood,
Colchis and our sire's realms, or fields with blood
Of slaughtered brother stained, go seek? What lands,
What seas must we find out at thy commands?
The Pontic Straits? through which that princely train
We safe brought home; when through the incensed main
And dangerous Symplegades, we fled
With thee, now turned adulterer to our bed?
Shall we for small Iolcos make? or steer
Unto Thessalian Tempe? what ways e'er
To thee we opened, 'gainst ourselves we closed.
Then whither send ye us? to what lands exposed?
To exile, an exiled wretch is sent
And yet no place assigned for banishment.
Yet go we must, so to command seems fit
To Creon's son-in-law, and we submit.

  Jas. When wrathful Creon sought thy life to have,
Moved by our tears, for death he exile gave.

  Med. We exile thought a punishment; but now
We find that for a favor you allow.

  Jas. Whilst yet thou mayst, get thee from hence conveyed;
The wrath of kings is heavy.

  Med. You persuade
This to endear you in Creusa's love;
You seek a hated strumpet to remove.

  Jas. Objects Medea love?

  Med. And treachery,
And murder too.

  Jas. What crime is there, 'gainst me
Thou canst object, deserves so foul a blame?

Med. All that we ever did.

Jas. Then 'tis your aim
To involve us in the guilt of your misdeeds.

Med. Those, those are thine. He to whose gain succeeds
The ill, is the ill's author. Though our fame
All should oppose, thou ought'st defend the same,
And say we're blameless: who should guiltless be
In thy repute, is guilty made for thee.

Jas. That life's a burden, which enjoyed brings shame

Med. That life discharge, enjoyed with loss of fame.

Jas. Rather appease thy wrath-incensed breast,
For thy poor children's sakes;

Med. No, we detest,
Abjure the thought; what? shall Creusa live,
And brothers to Medea's children give?

Jas. 'Twill be an honor when our exiled race
A queen shall with her kindred issue grace.

Med. Come never so unfortunate a day
To the already wretched, with alloy
Of baser blood, to mix our noble line;
Phœbus with Sisyphus his offspring join.

Jas. Why seek'st thou ruin on us both to bring?
Let me entreat thee to depart.

Med. The king
Could yet vouchsafe to hear us speak.

Jas. Declare
What's in my power to do for thee.

Med. Me! dare
Any mischief.

Jas. On either hand, see here
Two potent kings.

Med. Than those a greater fear,
Behold Medea! let us exercise
Our powers, and Jason be the victor's prize.

Jas. Wearied with mysteries, I yield; forbear;
So often tried, the turn of fortune fear.

Med. Mistress of fortune we have ever been.

Jas. Acastus there; here Creon's nearer spleen
Threatens destruction.

Med. Void thou either's harms;
Not 'gainst thy father-in-law to rise in arms,

Or stain with kindred's blood thy innocence,
Medea will. Guiltless with her fly hence.
  Jas. Who shall oppose, if they their powers combine,
And 'gainst us with united forces join?
  Med. Add Colchians too; Æetes general:
Scythians with Grecians join; we'll foil them all.
  Jas. I potent sceptres dread.
  Med. Rather take heed
You affect them not.
  Jas. Lest this our conference breed
Suspicion, let's cut short our long discourse.
  Med. Now, Jove, o'er all the heavens thy thunder force,
Stretch forth thy hand, thy vengeful flames prepare,
And from cracked clouds the world with horror scare.
Nor with delib'rate aim level thy throw,
Take him or me: whiche'er of us the blow
Shall sink, will guilty fall; if at us cast,
Thy thunder cannot miss.
  Jas. Resume at last
More sober thoughts, language more mild; if aught
In Creon's court, in exile may be thought
Easeful to thee, ask and the asked-for have.
  Med. Thou know'st we can, and use with scorn to wave
The wealth of kings; we only wish we might
Our children have companions in our flight;
That in their bosoms we our tears may shed.
More sons thou mayst expect from thy new bed.
  Jas. I must confess me willing to comply
With thy desires; forbid by piety.
Nor could I suffer this, though Creon's power
Should force me to it. For this alone implore
I life; of all my cares the only ease,
Sooner I could want breath, limbs, light, than these.
  Med. (aside). Loves he his children so! 'tis well, we ha'it:
Now know we where to wound him—we hope yet
We may our last words in their mindful breasts
Implant. [*Aloud.*] Embrace; seems this a just request?
This too, we with our latest speech entreat,
What our rash grief hath uttered, you'd forget,
And a more favorable memory
Of us retain; all passions buried be.
  Jas. All, all's forgot by us; and here we pray

Thou mayst the fervor of thy mind allay,
And gentle curb unto thy passions give.
Patience is misery's best lenitive. [*Exit*.
  Med. Gone! is it e'en so? hast thou forgotten me?
And all my merits slipped from thy memory?
No; we will ne'er slip thence. (*To herself.*) Now mind
  thy part;
Summon together all thy strength and art.
'Tis thy best use of ills to think there's none.

His Prophecy of America.

The chorus in the tragedy of "Medea" laments the building of the Argo, the first ship, and tells the progress of discovery, ending with a prophecy of the New World.

What was the purchase of so bold
A voyage, but a fleece of gold;
And greater mischief than the sea,
Medea: fit the freight to be
Of the first ship? The passive main
Now yields, and does all laws sustain.
Nor the famed Argo, by the hand
Of Pallas built, by heroes manned,
Does now alone complain she's forced
To sea; each petty boat's now coursed
About the deep; no bound'ry stands,
New walls by towns in foreign lands
Are raised; the pervious world in its old
Place leaves nothing. Indians the cold
Araxis drink, the Elbe, and Rhine
The Persians. The age shall come, in fine
Of many years, wherein the main
Shall loose the universal chain;
And mighty tracts of land be shown,
To search of elder days unknown;
New worlds by some new Tiphys found.
Nor Thule be earth's farthest bound.

LUCAN.

Lucan is the chief epic poet of the Silver Age, and shows the faults as well as the merits of his period. Marcus Annæus Lucanus was born at Corduba (Cordova), in Spain, A.D. 38. He was a nephew of Seneca, by whose writings the education and literature of the time were considerably affected. Going to Rome, Lucan soon attracted the favorable notice of the Emperor Nero by the excellence of his poetry. By imperial favor he was appointed quæstor and made a member of the college of augurs. Although a thorough republican at heart, he was a court poet, and sang the praises of his royal master. But soon he imprudently engaged with the emperor in a contest for supremacy in poetical skill and gained the prize, but lost place and preferment. He was prohibited not only from reciting his poetry in public, but also from exercising his rhetorical power at the bar. The poet joined Piso's conspiracy for the assassination of the emperor. The plot was detected, Lucan received capital sentence, and was allowed to choose the manner of his death. He ordered the physicians to open the arteries in his legs and arms, and as life ebbed out, repeated his own verses describing the death of Cato's soldier: "So the warm blood at once from every part ran purple poison down."

Of the many works of Lucan, only one has been preserved, the "Pharsalia." This rhetorical epic abounds in beautiful descriptions. Scenes, characters, events and incidents of war are treated with great vigor, but in too much detail. The narrative begins with Cæsar's crossing of the Rubicon and is continued to the time when that hero leaps into the sea at Alexandria and reaches his fleet in safety.

Though Lucan probably inclined to Pompey's side, he describes the rival leaders with equal vigor.

THE RIVALS, POMPEY AND CÆSAR.

THE sword is now the umpire to decide,
And part what friendship knew not to divide.
'Twas hard, an empire of so vast a size
Could not for two ambitious minds suffice;
The peopled earth, and wide extended main,
Could furnish room for only one to reign.
When dying Julia* first forsook the light,
And Hymen's tapers sunk in endless night,
The tender ties of kindred-love were torn,
Forgotten all, and buried in her urn.
Oh! if her death had haply been delayed,
How might the daughter and the wife persuade!
Like the famed Sabine dames, she had been seen
To stay the meeting war, and stand between:
On either hand had wooed them to accord,
Soothed her fierce father, and her furious lord,
To join in peace, and sheathe the ruthless sword.
But this the fatal sisters' doom denied;
The friends were severed, when the matron died.
The rival leaders mortal war proclaim,
Rage fires their souls with jealousy of fame,
And emulation fans the rising flame.

Thee, Pompey, thy past deeds by turns infest,
And jealous glory burns within thy breast;
Thy famed piratic laurel † seems to fade
Beneath successful Cæsar's rising shade;
His Gallic wreaths thou viewest with anxious eyes
Above thy naval crowns triumphant rise.

Thee, Cæsar, thy long labors past incite,
Thy use of war, and custom of the fight;
While bold ambition prompts thee in the race,
And bids thy courage scorn a second place.

---

* Julia, the daughter of Julius Cæsar, was married to Pompey.

† Pompey had won his first great reputation by clearing the Mediterranean of the pirates who had infested it, but Cæsar acquired yet greater fame by his conquest of Gaul.

Superior power, fierce faction's dearest care,
One could not brook, and one disdained to share.
Justly to name the better cause were hard,
While greatest names for either side declared:
Victorious Cæsar by the gods was crowned,
The vanquished party was by Cato owned.

   Nor came the rivals equal to the field;
One to increasing years began to yield,
Old Age came creeping in the peaceful gown,
And civil functions weighed the soldier down;
Disused to arms, he turned him to the laws,
And pleased himself with popular applause;
With gifts and liberal bounty sought for fame,
And loved to hear the vulgar shout his name;
In his own theatre rejoiced to sit,
Amidst the noisy praises of the pit.
Careless of future ills that might betide,
No aid he sought to prop his failing side,
But on his former fortune much relied.
Still seemed he to possess and fill his place;
But stood the shadow of what once he was;
So in the field with Ceres' bounty spread,
Uprears some ancient oak his reverend head;
Chaplets and sacred gifts his boughs adorn,
And spoils of war by mighty heroes worn.
But the first vigor of his root now gone,
He stands dependent on his weight alone;
All bare his naked branches are displayed,
And with his leafless trunk he forms a shade:
Yet though the winds his ruin daily threat,
As every blast would heave him from his seat;
Though thousand fairer trees the field supplies,
That rich in youthful verdure round him rise;
Fixed in his ancient state he yields to none,
And wears the honors of the grove alone.

   But Cæsar's greatness, and his strength, was more
Than past renown and antiquated power;
'Twas not the fame of what he once had been,
Or tales in old records and annals seen;
But 'twas a valor, restless, unconfined,
Which no success could sate, nor limits bind;
'Twas shame, a soldier's shame, untaught to yield.

That blushed for nothing but an ill-fought field;
Fierce in his hopes he was, nor knew to stay,
Where vengeance or ambition led the way;
Still prodigal of war whene'er withstood,
Nor spared to stain the guilty sword with blood;
Urging advantage, he improved all odds,
And made the most of fortune and the gods;
Pleased to o'erturn whate'er withheld his prize,
And saw the ruin with rejoicing eyes.
Such while earth trembles and heaven thunders loud,
Darts the swift lightning from the rending cloud;
Fierce through the day it breaks, and in its flight
The dreadful blast confounds the gazer's sight;
Resistless in its course delights to rove,
And cleaves the temples of its master Jove:
Alike where'er it passes or returns,
With equal rage the fell destroyer burns;
Then with a whirl full in its strength retires,
And re-collects the force of all its scattered fires.

Cato Re-weds the Widow Martia.

Cato the Younger, great-grandson of Cato the Censor, and a man of like severe character, is said to have given his wife Martia, with her father's consent, to his friend Hortensius, who had been childless. After the death of Hortensius, Martia returns to her former husband.

Now 'gan the sun to lift his dawning light,
Before him fled the colder shades of night;
When lo! the sounding doors are heard to turn,
Chaste Martia comes from dead Hortensius' urn.
Once to a better husband's happier bed,
With bridal rites, a virgin was she led.
When every debt of love and duty paid,
And thrice a parent by Lucina made;
The teeming matron, at her lord's command,
To glad Hortensius gave her plighted hand;
With a fair stock his barren house to grace,
And mingle by the mother's side the race.
At length this husband in his ashes laid,
And every rite of due religion paid,
Forth from his monument the mournful dame,
With beaten breasts, and locks dishevelled, came;

Then with a pale, dejected, rueful look,
Thus pleasing, to her former lord she spoke.
  "While nature yet with vigor fed my veins,
And made me equal to a mother's pains,
To thee obedient, I thy house forsook,
And to my arms another husband took:
My powers at length with genial labors worn,
Weary to thee and wasted I return.
At length a barren wedlock let me prove,
Give me the name, without the joys of love;
No more to be abandoned, let me come,
That "Cato's wife" may live upon my tomb.
Nor ask I now thy happiness to share,
I seek thy days of toil, thy nights of care:
Give me, with thee, to meet my country's foe,
Thy weary marches and thy camps to know;
Nor let posterity with shame record,
Cornelia* followed, Martia left, her lord.
  She said. The hero's manly heart was moved,
And the chaste matron's virtuous suit approved.
And though the times far differing thoughts demand,
Though war dissents from Hymen's holy band;
In plain unsolemn wise his faith he plights,
And calls the gods to view the lonely rites.
No genial bed, with rich embroidery graced,
On ivory steps in lofty state was placed.
But, as she was, in funeral attire,
With all the sadness sorrow could inspire,
With eyes dejected, with a joyless face,
She met her husband's, like a son's, embrace.
No Sabine mirth provokes the bridegroom's ears,
Nor sprightly wit the glad assembly cheers.
No friends, nor e'en their children, grace the feast,
Brutus attends, their only nuptial guest:
He stands a witness of the silent rite,
And sees the melancholy pair unite.
Nor he, the chief, his sacred visage cheered,
Nor smoothed his matted locks or horrid beard;
Nor deigns his heart one thought of joy to know,
But met his Martia with the same stern brow.

*The wife of Pompey.

(For when he saw the fatal factions arm,
The coming war, and Rome's impending harm,
Regardless quite of every other care,
Unshorn he left his loose neglected hair;
Rude hung the hoary honors of his head,
And a foul growth his mournful cheeks o'erspread.
No stings of private hate his peace infest,
Nor partial favor grew upon his breast;
But safe from prejudice, he kept his mind
Free, and at leisure to lament mankind.)
Nor could his former love's returning fire,
The warmth of one connubial wish inspire,
But strongly he withstood the just desire.
These were the stricter manners of the man,
And this the stubborn course in which they ran;
The golden mean unchanging to pursue,
Constant to keep the purposed end in view;
Religiously to follow nature's laws,
And die with pleasure in his country's cause.
He sought no end of marriage, but increase,
Nor wished a pleasure, but his country's peace:
That took up all the tenderest parts of life,
His country was his children and his wife.

Cæsar in the Storm at Sea.

Julius Cæsar, after having crossed the Adriatic into Macedonia in pursuit of Pompey, wished to return to Italy without the knowledge of his army, and embarked alone on a tempestuous night.

The boatman spread his canvas to the wind,
Unmoor'd his skiff, and left the shore behind.
Swift flew the nimble keel; and, as they passed,
Long trails of light the shooting meteors cast;
E'en the fixed fires above in motion seem,
Shake through the blast, and dart a quiv'ring beam;
Black horrors on the gloomy ocean brood,
And in long ridges rolls the threat'ning flood;
While loud and louder murmuring winds arise,
And growl from every quarter of the skies.
When thus the trembling master, pale with fear,
Beholds what wrath the dreadful gods prepare;

"My art is at a loss; the various tide
Beats my unstable bark on every side:
From the northwest the setting current swells,
While southern storms the driving rack foretells.
Howe'er it be, our purposed way is lost,
Nor can one relic of our wreck be tossed
By winds, like these, on fair Hesperia's coast.
Our only means of safety is to yield,
And measure back with haste the foamy field;
To give our unsuccessful labor o'er,
And reach, while yet we may, the neighb'ring shore."

But Cæsar, still superior to distress,
Fearless, and confident of sure success,
Thus to the pilot loud—"The seas despise,
And the vain threat'ning of the noisy skies.
Though gods deny thee yon Ausonian strand;
Yet go, I charge thee—go at my command.
Thy ignorance alone can cause thy fears,
Thou know'st not what a freight thy vessel bears;
Thou know'st not I am he to whom 'tis given
Never to want the care of watchful Heaven.
Obedient Fortune waits my humble thrall,
And always ready comes before I call.
Let winds and seas loud wars at freedom wage,
And waste upon themselves their empty rage;
A stronger, mightier demon is thy friend,
Thou and thy bark on Cæsar's fate depend.
Thou stand'st amazed to view this dreadful scene;
And wonder'st what the gods and Fortune mean!
Thy keel, auspicious, shall the storm appease,
Shall glide triumphant o'er the calmer seas,
And reach Brundusium's safer port with ease.
Nor can the gods ordain another now,
'Tis what I want, and what they must bestow."

Thus while in vaunting words the leader spoke,
Full on his bark the thund'ring tempest struck;
Off rips the rending canvas from the mast,
And whirling flits before the driving blast;
In every joint the groaning alder sounds,
And gaps wide-opening with a thousand wounds.
Now, rising all at once, and unconfin'd,
From every quarter roars the rushing wind:

First, from the wide Atlantic Ocean's bed,
Tempestuous Corus rears his dreadful head;
The obedient deep his potent breath controls,
And, mountain-high, the foamy flood he rolls.
Him the North-East, encount'ring fierce, defied,
And back rebuffeted the yielding tide.
The curling surges loud conflicting meet,
Dash their proud heads, and bellow as they beat;
While piercing Boreas, from the Scythian strand,
Ploughs up the waves and scoops the lowest sand.
Nor Eurus then, I ween, was left to dwell,
Nor showery Notus in the Æolian cell;
But each from every side his power to boast,
Ranged his proud forces to defend his coast.

Nor was that gloom the common shade of night,
The friendly darkness that relieves the light;
But fearful, black, and horrible to tell,
A murky vapor breathed from yawning hell:
So thick the mingling seas and clouds were hung,
Scarce could the struggling lightning gleam along.
Through nature's frame the dire convulsion strook,
Heaven groaned, the lab'ring pole and axis shook:
Uproar and chaos old prevailed again,
And broke the sacred elemental chain;
Black fiends, unhallowed, sought the best abodes,
Profaned the day and mingled with the gods.

At length the universal wreck appeared
To Cæsar's self e'en, worthy to be feared.
"Why all these pains, this toil of fate (he cries).
This labor of the seas, and earth and skies?
All nature and the gods at once alarmed,
Against my little boat and me are armed.
If, O ye powers divine! your will decrees
The glory of my death to these rude seas;
If warm, and in the fighting field to die,
If that, my first of wishes, you deny;
My soul no longer at her lot repines,
But yields to what your providence assigns;
Though immature I end my glorious days,
Cut short my conquest, and prevent new praise;
My life, already, stands the noblest theme,
To fill long annals of recording fame.

Far northern nations own me for their lord,
And envious factions crouch beneath my sword;
Inferior Pompey yields to me at home,
And only fills a second place in Rome.
My country has my high behests obeyed,
And at my feet her laws obedient laid;
All sov'reignty, all honors are my own,
Consul, dictator, I am all alone.
But thou, my only goddess and my friend,
Thou on whom all my secret prayers attend,
Conceal, O Fortune! this inglorious end.
Let none on earth, let none beside thee know,
I sunk thus poorly to the shades below.
Dispose, ye gods! my carcass as you please,
Deep let it drown beneath these raging seas;
I ask no urn my ashes to unfold,
Nor marble monuments, nor shrines of gold;
Let but the world, unknowing of my doom,
Expect me still and think I am to come;
So shall my name with terror still be heard,
And my return in every nation fear'd."

He spoke, and sudden, wondrous to behold,
High on a tenth huge wave his bark was rolled
Nor sunk again, alternate, as before,
But rushing, lodg'd, and fix'd upon the shore.
Rome and his fortune were at once restored,
And earth at once received him for her lord.

PETRONIUS ARBITER.

THE author of the famous "Satiræ," or "Satiricon," has been fairly identified with Petronius Arbiter, a master of revels of Nero's court. He won for himself the title "Arbiter Elegantiæ" by being the absolute authority on questions of taste in connection with the science of luxurious living. Tacitus in his "Annals" (Book XVI., chapters 18, 19) has drawn his portrait with a keen appreciation of his artistic nature, and yet in necessarily sombre colors. Petronius, says Professor Sellar, seems to have been possessed "of an easy, careless power, and a spirit which, if not courage in a good sense, was yet indifferent to death and capable of meeting calamity with Epicurean irony." He became Nero's most favored—at least, most desired—intimate; he spent his days in sleep and nights in dissipation; he was famous as an accomplished voluptuary. Nevertheless under this surface of dissolute character lay traits of the strongest fibre. He once served as a provincial governor, and again as a consul, and in each case acquitted himself with notable vigor. Knowing that Nero brooked no rivals near his throne, and that both Lucan with his "Pharsalia," and Seneca with his tragedies, were the objects of Nero's jealousy, Petronius may have resigned himself with Epicurean irony to the situation, and sought only to remain a courtier of supreme influence in Nero's imperial grace. There is very good reason to believe that his artistic sensibility was constantly shocked by Nero's atrocious vanities in art, music and poetry, and in the "Satiræ" occurs an episode of a poet stoned by the mob for reciting wofully bad doggerel on the theme of Troy, which apparently was intended as a dig at Cæsar. So nice was Petronius's affection for art that before his death (so says Pliny the Elder) he shattered a myrrhine vase of rare value in order to prevent it from falling into the hands of Nero. On the other hand, he may have committed this act of art iconoclasm in a spirit of pique at the all-powerful ruler, who had condemned him to death. The "Satiræ" may have been written for no other purpose than to amuse Nero with mimicry of the poets, artists, and vulgar rich freedmen around him, and they certainly reveal no such righteous rage as Juvenal's, or even such resigned satire as Martial's. Nero is certainly not satirized in the portrait of Trimalchio, whose prototype in real life M. Gaston Paris very plausibly judges to have been Pallas, the freedman of Claudius. And yet it is not too much to assume that Petronius wrote this remarkable work in a vein of Epicurean irony, of cynical humor. There remain only fragments of what was professedly a long novel, so to speak. A portion of even this was not discovered until the middle of the seventeenth century, in Paris (1664). There is no morality in this work of immoral sensualism, but it exhibits an admirable taste and brave cynicism, such as was displaced by Petronius in his enforced death. He had his veins opened and rebound again, thus prolonging a lingering departure during which he conversed not at all on serious matters, but listened, declares Tacitus, only to "lewd songs and light verses." Henryk Sienkiewicz, the Polish novelist, has made Petronius the central figure of his powerful and vivid romance, "Quo Vadis," and the above is his view of the Arbiter. Sienkiewicz has depicted him, no doubt, in excessively ideal colors, and given him much more tenderness of character than he really possessed, and yet he "has for the most part simply put color to Tacitus's marble." In this romance the disgrace of Petronius is connected with Nero's burning of Rome, and Petronius's attempt to save the Christians, on whom Tigellinus would fasten the blame.

Of the Satiræ it has been said that "perhaps next to a day spent amid the ruins of Pompeii nothing else makes us feel so near the actual daily life of Rome in the first century A.D. as this fragment." Petronius was not only the most truly humorous of all the Latin writers, but he was a master of characterization. He took, therefore, the old Roman Satura, or miscellany (mixed verse and prose), and created a new thing—the novel based on ordinary experience and contemporary life. He may be regarded even as a precursor of Cervantes and Le Sage. While he invented no actual plot, his work is a series of adventures befalling the moody philosopher, Encolpius. Besides the licentious adventures with Ascyltos and the boy Giton and with the fortune-hunters of Crotona, it includes the celebrated episode of the Matron of Ephesus. The great feature of the fragments is the "Cena Trimalchionis," the Banquet of Trimalchio. Although primarily a humorous satire on Neronic table-gluttony and the grotesque ostentation of the illiterate rich of Nero's day, with their retinue of "Cappadocian knights," this masterpiece still remains applicable in part as a satire on the "new rich" and the vulgar great of every generation.

Witty and obscene, the style of this work, prose and verse, is "the purest Latin of the Silver Age." Petronius invented the phrase "Horatii curiosa felicitas," and he himself produces many verbal felicities, as "woven wind." He speaks delightfully on art, music and poetry, and Sidonius Apollinaris ranked him with Cicero, Livy and Virgil, as one of the masters of Latin eloquence. In saying farewell to him we must re-echo Cowper's lament:

> Petronius, all the Muses weep for thee,
> But every tear doth scald thy memory!

The Banquet of Trimalchio.

A MAGNIFICENT first course was served up, for we were all reclined except Trimalchio, for whom, after a new fashion, the chief place was reserved. On the table stood an ass in Corinthian metal, with two panniers containing olives, white on one side, black on the other; and flanked by two silver dishes, on the borders of which was engraved Trimalchio's name with the weight of metal in each. There were also little salvers in the shape of bridges, on which were laid dormice strewed over with honey and poppy seed; and smoking-hot sausages on a silver gridiron, beneath which, representing black and live coals, lay plums and pomegranate grains.

We were in the midst of these dainties when Trimalchio himself was ushered in with a flourish of music, and was bolstered up on his couch with a number of little pillows, which set some indiscreet persons among us a-laughing. And well they might, for his shaven pate poked out of a scarlet mantle, which loaded his neck, and over the mantle he had put a napkin adorned with a purple border, with fringes that hung on either side. He had also a large gilded ring on the little finger of his left hand, and on the last joint of the finger next it a smaller ring that seemed of pure gold, but starred with steel. And to let us see that these were not the whole of his bravery, he stripped his right arm, which was adorned with a golden bracelet, and an ivory circle fastened with a glistening plate of gold.

Picking his teeth with a silver pin, "My friends," said he, "I had no mind to come yet to table; but lest my absence should keep you waiting, I deprived myself of my amusement. You will allow me, however, to finish my game."

A boy followed him with a draught-board of juniper wood and crystal dice; and I noticed one surpassing piece of luxury, for instead of black and white pieces he had medals of silver and gold. Meantime, whilst he was sweeping off his adversary's pieces, and we were still engaged with the first course, a machine was handed in with a basket on it, in which sat a hen carved of wood, her wings lying round and hollowed as if she was brooding. The musicians struck up, and two servants began immediately to search the straw under the hen, and drawing forth some peafowl's eggs distributed them among the guests.

At this Trimalchio turned towards us and said, "My friends, I gave orders that this hen should be set upon peafowl's eggs, but, by Hercules, I am afraid they are half hatched. However, we will try if they are yet eatable."

We took our spoons, each of which weighed at least half a pound, and began to break our paste eggs. For my part I had like to have thrown mine away, for it seemed to me to have a chicken in it; but hearing an old guest say, "There must be something good in this," I continued my search, and found a fine fat beccafico surrounded with yolk of egg, seasoned with pepper.

Trimalchio, having now left off his play, had been helped to everything on the table, and announced in a loud voice that if any one wished for more honeyed wine he might have it. The signal was given by the music, and the first course was removed by a company of singers; but a dish falling in the hurry, a servant took it up, which Trimalchio observing, boxed his ears and ordered him to throw it down again; and presently came the groom of the chambers with his broom, and swept away the silver dish with the rest of the litter.

He was followed immediately by two long-haired Ethiopians, with small leather bottles, such as are used for sprinkling the arena of the amphitheatre; and they poured wine on our hands, for no one offered us water. The master of the house, having been complimented on this piece of elegance, cried out, "Man is a lover of fair play." Then the old fellow gave orders that every man should have his own table; and, continued he, "We shall be less incommoded by heat when we are no longer crowded upon by these stinking servants."

At the same time there were brought in glass jars, close stopped with plaster, and with labels round their necks, on which was written, "Opimian Falernian, a hundred years old."

Whilst we were reading the labels, Trimalchio ejaculated, "O dear! O dear! to think that wine should be longer-lived than we poor manikins. Well, since it is so let us e'en drink till we can hold no more. There's life in wine. This is genuine Opimian, you may take my word for it. I did not put so good on my table yesterday, and I had much more respectable men than you to dine with me."

So we drank our wine, and mightily extolled all the fine things set before us; when in came a servant with a silver skeleton, so artfully put together that its joints and backbone turned every way. Having cast it a few times on the table, and made it assume various postures, Trimalchio cried out,

> Vain as vanity are we!
> Swift life's transient flames decay!
> What this is, we soon shall be;
> Then be merry whilst you may.

The applause we gave him was followed by the second course, which certainly did not come up to our expectation; yet the novelty of the thing drew every one's eyes upon it. It was a large circular tray with the twelve signs of the zodiac round it, upon every one of which the arranger had put an appropriate dish: on Aries ram's-head pies; on Taurus a piece of roast beef; on Gemini kidneys and lamb's fry; on Cancer a crown; on Leo African figs; on Virgo a young sow's haslet; on Libra a pair of scales, in one of which were tarts, in the other cheese-cakes; on Scorpio a little sea-fish of the same name; on Sagittarius a hare; on Capricorn a lobster; on Aquarius a goose; on Pisces two mullets; and in the middle there was a green turf, on which lay a honeycomb.

Meanwhile an Egyptian slave carried bread in a silver portable oven, singing at the same time in a very delicate voice a song in praise of wine flavored with rare herbs. But as we looked rather blank at the coarse fare before us, Trimalchio cried out, "Pray, gentleman, fall to: you see your dinner."

As he spoke, four fellows came dancing in to the sound of music, and took off the upper part of the tray; which being done, we saw beneath on a second tray crammed fowls, a sow's paps, and in the middle a hare fitted with wings to resemble Pegasus. We also remarked four figures of Marsyas standing at the several corners, and spouting a highly-seasoned sauce on some fish that swam in a very Euripus.

We all joined in the admiring exclamations begun by the domestics, and merrily fell to at what each liked best. "Cut!" said Trimalchio, who was not less delighted than ourselves with a device of the sort; and forth stepped the carver and began to cut up the meat, keeping time with the music, and with such antic gestures, you would have thought he was exerting himself to the sound of a hydraulic organ to win a chariot race.

Trimalchio nevertheless went on calling out, Cut, from time to time, in a low voice. Hearing the word so often repeated, I fancied there must be some joke connected with it, and therefore ventured to ask the guest who sat next above me what it meant. As he had often been present at these fooleries he replied, "Do you see that servant who is carving? His name is Cut; and therefore as often as Trimalchio cries Cut, he both calls and commands."

Not being able to eat any more, I turned to the same person to satisfy my curiosity in other particulars; and after leading the way with some pleasantries, "What woman is that," said I, "who is bustling about the room?"

"She is Trimalchio's wife," he replied, "her name is Fortunata, she counts her money by the bushel. As for what she was a little while ago, saving your favor, you would have been loth to take bread out of her hand; but now, no one knows why or wherefore she has got into heaven, as it were, and is Trimalchio's factotum: in short, if she says it is midnight at high noon he will believe her. He cannot tell his riches, he is so excessively wealthy; but this high-born lady has an eye to everything, and when you think least to meet her she is at your elbow. She drinks little, she is sober and a good adviser; but she has an ugly tongue, and in bed chatters like a magpie. If she like a body she likes him, and if she dislikes him she dislikes him in good earnest.

"As for Trimalchio, he has as much land as a kite can fly over; he has heaps upon heaps of money. There is more silver lying in his porter's lodge than another man's whole estate is worth. And as for his slaves, wheugh! by Hercules, I do not believe one-tenth of them know their own master, and they stand in such awe of him that he could make every dolt of them creep into a gimlet-hole. You must not imagine that he buys anything; he has all within himself, wool, chalk, pepper, nay, if you have a mind for hen's milk you'll get it. At first, I grant you, his wool was none of the best, for which reason he bought rams at Tarentum to improve his breed; he had bees fetched from Athens, that he might have Attic honey home-made; and that at the same time the native bees might be bettered by a cross with the Greek. It was only the other day he wrote to India for mushroom-seed; and he has not a single mule but was got by a wild ass. You see all these beds? There is not one of them but is wadded with the finest purple or scarlet wool. Oh, what a happy man he is!

"And don't turn up your nose at any of his fellow freedmen, mind you. They are very snug fellows. You see that one at the end there to the right? He is worth this moment his eight hundred thousand. Yet he began the world with nothing; it is not long since he used to carry wood on his back. They do say, but I don't know how true it may be, I only speak from hearsay, that he snatched off an Incubo's hat, and so found a treasure. For my part, I envy no man; if any god has stood his friend, well and good. He can still take a box on the ear for all that; he knows on which side his bread is buttered.

"But what think you of him you see in the freedman's place? How well off he was once! I don't upbraid him. He saw his money increase tenfold, but he went wrong at last. I don't suppose he has a hair on his head that is not mortgaged; though, by Hercules, it was not his fault, for there is not a better man living, but his rascally freedmen's, who choused him out of all. Let me tell you, when the pot no longer boils, and a man's fortune declines, farewell friends. And what was the handsome occupation he followed that you see him where he is? Why he was an undertaker. He used to keep a table like a king's—boars fed on Carian figs, huge pies, wild-fowl, stags—his cooks and pastry-cooks spilled more wine under the table than another man has in his cellar: it was more a dream of fancy than the life of a mortal man."

Trimalchio interrupted this pleasant chat; for the course had been removed, and as the company, now warm with wine, were beginning to engage in general conversation, he leaned on his elbow and said, "Pray commend this wine by your drinking; you must make your fish swim again. Do you imagine I can be content with such a supper as you saw just now boxed up as it were in a tray? 'Is Ulysses no better known?' Eh, what say you? Even at table we must remember our philology [classical learning].

"Peace to the bones of my good patron! It was his pleasure to make me a man among men. Nothing can come across me that is new to me, just as it was with him, whereof this tray supplies practical proof."

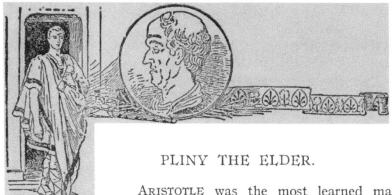

PLINY THE ELDER.

ARISTOTLE was the most learned man among the ancient Greeks. He was complete master of his learning, and having thoroughly digested and systematized his immense collection of observations, was able to appraise their true value, and to direct others to their proper use. Pliny the Elder was the most learned man among the Romans, but was mastered by his own learning. Unable to classify it properly or to fix its real value, he bequeathed to posterity a vast accumulation of miscellaneous information, in which important facts and worthless rubbish were mixed indiscriminately. Yet the huge piles of his multifarious gathering deeply impressed the imagination of his unlearned successors, and for a long time he was quoted with the reverence due to a master mind. Not only while the writings of Aristotle were lost, but for centuries after they were recovered, Pliny's "Natural History" was the standard encyclopædia of the world. The explanation of his influence lies partly in his credulity, which easily accepted extravagant statements of all sorts, and found ready echo among the later barbarians, who had acquired by conquest a material wealth and civilization which filled them with amazement. Not understanding what they saw, they were ready to believe any marvels.

Caius Plinius Secundus, to give him his classical designation, was born at Comum, now Como, in Northern Italy, in 23 A.D. At the age of sixteen he was studying at Rome under the Egyptian Apion. In early manhood he commanded a troop of cavalry under Pomponius in Germany, and his first treatise was on the "Art of Throwing the Javelin on Horseback." He returned to Rome to practice law, but was soon engaged in writing a biography of Pomponius, and a "History of the Wars in Germany." Under Nero he was made administrator of the revenues of Spain, and held this position until his friend Titus became emperor. Meantime this indefatigable writer composed a "History of His Own Times," and concluded his "Natural History," on which he had long been engaged, and which is the enduring monument of his peculiar fame. Pliny was now made prefect of the Roman fleet, having charge of the western Mediterranean. He was stationed near Naples when, in 79 A.D., the memorable eruption of Vesuvius took place, which buried Herculaneum and Pompeii. His zeal as a student of natural phenomena led him to expose himself to danger, and he perished in the catastrophe.

Out of the numerous works of this industrious writer the "Natural History" alone remains. It comprises thirty-seven books, and treats of everything in heaven and earth, from the nature of the Deity to the rotation of crops, and the best test for good eggs. Morals, medicine and the fine arts are discussed in his hap-hazard way, and he has preserved much information of the manners and customs of the ancient world. He was devoid of humor and full of prejudice, yet retained much of antique Roman virtue in a luxurious age.

The Qualities of the Dog.

Among the animals that are domesticated with mankind there are many circumstances that are deserving of being known: among these there are more particularly that most faithful friend of man, the dog, and the horse. We have an account of a dog that fought against a band of robbers in defending its master; and although it was pierced with wounds, still it would not leave the body, from which it drove away all birds and beasts. Another dog, in Epirus, recognized the murderer of its master in the midst of an assemblage of people, and, by biting and barking at him, extorted from him a confession of his crime. A king of the Garamantes, also, was brought back from exile by two hundred dogs, which maintained the combat against all his opponents. The people of Colophon and Castabala kept troops of dogs for the purposes of war; and these used to fight in the front rank and never retreat; they were the most faithful of auxiliaries, and yet required no pay. After the defeat of the Cimbri their dogs defended their movable houses, which were carried upon wagons. Jason, the Lycian, having been slain, his dog refused to take food, and died of famine. A dog, to which Darius gives the name of Hyrcanus, upon the funeral pile of King Lysimachus being lighted, threw itself into the flames; and the dog of King Hiero did the same. Philistus also gives a similar account of Pyrrhus, the dog of the tyrant Gelon; and it is said, also, that the dog of Nicomedes, King of Bithynia, tore Consingis, the wife of that king, in consequence of her wanton behavior, when toying with her husband.

Dogs are the only animals that are sure to know their masters, and if they suddenly meet him as a stranger, they will instantly recognize him. They are the only animals that will answer to their names, and recognize the voices of the family. They recollect a road along which they have passed, however long it may be. Next to man there is no living creature whose memory is so retentive. By sitting down on the ground we may arrest their most impetuous attack, even when prompted by the most violent rage.

In daily life we have discovered many other valuable qualities in this animal; but its intelligence and sagacity are more especially shown in the chase. It discovers and traces out the tracks of the animal, leading by the leash the sportsman who accompanies it straight up to the prey; and as soon as ever it has perceived it, how silent it is, and how secret but significant is the indication which it gives, first by the tail and afterwards by the nose!

When Alexander the Great was on his Indian expedition, he was presented by the King of Albania with a dog of unusual size; being greatly delighted with its noble appearance, he ordered bears, and after them wild boars, and then deer, to be let loose before it; but the dog lay down and regarded them with a kind of immovable contempt. The noble spirit of the general became irritated by the sluggishness thus manifested by an animal of such vast bulk, and he ordered it to be killed. The report of this reached the king, who accordingly sent another dog, and at the same time sent word that its powers were to be tried, not upon small animals, but upon the lion or the elephant; adding, that he had originally but two, and that if this one were put to death, the race would be extinct. Alexander, without delay, procured a lion, which in his presence was instantly torn to pieces. He then ordered an elephant to be brought, and never was he more delighted with any spectacle; for the dog, bristling up its hair all over the body, began by thundering forth a loud barking, and then attacked the animal, leaping at it first on the one side and then on the other, attacking it in the most skilful manner, and then again retreating at the opportune moment, until at last the elephant, being rendered quite giddy by turning round and round, fell to the earth, and made it quite re-echo with his fall.

The Evil Eye.

There are some persons who have the power of fascination with the eyes, and can even kill those on whom they fix their gaze for any length of time, more especially if their look denotes anger. A still more remarkable circumstance is the fact that these persons have two pupils in each eye. Apollonides says there are certain females of this description in Scythia; and Phylarchus states that a tribe of the Thibii in Pontus, and many other persons as well, have a double pupil in one eye, and in the other the figure of a horse. He also remarks that the bodies of these persons will not sink in water, even though weighed down with their garments.

Damon gives an account of a race of people not very much unlike them, whose perspiration is productive of consumption to the body of any other person that it touches. Cicero, also, one of our own writers, makes the remark that the glance of all women who have a double pupil is noxious.

A Fish that Can Stop a Ship.

We have now arrived at the culminating point of the wonders manifested to us by the operations of Nature. And even at the very outset, we find spontaneously presented to us an incomparable illustration of her mysterious powers: so much so, in fact, that beyond it we feel ourselves bound to forbear extending our inquiries, there being nothing to be found either equal or analogous to an element in which Nature quite triumphs over herself, and that, too, in such numberless ways. For what is there more unruly than the sea, with its winds, its tornadoes, and its tempests? And yet in what department of her works has Nature been more seconded by the ingenuity of man, than in this, by his inventions of sails and of oars? In addition to this, we are struck with the ineffable might displayed by the Ocean's tides, as they constantly ebb and flow, and so regulate the currents of the sea as though they were the waters of one vast river.

And yet all these forces, though acting in unison, and impelling in the same direction, a single fish, and that of a very diminutive size—the fish known as the "echeneïs"—possesses the power of counteracting. Winds may blow and storms may rage, and yet the echeneïs controls their fury, restrains their mighty force, and bids ships stand still in their career; a result which no cables, no anchors, from their ponderousness quite incapable of being weighed, could ever have produced! A fish bridles the impetuous violence of the deep, and subdues the frantic rage of the universe—and all this by no effort of its own, no act of resistance on its part, no act at all, in fact, but that of adhering to the bark! Trifling as this object would appear, it suffices to counteract all these forces combined, and to forbid the ship to pass onward in its way! Fleets, armed for war, pile up towers and bulwarks on their decks, in order that, even upon the deep, men may fight from behind ramparts as it were. But alas for human vanity!—when their prows, beaked with brass and iron, and armed for the onset, can thus be arrested and riveted to the spot by a little fish, no more than half a foot in length!

At the battle of Actium, it is said, a fish of this kind stopped the prætorian ship of Antony in its course, at the moment that he was hastening from ship to ship to encourage and exhort his men, and so compelled him to leave it and go on board another. Hence it was, that the fleet of Cæsar [Octavianus] gained the advantage in the onset, and charged with a redoubled impetuosity. In our own time, too, one of these fish arrested the ship of the Emperor Caius [Caligula] in its course, when he was returning from Astura to Antium: and thus, as the result proved, did an insignificant fish give presage of great events; for no sooner had the emperor returned to Rome than he was pierced by the weapons of his own soldiers. Nor did this sudden stoppage of the ship long remain a mystery, the cause being perceived upon finding that, out of the whole fleet, the emperor's five-banked galley was the only one that was making no way. The moment this was discovered, some of the sailors plunged into the sea, and, on making search about the ship's sides, they found an echeneïs adhering to the rudder. Upon its being shown to the emperor, he strongly expressed his indignation that such an obstacle as this should have impeded his progress, and have rendered powerless the hearty endeavors of some four hundred men. One thing, too, it is well known, more particularly surprised him, how it was possible that the fish, while adhering to the ship, should arrest it progress, and yet should have no such power when brought on board.

The Painter Apelles.

Apelles, of Cos, surpassed all the other painters who either preceded or succeeded him. Single-handed, he contributed more to painting than all the others together, and even went so far as to publish some treatises on the principles of the art. The great point of artistic merit with him was his singular charm of gracefulness, and this too, though the greatest of painters were his contemporaries. In admiring their works and bestowing high eulogiums upon them, he used to say that there was still wanting in them that ideal of beauty so peculiar to himself, and known to the Greeks as "Charis;" others, he said, had acquired all the other requisites of perfection, but in this one point he himself had no equal. He also asserted his claim to another great point of merit: admiring a picture by Protogenes, which bore evident marks of unbounded laboriousness and the most minute finish, he remarked that in every respect Protogenes was fully his equal, or perhaps his superior, except in this, that he himself knew when to take his hand off a picture,—a memorable lesson, which teaches us that over-carefulness may be productive of bad results. His candor, too, was equal to his talent; he acknowledged the superiority of Melanthius in his grouping, and of Asclepiodorus in the niceness of his measurements, or, in other words, the distances that ought to be left between the objects represented.

A circumstance that happened to him in connection with Protogenes is worthy of notice. The latter was living at Rhodes, when Apelles disembarked there, desirous of seeing the works of a man whom he had hitherto only known by reputation. Accordingly, he repaired at once to the studio; Protogenes was not at home, but there happened to be a large panel upon the easel ready for painting, with an old woman who was left in charge. To his inquiries she made answer that Protogenes was not at home, and then asked whom she should name as the visitor. "Here he is," was the reply of Apelles, and seizing a brush, he traced with color upon the panel an outline of a singularly minute fineness. Upon his return, the old woman mentioned to Protogenes what had happened. The artist, it is said, upon remarking the delicacy of the touch, instantly exclaimed that Apelles must have been the visitor, for that no other person was capable of executing anything so exquisitely perfect. So saying, he traced within the same outline a still finer outline, but with another color, and then took his departure, with instructions to the woman to show it to the stranger, if he returned, and to let him know that this was the person whom he had come to see. It happened as he anticipated; Apelles returned, and vexed at finding himself thus surpassed, took up another color and drew between both outlines, leaving no possibility of anything finer being executed. Upon seeing this, Protogenes admitted that he was defeated, and at once flew to the harbor to look for his guest. He thought proper, too, to transmit the panel to posterity, just as it was, and it always continued to be held in the highest admiration by all, artists in particular. I am told that it was burnt in the first fire which took place at Cæsar's palace on the Palatine Hill; but in former times I have often

Death and the Plowman.

stopped to admire it. Upon its vast surface it contained nothing whatever except the three outlines, so remarkably fine as to escape the sight: among the most elaborate works of numerous other artists it had all the appearance of a blank space; and yet by that very fact it attracted the notice of every one, and was held in higher estimation than any other painting there.

It was a custom with Apelles, to which he most tenaciously adhered, never to let any day pass, however busy he might be, without exercising himself by tracing some outline or other; a practice which has now passed into a proverb.* It was also a practice with him, when he had completed a work, to exhibit it to the view of the passers-by in some exposed place; while he himself, concealed behind the picture, would listen to the criticisms that were passed upon it; it being his opinion that the judgment of the public was preferable to his own, as being the more discerning of the two. It was under these circumstances, they say, that he was censured by a shoemaker for having represented the shoes with one shoe-string too little. The next day, the shoemaker, quite proud at seeing the former error corrected, thanks to his advice, began to criticize the leg; upon which Apelles, full of indignation, popped his head out, and reminded him that a shoemaker should give no opinion beyond the shoes, a piece of advice which has equally passed into a proverb.†

MARTIAL.

EPIGRAM, which had long flourished in the Greek language, was thoroughly naturalized in Latin, even before the time of Martial, but to him it chiefly owes its fame. Before his time the word epigram implied nothing more than a brief verse suitable for an inscription, but he added the sting or point, which henceforth became its characteristic.

Marcus Valerius Martialis was born at Bilbilis, in Spain, in 43 A.D. He tells us that his parents foolishly gave him a literary education. At Rome he lived in lodgings, up three

* *Nulla dies sine linea.* "No day without a line."
† *Ne sutor ultra crepidam.* "Let the shoemaker stick to his last."

flights of stairs; but, like Horace, he had also his "Sabine farm," the dimensions of which he humorously indicates by informing us that a cucumber could not lie straight on it. Yet the light-hearted poet tickled the public fancy till he had composed not less than 1,500 "Epigrams." Collected in fourteen books they have won universal fame. Martial is a keen satirist as well as a happy epigrammatist. Bores, whether literary or social, were his lawful prey: foibles, eccentricities, or extravagance of dress or manner were the objects of his attacks; and he spared nothing in the shape of affectation or hypocrisy. In his lighter verses, written merely to amuse, are found exquisite flights of fancy, brilliancy of description and graceful elegance. But Martial is censured for gross indecency, and the charge cannot be denied, though the poor excuse may be offered that he only complied with the perverted taste of his age. He himself declared, "Our page is wanton, but our life correct."

Martial's domestic life in Rome seems to have been a chronic genteel poverty, though he had the Emperor Domitian as his patron. After thirty-four years, he yearned to revisit the scenes of his youth and taste again the bliss of rural quiet and felicity. His desire was gratified, but he found to his dismay that the magnetism of Roman society still drew him towards the city. He was fortunate enough, however, to secure in marriage the hand of a handsome young Spanish lady, who he says compensated for all. Through his wife's devotion and modest little fortune, he was enabled to end his days in comfort and peace, A.D. 104.

Arria and Pætus.

When from her breast chaste Arria snatched the sword,
And gave the deathful weapon to her lord,
"My wound," she said, "believe me, does not smart;
But thine alone, my Pætus, pains my heart."

Not at Home.

May I not live, but, were it in my power,
With thee I'd pass both day and night each hour.

Two miles I go to see you; and two more
When I return; and two and two make four.
Often denied; often from home you're gone:
Are busy oft; and oft would be alone.
Two miles, to see you, give me no great pain:
Four, not to see you, go against the grain.

THE PRETTY GENIUS.

YES, you're a pretty preacher, sir, we know it;
Write pretty novels, are a pretty poet;
A pretty critic, and tell fortunes too;
Then, who writes farce or epigrams like you?
At every ball how prettily you nick it!
You fiddle, sing, play prettily at cricket.
Yet, after all, in nothing you excel,
Do all things prettily, but nothing well.
What shall I call you? say the best I can,
You are, my friend, a very busy man.

CHLOE.

I COULD resign that eye of blue,
   Howe'er its splendor used to thrill me;
And ev'n that cheek of roseate hue—
   To lose it, Chloe, scarce would kill me.

That snowy neck I ne'er should miss,
   However much I've raved about it;
And sweetly as that lip can kiss,
   I *think* I could exist without it.

In short, so well I've learned to fast,
   That sooth, my love, I know not whether
I might not bring myself at last
   —To do without you altogether.

THE ONLY SURE WEALTH.

YOUR slave will with your gold abscond,
   The fire your home lay low,
Your debtor will disown his bond,
   Your farm no crops bestow:

Your steward a mistress frail shall cheat;
Your freighted ship the storms will beat;
That only from mischance you'll save,
   Which to your friends is given;
The only wealth you'll always have
   Is that you've lent to heaven.

CHLOE'S KISSES.

COME, Chloe, and give me sweet kisses,
   For sweeter sure girl never gave;
But why, in the midst of my blisses,
   Do you ask me how many I'd have?

I'm not to be stinted in pleasure,
   Then, prithee, my charmer, be kind,
For, while I love thee above measure,
   To numbers I'll ne'er be confined.

Count the bees that on Hybla are playing;
   Count the flowers that enamel its fields;
Count the flocks that on Tempe are straying;
   Or the grain that rich Sicily yields.

Go, number the stars in the heaven;
   Count how many sands on the shore;
When so many kisses you've given,
   I still shall be craving for more.

To a heart full of love let me hold thee,
   To a heart, which, dear Chloe, is thine;
With my arms I'll forever enfold thee,
   And twist round thy limbs like a vine.

What joy can be greater than this is?
   My life on thy lips shall be spent;
But the wretch that can number his kisses,
   With few will be ever content.

THE AUTHOR'S RECOMPENSE.

'TIS not the city only doth approve
My muse, or idle ears my verses love.
The rough centurion, where cold frosts o'erspread
The Scythian fields, in war my books doth read.

My lines are sung in Britain far remote;
But yet my empty purse perceives it not.
What deathless numbers from my pen would flow,
What wars would my Pierian trumpet blow,
If, as Augustus now again doth live,
So Rome to me would a Mæcenas give?

The Girl of My Choice.

You ask, were I to change my life,
What kind of girl I'd take to wife?
Not one who coy or easy seems,
I hate alike the two extremes;
She satiates who at first complies,
She starves my love who long denies.
The maid must not, I'd call my own,
Say "No" too oft, or "Yes" too soon.

PLINY THE YOUNGER.

PLINY the Younger was, in his writings, an imitator of Cicero, and resembled that illustrious Roman in his virtues as well as his weaknesses. Like Cicero, he was conceited and vain-glorious. As to intellectual capacity, he stood below either Cicero or his own friend Tacitus, and he knew it; but he was a clever, cultivated man of wide sympathies, who took an active part in public life, and was well acquainted with many phases of society. A rather severe recent critic has pronounced him a prig.

Caius Plinius Cæcilius Secundus was born at Comum in 61 A.D. His father, C. Cæcilius, having died, he was adopted by his uncle, Pliny the Elder, who consulted the best interests of his charge. The young man began public life as an advocate in his nineteenth year. He held in succession some of the highest offices in the state, was a favorite with the emperor Trajan, and an intimate friend of Tacitus. Though not so indefatigably industrious as his uncle, the younger Pliny was always desirous to learn, and was never happier than when surrounded by his books and papers in his country retreat. Under Nerva he began to collect and publish his speeches, none of which have been preserved, with the exception of his panegyric on the Emperor Trajan for his own elevation to the consulate. The only works of Pliny which have reached us are his "Letters," which occupy ten books. They treat agreeably of art, literature, politics, town and country life, with here and there an anecdote of some distinguished man or woman of the time. They were written with a view to publication, and therefore have not the freshness of unpremeditated correspondence; yet a kind of modern element, both in thought and expression, makes Pliny more congenial than many earlier writers.[1]

> Companions of the Spring, the Thracian winds,
>   With kindly breath now drive the bark from shore;
> No frost, with hoary hand, the meadow binds,
>   Nor swoln with winter snow the torrents roar.
> The swallow, hapless bird! now builds her nest,
>   And in complaining notes begins to sing,
> That, with revenge too cruelly possessed,
>   Impious she punished an incestuous king.
> Stretched on the springing grass the shepherd swain
>   His reedy pipe with rural music fills;
> The god, who guards his flock, approves the strain,
>   The god, who loves Arcadia's gloomy hills.
>   —*Horace, from Ode 12, Bk. IV.*

[1] See Pliny's Letter Concerning the Christians.

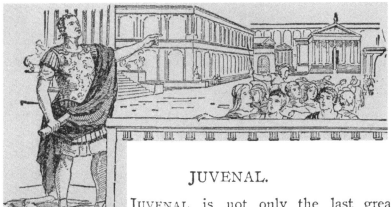

JUVENAL.

JUVENAL is not only the last great Roman satirist, but the last glowing ember of national life. The nature of his subject and the method of treating it make him a type for the world. Roman society had reached the stage of utter decay. The popular religion had become a thing of contempt and scorn, and there was nothing to take its place. Government was conducted by a system of corruption and bribery. Iniquity was established by law and maintained by the example of the great and powerful. People in high places, and of both sexes, were guilty of crimes for which the code of laws could find no name. Emperors in their abandon did not disdain to play the roles of buffoons and pantomimists. Moralists and Stoics were a sham, "counterfeiting the Curii, but living like bacchanals." Women were unsexed, and aping the manners of men, were equally unnatural and profligate. Such was the mass of moral pollution revealed under the search-light of the Roman satirist. He looked, and what he saw made him a pessimist of the severest type. Righteous indignation drove him to declamatory verse. He became the scourger of gross and open vices, encouraged by the example of a hateful tyrant.

Of Decimus Junius Juvenalis little is known except his writings. He is said to have been the son or ward of a wealthy freedman of Aquinum, a town noted also as the birthplace of St. Thomas Aquinas. It was not until he was advanced in life that he assumed the role of public satirist. Up to that time he had been an orator and rhetorician. Some verses written on Paris, a favorite actor of Domitian's, obtained for him a wider hearing. His first satire was written in Trajan's reign—about 100 A.D. After this he rose rapidly in public favor. At last he displeased the emperor by some lines reflecting on a new court favorite, and was assigned a military command in Upper Egypt. This was practically a sentence of banishment, and the bitterness of exile is said to have hastened his death.

The satires of Juvenal are sixteen in number, and exhibit all the vices of the age, whether in depraved literary tastes or moral obliquity. The author was a strict moralist, a social reformer, with a serious purpose, but without sympathy. He was stern, unyielding, and disposed to consign to perdition what he thought hopeless to recall. The nature of his subject gives terrible impulse to his natural eloquence, and drives him into the description of scenes and the use of language grossly offensive to modern taste. His style is vehement, lofty, impetuous, pitched in a high, rhetorical key. Tacitus lived in the same troublous times, when it was unsafe to publish the truth. When the danger was past, both wrote and condemned what was wrong, Tacitus giving the outside or public history, and Juvenal the inside or private view of Roman society. Thus the two great writers are mutually helpful and explanatory.

Dr. Samuel Johnson has given two noble imitations of Juvenal in his "London" and "The Vanity of Human Wishes." Our examples are taken from Gifford's more exact translations.

Domitian and the Turbot.

The degradation of the Roman Senate under Domitian is shown by their being hastily summoned by the emperor to decide how a fish should be cooked.

> It chanced that where the fane of Venus stands,
> Reared on Ancona's coast by Grecian hands,
> A turbot, wandering from the Illyrian main,
> Filled the wide bosom of the bursting seine.
> The mighty draught the astonished boatman eyes,
> And to the pontiff's table dooms the prize:
> For who would dare to sell it? who to buy?
> When the coast swarmed with many a practised spy,

Mud-rakers, prompt to swear the fish had fled
From Cæsar's ponds, ingrate! where long it fed,
And thus recaptured, claimed to be restored
To the dominion of its ancient lord! . . .

The wondering crowd, that gathered to survey
The enormous fish, and barred the fisher's way,
Satiate, at length retires; the gates unfold!
Murmuring, the excluded senators behold
The envied dainty enter.—On the man
To great Domitian pressed, and thus began:
"This, for a private table far too great,
Accept, and sumptuously your genius treat:
Haste to unload your stomach, and devour
A turbot, destined to this happy hour.
I sought him not;—he marked the toils I set,
And rushed, a willing victim, to the net."

Was flattery e'er so rank? yet he grows vain,
And his crest rises at the fulsome strain.
When to divine a mortal power we raise,
He looks for no hyperboles in praise.
But when was joy unmixed? no pot is found
Capacious as the turbot's ample round:
In this distress he calls the chiefs of state
(At once the objects of his scorn and hate),
And, after much debate, this question put—
"How say ye, Fathers! SHALL THE FISH BE CUT?"
"Oh, far be that disgrace," Montanus cries;
"No, let a pot be formed, of amplest size,
Within whose slender sides the fish, dread sire,
May spread his vast circumference entire!
Bring, bring the tempered clay, and let it feel
The quick gyrations of the plastic wheel:—
But, Cæsar, thus forewarned, make no campaign,
Unless your potters follow in your train!"

Montanus ended: all approved the plan,
And all the speech, so worthy of the man!
Versed in the old court luxury, he knew
The feasts of Nero and his midnight crew;
Where oft when potent draughts had fired the brain,
The jaded taste was spurred to gorge again.—
And, in my time, none understood so well
The science of good eating; he could tell

At the first relish, if his oysters fed
On the Rutupian or the Lucrine bed;
And from a crab's or lobster's color name
The country, nay, the district, whence it came.
  Here closed the solemn farce. The Fathers rise.
And each, submissive, from the presence hies:—
Pale, trembling wretches, whom the chief in sport
Had dragged astonished to the Alban court;
As if the stern Cicambri were in arms,
Or furious Catti threatened new alarms;
As if ill news by flying posts had come,
And gathering nations sought the fall of Rome!
And oh! that ever in such idle sport
Had lived the lord of that obsequious court;
Nor worse employed in savage scenes of blood,
That robbed the city of the brave and good—
While high-born cowards saw their brothers' doom,
And vengeance slumbered o'er the Lamian tomb;
But when he dared assail a vulgar tread,
Up rose the people, and the tyrant bled.

The Poet's Nature and Wants.

  But he, the bard of every age and clime,
Of genius fruitful and of soul sublime;
Who from the glowing mint of fancy pours
No spurious metal, fused from common ores,
But gold to matchless purity refined,
And stamped with all the godhead in his mind;
He, whom I feel, but want the power to paint,
Springs from a soul impatient of restraint,
And free from every care; a soul that loves
The Muses' haunts, clear founts and shady groves.
Never, no, never, did he wildly rave,
And shake his thyrsus in the Aonian cave,
Whom poverty kept sober, and the cries
Of a lean stomach, clamorous for supplies:
No! the wine circled briskly through their veins,
When Horace poured his dithyrambic strains!—
What room for fancy, say, unless the mind,
And all its thoughts, to poetry resigned,
Be hurried, with resistless force along,
By the two kindred powers of Wine and Song!

Oh! 'tis the exclusive business of a breast
Impetuous, uncontrolled,—not one distressed
With household cares,—to view the bright abodes,
The steeds, the chariots, and the forms of gods;
And the fierce Fury, as her snakes she shook,
And withered the Rutulian with a look!
Those snakes, had Virgil no Mæcenas found,
Had dropped, in listless length, upon the ground,
And the still slumbering trump groaned with no mortal
    sound.
Yet we expect from Lappa's tragic rage,
Such scenes as graced of old the Athenian stage:
Though he, poor man, from hand to mouth be fed,
And driven to pawn his furniture for bread!

The Degenerate Romans.

"Your ancient house!" No more. I cannot see
The wondrous merits of a pedigree:
No, Ponticus;—nor of a proud display
Of smoky ancestors, in wax or clay;
Æmilius, mounted on his car sublime;
Curius, half wasted by the teeth of time;
Corvinus, dwindled to a shapeless bust;
And high-born Galba, crumbling into dust.
  What boots it, on the lineal tree to trace,
Through many a branch, the founders of our race,
Time-honored chiefs; if, in their sight, we give
Loose rein to vice, and like low villains live?
Say, what avails it, that, on either hand,
The stern Numantii, an illustrious band,
Frown from the walls, if their degenerate race
Waste the long night at dice, before their face?
If, staggering to a drowsy bed, they creep
At that prime hour when, starting from their sleep,
Their sires the signal of the fight unfurled,
And drew their legions forth, that won the world?
  Say, why should Fabius, of th' Herculean name,
To the great altar vaunt his lineal claim,
If, softer than Euganean lambs, the youth
His wanton limbs with Ætna's pumice smooth,
And shame his rough-hewn sires? if greedy, vain,
If a vile trafficker in secret bane,

He blast his wretched kindred with a bust
For public vengeance to—reduce to dust!

  Fond man! though all the heroes of your line
Bedeck your halls, and round your galleries shine,
In proud display; yet take this truth from me—
Virtue alone is true nobility.
Set Cossus, Drusus, Paulus, then in view,
The bright example of their lives pursue;
Let them precede the statues of your race,
And these, when consul, of your rods take place.

  O give me inborn worth! Dare to be just,
Firm to your word, and faithful to your trust;
These praises hear, at least deserve to hear,
I grant your claim, and recognize the peer.
Hail! from whatever stock you draw your birth,
The son of Cossus or the son of Earth,
All hail! in you exulting Rome espies
Her guardian Power, her great Palladium rise;
And shouts like Egypt, when her priests have found
A new Osiris, for the old one drowned.

  But shall we call those noble, who disgrace
Their lineage, proud of an illustrious race?
Vain thought!

  "Away, away! ye slaves of humblest birth,
Ye dregs of Rome, ye nothings of the earth,
Whose fathers who shall tell? my ancient line
Descends from Cecrops." Man of blood divine!
Live, and enjoy the secret sweets which spring
In breasts affined to so remote a king!
Yet know, amid these "dregs," low grandeur's scorn,
Will those be found whom arts and arms adorn:
Some, skilled to plead a noble blockhead's cause,
And solve the dark enigmas of the laws;
Some, who the Tigris' hostile banks explore,
And plant our eagles on Batavia's shore:
While thou, in mean, inglorious pleasure lost,
With "Cecrops! Cecrops!" all thou hast to boast,
Art a full brother to the cross-way stone,
Which clowns have chipped the head of Hermes on:
For 'tis no bar to kindred, that thy block
Is formed of flesh and blood, and theirs of rock.

The Fall of Sejanus.

Sejanus, the Minister of Tiberius, encouraged his master in the most detestable practices, and ruled in Rome while the emperor lived in solitude on the island of Capreæ. But being detected in a conspiracy to usurp the empire, he was executed by the order of Tiberius. The satirist describes the overthrow not only of the fallen minister, but of the bronze statues which had been erected in his honor.

Some, Power hurls headlong from her envied height;
Some, the broad tablet, flashing on the sight,
With titles, names: the statues, tumbled down,
Are dragged by hooting thousands through the town;
The brazen cars torn rudely from the yoke,
And, with the blameless steeds, to shivers broke—
Then roar the flames! The sooty artist blows,
And all Sejanus in the furnace glows;
Sejanus, once so honored, so adored,
And only second to the world's great lord,
Runs glittering from the mould, in cups and cans,
Basins and ewers, plates, pitchers, pots and pans.
  "Crown all your doors with bay, triumphant bay!
Sacred to Jove, the milk-white victim slay;
For lo! where great Sejanus by the throng,
A joyful spectacle! is dragged along.
What lips! what cheeks! ha, traitor! for my part,
I never loved the fellow—in my heart."
  "But tell me, why was he adjudged to bleed?
And who discovered, and who proved the deed?"
  "Proved!—a huge wordy letter came to-day
From Capreæ." Good! what think the people? They—
They follow fortune, as of old, and hate,
With their whole souls, the victim of the state.
Yet would the herd, thus zealous, thus on fire,

Had Nursia* met the Tuscan's fond desire,
And crushed the unwary prince, have all combined,
And hailed Sejanus master of mankind!
  Lured by the splendor of his happier hour,
Wouldst thou possess Sejanus' wealth and power;
See crowds of suppliants at thy levee wait,
Give this to sway the army, that the state;
And keep a prince in ward, retired to reign
O'er Capreæ's crags, with his Chaldean train?
Yes, yes, thou wouldst (for I can read thy breast)
Enjoy that favor which he once possessed,
Assume all offices, grasp all commands,
The imperial Horse and the Prætorian Bands.
'Tis nature, this; e'en those who want the will,
Pant for the dreadful privilege to kill:
Yet what delight can rank and power bestow,
Since every joy is balanced by its woe!

SUETONIUS.

SUETONIUS, though said to have been a voluminous writer, is best known to modern times by one work, "The Lives of the Twelve Cæsars." He is not remarkable for keen historical sense, nor does he exhibit any insight into political and military affairs. The few particulars of his life are gathered from his own writings and the "Letters" of the Younger Pliny. Caius Suetonius Tranquillus (75-160 A. D.) gained considerable distinction as an advocate in the reign of Trajan, and was brought under the favorable notice of the Emperor Hadrian, who made him his private secretary. This position he lost by some breach of etiquette, or want of proper deference to the Empress Sabina. He then devoted himself to historical and literary studies. In his chief work each subject of biography is dissected, and his component parts labelled, "personal appearance, habits, character, civil studies, military studies, death, burial and subsequent events." The writer is minute in details, and indefatigable in collecting facts, whether they be savory or unsavory. Strangely enough he makes no use of the historians whose works are preserved,

*The Etruscan goddess of fortune.

but he was able to consult official documents, and had other sources of information now completely lost. The facts are judiciously selected, and the whole work is pervaded by an air of impartiality, which leaves an impress of truth quite as clearly as the fine-drawn pictures of Tacitus.

According to Pliny the Younger, Suetonius was an upright and learned man, whose good qualities became more conspicuous with acquaintance. Compared with his contemporaries he is faithful in the execution of his work. He never wilfully falsifies, nor does he shrink from the truth.

The Emperor Titus.

From his return to Rome Titus constantly acted as colleague with his father Vespasian, and, indeed, as regent of the empire. He triumphed with his father, bore jointly with him the office of censor, and was, besides, his colleague not only in the tribunitian authority, but in seven consulships. Taking upon himself the care and inspection of all offices, he dictated letters, wrote proclamations in his father's name, and pronounced his speeches in the senate, in place of the quæstor. He likewise assumed the entire command of the prætorian guards, although no one but a Roman knight had ever before been their prefect. In this he conducted himself with great haughtiness and violence, taking off, without scruple or delay, all those he had most reason to suspect, after he had secretly sent his emissaries into the theatres and camps to demand, as if by general consent, that the suspected persons should be delivered up to punishment. Among these he invited to supper A. Cæcina, a man of consular rank, whom he ordered to be stabbed on his departure, immediately after he had gone out of the room. To this act, indeed, he was provoked by an imminent danger; for he had discovered a writing under the hand of Cæcina, containing an account of a plot hatched among the soldiers. By these acts, though he provided for his future security, yet for the present he so much incurred the hatred of the people that scarcely any one came to the empire with a more odious character, or more universally disliked.

Besides his reputation for cruelty, he was charged with giving way to habits of luxury, as he often prolonged his revels till midnight with his riotous acquaintance. He was supposed, besides, to be of a rapacious disposition; for it is certain that in causes which came before his father he used to offer his interest for sale and take bribes. In short, people publicly expressed an unfavorable opinion of him, and said he would prove another Nero. This prejudice against him turned out, in the end, to his advantage, and enhanced his praises to the highest pitch when he was found to possess no vicious propensities, but, on the contrary, the noblest virtues. His entertainments were agreeable rather than extravagant; and he surrounded himself with such excellent friends that the succeeding princes adopted them as most serviceable to themselves and the state. He immediately sent away Berenice from the city, much against the inclinations of both. Some of his old eunuchs, though such accomplished dancers that they enjoyed an uncontrollable sway upon the stage, he was so far from treating with any extraordinary kindness that he would not so much as witness their performances in the crowded theatre. He violated no private right; and if ever man refrained from injustice, he did; nay, he would not accept of the customary and allowable offerings. Yet in munificence he was inferior to none of the princes before him. Having dedicated his amphitheatre [the Colosseum], and built some warm baths close by it with great expedition, he entertained the people with most magnificent spectacles. He likewise exhibited a naval fight in the old Naumachia, besides a combat of gladiators, and in one day brought into the theatre five thousand wild beasts of all kinds.

He was by nature extremely benevolent; for whereas all

the emperors after Tiberius, according to the example he had set them, would not admit the grants made by former princes to be valid unless they received their own sanction, he confirmed them all, by one common edict, without waiting for any applications respecting them. Of all who petitioned for any favor he sent none away without hopes. And when his ministers represented to him that he promised more than he could perform, he replied, "No one ought to go away downcast from an audience with his prince." Once at supper, recollecting he had done nothing for any one that day, he broke out with .that memorable and justly-admired saying, "My friends, I have lost a day." More particularly, he treated the people on all occasions with such courtesy that, on his presenting them with a show of gladiators, he declared "he should manage it, not according to his own fancy, but that of the spectators," and did accordingly. He denied them nothing, and very frankly encouraged them to ask what they pleased. Espousing the cause of the Thracian party among the gladiators, he frequently joined in the popular demonstrations in their favor, but without compromising his dignity or doing injustice. To omit no opportunity of acquiring popularity, he sometimes made use himself of the baths he had erected, without excluding the common people.

THE EMPEROR CALIGULA.

CALIGULA evinced the savage barbarity of his temper by the following indications. When flesh was only to be had at a high price for feeding his wild beasts, he ordered that criminals should be given them to be devoured. After disfiguring many persons of honorable rank, by branding them in the face with hot irons, he condemned them to the mines, to work in repairing the highways, or to fight with wild beasts; or, tying them by the neck and heels, would shut them up in cages, or saw them asunder.

Nor were these severities inflicted merely for crimes of

great enormity, but for making remarks on his public games, or for not having sworn by the Genius of the emperor. He compelled parents to be present at the execution of their sons; and to one who excused himself on account of indisposition, he sent his own litter. He burned alive the writer of a farce, for some witty verse which had a double meaning. A Roman knight, who had been exposed to the wild beasts, crying out that he was innocent, Caligula called him back, and, having had his tongue cut out, remanded him to the arena.

Even in the midst of his diversions, while gaming or feasting, this savage ferocity never forsook him. Persons were often put to the torture in his presence, while he was dining or carousing. At Puteoli, at the dedication of the bridge, he invited a number of people to come to him from the shore, and then suddenly threw them headlong into the sea; thrusting down with poles and oars those who, to save themselves, had got hold of the rudders of the ships. As often as he met with handsome men, who had fine heads of hair, he would order the back of their heads to be shaved, to make them look ridiculous. At a sumptuous entertainment, he fell suddenly into a violent fit of laughter, and when the consuls, who reclined next to him, respectfully asked him the occasion, "Nothing," replied he, "but that, upon a single nod of mine, you might both have your throats cut."

In profuse expenditure he surpassed all the prodigals that ever lived; inventing a new kind of bath, washing in precious unguents, both warm and cold, drinking pearls of immense value dissolved in vinegar, and serving up for his guests loaves and other victuals modelled in gold. He built two ships with ten banks of oars, the sterns of which blazed with jewels, while the sails were of various colors. They were fitted up with baths, galleries, and saloons, and supplied with a great variety of vines and fruit-trees. In these he would sail in the daytime along the coast of Campania, feasting amidst dancing and concerts of music.

The Philosopher in the Storm.

During the whole of the first night of our voyage a very stormy side-wind filled our vessel with water. At length, after much complaining, and sufficient employment at the pump, daylight appeared, but brought no diminution of our danger, nor cessation of the storm; but the whirlwinds seemed increasing, and the black sky, and the balls of fire, and the clouds, forming themselves into frightful shapes (which they called Typhons), appeared hanging over us ready to overwhelm the ship. In the company was a celebrated philosopher of the Stoic school, whom I had known at Athens, a man of some consequence, and rather distinguished for the good order in which he kept his pupils. Amidst all these dangers, and this tumult of sea and sky, I watched this man attentively, anxious to know the state of his mind, whether he was dauntless and unalarmed. I observed that he expressed no fear nor apprehensions, uttered no complaints like the rest, nor joined in their way of exclaiming, but in paleness and terror of countenance he differed but little from his neighbors.

When the sky grew clear, and the sea became calm, a certain rich Greek from Asia approached the Stoic; his wealth was proved from his expensive appearance, his quantity of baggage, and his train of attendants. "What is the reason," said he, in a bantering tone, "that, when we were in danger, you, who are a philosopher, were afraid, and looked pale, while I was neither afraid nor pale?" The philosopher doubted a little whether it was worth while to make any answer. "If," said he, "in so violent a storm I did discover a little fear, you are not worthy of being told the reason; but that follower of Aristippus shall give you an answer for me, who, upon a similar occasion, being asked by a man much like yourself why, as a philosopher, he was afraid, while he feared nothing, replied that there was not the same cause for fear in one as in the other, for the preservation of a worthless coxcomb was not an object worthy of much anxiety, but that he was concerned for the safety of an Aristippus." With this reply the Stoic got rid of the rich Asiatic.

CHAPTER XVII.

Architectural Wonders of Rome.

As the *agora* was the center of political life in Athens, so in Rome the arena of public action was the *forum*. The exact derivation of the word *forum* is uncertain, but it signified "market-place" or "common." The forum was almost as old as Rome itself, for when the Romans had a little settlement on the Palatine and the neighboring hills were occupied by Sabines and Etruscans, into the valley between the Palatine and the eastern hills the people used to gather to barter or take measures for the common good. In this early day the valley was wet and marshy, yet nevertheless, rude booths shortly sprang up for use on market days.

In its later years—even in its ruins—the forum recorded the various political stages through which the Romans passed. Traces of the monarchial years survived, monuments of the republic and its struggles stood by the side of imperial greatness. Each building and monument in the past and each stone in the ruins today has its story to tell—often a most eloquent and exciting story. Let us attempt to gain some general idea of this famous center of Rome.

In the first place, the very contour of the land determined that the forum must be comparatively small—scarcely larger than a modern city block. Some of the princes of later years had portions of the hills removed in order to give more space. The damp valley supplied excellent pasture and into it during the earliest years cattle and sheep were driven in the morning, to be driven back within the walls of the various hills for safe-keeping during the night. The northwestern end of the valley was somewhat higher than the rest, and here the fathers of the hamlets met for deliberations. This portion was later surrounded by a railing and reserved for the comitia.

The early Romans were farmers who industriously tilled the soil. When war broke out with nearby tribes they tied a bundle of hay to the top of a pole and marched out of the settlement to avenge insults offered or to repulse some bold assailant. When the war was over they returned to their fields again.

Quite as a natural result, their chief god was Saturn, god of agriculture, and in the southwestern end of the forum an altar was erected in his honor. We are told that an early statue of this god was hollow and kept filled with olive oil, while a real sickle was placed in his hand and his feet were adorned with fillets of wool. This would be quite in keeping with the conceptions of a primitive farming people.

In due time the path which had led from the eastern hills to Capitoline—or near it—became a street, known as the Via Sacra. It may have been called the Sacred Way, because of some special sacrifice offered in prehistoric times, or perhaps because the priests always passed through it on their way to the temple of Jupiter.

We have seen how important was fire in antiquity, and how carefully it was guarded because of the trouble of starting it again. For this reason the daughters of the chieftain gave special care to the task of replenishing the fire, and from embers thus kept burning in the chieftain's hut, his followers obtained coals for their hearths. In these primitive times the people lived in little round huts with thatched roofs—not unlike huts to be seen today in remote parts of Italy and Sicily.

As the different tribes united into one kingdom and one chieftain or king sufficed for all, he came down into the valley —neutral ground—to live. Here, too, the sacred fire was brought—tended still by his daughters. Altars were erected to Janus—god of gates or doors—and to Vulcan.

Tradition says that when Numa Pompilius became king he built a temple to Vesta—fire of the hearth. With the conservatism governing all matters pertaining to religion in all ages, although the round huts of early years had been replaced by houses of a different type, still the temple erected in honor of Vesta clung to the first shape. Indeed, through the round house or temple sacred to the flame we read back to the house of primitive years. Fires in Rome wiped out the Temple of Vesta several times, but no matter how costly the one which replaced it, the shape remained unchanged.

Near the Temple of Vesta was the Atrium—so-called from the *atrium,* or chief room of the house—built for the Vestal Virgins: maidens now chosen from the noble families to guard Vesta's fire. Near, too, was the Regia, the house for king and priest. In place of the altar of Janus, a temple was built for the god. During war its doors were open, so that mothers might enter to pray for husbands and sons; during periods of peace the doors were closed. We may judge what a military people were the Romans by the fact that only three times were the doors of this temple shut.

The forum was becoming such a noisy, busy place that Tullus Hostilius is credited with having built a house for the senate—named for him the Curia Hostilia. This was near the Comitium. Having now a place for the laws to be made, it was thought necessary to have a place to confine those who disobeyed them, and we find the *carcer,* or Mamertine prison soon provided. Of all Rome's prisons this was most loathsome. It consisted first of a mere cell underground—dark, cold and damp from the waters of a flowing spring. Later an upper story was added, and fortunate was he who was confined in this rather than the lower cell. As time went on, only those sentenced to death were imprisoned here. Our word *incarcerate* comes directly from the Latin, as is plain.

The elder Tarquin is supposed to have finally made the forum dry by draining off the water from springs by means of the Cloaca Maxima. This was a large sewer unlike any of our day. Instead of pipes, a channel was built of stones so skillfully fitted together that no cement was used, yet no water could leak out of it. This passed under the forum and carried the drainage of this formerly marshy district into the Tiber. The early Romans were proud of their Cloaca Maxima, and well might they be—for it endures to this day and still carries the water from this section to the river.

It was the elder Tarquin who is supposed to have regulated the size of the forum and to have ordered that all buildings adjoining it should front upon it and have porticoes upon the open area. Tarquin the Proud replaced the altar to Saturn by a temple, but his measures soon became so drastic that the people rose up and drove kings forever from their land.

Tradition says that the first structure to be erected upon the forum after the establishment of the republic was the Temple of Castor and Pollux. These were the twin gods, it will be remembered, who suddenly appeared at the head of the Roman army during the battle of Lake Regillus. Aided and encouraged by their presence, Roman fathers told their children, the Thirty Cities were defeated and great was the plunder of Rome. After the fray was ended two strange horsemen were seen to ride into the forum and bathe their horses in the fountain before the temple of Vesta.

> "Then like a flash away they passed,
> And no man saw them more."

In their gratitude the Romans built a temple to their memory for that day's visitation.

The Rostra probably dates from the granting of the tribunes to the common people. From this platform the tribunes and others addressed the people, and in front of it distinguished dead were brought for an oration to be made over them by one near of kin. The front of the platform was decked with the prows of ships taken as prizes in the battle of Antium—hence the name *rostra,* meaning beaks.

As Rome's influence abroad grew stronger and ambassadors visited the city, it was necessary to provide some place for their convenience until the senate should receive them; so in front of the Curia Hostilia an enclosed terrace, the Graecostasis, was reserved. Here foreign legates might stand and listen to the speeches from the Rostra, and here they might confer before giving replies to the senate.

To relieve the pressure in the forum, Cato built the first basilica—the Basilica Porcia. This style of building was new in Rome. It consisted mainly of porticoes, thus providing shelter from the hot sun and from the storm. Halls of justice —court-rooms—were usually built in the central portion of the basilica. This one was so successful that several others were erected, notably the Basilica Julia, started by Julius Caesar and completed by his nephew, Augustus.

We have seen what havoc the Gauls brought to Rome upon their first early invasion. They plundered and laid waste without restraint, and when the terrified Romans who, caught unawares, had taken refuge where they might, returned to find their city in ruins, they were upon the point of leaving forever the scene of such disorder. Yet some of the stronger hearts incited the rest not to abandon the home of their fathers—rather to stay and rebuild the sacred temples. This counsel prevailed, and finally over the lower end of the restored forum the first triumphal arch was built—the Arch of Fabius, who had finally marched against the bold invaders and given them such a blow that they never forgot the power of Rome. This arch was to stand as a warning to any who might be rash enough to invade Roman territory. Arch after arch was erected to Rome's great men in the future—one was raised to the honor of Augustus, another to Titus, one to Hadrian, and to others who deserved them less.

The wars of conquest preceding the establishment of the principate brought countless wealth to Rome and enabled Augustus and later princes to add materially to the glories of the capital. In fact, Augustus' statement that he found the city in brick and left it in marble was literally true. Building after building upon the Roman forum was pulled down, only to be replaced by others which preserved the style of the first but were more pleasing to the eye. New ones were added by each succeeding prince.

The Golden Milestone or Miliarium Aureum, was set up by Augustus near the Temple of Saturn. Upon it were engraved the names of the principal towns to be reached from the thirty-seven gates of Rome, together with the distance of each from the capital. Another stone was erected on the spot supposed to be the center of the empire.

While some of the more important buildings on the forum have been enumerated, nothing has been said of the state treasury which for many years was located in the lower story of the Temple of Saturn, or the Tabularium, wherein were kept the records of state, treaties, decrees of the senate and the laws—all described on tablets of bronze. The Temple of Vespasian, erected by his son, and another built by Augustus to the divinity of Julius Caesar, were also famous.

At the lower end of the forum the Flavian princes erected

their huge amphitheater, which has been mentioned in an earlier chapter. The Circus Maximus and various baths were also discussed before.

And what is left of it all? After the Teutons came down from the north and destroyed for years and years until they were satisfied, Rome was practically left in ruins. The forum became a heap of rubbish and kind nature spread a green mantle over the unsightly spot—as she always tries to cover the desolation wrought by man. Once again the forum became a pasturage, herds of cattle wandering where Rome's mighty ones had walked. In comparatively modern times, with the spirit of reverence for the past and the desire to learn more of it, men have set to work to lay bare such remains as still exist. Columns have been raised again; others standing have been cleared of rubbish that partially concealed them. One column here, three there, and eight in a third place, mark the spots where once stood splendid temples. All around has sprung up the new city—modern Rome, so unlike the earlier capital—and he today who views it all for the first time is doomed to disappointment. If he be a student of the past, he resents the infringement of the new upon the old. Yet a longer acquaintance, and the keen disappointment of first sight has abated and day by day his imagination reconstructs it as it once was. Columns multiply, buildings rise up again, and fancy pictures the forum as it once stood—the glory of Rome.

THE COLISEUM.

Type of the antique Rome! Rich reliquary
Of lofty contemplation left to Time
By buried centuries of pomp and power!
At length—at length—after so many days
Of weary pilgrimage and burning thirst,
(Thirst for the springs of lore that in thee lie,)
I kneel, an altered and an humble man,
Amid thy shadows, and so drink within
My very soul thy grandeur, gloom, and glory;

Here, where a hero fell, a column falls!
Here, where a mimic eagle glared in gold,
A midnight vigil holds the swarthy bat!
Here, where the dames of Rome their gilded hair
Waved to the wind, now wave the reed and thistle!
Here, where on golden throne the monarch lolled,
Glides, spectre-like, unto his marble home,
Lit by the wan light of the horned moon,
The swift and silent lizard of the stones!
But stay! These walls—these ivy-clad arcades—
These mouldering plinths—these sad and blackened shafts—
These vague entablatures—this crumbling frieze—
These shattered cornices—this wreck—this ruin—
These stones—alas! these gray stones—are they all—
All of the famed and the colossal left
By the corrosive Hours to Fate and me?

"Not all!" the echoes answered me. "Not all!
Prophetic sounds and loud, arise forever
From us, and from all Ruin, unto the wise,
As melody from Memnon to the Sun.
We rule the hearts of mightiest men!—we rule
With a despotic sway all giant minds!
We are not impotent—we pallid stones.
Not all our power is gone!—not all our fame!—
Not all the magic of our high renown!—
Not all the wonder that encircles us!—
Not all the mysteries that in us lie!—
Not all the memories that hang upon
And cling around about us as a garment,
Clothing us in a robe of more than glory."   —*Poe.*

CHAPTER XVIII.

Italy of Today.

The transcendent beauty of Italy has been proverbial. No land received a more abundant outpouring from Nature's store than this "pearl of the Mediterranean." Beauty is manifest in many forms, and combined with diversified landscape there are everywhere evidences of long occupation by man. Ruined castles, broken walls—silent witnesses of a storied past—are commingled with olive orchards and fruitful vines—the pride of today.

Italy should be left unvisited by those who favor foreign lands only with a brief sojourn devoted largely to passing unfavorable criticism upon what is not justly estimated or understood. This is a country where care does not oppress and where poverty, however keen, is not allowed to dominate. The poorest peasant basks in the glorious sunshine and drinks to the full the voluptuous beauty around him. Only upon those who approach in a worshipful mood does Italy smile as she only can. Those who give themselves up to her influence forgetful of time or tide, grow presently to feel the mysterious fascination which henceforward entices them to return.

Every variety of mountain may be found in the peninsula. On the north the snow-bound Alps stand guard; although armies have poured over them not infrequently, the toll exacted by these silent warders deterred the less doughty from an attempt. Throughout the entire length stretch the Apennines, the backbone of the peninsula. Lower than the Alps, their summits rise in irregular peaks above the line of cultivation. In the south, volcanic mountains stand, and in most southern Italy and Sicily are ranges too rough for cultivation, cactus-covered or overlaid with sulphur dust.

Sometimes the mountains jut into the Mediterranean, producing the pleasing effect of combined mountain and sea; everywhere they are crowned by little towns, at first glance seemingly inaccessible. Two enemies drove people to the hills for habitation—malaria, which lurked in the plains, and plunderers, against whom stout defense was needed.

As might be expected in a land where mountains pierce the snow line, rivers and waterfalls are abundant. Few streams are suited to commerce, but many lend charm to the eye. Besides the immortal Tiber, the Arno gives Florence added interest; the Adige contributes in no small measure to Verona's beauty, and the Po, with its tributaries and willow-bordered canals, is the most conspicuous feature in the great plain of Lombardy.

At the foot of the Alps lie Italy's largest lakes: Maggiore, Como, Garda, and Lugano. Flanked by mountains on the north, they touch the fertile plain upon the south and have for centuries been popular as sites for castles and country places.

Nor can the sea be for a moment forgotten. The Bay of Naples is world-renowned, and numerous other bays, if their waters are less sapphire, offer a variety of coastlines: some rocky, some sand-rimmed. The peculiar situation of Venice, built on a series of lagoons, has given it scenic effects unlike that of other cities, and dozens of towns and scores of hamlets owe their commanding views to the proximity of the water.

Between mountain ranges and traversed by irregular spurs, lie the plains—the food-producing districts of Italy. Arable land is so limited that every square foot is seized upon by the industrious farmer, while tillable areas are added by terracing naked rocks with soil brought from away. The agricultural character of the country is at once apparent; only two Italian cities reach the half-million mark and less than ten have one hundred thousand people. The population is widely diffused, not massed.

Had Italy been a land of forbidding skies, sterile soil and severe climate, her history would have been far different. Her beauty was her curse. Napoleon cheered his disheartened soldiers by picturing the luxury that awaited them in the valley to which they would shortly descend. The reports of its richness and productivity, as well as the accumulated wealth of many towns, made enemies watchful of the slightest opportunity to creep in. When we read of centuries of strife when community fought against community, citizen against citizen, until blood ran riot in the streets, and men lived behind barricades; when army after army was brought thither to share the spoils, and reformer vied with barbarian in seeking what he could destroy, the wonder is not that so little remains of ancient and mediæval Italy but that aught survived the ruthless devastation.

Fortunate is the one who enters Italy by the great highway of waters. Far better is it to revel in modern European cities after wandering among the shrines of antiquity than to reverse the order and approach overland from the north.

Sicily was once a part of the peninsula. Though separated for ages, her history cannot be considered apart from that of the mainland. The name signifies "Island of the Sun," and is most appropriate. The delightful climate has caused invalids to flock thither in recent years, to bask in the warm sunshine while rigorous winter holds the north in its grasp. Nor are health-seekers alone attracted. The yachtsman and motorist find Sicily a joy; those who love to study ancient remains may likewise pass months pleasantly, for some forty Greek temples may be visited; several old theaters are to be seen; one of the most beautiful churches in all Christendom is here, the Chapel of Palermo; while for music-lovers, the largest opera house in the world has been built.

Palermo is famed for its museum, its palm-gardens and mosaics; Syracuse for its Greek remains and its catacombs; Taormina for its views of Mount Etna and its Græco-Roman ruins. Even a short sojourn may be gratifying. Sicily is unique also in being one place where the supply for real curios is still equal to the demand.

"See Naples and die!" exclaimed an enthusiast long ago, and the phrase is still repeated. And yet it is the bay, not the city, that calls for extravagant praise. The waters are of such an intense blue and the expanse of tranquil sea so inspiring, that once seen, the sight is never to be forgotten. The town rises in terraces, resplendent with vineyards and orange gardens; flowers hang over the water's edge and are mirrored in its depths.

"The beauty of the Bay of Naples, as seen from Naples itself, is of the majestic order. It is a vast body of water with mountains for its sides, and a chain of turquoise islands to break the monotony of its wide mouth. Even with Vesuvius beheaded like Conradin, we have here a rare pageant of mountains; Naples, a mountain covered with a hundred thousand houses in faded rainbow tints; Vesuvius, a garden showing its brown earth; and the mountains of the Sorrento peninsula, making a blue sierra in the hot noon—what a horizon they make!"

Southern Italy is more oppressed by poverty than the central and northern portions, and Naples unfortunately harbors more squalor and dreadful need than any other city of its size. Even the most abject sections of our slums could scarcely parallel the revolting scenes of the Neapolitan center. Yet woe betide the traveler whose heart is moved by some especially appealing sight to empty his purse; his steps are dogged by scores of beggars who hardly allow him to escape.

Mediæval and modern Naples are joined by the thoroughfare long called the Toledo, now *Strada Roma*. Only Joppa Gate and the famous bridge of Constantinople afford opportunity to watch such varied types of humanity as incessantly move to and fro. The unusual noises of Naples jar upon the traveler's ears. The venders' cries fall unheeded upon the natives, but the great volume and variety cause visitors to long remember them. Sights, too, which it would be hard to parallel, strike the eye. At Christmas time flocks of turkeys are driven through the city; they are halted before each house; each householder selects his bird, whereupon the remainder are driven along to the next buyer. Not only are cows milked in the streets before the consumer's eyes, but goats are brought to the highest floor of tenement buildings and milked before each door. Surely Naples offers discouraging difficulties to the middleman.

It is doubtful whether Americans would value imported macaroni if they could see it drying. The use of machinery has now removed many of the earlier objectionable features, but it is still dried in the dusty streets, under conditions which pure food commissions would never permit. Even if accidentally dropped in the mud, it needs but another washing and drying before given a fancy label and shipped to some foreign port.

Villa Nazionale, a park laid out by the Bourbon kings;

Museo Nazionale, a delight to lovers of antiques; and the Castle of St. Elmo attract the stranger. The building now used as a museum was constructed for cavalry barracks in the sixteenth century and in 1790 was appropriated by the Bourbons for collections of antiquities. It is especially interesting today because it has become the repository for the many finds at Pompeii and Herculaneum—valuable for the light they throw upon Græco-Italian life. St. Elmo was impregnable until the late inventions of war guns, having huge walls, subterranean passages and unlimited water supply. It is used today as a prison and hence not open to visitors.

Many enticing places lie near Naples. The rocky island of Capri, coral-caved, with its colored grottos, surpasses one's wildest imaginative flight. Curious reflections of light render some grottos blue, others green, others red, and call to mind the poet's exclamation of "the light that never was on land or sea." Capri is rich also in wild flowers, some of the choicest orchids being native.

Amalfi, a town of superb setting, gives today no indication of its remarkable history. Time was when its fleets rivaled those of Genoa and Pisa; when as a republic it was powerful in Italy. Today it numbers but three thousand people, many of whom find employment in the flourishing paper mills.

Pompeii, that strange, deserted habitation of man, remains an eloquent memorial of the tragedy enacted on the twenty-fourth of August, '79. A gay resort of Rome's profligate nobles, its care-free life was checked by a catastrophe unparalleled before or since. None can wander through its streets, view its unroofed walls, and study its remains without feeling the reality of a calamity removed in point of time almost two thousand years.

Rome, the capital of modern Italy, once the mistress of the world, is the magnet toward which all travelers in the peninsula are drawn. It is possible to go from the seashore to Rome by boat, although little is to be seen that way except the Campagna—that "green motionless sea of silence." This is the name applied to the vast undulating waste that reaches southwest of Rome, between the city and the sea and far to the south. Once cultivated, it lies today untouched, serving as pasturage for the half-wild cattle that roam over it.

Somewhat as the desert impresses those who view it does this expanse of land affect those who see it in the varying lights of day and sunset. Through it the Tiber wanders, serpent-like.

The whole city of Rome is one vast museum, in spite of the fact that it is also a rapidly growing metropolis. Visitors are often at first disappointed to find the past so interlinked with the present. However, the immensity of Rome is overpowering. A lifetime would be too brief to exhaust its wonders. He whose sojourn must be brief should confine his attention to the more prominent sights—not attempt to hurriedly scan the whole. Standing by the Tiber, one recalls the part the river played in the foundation of the first rude hamlet. The remains of Horatio's bridge bring back a flood of associations. The "seven hills" have been much reduced in height and some of them have been rendered scarcely recognizable because of new streets cut through them. Aventine, from whose summit the nobility were wont to watch the races in the Circus Maximus, is now the site of a new Benedictine College. Two churches, one dedicated to Saint Alexis, the other to Saint Sabina, are also there. On Esquiline may be seen the domes of other churches and particularly the campanile of S. Marie Maggiore. This is the largest of eighty churches in Rome dedicated to the Mother Mary. On Quirinal is the vast palace, once the abode of popes, now the palace of the king of Italy; Viminal is almost lost in new streets.

Capitol Hill, once the city's center, owes its present arrangement of buildings to Michael Angelo; the museum stands on one side, the Palace of the Conservators on the other. It will be remembered that the hill was originally steep and rocky and that it was crowned by the Temple of Jupiter. Only one of the old buildings remain—the Tabularium—or public record office, now the basement in the Palace of the Senator. A few rich legacies of the past are preserved in the museum—the Faun of Praxiteles and the Dying Gladiator being most widely known.

Over the Mamertine Prison has been erected the church of St. Joseph of the Carpenters. The Forum has been excavated in part and invaluable discoveries have resulted.

Across the Tiber and to the north is the great palace of the Vatican and more conspicuous still, the Basilica of St.

Peter's. This mountain of art is believed to cover the tomb of St. Peter. It is the largest church in the world and exemplifies as far as stone and mortar can, the tremendous part the Church has played in the world's history. Simply to cross from one side of the building to the other is quite a journey. Its vast proportions defy description. Although earlier buildings have been erected on this site, as it stands now it was begun in 1508 and dedicated in 1626. Three famous architects labored upon it and several others either added to or detracted from its imposing effect. The conception originated with Bramante; Michael Angelo designed the first dome.

The Vatican, with its reputed seven thousand rooms, is likewise the result of many hands and many minds. It is rambling and exemplifies no unified plan. It was used by the papacy after the period of papal residence at Avignon for its safety, and during the tumultuous Middle Ages was prepared as a fortress to withstand a siege. Succeeding popes have beautified and enlarged it until it serves not only as a palace for the pope and the cardinals, but contains rich museums, libraries, picture galleries, offices, offices for church administration and suites of apartments devoted to a wide variety of uses.

The Corso, the narrow street extending from the foot of Capitoline to the Porte del Popolo, is the great thoroughfare today. Via Nazionale and Corso Vittorio Emanuele are new streets and have been made wider. More interesting to readers of Latin literature is the Via Appia—the great artery that connected Rome first with Capua and later with the Adriatic. It was built of hexagonal slabs of hard lava fitted closely together. So well was it constructed that recently repaired, it supplies a highway of travel today. An ancient law made it prohibitive to inter the dead within the city walls. The Romans burned their dead and preserved the ashes in urns. They adopted the plan of building tombs along the highways; only prominent patrician families were buried along the Appian Way. As wealth increased, as a result of foreign conquests, these ancestral tombs became more splendid and elaborate. Instead of choosing quiet and secluded places for their dead, they preferred to leave them where life was gayest and it was no unusual sight to find a tomb by the side of a circus.

The Appian Way, at its greatest width is about twenty-six feet; formerly at intervals seats were built for the weary traveler; inns were scattered along the route and statues of the gods stationed here and there. At intervals of 5,000 feet, milestones were erected.

The early Christians buried their dead. Under the ban of the law, they were refused burial in the cemeteries. The exigencies of the times, therefore, led them to appropriate certain galleries or passages beneath the city and to construct others. These are known as catacombs. They were originally called Caemeteria, meaning places of sleep, rest and repose. Later the present name was given them, its exact derivation being uncertain.

The catacombs form a network of subterranean passages outside the walls and beneath the city. It was formerly believed that these tunnels were all connected and that they even gave access to the sea. Modern examination has shown, on the contrary, that several of the catacombs—there were forty-six in Rome—were wholly isolated and that while originally clearly defined, because of their great extent, they grew into a labyrinth. Cut in the soft tufa, they were about two feet wide and were lined on either side by niches just large enough to receive a body. These were sealed by slabs of marble or by cemented tiles. The name of the deceased was often carved in the marble or painted on the tiles. During periods of persecution greater precaution was taken; sometimes only the imprint of a shell or tiny object was made in the soft cement to identify the place for relatives. However, it has to be granted that the respect of the Romans for the dead would have prevented any wholesale sacrilege of those interred.

At intervals these narrow galleries led into small rooms, cut in square or rectangular form. These were used as assembly places for groups of worshippers and were also sought as places of refuge during times of danger. Light and air were obtained by means of shafts, so constructed that one frequently supplied air for several passages.

As their numbers increased, the Christians found it necessary to increase their burial area and tier upon tier of these galleries were made. Sometimes stairways lead to as many as five stories. Students of early Christian art find here the first examples. The walls of the rooms were painted with sacred pictures. Symbols were used to represent things holy and we find often the picture of the Good Shepherd, who cares for his sheep. The Catacombs of St. Callixtus were located beneath the Appian Way. Other cities have series of catacombs but far less extensive than those of Rome.

The most recent architectural triumph in Rome has been the new capitol. Whereas the first object that previously struck the eye was St. Peter's, this stupendous structure on the site of the old Temple of Juno, on the brow of Capitoline, is now first seen. The wide stairs leading up to it are imposing. Built of white Brescia marble, it stands as a mighty monument to New Italy.

Tuscany contains many places that divert the attention of the traveler; the lover of art must always place Florence first —"the flower of cities—the city of flowers." Unlike many another ancient center, modern Florence does not leave her monuments unused. Whether he will or no, the stranger must take heed of them. What was once a royal palace serves as a picture gallery; another, as a town hall; the palace of the Podestà, as a museum. All roads seem to meet at the Cathedral. In short, art is brought before one at every turn.

The Arno divides the city in two unequal parts. The mountains form an amphitheater open to the west, and with such a setting a center of the fine arts grew up. It abounds in monuments of all ages since the second thousand years began, but the age of the Medici was particularly prolific. Besides churches and palaces, there are bridges, fountains, columns and statuary to examine. The very flower girls around Giotto's campanile are fascinating.

Siena is almost a rival of Florence in Renaissance art. Tradition connects its founding with the son of Remus. The strife between these two cities lasted for centuries and ended only with Siena's annexation to the dominions of Florence. Only the Doge's palace in Venice was more beautiful than the civic palace of Siena. Its cathedral has glaring faults but is, nevertheless, a rich repository of painting.

Pisa, a town of some thirty thousand, is becoming known as the headquarters for Italian racing; but it has had a wonderful history. It was once the rival of Genoa and Venice.

Defeated by Genoa, it later became a dependency of Florence, after which its history was less tempestuous.

Pisa is usually associated with the Leaning Tower—built as a campanile for the great cathedral. Probably there was no intention of constructing anything architecturally phenomenal, but it is surmised that the ground sank on one side before the building was completed and the upper stories were added in a way to relieve the strain. The bells suspended in the top of the belfry are very heavy and it is hard for the spectator to realize that the whole structure is not ready to fall and crush him. The marble used in this tower and in the cathedral to which it belongs, came from Carrara, the famous marble quarries. Known to the Romans and lost sight of until the eleventh century, the most beautiful marble in the world is obtained here. Carrara presents a curious spectacle to the sightseer. About four hundred and fifty quarries are near by; these supply most of the marble used throughout Italy and in many other lands where the finest quality is desired. Although so many quarries are being worked, only six yield the exquisite quality desired for the rarest statuary. The Albissima quarry, now owned by the American Marble Trust, once furnished the marble used by Michael Angelo. In modern times it supplied marble for the construction of Garfield's monument in Cleveland.

The whole town is filled with sculptors and works of art are to be seen on every hand.

Venice could supply entertainment and diversion for the summers of a lifetime. Unique in situation, rich in history, prolific in works of art, volumes have been written about it and much is left unsaid. Because it is so unlike other places, some call it artificial and unreal; why paint it, they ask—since it is itself but a picture. Yet Venice has known the stern realities of life—none better. The splash of the oar in the darkness recalls the years when few knew what the sound might portend. Today, with its canals mirroring the lights of sunset, it seems of "such stuff as dreams are made of," and if one were to paint just one characteristic object, it would be a Venetian gondola—if to record but one sound, the song of the gondolier.

Milan is a big city, with greater evidences of modern

activity than any other in Italy. For this reason it repels many visitors who resent seeing the present when they expected to witness memorials of the past. Still Milan is not lacking in venerable remains. So long as her cathedral with its two thousand statues and its myriads of spires shimmers in the sunlight and stands a mystical phantom in the moonlight, one cannot forget the past in its midst. Nor is it all that the city affords. While not thrust upon one with the same insistence as those in other places, there are many survivals of the period when Italian art was in its flower.

Finally, of the large cities which the tourist in Italy would not wish to omit, Genoa must be mentioned. At any season of the year it is enjoyable. While architecturally gratifying and picturesque in situation, its shipping industries make it more prosperous than other Italian centers, with the possible exception of Milan. Having no imposing picture gallery, it possesses many worthy paintings. And beyond its local importance, for centuries to come, it may be, men will thrill at the sound of the word Genoa because it gave birth to a man whose undaunted courage had such a far-reaching influence upon the world's subsequent history.

THE MIDDLE AGES

The Forest Children.

I wish to give you some general conception of the causes which urged our Teutonic race to attack and destroy Rome.
And I shall begin, if you will allow me, by a parable, a myth, a saga, such as the men of whom I am going to tell you loved; and if it seem to any of you childish, bear in mind that what is childish need not therefore be shallow. I know that it is not history. But I beg you to bear in mind that I am not here to teach you history. No man can do that. I am here to teach you how to teach yourselves history. I will give you the scaffolding as well as I can; you must build the house.

Fancy to yourself a great Troll-garden, such as our forefathers dreamed of often fifteen hundred years ago;—a fairy palace, with a fairy garden; and all around the primæval wood. Inside the Trolls dwell, cunning and wicked, watching their fairy treasures, working at their magic forges, making and making always things rare and strange; and outside, the forest is full of children; such children as the world had never seen before, but children still: children in frankness, and purity, and affectionateness, and tenderness of conscience, and devout awe of the unseen; and children too in fancy, and silliness and ignorance, and caprice, and jealousy, and quarrelsomeness, and love of excitement and adventure, and the mere sport of overflowing animal health. They play unharmed among the forest beasts, and conquer them in their play; but the forest is too dull and too poor for them; and they wander to the walls of the Troll-garden, and wonder what is inside. One can conceive easily for oneself what from that moment would begin to happen. Some of the more adventurous clamber in. Some, too, the Trolls steal and carry off into their palace. Most never return: but here and there one escapes out again, and tells how the Trolls killed all his comrades: but tells, too, of the wonders he has seen inside, of shoes of swiftness, and swords of sharpness, and caps of darkness; of charmed harps, charmed jewels,

Mosaic.—Worship of the Magi.—Sixth Century

and above all of the charmed wine: and after all, the Trolls were very kind to him—see what fine clothes they have given him—and he struts about awhile among his companions; and then returns, and not alone. The Trolls have bewitched him, as they will bewitch more. So the fame of the Troll-garden spreads; and more and more steal in, boys and maidens, and tempt their comrades over the wall, and tell of the jewels, and the dresses, and the wine, the joyous maddening wine, which equals men with gods; and forget to tell how the Trolls have bought them, soul as well as body, and taught them to be vain, and lustful, and slavish; and tempted them, too often, to sins which have no name.

But their better nature flashes out at times. They will not be the slaves and brutes in human form, which the evil Trolls would have them; and they rebel, and escape, and tell of the horrors of that fair foul place. And then arises a noble indignation, and war between the Trolls and the forest-children. But still the Trolls can tempt and bribe the greedier or the more vain; and still the wonders inside haunt their minds; till it becomes a fixed idea among them all, to conquer the garden for themselves and bedizen themselves in the fine clothes, and drink their fill of the wine. Again and again they break in: but the Trolls drive them out, rebuild their walls, keep off those outside by those whom they hold enslaved within; till the boys grow to be youths, and the youths men: and still the Troll-garden is not conquered, and still it shall be. And the Trolls have grown old and weak, and their walls are crumbling away. Perhaps they may succeed this time—perhaps next.

And at last they do succeed—the fairy walls are breached, the fairy palace stormed—and the Trolls are crouching at their feet, and now all will be theirs, gold, jewels, dresses, arms, all that the Troll possesses—except his cunning.

For as each struggles into the charmed grounds, the spell of the place falls on him. He drinks the wine, and it maddens him. He fills his arms with precious trumpery, and another snatches it from his grasp. Each envies the youth before him, each cries—Why had I not the luck to enter first? And the Trolls set them against each other, and split them into parties, each mad with excitement, and jealousy, and wine, till, they scarce know how, each falls upon his fellow, and all upon those who are crowding in from the forest, and they fight and fight, up and down the palace halls, till their triumph has become a very feast of the Lapithae, and the Trolls look on, and laugh a wicked laugh, as they tar them on to the unnatural fight, till the gardens are all trampled, the finery torn, the halls dismantled, and each pavement slippery with brothers' blood. And then, when the wine is gone out of them, the survivors come to their senses, and stare shamefully and sadly round. What an ugly, desolate, tottering ruin the fairy palace has become! Have they spoilt it themselves or have the Trolls bewitched it? And all the fairy treasure—what has become of it no man knows. Have they thrown it away in their quarrel? Have the cunningest hidden it? Have the Trolls flown away with it to the fairy land beyond the Eastern mountains? Who can tell? Nothing is left but recrimination and remorse. And they wander back again into the forest, away from the doleful ruin, carrion-strewn, to sulk each apart over some petty spoil which he has saved from the general wreck, hating and dreading each the sounds of his neighbor's footstep.

What will become of the forest children, unless some kind saint or hermit comes among them, to bind them in the holy bonds of brotherhood and law?

This is my saga; and it is a true one withal. For it is neither more nor less than the story of the Teutonic tribes, and how they overthrew the Empire of Rome.

Menzel, who, though he may not rank very high as a historian, has at least a true German heart, opens his history with a striking passage:

"The sages of the East were teaching wisdom beneath the palms; the merchants of Tyre and Carthage were weighing their heavy anchors, and spreading their purple sails for far seas; the Greek was making the earth fair by his art, and the Roman founding his colossal empire of force, while the Teuton sat, yet a child, unknown and naked among the forest beasts: and yet unharmed and in his sport he lorded it over them; for the child was of a royal race, and destined to win glory for all time to come."

To the strange and complicated education which God appointed for this race, and by which he has fitted it to become, at least for many centuries henceforth, the ruling race of the world, I wish to call your attention in my future lectures. To-day, I wish to impress strongly on your minds this childishness of our forefathers. For good or for evil they were great boys—as boys with the strength of men might well be. Try to conceive such to yourselves, and you have the old Markman, Allman, Goth, Lombard, Saxon, Frank. And the notion may be more than a mere metaphor. Races, like individuals, it has been often said, may have their childhood, their youth, their manhood, their old age, and natural death. It is but a theory—perhaps nothing more. But at least, each race has its childhood. Their virtues, and their sad failings, and failures, I can understand on no other theory. The nearest type which we can see now is I fancy, the English sailor, or the English navvy. A great, simple, honest baby—full of power and fun, very coarse and plain spoken at times: but if treated like a human being, most affectionate, susceptible, even sentimental and superstitious; fond of gambling, brute excitement, childish amusements in the intervals of enormous exertion; quarrelsome among themselves, as boys are, and with a spirit of wild independence which seems to be strength; but, which, till it be disciplined into loyal obedience and self-sacrifice, is mere weakness; and beneath all a deep practical shrewdness, an indomitable perseverance, when roused by need. Such a spirit as we see to this day in the English sailor—that is the nearest analogue I can find now. One gets hints here and there of what manner of men they were, from the evil day, when, one hundred and two years before Christ, the Kempers and Teutons, ranging over the Alps toward Italy, 300,000 armed men and 15,000 mailed knights with broadswords and lances, and in their helmets the same bulls' horns, wings, and feathers which one sees now in the crests of German princes, stumbled upon Marius and his Romans, and were destroyed utterly, first the men, then the women, who like true women as they were, rather than give up their honour to the Romans, hung themselves on the horns of the wagon-oxen, and were trampled to death beneath their feet; and then the very dogs, who fought on when men and women were all slain—from that fatal day, down to the glorious one, when, five hundred years after, Alaric stood beneath the walls of Rome, and to their despairing boasts of the Roman numbers, answered, "Come out to us then, the thicker the hay, the easier mowed,"—for five hundred years, I say, the hints of their character are all those of a boy-nature.

They were cruel at times: but so are boys—much more cruel than grown men, I hardly know why—perhaps because they have not felt suffering so much themselves, and know not how hard it is to bear. There were varieties of character among them. The Franks were always false, vain, capricious, selfish, taking part with the Romans whenever their interest or vanity was at stake—the worst of all Teutons, though by no means the weakest—and a miserable business they made of it in France, for some five hundred years. The Goths, Salvian says, were the most ignavi of all of them; great lazy lourdans; apt to be cruel, too, the Visigoths at least, as their Spanish descendants proved to the horror of the world: but men of honour withal, as those old Spaniards were. The Saxons were famed for cruelty—I know not why, for our branch of the Saxons has been, from the beginning of history, the least cruel people in Europe; but they had the reputation—as the Vandals had also—of being the most pure; *Castitate venerandi*. And among the uncivilized people coldness and cruelty go often together. The less passionate and sensitive the nature, the less open to pity. The Caribs of the West Indies were famed for both, in contrast to the profligate and gentle inhabitants of Cuba and Hispaniola; and in double contrast to the Red Indian tribes of North America, who combined, from our first acquaintance with them, the two vices of cruelty and profligacy, to an extent which has done more to extirpate them than all the fire-water of the white man.

But we must be careful how we compare our forefathers with these, or any other savages. Those who, like Gibbon, have tried to draw a parallel between the Red Indian and the Primaeval Teuton, have done so at the expense of facts. First, they have overlooked the broad fact that while the Red Indians have been, ever since we have known them, a decreasing race, the Teutons have been a rapidly increasing one; in spite of war, and famine, and all the ills of the precarious forest life, proving their youthful strength and vitality by a reproduction unparalleled, as far as I know, in history, save perhaps by that noble and young race, the Russian. These writers have not known that the Teuton had his definite laws, more simple, doubtless, in the time of Tacitus than in that of Justinian, but still founded on abstract principles so deep and broad that they form the groundwork of our English laws and constitution; that the Teuton creed concerning the unseen world, and divine beings, was of a loftiness and purity as far above the silly legends of Hiawatha as the Teuton morals were above those of a Sioux or a Comanche. Let any one read honest accounts of the Red Indians; let him read Catlin, James, Lewis and Clarke, Shoolbred; and first and best of all, the old "Travaile in Virginia," published by the Hakluyt Society; and then let him read the Germania of Tacitus, and judge for himself. For my part, I believe that if Gibbon was right, and if our forefathers in the German forests had been like Powhattan's people as we found them in the Virginian forests, the Romans would not have been long in civilizing us off the face of the earth.

No. All the notes which Tacitus gives us are notes of a young and strong race; unconscious of its own capabilities, but possessing such capabilities that the observant Romans saw at once with dread and awe that they were face to face with such a people as they had never met before; that in their hands, sooner or later, might lie the fate of Rome. Mad Caracalla, aping the Teuton dress and hair, listening in dread to the songs of the Allman Alrunas, telling the Teutons that they ought to come over the Rhine and destroy the empire, and then, murdering the interpreters, lest they should repeat his words, was but babbling out in an insane shape the thought which was brooding in the most far-seeing Roman minds. He felt that they could have done the deed; and he felt rightly, madman as he was. They could have done it then, if physical power and courage were all that was needed, in the days of the Allman war. They could have done it a few years before, when the Markmen fought Marcus Aurelius Antoninus; on the day when the Caesar, at the advice of his augurs, sent two lions to swim across the Danube as a test of victory; and the simple Markmen took them for big dogs, and killed them with their clubs. From that day, indeed, the Teutons began to conquer slowly, but surely. Though Antoninus beat the Markmen on the Danube, and recovered 100,000 Roman prisoners, yet it was only by the help of the vandals; from that day the empire was doomed, and the Teutons only kept at bay by bribing one tribe to fight another, or by enlisting their more adventurous spirits into the Roman legions, to fight against men of their own blood—a short-sighted and suicidal policy; for by that very method they were teaching the Teuton all he needed, the discipline and the military science of the Roman.

But the Teutons might have done it a hundred years before that, when Rome was in a death agony, and Vitellius and Vespasian were struggling for the purple, and Cavilis and the fair Velleda, like Barak and Deborah of old, raised the Teuton tribes. They might have done it before that again, when Hermann slew Varus and his legions in the Teutoburger Wald; or before that again, when the Kempers and Teutons burst over the Alps, to madden themselves with the fatal wines of the rich south. And why did the Teutons not do it? Because they were boys fighting against cunning men. Boiorich, the young Kemper, riding down to Marius' camp, to bid him fix the place and time of battle—for the Teuton thought it mean to use surprises and stratagems, or to conquer save in fair and open fight—is the type of the Teuton hero; and one which had no chance in a struggle with the cool, false, politic Roman, grown grey in the experience of the forum and of the camp, and still as physically brave as his young enemy. Because, too, there was no unity among them; no feeling that they were brethren of one blood. Had the Teuton tribes, at any one of the great crises I have mentioned, and at many a crisis afterwards, united for but three years, under the feeling of a common blood, language, interest, destiny, Rome would have perished. But they could not learn that lesson. They could not put aside their boyish quarrels.

They never learnt the lesson till after their final victory, when the Gospel of Christ—of a Being to whom they all owed equal allegiance, in whose sight they were all morally equal—came to unite them into a Christendom.

And it was well that they did not learn it sooner. Well for them and for the world, that they did not unite on any false ground of interest or ambition, but had to wait for the true ground of unity, the knowledge of the God-man, King of all nations upon earth.

Had they destroyed Rome sooner, what would not they have lost? What would not the world have lost? Christianity would have been stifled in its very cradle; and with Christianity all chance—be sure of it—of their own progress. Roman law, order, and discipline, the very things which they needed to acquire by a contact of five hundred years, would have been swept away. All classic literature and classic art, which they learnt to admire with an almost superstitious awe, would have perished likewise. Greek philosophy, the germs of physical science, and all that we owe to the ancients, would have perished; and we should have truly had an invasion of the barbarians, followed by truly dark ages, in which Europe would have had to begin all anew, without the help of the generations which had gone before.

Therefore it was well as it was, and God was just and merciful to them and to the human race. They had a glorious destiny, and glorious powers wherewith to fulfill it: but they had, as every man and people has, before whom there is a noble future, to be educated by suffering. There was before them a terrible experience of sorrow and disappointment, sin and blood, by which they gained the first consciousness of what they could do and what they could not. Like Adam of old, like every man unto this day, they ate of the tree of the knowledge of good and evil, and were driven out of the paradise of unconsciousness; they had to begin again sadder and wiser men, and eat their bread in the sweat of their brow, and so to rise, after their fall, into a nobler, wiser, more artificial, and therefore more truly human and divine life, than that from which they had at first fallen, when they left their German wilds.

One does not, of course, mean the parallel to fit in all details. The fall of the Teuton from the noble simplicity in which Tacitus beheld and honoured him, was a work of four centuries; perhaps it was going on in Tacitus' own time. But the culminating point was the century which saw Italy conquered, and Rome sacked, by Visigoth, by Ostrogoth, by Vandal, till nothing was left save fever-haunted ruins. Then the ignorant and greedy child, who had been grasping so long after the fair apples of Sodom, clutched them once and for all, and found them turn to ashes in his hands.

Yes—it is thus that I wish you to look at the Invasion of the Barbarians, Immigration of the Teutons, or whatsoever name you may call it. Before looking at questions of migration, of ethnology, of laws, and of classes, look first at the thing itself;

and see with sacred pity and awe, one of the saddest and grandest tragedies ever performed on earth. Poor souls! And they were so simple withal. One pities them, as one pities a child who steals apples, and makes himself sick with them after all. It is not the enormous loss of life which is to me the most tragic part of the story; it is that very simplicity of the Teutons. Bloodshed is a bad thing, certainly; but after all nature is prodigal of human life—killing her twenty thousand and her fifty thousand by a single earthquake; and as for death in battle—I sometimes am tempted to think, having sat by many death beds, that our old forefathers may have been right, and that death in battle may be a not unenviable method of passing out of this troublesome world. Besides, we have no right to blame those old Teutons, while we are killing every year more of her Majesty's subjects by preventable disease, than ever they killed in their bloodiest battle. Let us think of that, and mend that, ere we blame the old German heroes. No, there are more pitiful tragedies than any battlefield can show; and first among them, surely, is the disappointment of young hopes, the degradation of young souls.

One pities them, I say. And they pitied themselves. Remorse, shame, sadness, mark the few legends and songs of the days which followed the fall of Rome. They had done a great work. They had destroyed a mighty tyranny; they had parted between them the spoils wrung from all the nations; they had rid the earth of a mighty man-devouring ogre, whose hands had been stretched out for centuries over all the earth, dragging all virgins to his den, butchering and torturing thousands for his sport; foul, too, with crimes for which their language, like our own (thank God) has scarcely found a name. Babylon, the Great, drunken with the blood of the saints, had fallen at last before the simple foresters of the north : but if it looks a triumph to us, it looked not such to them. They could only think how they had stained their hands in their brothers' blood. They had got the fatal Nibelungen hoard: but it had vanished between their hands, and left them to kill each other, till none was left.

You know the Nibelungen Lied? That expresses, I believe, the keynote of the old Teuton's heart, after his work was done. Siegfried murdered by his brother-in-law; fair Chriemhild turned into an avenging fury; the heroes hewing each other down, they scarce know why, in Hunnish Etzel's hall, till Hagen and Gunther stand alone; Dietrich of Bern going in, to bind the last surviving heroes; Chriemhild shaking Hagen's gory head in Gunther's face, himself hewed down by the old Hildebrand, till nothing is left but stark corpses and vain tears—while all the while the Nibelungen hoard, the cause of all the woe, lies drowned in the deep Rhine until the judgment day. What is all this, but the true tale of the fall of Rome, of the mad quarrels of the conquering Teutons? The names are confused, mythic; the dates and places all awry; but the tale is true—too true. *Mutato nomine fabula narratur.* Even so they went on, killing, till none were left. Deeds as strange, horrible, fratricidal, were done, again and again, not only between Frank and Goth, Lombard and Gepid, but between Lombard and Lombard, Frank and Frank. Yes, they were drunk with each other's blood, those elder brethren of ours. Let us thank God that we did not share their booty, and perish, like them, from the touch of the fatal Nibelungen hoard. Happy for us Englishmen, that we were forced to seek our adventures here, in this lonely isle; to turn aside from the great stream of Teutonic immigration; and settle here, each man on his forest-clearing, to till the ground in comparative peace, keeping unbroken the old Teutonic laws, unstained the old Teutonic faith and virtue, cursed neither with poverty nor riches, but fed with food sufficient for us. To us, indeed, after long centuries, peace brought sloth, and sloth foreign invaders and bitter woes: but better so, than that we should have cast away alike our virtue and our lives, in that mad quarrel over the fairy gold of Rome.

—From *The Roman and the Teuton,* Charles Kingsley.

CHAPTER I.
INTRODUCTORY.

By the *Middle Ages,* we refer to the years intervening between the fall of Rome and the beginning of the Renaissance. It was once customary to designate these as the Dark Ages, but the more we learn of them the more we become persuaded that they were by no means so dark as was formerly supposed. After the passing of the first two or three hundred years following the collapse of Rome, forces of tremendous importance for the future were already at work. Unfortunately, sufficient means for an adequate understanding of the Middle Ages have not been available. Few records were kept or chronicles made during the first portion of the period, and when writings became more general they did not necessarily treat of subjects absorbing to us today. Certain it is that the field of mediaeval history lies still largely unworked, and many questions yet unsolved will probably be cleared up in the future.

As has already been shown, the northern boundaries of the Roman Empire were for a long time the Rhine and Danube rivers. North of Italy and south of these rivers the territory had been Romanized to a considerable extent. North of these boundary streams dwelt the Teutons—children of the forests; save on the very border-land they had remained almost wholly untouched by Latin civilization.

When at last Rome's armies weakened, and along the frontier the firm authority of the Eternal City was no longer sternly supported, the stream of barbarous hordes poured across a line previously regarded as impassable, and Rome, conquered not by foreigners but internal weaknesses, collapsed.

The Teutons.

Of the Teutons we may learn from the writings of Cæsar, Tacitus, and other Roman writers. They were vigorous people in the first strength of a young race. Almost untouched by civilizing influences, they brought utter destruction as they poured unceasingly into the old Roman Empire.

Of the many Germanic tribes and their wanderings we need not here treat. Suffice it to say that the first two centuries after the fall of Rome are expressively designated as the age of the *Wandering of the Nations*. Settled at length in one portion of the empire or another, Europe passed through a long *Transition Period*. During this indefinite age the Teutonic invaders gradually assimilated much of the surviving culture of antiquity. They dropped many of their fierce northern ways for more highly developed ways of the Romans. Most of all, the greater portion of the Germans became imbued with the fundamental teachings of Christianity. This alone accounts for the fact that the people of southern Europe did not suffer even more than they did.

Of the Teutonic peoples, the Franks soon asserted themselves most powerfully. Uniting more effectively under their chieftain Clovis, they subdued the Burgundians and established their power in western Europe. They were later ruled by the Merovingian kings. Nevertheless, the Mayors of the Palace became in fact stronger than the weak kings whom they served. When the Saracens threatened to overthrow the civilization of Western Europe and replace it by their own, it was Charles, Mayor of the Palace—not the Merovingian king—who rallied Christian forces and defeated the Moors at the battle of Tours. It was on this occasion that he won the name *Martel*—the hammer—because he hammered away so effectually against his enemies on the battlefield. Still, Charles Martel never bore the kingly title. His son, Pippin III., felt ambitious to do so and appealed to the Pope, asking who should bear the name of king, he to whom the title passed in hereditary line or he who performed the functions of king. The Pope held in grateful memory the work of Martel on that fateful day when Europe stood aghast at the danger threatening, and replied that it seemed but reasonable that the one who discharged the duties of a king should be so in fact. Thus supported by the highest authority in Christendom, Pippin III. deposed the weak survivor of his line and assumed the title *King of the Franks.*

When, not long after, Italy was disturbed by the Lombards, who wished to extend their territories, the Pope called upon Pippin to aid him against them. This the Frankish king was glad to do, presenting the Pope with some of the territories in question. Thus was the basis laid for the temporal power of the Pope and thus the Papal States had their beginning.

CHARLEMAGNE.

When Pippin died, his kingdom was left to his sons, Carloman and Charles. Shortly after Carloman died and Charles ruled alone. Charlemagne—the great Charles—reigned forty-six years. He was a brave warrior and an able statesman, and his is beyond all question the greatest name on the pages of history after the passing of Rome's last great statesman to the dawn of modern times.

Much of Charlemagne's reign was filled with campaigns—he is reputed to have conducted fifty. His services were early called into action by the Pope, who was again disturbed by the persistent Lombards. Then began a long intermittent war with the Saxons—a branch of the Teutonic race that still clung tenaciously to ancestral ways. Einhard, who wrote a Life of Charlemagne from his own personal knowledge and observation, speaks of this Saxon war which broke out after the war with the Lombards:

"At the conclusion of this struggle, the Saxon war, that seems to have been only laid aside for the time, was taken up again. No war ever undertaken by the Frank nation was carried on with such persistence and bitterness, or cost so much labor, because the Saxons, like almost all the tribes of Germany, were a fierce people, given to the worship of devils, and hostile to our religion, and did not consider it dishonorable to transgress and violate all law, human and divine. Then there were peculiar circumstances that tended to cause a breach of peace every day. Except for a few places, where large forests or mountain-ridges intervened and made the bounds certain, the line between ourselves and the Saxons passed almost in its whole extent through an open country, so that there was no end to the murders, thefts, and arsons on both sides. In this way the Franks became so embittered that they at last resolved to make reprisals no longer, but to come to open war with the Saxons. Accordingly war was begun against them, and was waged for thirty-three successive years with great fury; more, however, to the disadvantage of the Saxons than of the Franks. It could doubtless have been brought to an end sooner had it not been for the faithlessness of the Saxons. It is hard to say how often they were conquered, and, humbly submitting to the king, promised to do what was enjoined upon them, gave without hesitation the required hostages, and received the officers sent them from the king. They were sometimes so much weakened and reduced that they promised to renounce the worship of devils, and to adopt Christianity; but they were no less ready to violate these terms than prompt to accept them, so that it is impossible to tell which came easier to them to do; scarcely a year passed from the beginning of the war without such changes on their part. But the king did not suffer his high purpose and steadfastness—firm alike in good and evil fortune—to be wearied by any fickleness on their part, or to be turned from the task that he had undertaken; on the contrary, he never allowed their faithless behavior to go unpunished, but either took the field against them in person, or sent his counts with an army to wreak vengeance and exact righteous satisfaction. At last, after conquering and subduing all who had offered resistance, he took ten thousand of those that lived on the banks of the Elbe, and settled them, with their wives and children, in many different bodies here and there in Gaul and Germany. The war that had lasted so many years was at length ended by their acceding to the terms offered by the king; which were renunciation of their national religious customs and the worship of devils, acceptance of the sacraments of the Christian faith and religion, and union with the Franks to form one people."[1]

By such untiring efforts Charlemagne extended his boundaries and widened his possessions until he ruled northern Italy, what is now France, most of Germany and the Low Countries. It is surmised that he was considering whether he might not assume the title of Emperor. As it happened just then in the East, a woman occupied the throne, and the West was loath to

[1] Einhard: Life of Charlemagne.

recognize her as successor of the Cæsars. Accordingly on Christmas Day, as Charlemagne knelt at the altar in one of the basilicas, Pope Leo III. placed a crown upon the head of the worshipping king, proclaiming him Emperor and Augustus. Charlemagne is said to have later remarked that had he known what the Pope intended to do, he would have remained away from the service. The fact that the *Pope* placed the crown upon the head of the *Emperor* was not to be forgotten.

It had been Pope Leo's plan to withdraw the capital from the East to the West again. This was not accomplished; rather, it was understood that the line of western emperors was once more restored—that under Charlemagne the old empire of Rome was again brought into being. After Charlemagne's death his empire fell apart, but it was re-united under Otto the Great and henceforth the *Emperor* became a potent factor in European affairs.

In peace Charlemagne was quite as efficient as in war. He organized his empire and established itinerant officers whose duty it was to visit various parts of the realm and see that justice was properly administered. He built monasteries and founded schools and gave his personal supervision to religious and educational concerns. Most famous of the schools was the so-called Palace school, taught by Alcuin, whom Charlemagne brought to his court to instruct his children. When his time permitted, the great king would himself attend Alcuin's classes, interesting himself in all branches of learning.

" The plan that he adopted for his children's education was, first of all, to have both boys and girls instructed in the liberal arts, to which he also turned his own attention. As soon as their years admitted, in accordance with the custom of the Franks, the boys had to learn horsemanship, and to practice war and the chase, and the girls to familiarize themselves with cloth-making, and to handle distaff and spindle, that they might not grow indolent through idleness, and he fostered in them every virtuous sentiment."[2]

Alcuin's school will be considered again in connection with mediaeval education. Here it is significant to note the attitude of the Emperor Charlemagne toward learning itself.

Charlemagne made a great impression upon his age. To

[2]Einhard: Life of Charlemagne.

all classes he embodied the ideal of the times. It is curious and amusing to find how often he was quoted to prove discordant theories. For example, Charlemagne because of his ardent interest in religious matters and his unfaltering support of the Church, was very popular with churchmen. We find monks who wished to impress upon their younger brothers the virtue of fasting, representing Charlemagne as eating so little that we well know no active man could have partaken so sparingly and preserved his health. On the other hand, some of his admirers considered bodily strength and noble stature greatly to be desired, and these enumerated the number of dishes Charlemagne consumed at one meal—far too many for any man to have possibly encompassed.

In literature, Charlemagne was the hero around which marvelous tales centered. Nor is it surprising when we think of the many achievements of the great king that his contemporaries valued him so highly. He was by far the greatest light of his age, and long after his death his influence was felt in many directions. After the wide empire had fallen in pieces because of the inability of his sons to rule, yet the *idea* of an empire remained and the empire itself was much easier restored than it had been in the beginning created.

CHARLEMAGNE.

"Charles was large and strong, and of lofty stature, though not disproportionately tall (his height is well known to have been seven times the length of his foot); the upper part of his head was round, his eyes very large and animated, nose a little long, hair fair, and face laughing and merry. Thus his appearance was always stately and dignified, whether he was standing or sitting; although his neck was thick and somewhat short, and his belly rather prominent; but the symmetry of the rest of his body concealed these defects. His gait was firm, his whole carriage manly, and his voice clear, but not so strong as his size led one to expect. His health was excellent, except during the four years preceding his death, when he was subject to frequent fevers; at the last he even limped a little with one foot. Even in those years he consulted rather his own inclinations than the advice of physicians, who were almost hateful to him, because they wanted him to give up roasts, to which he was accustomed, and to eat boiled meat instead. In accordance with the national custom, he took frequent exercise on horseback and in the chase, accomplishments in which scarcely any people in the world can equal the Franks. He enjoyed the exhalations from natural warm springs, and often practised swimming, in which he was such an adept that none could surpass him; and hence it was that he built his palace at Aix-la-Chapelle, and lived there constantly during his latter years until his death. He used not only to invite his sons to his bath, but his nobles and friends, and now and then a troop of his retinue or body-guard, so that a hundred or more persons sometimes bathed with him.

He used to wear the national, that is to say, the Frank dress —next his skin a linen shirt and linen breeches, and above these a tunic fringed with silk; while hose fastened by bands covered his lower limbs, and shoes his feet, and he protected his shoulders and chest in winter by a closely fitting coat of otter or marten skins. Over all he flung a blue cloak, and he always had a sword girt about him, usually one with a gold or silver hilt and belt; he sometimes carried a jeweled sword, but only on great feast-days or at the reception of ambassadors from foreign nations. He despised foreign costumes, however handsome,

Farming in Luzon—As in Middle Ages.

and never allowed himself to be robed in them, except twice in Rome, when he donned the Roman tunic, chlamys, and shoes; the first time at the request of Pope Hadrian, the second to gratify Leo, Hadrian's successor. On great feast-days he made use of embroidered clothes, and shoes bedecked with precious stones; his cloak was fastened by a golden buckle, and he appeared crowned with a diadem of gold and gems; but on other days his dress varied little from the common dress of the people.

Charles was temperate in eating, and particularly so in drinking, for he abominated drunkenness in anybody, much more in himself and those of his household; but he could not easily abstain from food, and often complained that fasts injured his health. He very rarely gave entertainments, only on great feast-days, and then to large numbers of people. His meals ordinarily consisted of four courses, not counting the roast, which his huntsmen used to bring in on the spit; he was more fond of this than of any other dish. While at table, he listened to reading or music. The subjects of the readings were the stories and deeds of olden time; he was fond, too, of St. Augustine's books, and especially of the one entitled "The City of God." He was so moderate in the use of wine and all sorts of drink that he rarely allowed himself more than three cups in the course of a meal. In summer, after the midday meal, he would eat some fruit, drain a single cup, put off his clothes and shoes, just as he did for the night, and rest for two or three hours. He was in the habit of awaking and rising from bed four or five times during the night. While he was dressing and putting on his shoes, he not only gave audience to his friends, but if the Count of the Palace told him of any suit in which his judgment was necessary, he had the parties brought before him forthwith, took cognizance of the case, and gave his decision, just as if he were sitting on the judgment-seat. This was not the only business that he transacted at this time, but he performed any duty of the day whatever whether he had to attend to the matter himself or to give commands concerning it to his officers.

Charles had the gift of ready and fluent speech, and could express whatever he had to say with the utmost clearness. He was not satisfied with command of his native language merely, but gave attention to the study of foreign ones, and in par ticular was such a master of Latin that he could speak it as well as his native tongue; but he could understand Greek better than he could speak it. He was so eloquent, indeed, that he might have passed for a teacher of eloquence. He most zealously cultivated the liberal arts, held those who taught them in great esteem, and conferred great honours upon them. He took lessons in grammar of the deacon Peter of Pisa, at that time an aged man. Another deacon, Albin of Britain, surnamed Alcuin, a man of Saxon extraction, who was the greatest scholar of the day, was his teacher in other branches of learning. The King spent much time and labour with him studying rhetoric, dialectics, and especially astronomy; he learned to reckon, and used to investigate the motions of the heavenly bodies most curiously, with an intelligent scrutiny. He also tried to write, and used to keep tablets and blanks in bed under his pillow, that at leisure hours he might accustom his hand to form the letters; however, as he did not begin his efforts in due season, but late in life, they met with ill success.

He cherished with the greatest fervour and devotion the principles of the Christian religion, which had been instilled into him from infancy. Hence it was that he built the beautiful basilica at Aix-la-Chapelle, which he adorned with gold and silver and lamps, and with rails and doors of solid brass. He had the columns and marbles for this structure brought from Rome and Ravenna, for he could not find such as were suitable elsewhere. He was a constant worshipper at this church as long as his health permitted, going morning and evening, even after nightfall, besides attending mass; and he took care that all the services there conducted should be administered with the utmost possible propriety, very often warning the sextons not to let any improper or unclean thing be brought into the building, or remain in it. He provided it with a great number of sacred vessels of gold and silver, and with such a quantity of clerical robes that not even the doorkeepers, who fill the humblest office in the church, were obliged to wear their every-day clothes when in the exercise of their duties. He was at great pains to improve the church reading and psalmody, for he was well skilled in both, although he neither read in public nor sang, except in a low tone and with others. .

He was very forward in succouring the poor, and in that

gratuitous generosity which the Greeks call alms, so much so that he not only made a point of giving in his own country and his own kingdom, but when he discovered that there were Christians living in poverty in Syria, Egypt, and Africa, at Jerusalem, Alexandria, and Carthage, he had compassion on their wants, and used to send money over the seas to them. The reason that he zealously strove to make friends with the kings beyond the seas was that he might get help and relief to the Christians living under their rule. He cherished the Church of St. Peter the Apostle at Rome above all other holy and sacred places, and heaped its treasury with a vast wealth of gold, silver, and precious stones. He sent great and countless gifts to the popes; and throughout his whole reign the wish that he had nearest at heart was to re-establish the ancient authority of the city of Rome under his care and by his influence, and to defend and protect the Church of St. Peter, and to beautify and enrich it out of his own store above all other churches. Although he held it in such veneration, he only repaired to Rome to pay his vows and make his supplications four times during the whole forty-seven years that he reigned.

When he made his last journey thither, he had also other ends in view. The Romans had inflicted many injuries upon the Pontiff Leo, tearing out his eyes and cutting out his tongue, so that he had been compelled to call upon the King for help. Charles accordingly went to Rome, to set in order the affairs of the church, which were in great confusion, and passed the whole winter there. It was then that he received the titles of Emperor and Augustus, to which he at first had such an aversion that he declared that he would not have set foot in the church the day that they were conferred, although it was a great feast-day, if he could have foreseen the design of the Pope. He bore very patiently with the jealousy which the Roman emperors showed upon his assuming these titles, for they took this step very ill; and by dint of frequent embassies and letters, in which he addressed them as brothers, he made their haughtiness yield to his magnanimity, a quality in which he was unquestionably much their superior."

—*From Einhard's Life of Charlemagne.*

CHAPTER II.

The Early Church.

We have spoken of the tremendous change Christianity wrought in the Germanic tribes that spread over the old Roman empire. When in 313 A. D. the Milan Decree granted toleration to the Christians, it was found that they already possessed a well organized church and band of workers. Let us see how this had come about.

Organization is natural to people and each naturally organizes new departments in accordance with the plan most familiar. Speaking of the prevailing tendency for organization in America, some one once said that if a number of scientists should be convened for the discussion of a newly discovered plant in Europe, they would come together and discuss it. But if the same kind of an assembly were convened in America, the men would meet, elect officers, appoint committees and frame a fitting constitution. Then if one returned for a second meeting, he would probably hear the new plant discussed. Just as the spirit of organization is strong among us today, so was it strong in Rome. No people have ever surpassed the Romans in perfect and efficient organization. Naturally, when Christianity gained a foothold in Rome, it had to be given an organized form to be adequately understood.

We have seen in an earlier chapter that during the first century after Christ his loyal followers, with their strong and simple faith, many of whom had known Christ or his apostles, met in little companies and sang and praised God. Christ had said he would come again, and his own waited for him. In the second century, a change came about. Those who had been in touch with Christ or his disciples had passed away. It became apparent that he had not meant to reveal himself on earth. New people constantly joining the ranks needed to be trained; the old needed cheer and comfort; it was necessary also to send news from one little body of worshippers to another. Not with any interest in this world, then, but to make ready for the next, the people felt the necessity of a leader. Undoubtedly some old man had from the beginning taken a sort of leadership—for, as Hatch explains, *wherever two people meet together, one is always the leader.* This leader, or *presbyter,* looked after the poor and presided at the love-feast. Deacons passed around the wine and bread, and where several congregations met together to celebrate the Agape, the oldest presbyter, or most able, became the presbyter of the presbyters, or the *bishop*.

At first the presbyters and bishops still followed their means of livelihood, but presently their church duties became so constant and exacting that they had time for these alone. Moreover, in the second century it came to be taught that he who honored a bishop, honored God. This was the origin of the distinction between laity and clergy. New duties required new officers and this tended to separate the two classes still more.

At first, as we have previously learned, Christianity was scorned and scoffed at by the Romans and no heed given it; then, as its numbers continued to increase, measures were taken to stamp it out as dangerous to the state. Sometimes for years together, persecutions would be carried on with the avowed purpose of weeding out the new faith. During such times the Christians would practically disappear, hold meetings in secret, and pass much of the time in the labyrinth of catacombs which tunneled the city and which had for long been used as burial places for the wealthy. Sometimes the Christians would come forward in such numbers that those carrying on the persecutions would be out-wearied and the matter would drop again. In 313 A. D. the Milan Decree granted toleration and not long after, privileges were extended to Christians. At length in 392 A. D. Christianity became the state religion and now it was the worshippers of the old religions who were persecuted and obliged to hold meetings in secret—as the Christians before had been.

The celebrated council of Nicaea, the first general council of Christianity, was convened by the Emperor Constantine at Nicaea in Asia Minor A. D. 325 for the purpose of settling certain differences that had arisen in the church respecting the doctrines of Arius, which at that time had assumed serious proportions. This council was attended by a large number of bishops, upwards of two hundred and fifty, of whom the greater part came from the East. In addition there were also presbyters, deacons and other followers of Christ from all parts of the Christian world. At this council the doctrines advocated by Arius were branded as heresy and the excommunication of Arius from the church decreed by the council, and for its future guidance the Nicene creed with its more clearly defined articles of faith was adopted by the assembled council. Christianity given now a sure footing in the empire, the next two centuries were concerned with an effort to eliminate pagan customs. In 413 A. D. a monk, visiting Rome, looked in upon some gladiatorial games. He was horrified by what he saw and interfered. He was killed, and the death of a monk in this way so shocked the sense of the people that from that time forward these demoralizing games were discontinued.

In conflict with the older religions, Christianity, as might be expected, underwent many changes. If any one doubts this, let him read the teaching of Christ as recorded by those who wrote the Apostles, and compare with them the Christian teachings of later times. Indeed, it was this ability of Christianity to expand that has given it vitality for so many ages. As soon as the highest ideals of a religion are formulated, the religion must crystalize and its worshippers stagnate. Even the church ceremonies and sacred days were taken over from antiquity. The baptism, supper, incense, bells, lights, procession of priests, etc., were borrowed. The idea of demons came from Germany—perhaps from Babylonia in the first instance. The conception of angels long current came from Persia. Expanding in this way, incorporating what it could use from every nation, Christianity won in the struggle and in 529 A. D. schools of Greek philosophy were closed in Athens and about the same time in Alexandria.

Beginnings of the Papacy.

From the first, the importance of a bishop depended upon the city he represented. Quite naturally, the large centers kept more closely in touch with affairs than those remote from them. The bishops from the cities were deferred to by the bishops from smaller towns, and in the very nature of things, the bishop of Rome was the one to whom all gave homage and in whom all placed confidence. Rome was still the old center of the empire—the *Eternal City*. The very name of Rome had possessed magic power for ages. Here in the first three centuries, the emperor still had his capital. Here was the largest congregation. By the fourth century, the Petrine theory was sufficiently established. This held that Christ had given the congregation of Rome into Peter's keeping, that Peter was the representative of God on earth and the bishops who succeeded him were his successors and consequently they, too, represented God on earth. It has well been said that the history of the primacy of Rome is the history of a theory.

In 270 A. D. the emperor Aurelian said he would not recognize any bishop not previously recognized by the bishop of Rome. This was a great boon for the Roman bishop.

When Constantine moved the capital of his empire from Rome to Constantinople, he left the West without anyone to represent authority as emperors before had done. Thus it came about that the people turned to the Pope for help which otherwise they would have sought from the emperor. When Attila came before the gates of Rome and the terrified people knew not where to seek help, it was the Pope who went out to meet him and by his very presence and confidence saved Rome from destruction. It followed naturally and rightly that the people regarded the Pope as possessed of more than usual power and that their reverence for him was doubly increased. By the time of Charlemagne, the Pope was recognized by people and kings as the greatest spiritual authority on earth.

The Papacy, thus established, developed such power that it shortly came into conflict with the emperors. Pope Gregory VII. was one of the powerful Popes who held tenaciously to the theory that the Pope was superior to the Emperor—a theory rejected by all strong emperors. He realized that if this claim was to be given force, the church must institute several reforms. Two crying abuses of his day were the corruption of the clergy and the purchase of church offices. The reforms he instituted are known as the enforcement of celibacy and the suppression of simony. While he did not see the accomplishment of these needed corrections in his day, they nevertheless were eventually realized.

Gregory felt that Christendom should constitute a great

empire, with the Pope at its head—superior to the Emperor, who should receive his authority from the Pope as God's representative on earth. This was a mighty ideal for the Papacy to proclaim and for centuries the struggle to realize it absorbed a considerable amount of energy whenever a strong Emperor and a strong Pope ruled at the same time. When one or the other was weak, the conflict subsided temporarily.

The institution of monasticism early found a place in the Christian Church. The idea of living in isolation that one might thereby save his soul came into Europe with caravans from the East. Ascetics had existed in considerable numbers in India and other Asiatic countries from early times. They found virtue in torturing their bodies, suffering, and in living apart from the world. Such beings may be seen today in the East—most repulsive, many of them. Their interests are almost invariably selfish; they seek salvation for themselves alone.

Affairs were in such disorder in Europe that the idea of withdrawing from worldly concerns and living a quiet life in meditation and prayer must have seemed attractive indeed to many. With the slaughter that accompanied the invasion, whole communities were wiped out of existence and accidental survivors found solace only in the teachings of Christianity.

At first, certain Christians withdrew from the world after the fashion of the East, living lives of austerity and physical suffering. Sometimes men simply fled from the disordered scenes to find solitude in the desert. However, the Western man has ever been more active than his Eastern brother—less given to hair-splitting philosophies and more given to expending effort along some chosen direction. While in Egypt the example of St. Anthony was leading men to forsake the world and renounce all social relationships, and was peopling whole desert regions, the more rigorous climate of the West did not allure to such a careless existence. Little communities of men, rather, who had a common desire to retire from society, with its temptations and dangers, sprang up in various places. Fortunately there shortly arose a monk possessed of great organizing ability. He foresaw the result if men were to drift into lives of idleness and irregularity under the name of religion and he promptly formulated rules for their observance.

Poverty, chastity and obedience were the three vows required of him who would enter a monastery. By poverty was meant the renunciation of all worldly goods; whatever one owned was to be disposed of or to become the property of the order; by chastity, the monk was to remain unmarried and to live a pure life; by obedience, he pledged himself to obey implicitly the abbot and the rules of his order. A portion of each day was to be spent by the monks in manual labor. This dignified daily toil and led to the reclaiming and cultivation of wide areas of useless land. In the settlement of forests or land which had sunk into a wilderness, the labor of the monks became a potent factor. Another part of the day was reserved for sacred reading. According to their abilities, monks were assigned special duties: some were educated and could teach the rest; some were expert copyists and multiplied the copies of books in their possession; some became eloquent preachers. Many were ignorant creatures who could only perform the most simple tasks.

In an age when travel was slow and uncertain, when inns were unknown, and life away from regular thoroughfares insecure, the monasteries offered the most welcome hospitality. Hither the helpless came for aid, nor were they turned aside. Schools had fallen into decay almost everywhere, but in the monasteries learning was still fostered; boys giving evidence of special ability could be sent thither to be taught by the monks.

It was not strange that in an age as rough as the one we are studying, evil fellows now and then would use the monastery as a means of carrying out their plans. Now and then some would-be murderer used the monastery to hide his crime and escape punishment. This was only to be expected. But a much larger number of evil men were recalled from paths of crime and made useful beings; others who lacked strength to stand by themselves were awakened to their possibilities by the discipline of their order.

As time went on, the faithful made presents of considerable wealth to the monasteries and these finally grew to be possessed of large means. It sometimes happened then that the monks lapsed into the ways of luxury and lived in affluence and ease. Yet even so, there was sure to arise among them men like Bernard of Clairvaux who mercilessly assailed the self-indulgence and laxity of the cloisters. Such men, in their utter poverty, living lives shorn of the barest comforts, wielded wide authority and commanded the obedience of kings and statesmen.

It is difficult to realize what the Middle Ages would have been had monastic life been eliminated. From the monasteries courageous men set out to establish outlying missions; they converted the people to the Christian faith and taught them to perform their tasks more intelligently. They kept whatever records of the past remain to us in several fields, and prevented learning in the West from becoming extinct. We today owe more to the mediæval monk than we probably ever realize and but for the labor of these unselfish men history in Europe would have been quite other than it proved.

SYMBOLS USED BY EARLY CHRISTIANS.

THE MONK AS A CIVILIZER.

"The monasteries were the refuges, whither the weak escaped from the competition of the strong. Thither flocked the poor, the crippled, the orphan, and the widow, all, in fact, who could not fight for themselves. There they found something like justice, order, pity, help. Even the fool and the coward, when they went to the convent-door, were not turned away. The poor half-witted rascal, who had not sense enough to serve the king, might still serve the abbot. He would be set to drive, plough, or hew wood—possibly by the side of a gentleman, a nobleman, or even a prince—and live under equal law with them; and under, too, a discipline more strict than that of any modern army; and if he would not hew the wood, or drive the bullocks, as he ought, then the abbot would have him flogged soundly till he did; which was better for him, after all, than wandering about to be hooted by the boys, and dying in a ditch at last.

The coward, too—the abbot could make him of use, even though the king could not. There were, no doubt, in those days, though fewer in number than now, men who could not face physical danger, and the storm of the evil world—delicate, nervous, imaginative, feminine characters; who, when sent out to battle, would be very likely to run away. Our forefathers, having no use for such persons, used to put such into a boghole, and lay a hurdle over them, in the belief that they would sink to the lowest pool of Hela for ever more. But the abbot had great use for such. They could learn to read, write, sing, think; they were often very clever; they might make great scholars; at all events, they might make saints. Whatever they could not do, they could pray. And the united prayer of those monks, it was then believed, could take heaven by storm, after the course of the elements, overcome Divine justice, avert from mankind the anger of an offended God. Whether that belief were right or wrong, people held it; and the man who could not fight with carnal weapons, regained his self-respect, and therefore his virtue, when he found himself fighting, as he held, with spiritual weapons against all the powers of darkness. The first light in which I wish you to look at the old monasteries, is as defences for the weak against the strong.

But what has this to do with what I said at first, as to the masses having no history? This: that through these monasteries the masses began first to have a history; because through them they ceased to be masses, and became first, persons and men, and then, gradually, a people. That last the monasteries could not make them: but they educated them for becoming a people; and in this way: They brought out, in each man, the sense of individual responsibility. They taught him, whether warrior or cripple, prince or beggar, that he had an immortal soul, for which each must give like account to God.

Do you not see the effect of that new thought? Treated as slaves, as things and animals, the many had learned to consider themselves as things and animals. And so they had become " a mass," that is, a mere heap of inorganic units, each of which has no spring of life in itself, as distinguished from a whole, a people, which has one bond, uniting each to all. The " masses " of the French had fallen into that state, before the Revolution of 1793. The "masses" of our agricultural labourers,—the " masses " of our manufacturing workmen, were fast falling into that state in the days of our grandfathers. Whether the French masses have risen out of it, remains to be seen. The English masses, thanks to Almighty God, have risen out of it; and by the very same factor by which the middle-age masses rose—by Religion. The great Methodist movement of the last century did for our masses what the monks did for our forefathers in the middle ages. Wesley and Whitfield, and many another noble soul, said to Nailsea colliers, Cornish miners, and all manner of drunken, brutalized fellows, living like the beasts that perish—' Each of you—thou and thou and thou—stand apart and alone before God. Each has an immortal soul in him, which will be happy or miserable forever, according to the deeds done in the body. A whole eternity of shame or of glory lies in you—and you are living like a beast.' And in proportion as each man heard that word, and took it home to himself, he became a new man, and a true man. The preachers may have mixed up words with their message with which we may disagree, have appealed to low hopes and fears which we should be ashamed to bring into our calculations;—so did the monks; but they got their work done somehow; and let us thank them, and the old Methodists, and any man who will tell men, in whatever clumsy and rough fashion, that they are not things, and pieces of a mass, but persons, with an everlasting duty, an everlasting right and wrong, an everlasting God in whose presence they stand, and who will judge them according to their works. True, that is not all that men need to learn. After they are taught, each apart, that he is a man, they must be taught, how to be an united people; but the individual teaching must come first; and before we hastily blame the individualizing tendencies of the old Evangelical movement, or that of the middle-age monks, let us remember, that if they had not laid the foundation, others could not build thereon.

Besides, they built themselves, as well as they could, on their own foundation. As soon as men begin to be really men, the desire of corporate life springs up in them. They must unite; they must organize themselves. If they possess duties, they must be duties to their fellow-men; if they possess virtues and graces, they must mix with their fellow-men in order to exercise them.

The solitaries of the Thebaid found that they became selfish wild beasts, or went mad, if they remained alone; and they formed themselves into lauras, "lanes" of huts, convents, under a common abbot or father. The evangelical converts of the last century formed themselves into powerful and highly organized sects. The middle-age monasteries organized themselves into highly artificial communities round some sacred spot, generally under the supposed protection of some saint or martyr, whose bones lay there. Each method was good, though not the highest. None of them rises to the idea of a people, having one national life, under one monarch, the representative to each and all of that national life, and the dispenser and executor of its laws. Indeed, the artificial organization, whether monastic or sectarian, may become so strong as to interfere with national life, and make men forget their real duty to their king and country, in their self-imposed duty to the sect or order to which they belong. The monastic organization indeed had to die, in many countries, in order that national life might develop itself; and the dissolution of the monasteries marks the birth of an united and powerful England. They or Britain must have died. An imperium in imperio—much more many separate imperia—was an element of national weakness, which might be allowed in times of peace and safety, but not in times of convulsion and of danger.

You may ask, however, how these monasteries became so powerful, if they were merely refuges for the weak? Even if they were (and they were) the homes of an equal justice and order, mercy and beneficence, which had few or no standing-places outside their walls, still, how, if governed by weak men, could they survive in the great battle of life? The sheep would have but a poor life of it, if they set up hurdles against the wolves, and agreed at all events not to eat each other.

The answer is, that the monasteries were not altogether tenanted by incapables. The same causes which brought the low-born into the monasteries, brought the high-born, many of the very highest. The same cause which brought the weak into the monasteries, brought the strong, many of the very strongest.

The middle-age records give us a long list of kings, princes, nobles, who having done (as they held) their work in the world outside, went into those convents to try their hands at what seemed to them (and often was) better work than the perpetual coil of war, intrigue, and ambition, which was not the crime, but the necessary fate, of a ruler in the middle ages. Tired of work, and tired of life; tired, too, of vain luxury and vain wealth, they fled to the convent, as to the only place where a man could get a little peace, and think of God, and his own soul; and recollected, as they worked with their own hands by the side of the lowest-born of their subjects, that they had a human flesh and blood, a human immortal soul, like those whom they had ruled. Thank God that the great have other methods now of learning that great truth; that the work of life, if but well done, will teach it to them: but those were hard times, and wild times; and fighting men could hardly learn, save in the convent, that there was a God above who watched the widows' and the orphans' tears, and when he made inquisition for blood, forgot not the cause of the poor.

Such men and women of rank brought into the convent, meanwhile, all the prestige of their rank, all their superior knowledge of the world; and became the patrons and protectors of the society; while they submitted, generally with peculiar humility and devotion, to its most severe and degrading rules. Their higher sensibilities, instead of making them shrink from hardship, made them strong to endure self-sacrifices, and often self-tortures, which seem to us all but incredible; and the lives, or rather living deaths, of the noble and princely penitents of the early middle ages, are among the most beautiful tragedies of humanity,

To these monasteries, too, came the men of the very highest intellect, of whatsoever class. I say, of the very highest intellect. Tolerably talented men might find it worth while to stay in the world, and use their wits in struggling upward there. The most talented of all would be the very men to see a better "carrière ouverte aux talens" than the world could give; to long for deeper and loftier meditation than could be found in the court; for a more divine life, a more blessed death, than could be found in the camp and the battle-field.

And so it befalls, that in the early middle age the cleverest men were generally inside the convent, trying, by moral influence and superior intellect, to keep those outside from tearing each other to pieces.

But these intellects could not remain locked up in the monasteries. The daily routine of devotion, even of silent study and contemplation, was not sufficient for them, as it was for the average monk. There was still a reserve of force in them, which must be up and doing; and which, in a man inspired by that Spirit which is the Spirit of love to man as well as to God, must needs expand outwards in all directions, to Christianize, to civilize, to colonize.

To colonize. When people talk loosely of founding an abbey for superstitious uses, they cannot surely be aware of the state of the countries in which those abbeys were founded; either primeval forest, hardly tilled common, or to be described by that terrible epithet of Domesday-book, "wasta"—wasted by war. A knowledge of that fact would lead them to guess that there were almost certainly uses for the abbey which had nothing to do with superstition; which were as thoroughly practical as those of a company for draining the bog of Allen, or running a railroad through an American forest. Such, at least, was the case, at least for the first seven centuries after the fall of Rome; and to these missionary colonizers Europe owes, I verily believe, among a hundred benefits, this which all Englishmen will appreciate; that Roman agriculture not only revived in the countries which were once the Empire, but spread from thence westward and northward, into the principal wilderness of the Teuton and Sclavonic races.

Surely such men as St. Sturmi were children of wisdom, put what sense on the word you will. In a dark, confused, lawless, cut-throat age, while everything was decided by the sword, they found that they could do no good to themselves, or any man, by throwing their sword into either scale. They would be men of peace, and see what could be done so. Was that not wise? So they set to work. They feared God exceedingly, and walked with God. Was not that wise? They wrought righteousness, and were merciful and kind, while kings and nobles were murdering around them; pure and temperate, while other men were lustful and drunken; just and equal in all their ways, while other men were unjust and capricious; serving God faithfully, according to their light, while the people round them were half or wholly heathen; content to do their work well on earth, and look for their reward in heaven, while the kings and nobles, the holders of the land, were full of insane ambition, every man trying to seize a scrap of ground from his neighbor, as if that would make them happier. Was that not wise? Which was the wiser, the chief killing human beings, to take from them some few square miles which men had brought into cultivation already, or the monk, leaving the cultivated land, and going out into the backwoods to clear the forest, and till the virgin soil? Which was the child of wisdom, I ask again? And do not tell me that the old monk worked only for fanatical and superstitious ends. It is not so. I know well his fanaticism and his superstition, and the depths of its ignorance and silliness: but he had more in him than that. Had he not, he would have worked no lasting work. He was not only the pioneer of civilization, but he knew that he was such. He believed that all knowledge came from God, even that which taught a man to clear the forest, and plant corn instead; and he determined to spread such knowledge as he had wherever he could. He was a wiser man than the heathen Saxons, even than the Christian Franks, around him; a better scholar, a better thinker, better handicraftsman, better farmer; and he did not keep his knowledge to himself. He did not, as some tell you, keep the Bible to himself. It is not so; and those who say so, in this generation, ought to be ashamed of themselves. The monk knew his Bible well himself, and he taught it. Those who learnt from him to read, learnt to read their Bibles. Those who did not learn (of course the vast majority in days when there was no printing), he taught by sermons, by pictures, afterward by mystery and miracle plays. The Bible was not forbidden to the laity till centuries afterwards—and forbidden then, why? Because the laity throughout Europe knew too much about the Bible, and not too little. Because the early monks had so ingrained the mind of the masses, throughout Christendom, with Bible stories, Bible personages, the great facts, and the great doctrines, of our Lord's life, that the masses knew too much; that they could contrast too easily, and too freely, the fallen and profligate monks of the 15th and 16th centuries, with those Bible examples, which the old monks of centuries before had taught their forefathers. Then the clergy tried to keep from the laity, because it testified against themselves, the very book which centuries before they had taught them to love and know too well. In a word, the old monk missionary taught all he knew to all who would learn, just as our best modern missionaries do; and he was loved, and obeyed, and looked on as a superior being, as they are.

Of course he did not know how far civilization would extend. He could not foretell railroads and electric telegraphs, any more than he could political economy, or sanitary science. But the best that he knew, he taught—and did also, working with his own hands. He was faithful in a few things, and God made him ruler over many things. For out of those monasteries sprang—what did not spring? They restored again and again sound law and just government, when the good old Teutonic laws, and the Roman law also, was trampled under foot amid the lawless strife of ambition and fury. Under their shadow sprang up the towns with their corporate rights, their middle classes, their artisan classes. They were the physicians, the alms-givers, the relieving officers, the schoolmasters of the middle-age world. They first taught us the great principle of the division of labour, to which we owe, at this moment, that England is what she is, instead of being covered with a horde of peasants, each making and producing everything for himself and starving each upon his rood of ground. They transcribed or composed all the books of the then world; many of them spent their lives in doing nothing but writing; and the number of books, even of those to be found in single monasteries, considering the tedious labour of copying, is altogether astonishing. They preserved to us the treasures of classical antiquity. They discovered for us the germs of all our modern inventions. They brought in from abroad arts and new knowledge; and while they taught men to know that they had a common humanity, a common Father in heaven, taught them also to profit by each one's wisdom instead of remaining in isolated ignorance. They, too, were the great witnesses against feudal caste. With them was neither high-born nor low-born, rich nor poor: worth was their only test; the meanest serf entering there might become the lord of knights and vassals, the counsellor of kings and princes. Men may talk of democracy—those old monasteries were the most democratic institutions the world had ever till then seen. "A man's a man for a' that," was not only talked of in them, but carried out in practice—only not in anarchy, and as a cloak for licentiousness: but under those safeguards of strict discipline, and almost military order, without which men may call themselves free, and yet be really only slaves to their own passions. Yes, paradoxical as it may seem, in those monasteries was preserved the sacred fire of modern liberty, through those feudal centuries when all the outside world was doing its best to trample it out. Remember, as a single instance, that in the Abbot's lodging at Bury St. Edmunds, the Magna Charta was drawn out, before being presented to John at Runymede. I know what they became afterwards, better than most do here; too well to defile my lips, or your ears, with tales too true. They had done their work, and they went. Like all things born, in time they died; and decayed in time; and the old order changed, giving place to the new; and God fulfilled himself in many ways. But in them, too, he fulfilled himself. They were the best things the world had seen; the only method of Christianizing and civilizing semi-barbarous Europe. Like all human plans and conceptions, they contained in themselves original sin; idolatry, celibacy, inhuman fanaticism; these were their three roots of bitterness; and when they bore the natural fruit of immorality, the mon-

MINIATURE.—QUEEN OF SHEBA BEFORE SOLOMON.

asteries fell with a great and just destruction. But had not those monasteries been good at first, and noble at first; had not the men in them been better and more useful men than the men outside, do you think they would have endured for centuries? They would not even have established themselves at all. They would soon, in those stormy times, have been swept off the face of the earth. Ill used they often were, plundered and burnt down. But men found that they were good. Their own plunderers found that they could not do without them; and repented, and humbled themselves, and built them up again, to be sentries of justice and mercy and peace, amid the wild weltering sea of war and misery. For all things endure, even for a generation, only by virtue of the good which is in them. By the Spirit of God in them they live, as do all created things; and when he taketh away their breath they die, and return again to their dust."

—*Extract from essay by Charles Kingsley.*

THE RULE OF ST. BENEDICT.

Prologue.

We are about to found, therefore, a school for the Lord's service; in the organization of which we trust that we shall ordain nothing severe and nothing burdensome. But even if, the demands of justice dictating it, something a little irksome shall be the result, for the purpose of amending vices or preserving charity;—thou shalt not therefore, struck by fear, flee the way of salvation, which can not be entered upon except through a narrow entrance. But as one's way of life and one's faith progresses, the heart becomes broadened, and, with the unutterable sweetness of love, the way of the mandates of the Lord is traversed. Thus, never departing from His guidance, continuing in the monastery in His teaching until death, through patience we are made partakers in Christ's passion, in order that we may merit to be companions in His kingdom.

Concerning the Kinds of Monks and Their Manner of Living.

It is manifest that there are four kinds of monks. The cenobites are the first kind; that is, those living in a monastery, serving under a rule or an abbot. Then the second kind is that of the anchorites; that is, the hermits—those who, not by the new fervour of a conversation but by the long probation of life in a monastery, have learned to fight against the devil, having already been taught by the solace of many. They, having been well prepared in the army of brothers for the solitary fight of the hermit, being secure now without the consolation of another, are able, God helping them, to fight with their own hand or arm against the vices of the flesh or of their thoughts.

But a third very bad kind of monks are the sarabaites, approved by no rule, experience being their teacher, as with the gold which is tried in the furnace. But, softened after the manner of lead, keeping faith with the world by their works, they are known through their tonsure to lie to God. These, being shut up by twos or threes, or, indeed, alone, without a shepherd, not in the Lord's but in their own sheep-folds—their law is the satisfaction of their desires. For whatever they think good or choice, this they call holy; and what they do not wish, this they consider unlawful. But the fourth kind of monks is the kind which is called gyratory. During their whole life they are guests, for three or four days at a time, in the cells of the different monasteries, throughout the various provinces; always wandering and never stationary, given over to the service of their own pleasures and the joys of the palate, and in every way worse than the sarabaites. Concerning the most wretched way of living of all of such monks it is better to be silent than to speak. These things therefore being omitted, let us proceed with the aid of God, to treat of the best kind, the cenobites.

What the Abbot Should be Like.

An abbot who is worthy to preside over a monastery ought always to remember what he is called, and carry out with his deeds the name of a Superior. For he is believed to be Christ's representative, since he is called by His name, the apostle saying: "Ye have received the spirit of adoption of sons, whereby we call Abba, Father." And so the abbot should not—grant that he may not—teach, or decree, or order, any thing apart from the precept of the Lord; but his order or teaching should be sprinkled with the ferment of divine justice in the minds of his disciples. Let the abbot always be mindful that, at the tremendous judgment of God, both things will be weighed in the balance: his teaching and the obedience of his disciples. And let the abbot know that whatever the father of the family finds of less utility among the sheep is laid to the fault of the shepherd.

Concerning Obedience.

The first grade of humility is obedience without delay. This becomes those who, on account of the holy service which they have professed, or on account of the fear of hell or the glory of eternal life consider nothing dearer to them than Christ: so that, so soon as anything is commanded by their superior, they may not know how to suffer delay in doing it, even as if it were a divine command. Concerning whom the Lord said: "As soon as he heard of me he obeyed me." And again he said to the learned men: "He who heareth you heareth me." Therefore let all such, straightway leaving their own affairs and giving up their own will, with unoccupied hands and leaving incomplete what they were doing—the foot of obedience being foremost—follow with their deeds the voice of him who orders.

Concerning Silence.

Let us do as the prophet says: "I said, I will take heed to my ways that I sin not with my tongue, I have kept my mouth with a bridle: I was dumb with silence, I held my peace even from good; and my sorrow was stirred." Here the prophet shows that if one ought at times, for the sake of silence, to refrain from good sayings; how much more, as a punishment for sin, ought one to cease from evil words.   And therefore, if anything is to be asked of the prior, let it be asked with all humility and subjection of reverence; lest one seem to speak more than is fitting. Scurrilities, however, or idle words and those exciting laughter, we condemn in all places with a lasting prohibition: nor do we permit a disciple to open his mouth for such sayings.

Concerning Humility.

The sixth grade of humility is, that a monk be contented with all lowliness or extremity, and consider himself with regard to everything which is enjoined on him, as a poor and unworthy workman; saying to himself with the prophet: "I was reduced to nothing and was ignorant; I was made as the cattle before thee, and I am always with thee." The seventh grade of humility is, not only that he, with his tongue, pronounce himself viler and more worthless than all; but that he also believe it in the innermost workings of his heart; humbling himself and saying with the prophet, etc.   The eighth degree of humility is that a monk do nothing except what the common rule of the monastery, or the example of his elders, urges him to do. The ninth degree of humility is that a monk restrain his tongue from speaking; and, keeping silence, do not speak until he is spoken to. The tenth grade of humility is that he be not ready, and easily inclined, to laugh. The eleventh grade of humility is that a monk, when he speaks, speaks slowly and without laughter, humbly with gravity, using few and reasonable words; and that he be not loud of voice.

The twelfth grade of humility is that a monk shall not only with his heart but also with his body, always show humility to all who see him: that is, when at work, in the oratory, in the monastery, in the garden, on the road, in the fields. And everywhere, sitting or walking or standing, let him always be with head inclined, his looks fixed upon the ground; remembering every hour that he is guilty of his sins. Let him think that he is already being presented before the tremendous judgment of God, saying always to himself in his heart what that publican of the gospel, fixing his eyes on the earth, said: "Lord I am not worthy, I a sinner, so much as to lift up mine eyes unto Heaven."

Concerning the Divine Offices at Night.

In the winter time, that is from the Calends of November until Easter, according to what is reasonable, they must rise at the eighth hour of the night, so that they rest a little more than half the night, and rise when they have already digested. But let the time that remains after vigils be kept for meditation by those brothers who are in any way behind hand with the psalter or lessons. From Easter, moreover, until the aforesaid Calends of November, let the hour of keeping vigils be so arranged that, a short interval being observed in which the brethren may go out for the necessities of nature, the matins, which are always to take place with the dawning light, may straightway follow.

How the Monks Shall Sleep.

They shall sleep separately in separate beds. They shall receive positions for their beds, after the manner of their characters, according to the dispensation of their abbot. If it can be done, they shall all sleep in one place. If, however, their number do not permit it, they shall rest by tens or twenties, with elders who will concern themselves about them. A candle shall always be burning in that same cell until early in the morning. They shall sleep clothed, and girt with belts or with ropes; and they shall not have their knives at their sides while they sleep, lest perchance in a dream they should wound the sleepers. And let the monks be always on the alert; and, when the signal is given, rising without delay, let them hasten to mutually prepare themselves for the service of God—with all gravity and modesty, however. The younger brothers shall not have beds by themselves, but intersperse among those of the elder ones. And when they rise for the service of God, they shall exhort each other mutually with moderation, on account of the excuses that those who are sleepy are inclined to make.

Whether the Monks Should Have Anything of Their Own.

More than anything else is this special vice to be cut off root and branch from the monastery, that one should presume to give or receive anything without the order of the abbot, or should have anything of his own. He should have absolutely not anything: neither a book, nor tablets, nor a pen—nothing at all. For indeed it is not allowed to the monks to have their own bodies or wills in their own power. But all things necessary they must expect from the Father of the monastery; nor is it allowable to have anything which the abbot did not give or permit. All things shall be common to all, as it is written: "Let not any man presume to call anything his own." But if any one shall have been discovered delighting in this most evil vice: being warned once and again, if he do not amend, let him be subjected to punishment.

Concerning Infirm Brothers.

Before all, and above all, attention shall be paid to the care of the sick; so that they shall be served as if it were actually Christ. For He himself said: "I was sick and ye visited me." And: "Inasmuch as ye have done it unto one of the least of these ye have done it unto me." But let the sick also consider that they are being served to the honour of God; and let them not offend by their abundance the brothers who serve them: which (offenses) nevertheless are patiently to be borne, for, from such, a greater reward is acquired. Wherefore let the abbot take the greatest care lest they suffer neglect. And for these infirm brothers a cell by itself shall be set apart, and a servitor, God-fearing, and diligent and careful. The use of baths shall be offered to the sick as often as it is necessary: to the healthy, and especially to youths, it shall not be so readily conceded. But also the eating of flesh shall be allowed to the sick, and altogether to the feeble, for their rehabilitation. But when they have grown better, they shall all, in the usual manner, abstain from flesh. The abbot, moreover, shall take the greatest care lest the sick are neglected by the cellarer or by the servitors: for whatever fault is committed by the disciples rebounds upon him.

Concerning the Daily Manual Labor.

Idleness is the enemy of the soul. And therefore, at fixed times, the brothers ought to be occupied in manual labour; and again, at fixed times, in sacred reading. Therefore we believe that, according to this disposition, both seasons ought to be arranged; so that, from Easter until the Calends of October, going out early, from the first until the fourth hour they shall do what labour may be necessary. Moreover, from the fourth hour until about the sixth, they shall be free for reading. After the meal of the sixth hour, moreover, rising from table, they shall rest in their beds with all silence; or, perchance, he that wishes to read may so read to himself that he do not disturb another. And the nona (the second meal) shall be gone through with more moderately about the middle of the eighth hour; and again they shall work at what is to be done until Vespers. But, if the exigency or poverty of the place demands that they be occupied by themselves in picking fruits, they shall not be dismayed: for then they are truly monks if they live by the labours of their hands; as did also our fathers and the apostles. Let all things be done with moderation, however, on account of the faint-hearted.

Concerning the Reception of Guests.

All guests who come shall be received as though they were Christ; for He Himself said: "I was a stranger and ye took me in." And to all, fitting honour shall be shown; but, most of all, to servants of the faith and to pilgrims. When, therefore. a guest is announced, the prior of the brothers shall run to meet him, with every office of love.

Concerning the Doorkeepers of the Monastery.

At the door of the monastery shall be placed a wise old man who shall know how to receive a reply and to return one; whose ripeness of age will not permit him to trifle. Which doorkeeper ought to have a cell next to the door; so that those arriving may receive a reply. And straightway, when any one has knocked, or a poor man has called out, he shall answer, " Thanks be to God! " or shall give the blessing; and with all the gentleness of the fear of God he shall hastily give a reply with the fervour of charity. And if this doorkeeper need assistance he may receive a younger brother.

A monastery, moreover, if it can be done, ought so to be arranged that everything necessary—that is, water, a mill, a garden, a bakery—may be made use of, and different arts be carried on, within the monastery; so that there shall be no need for the monks to wander about outside. For this is not at all good for their souls. We wish, moreover, that this Rule be read very often in the congregation; lest any of the brothers excuse himself on account of ignorance.

Concerning the Fact that Not Every Just Observance is Decreed in This Rule.

We have written out this Rule, indeed, that we may show those observing it in the monasteries how to have some honesty of character, or beginning of conversion. But for those who hasten to the perfection of living, there are the teachings of the Holy Fathers: the observance of which leads a man to the heights of perfection. For what page, or what discourse, of Divine authority of the Old or the New Testament is not a most perfect rule for human life? Or what book of the holy Catholic Fathers does not trumpet forth how by the right path we shall come to our Creator. Also the reading aloud of the Fathers, and their decrees, and their lives; also the Rule of our holy Father Basil—what else are they except instruments of virtue for well-living and obedient monks? We, moreover, blush with confusion for the idle, and the evilly living and the negligent. Thou, therefore, whoever doth hasten to the celestial fatherland, perform with Christ's aid this Rule written out as the least of beginnings: and then at length, under God's protection, thou wilt come to the greater things that we have mentioned; to the summits of learning and virtue.

—*Translated in Henderson's Historical Documents.*

ST. PETER BESTOWING TEMPORAL POWER ON THE KING, SPIRITUAL POWER ON THE POPE.

CHAPTER III.

THE FEUDAL SYSTEM.

From the ninth to the fifteenth centuries political organization and social life in Europe were largely founded upon the feudal system. Sooner or later, nearly all European countries came under its sway, and without some knowledge of it and its workings no understanding of the Middle Ages is possible.

The theory of feudalism is simple; as it worked out, it gave rise to a large number of complex details and modifications, and if one seeks to gain some insight into it from abundant historical treatises, he is sometimes bewildered by technical terms and phrases peculiar to this subject alone. While there are many questions still in dispute among authorities, it is not difficult to grasp the fundamental ideas involved in this particular phase of social relationship. We must look to the peculiar conditions of the times and to certain surviving ideas of both Roman and German for the beginnings of this system and its control in Europe.

After the breaking up of Charlemagne's empire, centralized government was very weak; indeed, it sometimes appears to have been completely crushed out. Nevertheless, during the greater portion of the later Middle Ages, the state in theory was absolute. However, in theory alone was this the case.

The Teutons, who came into the old Roman empire in such limitless hordes during the fourth and fifth centuries, placed small value upon land. In their native home, land had been abundant, and when they pushed south they were able to win as much territory as they wished in almost any direction. However, as conditions became more settled and incoming tribes materially increased the population, land grew in importance. Men became more and more dependent upon its yield for their sustenance.

The ties between chieftain and followers, or between king and nobles, were by no means absolute, and kings used every effort to bind warriors to themselves. When a king conquered the territory of a people, he not infrequently appropriated a large portion of it for himself—leaving the remainder, it might be, to the original possessors, subject to dues. The territory gained in this way the king would divide among his brave leaders, he promising it to them and theirs and insuring them security in possession of it; they, on the other hand, swearing to serve him in time of war and to bring to his cause a stated number of warriors.

These tracts of land presented as gifts from the king were in most instances too extensive to be even supervised by the nobles who received them, but each on his own account would divide the entire grant into several smaller portions, bestowing them upon several knights, it might be, reserving a considerable amount for his personal use. The knights in their turn would swear to support the lord in his wars and to furnish him so many fighting men. The lord or noble would accept their homage, promising in his turn that they would be left in possession of the grant. The knight, whose life was probably spent in military expeditions, would parcel out his territory among so many tillers of the soil. These might be freemen or serfs. To the freeman the land was often granted indefinitely. Provided the conditions of the grant were met, he might will it to his heirs or transfer his possession. The serf belonged to the soil and was transferred with it, as were the trees and buildings thereon.

Thus, we see, feudalism was a system of land tenure; from the king, through the lord, under-lord, down indefinitely to the peasant and the serf, protection was promised on one side—service and feudal dues upon the other.

Let us now consider a particular example to make the matter plainer. Let us suppose an estate to be in the possession of a lord who might have received it directly from the king, or from a more powerful lord. In either case, the conditions would be similar. This estate consists of two principal parts: the portion reserved for the personal use of the lord, whereon are located his house and out-buildings; secondly, the remainder, which is divided among several peasants. As a rule the peasants had cottages clustering around the lord's dwelling, forming a little village. The Latin word for domain—villa—in France grew into *ville;* the peasants on the ville called themselves *villeins,* and the settlement made up of their dwellings was called a *village.* The service and feudal dues exacted by the lord differed widely, but one illustration is sufficient for our purpose.

One domain was made up of the owner's reserve, house and other buildings, six fields of arable land containing approximately 865 acres, 42 acres of vineyards, 35 acres of meadow, and woodland enough for the fattening of fifty hogs. This was granted out in small parcels to both freemen and serfs. One free peasant having a wife and two children had two holdings. For each he paid one ox, did the fall work on one-half an acre of the reserve, did carting and odd jobs, gave three pullets and fifteen eggs. In addition to this he paid various feudal fees. On the same domain there was another peasant having a wife and five children. He had one free holding containing 30 acres, one acre in grapes and two-thirds acre in meadow. He paid the same. Finally, we may note one serf having a wife and two children who had one servile holding. It consisted of six acres in arable land, one in grapes, and two-thirds of an acre of meadow. For this he cultivated eight acres of vineyard, paid four measures of wine, six quarts of mustard, three pullets and fifteen eggs, besides doing odd jobs as directed. There were 117 holdings on this estate, some free, some servile.

Seldom if ever did one holding consist of many acres lying together; as a rule it was made up of a given number of acres of tillable soil, of meadow, woodland and vineyard—if in the southern countries. Even in a country where only one or two kinds of crops were raised, the holding was made up of different allotments, some to be left to fallow while the others were tilled.

The requirements of the lord varied in different parts of the country—more especially in different countries. Yet there was a similarity after all—custom largely regulating the matter.

It is not so difficult to explain the existence of the villeins as that of the serfs. In all civilized ages and countries some people have possessed and others have not. The peasant of the

Middle Ages may be easily compared to the man who today rents land from another. Neither render personal service; both are tillers of the soil. With the serf the matter was somewhat different.

It is supposed that the serfs of the Middle Ages were the descendants of the Roman slaves; sometimes they may have been prisoners taken in war. Their condition was considerably better than that of the Roman slaves, for the master on the estate was dependent upon the industry of the serf, and it was to his own interest to make conditions for him tolerable. Serfs were no longer sold. They belonged to the soil; they could marry and their marriages were recognized. As they became tillers of the soil, they merged from slavery into serfdom. As in the case of the villein, no general government stipulated what should be required of them, but here again custom largely controlled.

In addition to the service demanded of the serfs, like the free peasants, they were subject to certain feudal taxes or dues. In the first place, there was a kind of poll-tax levied; then there was a fee required of a serf who married outside the estate. If serfs belonging to an estate married there was no fee exacted, because the service of both remained to the owner; but if one married in such a way as to be required to leave the estate, this was a loss to the master and the privilege had to be purchased. Third, there was the right of *mortmain:* the right of the owner to take back the holding of a serf at his death unless he had a child still living with him. This seems to have given way to a fee demanded of the heirs if they would retain the holding; sometimes only a cow or an ox was demanded.

The owner could not dismiss the serf nor could he leave without the owner's consent. If he left without this consent he could be recovered, or the master could confiscate all his possessions. Still another fee could be collected if the serf wished to purchase his freedom. Sometimes whole villages bought their freedom, being retained as villeins upon the estate.

Viewed from some standpoints, the position of the villeins was not an oppressive one. The relation between the villein and the owner is comparable to that existing between tenant and landlord—like that to be found today where men still farm on shares. The villein held possession of the land in exchange for so much produce. The lord could not deprive him of it so long as he fulfilled his obligations, nor could the owner increase the rent. The villein might even sell his holding, provided the conditions of the agreement with the lord were kept.

The relationship existing between the lord and the villein was a very close one. It is hard for us to understand how such an intimate relation ever developed. Some have sought to find its origin in Roman customs, others have felt sure it arose from an old German relation. It has given rise to much controversy and is not yet fully understood. Whatever may have been its origin, the relation certainly existed. The vassal —and whatever freeman served another was his vassal—was bound to fight for his lord, give him his horse if he was unhorsed in battle, offer himself as a ransom if the lord was taken prisoner. In every situation wherein the lord was endangered, the vassal was bound to offer himself as his lord's protector. The same relationship existed whether the over-lord was powerful or petty, king or noble, knight or churchman. Moreover, the over-lord had the right to fine the vassal in his court, try him for serious crimes, and punish him according to his judgment—even to banishment and death.

Whatever the precedent for such a relationship in Roman or Teutonic custom, in Mediaeval Europe it arose in several ways. The king, as we have seen, needed fighting men, and to bind lords to himself he not only made them gifts of land—*he shared his sovereignty with them.* Ordinarily citizens owe allegiance to their government, whatever kind it be. For the government they perform military service, for its support they pay taxes, in its courts they are judged. Now the king to win support voluntarily gave up some of his prerogatives—which he may not have greatly valued at the time, or which he may have expected to win back—to satisfy lords whose influence and strength he needed. This resulted, as we might expect, not in a well centralized government, but in a number of petty states within the state, a nobility struggling within itself for prepondering power, and a great mass of people, subjects of a king, to be sure, but unconscious of any save the lord in whose wars they fought, in whose protection they lived, for whose support they worked, and who, in short, combined in himself law-making, judiciary and executive powers.

Not always did the lords receive their sovereignty from the king. Sometimes they usurped power during times of disturbance: A new king coming to the throne did not always know what grants had previously been made. A lord's strength was also increased when men having their own small holdings came voluntarily to him whose strength was sufficient to protect them in troublous times, and surrendered to him their lands that they might become his vassals.

In early times, vassals were able to discriminate between the earlier and just exactions demanded of them and those that were later and unjust. Nevertheless, after an unjust exaction had been complied with for a considerable time, custom sanctioned it. Herein we find an explanation for those petty, annoying requirements which, for example, so enraged the peasants of France prior to the revolution and which, surviving to comparatively recent times, seem so surprising. As one reads back step by step, through different feudal stages, it is hardly possible to separate the original from the later requirements.

Besides the head tax and the redemption tax, already mentioned, the lord received several regular taxes from the free peasants. A farm tax was annually collected, and to this was sometimes added a house, or chimney tax. The *taille* seems to have been a charge levied annually against tenants. This was payable in money.

If the peasant transferred his holding, he paid the lord a fee; he also was required to pay toll at bridges, gates, ports, etc., and the lord demanded the privilege of putting his produce upon the market before the peasant. Certain monopolies were also held by the lord: the peasant must have his wheat ground at the lord's mill; his bread baked at the lord's oven; his grapes pressed at the lord's wine-press, etc., and toll was taken for each. If he cut wood in the lord's forest for fuel, he had to pay a fee; for pasturing his cattle he paid another, and a third if he fished in the lord's streams. Besides, the lord's weights and measures had to be used on all occasions.

Probably these were among the unjust exactions that custom gradually sanctioned.

We have already noted the lord's power as judge over those on his domain. Contracts stipulated fines for failure to pay dues or failure to pay them promptly; for slight misdemeanors and more serious ones; finally, the lord could place heavy penalties upon his feudal subjects. However, it must not be supposed that this last was very commonly resorted to.

One of the annoying requirements was that made by the lord for his entertainment when he visited an estate upon which he did not live. The vassals must needs entertain him and his train, feed his horses, dogs, etc. This grew to be such an injustice that custom limited such visits to three per year, and finally a tax was accepted in its place.

The following extract is taken from a not exaggerated rehearsal of the peasant's grievances—the estate in this case belonging to an ecclesiastical order:

"The tenants must fetch stone, mix mortar, and serve the masons. Toward the last of June, on demand they must mow and turn hay and draw it to the manor-house. In August they must reap the convent's grain, put it in sheaves and draw it in. For their tenure they owe the champart: they cannot remove their sheaves before they have been to seek the assessor of the champart, who deducts his due, and they must cart his part to the champart-barn; during this time their own grain remains exposed to the wind and rain. On the eighth of September the villein owes his pork-due, one pig in eight; he has the right to take out two; the third choice belongs to the seigneur. On the ninth of October he takes the cens. At Christmas he owes his chicken-due; also the grain-due of two setiers of barley, and a quart of wheat. On Palm Sunday he owes his sheep-due; and if he does not pay it on the day set the seigneur fines him, arbitrarily. At Easter he owes corvée: by the way of corvée he must plough, sow and harrow. If the villein sells his land, he owes the seigneur the thirteenth part of its value. If he marries his daughter to any one outside the seigneury, he pays a marriage-right of three sous. He is subjected to the mill-ban and the oven-ban; his wife goes to get bread; she pays the customary charges; the woman at the oven grumbles—for she is 'very proud and haughty'—and the man at the oven complains of not having his due; he swears that the oven will be poorly heated and that the villein's bread will be all raw and not well browned."

When one considers that in addition to these various duties already cited the peasant had to help build and repair roads and bridges, repair the castle, and construct its fortifications, guard the walls when danger threatened, and even follow the master upon some war he might be undertaking for his own personal gratification and gain, it is not hard to understand the discontent that finally permeated all feudal countries.

When the Normans crossed the English channel and conquered England, William the Conqueror introduced the feudal system into the island shorn of several of its most flagrant faults.[1] He compelled vassals all over the land to take the oath of fealty to him first, to the feudal lord afterwards. Moreover, he established courts wherein all subjects might state their grievances. For this reason feudalism never developed here as it did on the continent. Furthermore, it must be remembered that there was no established way for this organization to develop; there grew up so many differences and irregularities from any general plan which might be explained that so far there has never been any adequate and exhaustive work on the subject. If a rule seems in a fair way to be established, other data seems directly to disprove its universality.

When the usual means of social protection fail, unusual ones will always arise. In Mediaeval Europe, poor means of communication, poor roads, and distances out of all proportion to the means of overcoming them, brought a demand for local rather than central control. Generally speaking, the overseer of a domain, whether lord or vassal, comprehended the needs of his locality better than a remote king whose years were filled with foreign wars possibly could. In an age when might made right, the lord brought a feeling of protection that the king was yet unable to give. In many cases the lord was loved by his vassals, and for generations together prosperity and contentment obtained on a domain. Yet as society became more settled, the king looked with disfavor upon the nobles who usurped his rights and allowed him to be scarcely more

[1] There may have been some form of feudalism in England before the Conquest, but we know practically nothing of it.

powerful than they. Also the dissatisfaction felt by royalty was augmented by that of the common people, who in plenty of cases had reason to hate the nobles for their thoughtless, irresponsible ways.

When the nobles were not fighting they liked best of all to hunt, and this sport gave rise to many attendant troubles. Large tracts of land were often turned into great reserves for the sole pleasure of the lord. Not infrequently peasants were turned away from homes they had long occupied so that the selfishness of the nobility might be gratified. The game abounding in these reserves was guarded for the special enjoyment of the lord, and peasants were even put to death for killing wild animals for food. Moreover, when the chase grew hot, a troop of horsemen might gallop after the fleeing game, across meadows and grain fields. Many a peasant saw his year's work laid waste by these lords in their scurry for some animal bent upon preserving its life. Of course, he had absolutely no redress.

Feudalism fostered marked social distinctions. At the top was an aristocracy, except in war idle and of no particular strength to a country. Each sought to aggrandize himself at the expense of the whole. Finding himself stronger than the king, many a lord attempted to make himself supreme. Such a state of affairs was unsatisfactory to all save the nobles themselves, who were content to monopolize the benefits of the age to the detriment of other social classes. Gradually, however, the common people asserted themselves. First in the towns they united for the common good and purchased their freedom. The free towns multiplied, and more and more the strength of the feudal lords was checked.

Finally the employment of gun-powder for purposes of war rendered the feudal cavalry no longer useful. This forever broke the strength of the feudal knights.

The dawn of modern history witnessed the decline of the feudal system and the growth of national spirit. Only here and there did the obligations live on when the reason for them had passed and real power and protection were vested in a national government.

Closely allied to this subject is chivalry, to be considered in another chapter.

CHAPTER IV.

Religious Wars—The Crusades.

Religious wars occupy a considerable place in mediaeval history, being waged for the most part between Christians and Mohammedans. Occasionally they occurred between orthodox Christians and heretics, but these demonstrations never reached such proportions as the ones made against those of an entirely different faith.

It may be remembered that Christians were in the beginning a peace-loving body, opposed to war or any show of violence whatever. Centuries of conflict had brought about a decided change in this regard. As a matter of fact, the Teutons now made up the great body of Christians. Fighters to begin with, when they became Christians they became, by very necessity of the case, fighting Christians. Yet earlier still Constantine had transformed a religion of peace into one of war by placing his sword above the cross.

The new aspect given the faith by this action of Constantine and the fighting tendencies contributed by the Germans were but factors. Religion is but one phase of culture, and humanity in the Middle Ages had as a whole attained to no advanced stage in the assimilation of cultural elements. Men loved fighting and were still cruel and brutal. In reading the chronicles of the Crusades, one is appalled by the cruelty allowed—even sanctioned—by the most intelligent leaders.

The Germans brought with them the trial by ordeal, as a means of determining innocence or guilt, when they pushed into southern Europe. With the belief that to the innocent would be given the victory, men and women were required to demonstrate their innocence or guilt by submitting to the ordeal of hot or cold water, or by fire. If one were accused and yet protested his innocence, in the presence of witnesses he might plunge his arm into a kettle of boiling water. The rapidity by which the arm healed indicated whether or not he had committed the crime attributed to him. Or perhaps he accused would be thrown into a lake. If he sank, he was innocent—for the water would receive only the pure in heart. Trial by battle was most popular, and churchmen and monasteries often maintained champions who represented them when they were assailed.

Thus it came to be universally accepted that God would give victory to the right, and hence it might be a sacred duty to fight and so become an instrument through which righteousness should assert itself. So prevalent did fighting and dueling become that Europe generally was the arena for quarreling nobles, knights, and men of whatever quality, save the peasants and serfs. To such lengths did disorders of this sort go that the Church undertook to stop them and issued what was known as the Peace of God. By this men were threatened with excommunication if they engaged in private battles. But so great was the love of fighting that men willingly braved the threats of hell-fire rather than renounce their dueling. Finally the Church sought to mitigate rather than utterly forbid the practice, and made it unlawful to fight between Thursday evening and Monday morning. This was known as the Truce of God.

From the time of the repulse of the Saracens at the battle of Tours, there had been intermittent war between Christians and Mohammedans. Especially was this the case in Spain. Indeed, it ceased only in the final repulsion of the Moors in the fifteenth century. Deep hatred existed between men of the two religions, and this hatred was fanned into a flame in the latter part of the eleventh century.

Throughout the Middle Ages it was regarded as meritorious to visit the tomb or shrine of some saint or holy person. Often those in poor health felt restored by such visits and the afflicted found relief from their troubles at a favorite shrine. The custom was not in the least peculiar to Christians. The faithful Mohammedan still hopes to pay a visit to the sacred city of Mecca sometime during his life, and among the religious of nearly all countries some spots have been—frequently are still—thought sacred.

If the pious Christian in the Middle Ages felt his sins forgiven and his health restored by a visit to the tomb of some holy saint, even more did he venerate a pilgrimage to the land where had lived and died the founder of his faith. To reach Palestine in general and Jerusalem in particular was his fondest desire. For years palmers had returned from such pilgrimages bearing the palm of the Holy Land, and all who saw them envied them the journey they had made, and listened with wonder to the stories they recounted. Although the Saracens dominated Syria—and all western Asia from the Mediterranean to the Indus, from the Caspian to Spain—they had allowed Christians free access to their sacred places. However, the Seljuk Turks had finally wrested Spain from the Arabians and, although the Turks became Mohammedans, they were by no means so tolerant as the Saracens, and put obstacles at once in the way of visiting Christians. Returning home, palmers complained bitterly of the harsh treatment and the insults they had received.

The Turks were threatening Constantinople, having already won certain territories from the eastern emperor. In his dismay, Emperor Alexis appealed to the pope for aid against the Mohammedans. Pope Urban II was now occupying the papal chair, and he was not only a pope—he possessed the qualities of a shrewd politican as well. He saw the responsibility of regaining spiritual control over the eastern empire —as he had continued to hold over the western. For this reason he called a council to consider the situation in the East. It met in Italy, but accomplished little. He thereupon appointed a new council, to meet this time in Clermont, in the land of the Franks. They at least were not likely to remain deaf to the call of a sacred war; nor did they. The following spring found the call to arms in behalf of the sacred places of the Christians echoing everywhere. The pope preached a crusade, monks and churchmen urged it, and the Church was a strong medium through which to reach the people. In the Middle Ages, the Church had a firm hold upon men, and, whether or not they obeyed its injunctions in all particulars, they were glad to have so excellent a reason for setting out upon a military campaign.

All classes of society were attracted by the crusaders' cry. The oppressed peasants and serfs were glad of an opportunity to abandon a life which had become well-nigh intolerable. Some were stimulated to go by the hope of extending trade; some loved adventure, and for this alone joined the ranks. Probably the great majority at the outset were actuated by generous and religious motives. They felt keenly the insults offered their brother Christians, and they chafed at the idea of the localities held sacred by the Christian world being in the hands of the unbelievers. However self-seeking and greedy they later became, this motive was undoubtedly powerful at the beginning. For a time they acted under the spell thrown around them by the fiery speeches of religious preachers.

The difficulty of carrying out the plan as it had been quickly formulated—to march to Jerusalem and rescue it from the hands of the Mohammedans and establish a kingdom under control of the Latin Church in Palestine—was apparent from the start. It was almost impossible under the circumstances to get concerted action. Before the main army was ready, two detachments under fanatic leaders set out alone. Had the Saracens and Turks united, probably none of the crusading armies would have accomplished anything, but as it happened they were at this time quarreling and the Turks themselves were not united. Nevertheless, such stray bands as those that set out under Walter the Penniless came to naught. Those who made up their numbers were not prepared for the difficulties they had to encounter. They were not adequately prepared for the rigor of the march, and hundreds and thousands fell by the wayside.

The main stream that set out under the leadership of Robert of Normandy, Godfrey of Bouillon, Raymond of Toulouse and others, fared better. The emperor of the East was almost as alarmed by their numbers as he had previously been by the proximity of the Turks, and he persuaded them to move on as soon as possible. They captured Nicaea, which he promptly claimed. Antioch was captured and at length the city of Jerusalem. Terrible was the slaughter of the Mohammedans, who had held out as long as possible within the city. The crusaders fought with the ferocity that rings through the Book of Joshua. One crusader sent word to those at home that if they would know what happened there, he would say that the crusaders' horses rode to their knees through blood of the Saracens.

Each leader was eager for self-aggrandizement, and what to do with conquered territory was a problem. Finally a Latin kingdom was set up with Godfrey of Bouillon at the head. He would not accept the title of king, but called himself the *Defender of the Holy Sepulcher*.

From the time the first crusaders set out—in 1096 A. D.— until the end of the kingdom of Jerusalem in 1291, men were journeying back and forth between different parts of Europe and the East. The crusade continued, although for years at a time there would be no fighting. Sometimes a wave of indignation would spread through Europe, caused by some movement of the Turks, and a great stream of humanity would pour out again to the field of action; such occasions have come to be known as the Second Crusade, Third Crusade, etc. Eight crusades are thus often enumerated. In 1146 Edessa fell into the hands of the Turks and the population was sold into slavery. Then it was that St. Bernard of Clairvaux preached a crusade. This proved unsuccessful, and the crusaders returned home saying they had accomplished "all that God willed and the people of the country permitted."

In 1187 Saladin, the sultan of Egypt, captured Jerusalem. Now it was that three kings, Richard I of England, Philip Augustus of France, and Frederick Barbarossa of Germany, were moved to undertake the so-called Third Crusade. Frederick Barbarossa was drowned while crossing a stream; Richard the Lion-Hearted was taken prisoner when returning through Germany, where the Emperor Henry VI held him for ransom. The result of the crusade was a truce agreed to by Saladin. It was to last three and one-half years and by it the Christians were allowed free access to the holy places. The Fourth Crusade was diverted from its purpose by the Venetians, who saw good opportunity to further their commerce. Constantinople was captured and a Latin kingdom set up. Unfortunately, the city was sacked and relics of priceless worth destroyed. The kingdom thus established maintained itself until the year 1453, when the Turks finally captured Constantinople.

Several crusades followed, most atrocious being the Childrens' Crusade. We may well pause for a moment to ponder over this crusade, not for its accomplishment, for it accomplished absolutely nothing, but it shows to what extremities feeling in the Middle Ages could go when religion gave sanction to a cause.

A French peasant lad of about 12 years became excited about the crusade. Small wonder was it that even the babes began to talk of a movement that was reaching into the second hundred years, and for which every village had sent out its offering of men and money. He thought that he was called to preach a crusade among the children. This was a credulous age and people of ripe years took up the cry and said those who had already gone forth had been too worldly-minded and now the purity of childhood would show to the rest how great had been their lack of faith. We can hardly believe our eyes today as we read of the 20,000 or more children who set out from Germany and the 30,000 from France, to win back Jerusalem from the Turks! The majority of them were boys averaging about 12 years, although many girls went, too, and the companies were swelled with women and men of the worst types. Nor is it to be imagined that all the grown people of Europe had become temporarily bereft of their senses. Many foresaw exactly how the matter would result and tried their best to divert the children from their wild purpose. Cities along the line of march even offered to care for the children and let them grow into citizenship if they would but halt from their vain attempt. But just as wise heads used their influence in this way, deluded ones encouraged the children, and we know very well that had not many parents believed in the undertaking, the children would not have been permitted to organize themselves and go about singing and preaching the cause. Such a demonstration in our time would be impossible, but it must be remembered that human intelligence has passed through many a broadening experience since that day.

The thousands of children who marched over the mountains and into Italy continued until they could go no farther, and such as remained and had strength and courage turned back. But by the time they reached their native towns, they had for the most part become utterly demoralized and abandoned. Even those who reached their homes in a weak, exhausted condition, did not know where they had been and were crushed by their disappointments and weary toil.

Those who set sail from Marseilles were many of them shipwrecked. They fared much better than those who survived only to be sold into slavery.

Never was it possible to create so great ardour again. While four minor crusades were undertaken, they were of small importance when compared with the earlier ones. Lesser ones were directed against the Moors in Spain, but the whole sympathy of Mediaeval Europe was probably never so completely with the movements as it had formerly been.

It has been apparent that the crusaders failed to accomplish their purpose—namely, to win and hold Palestine as a Latin kingdom. Nevertheless the crusades bore great results for Europe and European civilization. To say nothing of staying the power of the Turks for 200 or 300 years, they accomplished other results quite as important. Trade was given new channels through which to operate, and much wealth accrued to Europe; especially did it come into the hands of the middle class, who made quick use of it to gain freedom from feudal exactions. Towns purchased their freedom from lords who needed large sums of money; individuals freed themselves from claims upon them. To be sure, the rise of free towns was the more important result, for within these centers life went forward with fresh impulses, and great things came out of them.

Feudalism received a blow from which it never rallied. One by one, in country after country, power was wrested from the nobles and the way was left for the rise of nations and national feeling.

Literature and learning received wide contributions. Much of the old Greek and Roman learning, overthrown in the West, had lived on in the East. In Europe Greek had been practically a forgotten tongue during the Middle Ages. Now through eastern channels it was given back to the West, together with Greek masterpieces and Greek thought. The East had its own literature and songs and productions, which the crusaders brought back, contributing to the literatures of Europe new conceptions and rich imagery. Especially were the crusaders affected by the culture of the East. In many branches of learning the people of the East were far in advance of the West. Contact between the two continents gave all cultural elements new impulses and paved the way for the wonders of the Renaissance.

A KNIGHT TEMPLAR.

KNIGHT IN ARMOR.

The Children's Crusade.

"Of all the strange armies which those days of strange sights had witnessed, this was the most notable. There were no mailed soldiers, who marched beneath feudal banners that had waved over battlefields in Europe and in Asia; there were no chargers that carried strong warriors who held well-used swords; nor yet were there pilgrims of mature years, who had set out, unarmed, to pray in consecrated spots. It was an army of children, who were actually departing to recover possession of a land in whose behalf many a host had died in vain. In the van we see Nicholas, probably accompanied by an escort and attendants. Then the line stretches with varying regularity for several miles, and, over the uniformed ranks of little ones, rise the crosses and banners that are proudly carried. We see, among the numbers, the many adults who desired to share the glory of the enterprise or to plunder and corrupt. There were women who came to profit in their baseness or suffer in their weakness, and girls who were destined to a bitter lot of shame, instead of a rest in Palestine. And priests and monks were there, some to rob, and some to pray. But the mass were boys of about 12 years of age. They gave character to the army, and it is with them that we are concerned. They came from mansion and from hovel, from luxury and from want; the pedigree of princes was possessed by those who walked by the side of humble serfs.

As they marched along, they beguiled the time with narrative and song. As to the former, there was among them a store which was not soon exhausted.

The children from the castle told of knightly deeds by men of famous names, and to the more credulous peasants, repeated what they had so often heard from their proud kindred, who had won such fame in conflict. They who had never before spoken with the despised boor forgot their station and wearied not to answer questions concerning the life of the noble-born, which had been almost as sacred and revered in the cabins of the lowly as the associations of the Holy Land. The serf child could only tell of obscurer feats of arms and of less exalted deeds, which his kindred had known; but yet each was ready to hear the wonderful stories of the other. In this way, throughout the host, the spirit of the cause was kept alive, and their minds were inflamed into resolution to surpass the achievement of squire, and knight, and baron. The fame of the heroes who had fallen, to be immortal in song, or who had survived to receive the love of woman and the envy of man, was yet to pale before the lustre of the deeds of God's own army.

And songs, too, whiled away the tedious hours of wandering, as well as aided in sustaining their spirits. Chroniclers expressly say that singing formed a marked feature in their journey. They sang many lyrics which returned pilgrims and warriors had taught them, but which, it is sad to say, have been lost. They also composed many of their own, which have shared the same fate. It is natural to wish most earnestly that some of these had survived, that thence we might learn something of the children's feelings, and that we might enter into a fuller sympathy with them, in reading the words which conveyed their emotions. But, although we have not the language of these songs, we can well imagine their themes. The constant subjects were the restoration of the Holy Sepulchre, and the glory of that triumph. We need not labor much to realize the ardor which nerved them to endure fatigue, when, their little hearts bounding with excitement, they shouted in spirited tunes the expressions of the hopes and dreams of years.

From the oblivion of ages there has survived, however, only one of the hymns which were sung by them. It was brought by the recruits from Westphalia, and had been sung by many a pilgrim before, on the way to Palestine. Its words and air, so well adapted to this present assemblage, made it popular, and it delights the Christian of today by the evidence which it affords that there lingered yet some appreciation of the truth of the Gospel, some love to the Saviour. It seems as a gleam of light in the darkness of the age. Listen, then, children of the nineteenth century, to words which other children sang as they marched along the Rhine, nearly seven hundred years ago.

Let us quote it first in the original, in which these little crusaders were wont to sing it, having modernized its antique German:

"Schönster Herr Jesus,
 Herrscher aller Erden,
Gottes und Maria Sohn;
 Dich will ich lieben,
 Dich will ich ehren,
Du, meiner Seele Freud' und Kron!

"Schön sind die Felder,
 Noch schöner sind die Wälder,
In der schönen Frühlingszeit;
 Jesus ist schöner,
 Jesus ist reiner,
Der unser traurig Herz erfreut.

"Schön leuchtet die Sonne,
 Noch schöner leuchtet der Monde,
Und die Sternlein allzumal;
 Jesus leuchtet schöner,
 Jesus leuchtet reiner,
Als all' die Engel im Himmelsaal."

TRANSLATION.

"Fairest Lord Jesus,
 Ruler of all nature,
Thou of Mary and of God the Son!
 Thee will I cherish,
 Thee will I honor,
Thee my soul's glory, joy, and crown!

"Fair are the meadows,
 Fairer still the woodlands,
Robed in the blooming garb of spring;
 Jesus is fairer,
 Jesus is purer,
Who makes our saddened heart to sing.

"Fair is the sunshine,
 Fairer still the moonlight,
And the sparkling, starry host;
 Jesus shines brighter,
 Jesus shines purer,
Than all the angels heaven can boast."

How welcome is such a hymn from the past ages, and how does it add to our interest in these youths who used it!

Thus singing their songs, they passed on southwards, seeking Palestine. But it is natural to inquire if they did not know that the Mediterranean intervened; and if so, how did they expect to cross it? Did their leaders not have an answer ready for this question? We find, as a feature of curious interest, that they who had excited and promoted the Crusade had promised that the Lord would provide a pathway through that great sea to the land beyond its waters. Availing themselves of a home argument, they pointed to the fearful drought which is recorded to have prevailed that summer, as evidence from heaven that the army was to pass, like Israel's hosts, through the sea, for they said that the Mediterranean was drying up for this end. This was asserted in reply to the natural objections that there would not be enough vessels to carry such a vast number, or that, if they were obtained, the young pilgrims would lack money to pay for their transportation and their food. The story was believed, and the children were buoyed up and encouraged on the march by the anticipation of so signal an interference in their behalf. Surely, said they, if we are thus to triumph over the deep waters, as did the people of God in old times, we must win an equal success, and rest in the same land, by virtue of the same divine aid.

They journeyed onward through the domains of the lords and nobles who owed allegiance to France, or to the Empire. Their fame may have preceded them, or it may not, yet their arrival was always the signal of commotion in every village, where they won new recruits from the astonished and enraptured children. Each member of the host told, in his own words, the same title of a celestial call and of a certain success, and repeated, with embellishments of his own invention, the appeal in behalf of the defiled Tomb of Christ. If night overtook them by any town or hamlet, they sought shelter where they could find it. One chronicler tells us that no city on the way could contain the army. Some slept in houses, where the kind-hearted or the sympathizing invited them to rest; others reposed in the streets and market places; while they who could find no space within, lay down without the walls. But if, as was generally the case, the darkness found them in the open country, they passed the night in the barns and hovels, under the trees of the forest, or on the green bank of some stream, and the angel of sleep closed their heavy eyelids under the starlight. The day's march was wearisome to little ones who had never before been out of sight of home, and therefore they soon fell asleep, wherever it was. When morning came they ate whatever they had in their wallets, or what they begged or bought as they went. The line of march was again formed, the banners unfurled, the crosses uplifted, and, with the morning sun they began another day of fatigue. At noon they rested by some brook to eat their scanty meal and quench their thirst, and again started to wander on through the quiet hours of afternoon, until the welcome sunset reminded them that they had passed another stage of their journey to distant—oh so distant!—Palestine.

—*From the Children's Crusade, by G. Z. Gray.*

CRUSADERS.

Ordeal of Hot Water Undertaken by a Priest to Confute a Heretic!

An Arian presbyter disputing with a deacon of our religion made venomous assertions against the Son of God and the Holy Ghost, as is the habit of that sect. But when the deacon had discoursed a long time concerning the reasonableness of our faith and the heretic, blinded by the fog of unbelief, continued to reject the truth, according as it is written, "Wisdom shall not enter the mind of the wicked," the former said: "Why weary ourselves with long discussions? Let acts approve the truth; let a kettle be heated over the fire and someone's ring be thrown into the boiling water. Let him who shall take it from the heated liquid be approved as a follower of the truth, and afterwards let the other party be converted to the knowledge of this truth. And do thou also understand, O heretic, that this our party will fulfil the conditions with the aid of the Holy Ghost; thou shalt confess that there is no discordance, no dissimilarity in the Holy Trinity." The heretic consented to the proposition and they separated after appointing the next morning for the trial. But the fervor of faith in which the deacon had first made this suggestion began to cool through the instigation of the enemy. Rising with the dawn he bathed his arm in oil and smeared it with ointment. But nevertheless he made the round of the sacred places and called in prayer on the Lord. What more shall I say? About the third hour they met in the market place. The people came together to see the show. A fire was lighted, the kettle was placed upon it, and when it grew very hot the ring was thrown into the boiling water. The deacon invited the heretic to take it out of the water first. But he promptly refused, saying, "Thou who didst propose this trial are the one to take it out." The deacon, all of a tremble, bared his arm. And when the heretic presbyter saw it besmeared with ointment, he cried out:

"With magic arts thou hast thought to protect thyself, that thou hast made use of these salves, but what thou hast done will not avail." While they were thus quarreling there came up a deacon from Ravenna named Iacinthus and inquired what the trouble was about. When he learned the truth he drew his arm out from under his robe at once and plunged his right hand into the kettle. Now the ring that had been thrown in was a little thing and very light, so that it was thrown about by the water as chaff would be blown about by the wind; and searching for it a long time he found it after about an hour. Meanwhile the flame beneath the kettle blazed up mightily, so that the greater heat might make it difficult for the ring to be followed by the hand; but the deacon extracted it at length and suffered no harm, protesting rather that at the bottom the kettle was cold, while at the top it was just pleasantly warm. When the heretic beheld this he was greatly confused and audaciously thrust his hand into the kettle, saying, "my faith will aid me." As soon as his hand had been thrust in all the flesh was boiled off the bones clear up to the elbow. And so the dispute ended.

Ordeal of Glowing Ploughshares Undergone by Queen Emma.[1]

The queen was brought at the king's command from Whewell to Winchester and throughout all the night preceding her trial she kept her vigil at the shrine of St. Swithin.

On the appointed day the clergy and the people came to the church and the king himself sat on the tribunal. The queen was brought before her son and questioned whether she was willing to go through with what she had undertaken.

Nine glowing ploughshares were placed on the carefully-swept pavement of the church. After these had been consecrated by a short ceremony the queen's shoes and stockings were taken off; then her robe was removed and her cloak thrown aside, and, supported by two bishops, one on either side, she was led to the torture. The bishops who led her were weeping and those who were much more afraid than she were encouraging her not to fear. Uncontrollable weeping broke out all over the church and all voices were united in the cry "St. Swithin, O St. Swithin, help her!" If the thunder had pealed forth at this time the people would not have heard it, with such strength, with such a concourse of voices did the shout go

[1] From University Translations and Reprints, U. of Pa.

up to heaven that St. Swithin should now or never hasten to her aid. God suffers violence and St. Swithin is dragged by force from Heaven. In a low voice the queen offered this prayer as she undertook the ordeal: "O God, who didst free Susanna from the wicked elders and the three youths from the fiery furnace, from the fire prepared for me deign to preserve me through the merits of St. Swithin."

Behold the miracle! With the bishops directing her feet, in nine steps she walked upon the nine ploughshares, pressing each one of them with the full weight of her whole body; and though she thus passed over them all, they neither saw the iron nor felt the heat. Therefore she said to the bishops: "Am I not to obtain that which I especially sought? Why do you lead me out of the church when I ought to be tried within it?" For she was going out and yet did not realize that she had gone through the ordeal. To which the bishops replied as well as they could through their sobs: "O lady, behold, you have already done it; the deed is now accomplished which you think must yet be done." She gazed and her eyes were opened; then for the first time she looked about and understood the miracle. "Lead me," she said, "to my son, that he may see my feet and know that I have suffered no ill."

Ordeal of the Cross.

(Note: In the ordeal of the cross the two litigants were placed standing before a crucifix with their arms outstretched. The one who was able to maintain this position the longer won his case.)

If a dispute, contention or controversy shall arise between the parties regarding the boundaries or limits of their kingdoms of such a nature that it cannot be settled or terminated by human evidence, then we desire that for the decision of the matter the will of God and the truth of the dispute may be sought by means of the judgment of the cross, nor shall any sort of battle or duel ever be adjudged for the decision of any such question.

It is enacted that hereafter no one shall presume to undertake any sort of ordeal of the cross; lest that which was glorified by the passion of Christ should be brought into contempt through anyone's temerity.

A Church Built for the Host by Bees.

I have heard that a certain rustic, wishing to become wealthy and having many hives of bees, asked certain evil men how he could get rich and increase the number of his bees. He was told by some one that if he would retain the sacred communion on Easter and place it in one of his hives, he would entice away all of his neighbor's bees, which leaving their own hives, would come to the place where the body of our Lord was and there would make honey. He did this.

Then all the bees came to the hive where the body of Christ was, and just as if they had felt compassion for the irreverence done to it, by their labor they began to construct a little church and to erect foundations and bases and columns and an altar with like labor, and with the greatest reverence they placed the body of our Lord upon the altar. And within that little beehive they formed that little church with wonderful and the most beautiful workmanship. The bees of the vicinity leaving their hives came together at that one; and over that structure they sang in their own manner certain wonderful melodies like hymns.

The rustic hearing this, wondered. But waiting until the fitting time for collecting the swarm of bees and the honey comb, he found nothing in his hives in which the bees had been accustomed to make honey; finding himself impoverished through the means by which he had believed that he would be enriched, he went to that one where he had placed the host, where he saw the bees had come together. But when he approached, just as if they had wanted to vindicate the insult to our Saviour, the bees rushed upon the rustic and stung him so severely that he escaped with difficulty, and suffering greatly. Going to the priest he related all that he had done and what the bees had done. The priest, by the advice of his bishop, collected his parishioners and went in procession to the place. Then the bees, leaving the hive, rose in the air, making sweet melody. Raising the hive they found within the noble structure of that little church the body of our Lord placed upon the altar. Then returning thanks they bore to their own church that little church of the bees constructed with such skill and elegance and with praises placed it on the altar.

By this deed those who do not reverence but offer insult instead to the sacred body of Christ or the sacred place where it is, ought to be put to great confusion.

Horrible Death of a Blasphemer of the Virgin.[2]

Also near Cluny, as I have heard from many, it happened recently, namely, in the year of our Lord 1246, when I was there, that a certain tavernkeeper on the Saturday before Advent, in selling wine and taking his pay, blasphemed Christ during the whole day. But when about the ninth hour, in the presence of a multitude of men, he had sworn by the tongue of the Blessed Virgin, by blaspheming her he lost the use of his tongue, and by speaking basely of her, suddenly stricken in the presence of the multitude, he fell dead.

[1,2] These two selections are taken from the University Translations and Reprints, U. of Pa.

CHAPTER V.

Schools and Education in the Middle Ages.

The schools maintained during the principate disappeared as a natural consequence after the fall of Rome. Life itself was uncertain during those years in which the Teutons swayed back and forth in their southward marches. The Eternal City was pillaged and sacked. All Roman institutions suffered and many collapsed. Even when peace settled for a time over Italy, learning had scarce time to make a faint beginning ere another era of disorder crushed it out. Probably throughout the Middle Ages there were scholarly men and in all centuries some children were taught, but they were long the favored few and we know little about Roman schools after the Germanic invasion.

The matter of education is always quickly affected by unsettled conditions. Boys are needed to serve in the armies in times of war or to stay at home while others join the ranks. So it was in the early Middle Ages. The Germans who conquered the vast territories of Rome were wholly unlettered, but they soon realized the need of training in the management of the lands they won. They understood in a vague way that they needed the mental grasp of the conquered Romans and assimilated quickly what they could. However, until the time of Charlemagne learning was confined to the monasteries.

Another reason for the decline of learning is to be found in the hostile attitude taken toward it by the early Church. Immorality had so thoroughly permeated all conditions of society and all classes that it was at first difficult for the early Christians to discriminate between what was good and what evil in Roman civilization. To be sure, the early Christians in Rome were Romans, but in their desire to break absolutely with the corruption of their day, they at first discarded much that was noble. It was St. Augustine who in a measure saved classical learning for the monks by pointing out that with the dross there were veins of gold and silver and these should be sought by the devout. Augustine did a great deal to formulate the teachings of the Church and to broaden religious thought.

A third reason for the decline of learning was that the curriculum of the monastic schools—the only schools for a considerable period—was adapted to the monk or priest alone. It was not in the least designed for men of affairs. For this reason the aggressive youth of the time was generally found in the world of activity.

Against these causes for the falling away of learning we may well note why it survived at all. The first reason has already been pointed out—the Germans felt the urgent need of it. Again, within the monastery the spark was kept alive until conditions allowed it to burst into the flame of the Renaissance. Finally, missionaries carried it from Rome to remote districts, where often, as for example, in Ireland, it was tenderly fostered.

For several centuries two forces were at work to hold down free thought. One was the inordinate value placed upon authority; the second, the attitude of the Church. Men were not concerned with what they themselves thought, but in citing as many opinions from earlier writers as they could. Great weight was placed upon any authority whatever. This is somewhat difficult to grasp in an age when all authority is questioned and none accepted until it has been proved beyond doubt.

Perhaps the second force binding free thought in mediaeval times is just as difficult for our age to understand. In the more civilized countries today the Church does not attempt to control the thoughts of men. This was quite the reverse in years gone by. Considerable freedom of thought was permissible so long as one held to the Church, but to break with it was heresy, and heresy was severely punished.

Learning was divided into seven branches: grammar, rhetoric, dialectics, music, arithmetic, geometry and astronomy. The first three were the more elementary; the remaining four, the studies for advanced students. The text-books were dull and uninteresting. The grammar of Donatus was used for nearly a thousand years. Like many text-books of the time, it was prepared in the form of question and answer. It contained as much matter as would be found on eight of our printed pages. Priscian wrote another, somewhat longer. By memorizing the contents of these two books one might master all knowledge of the subject of grammar.

Music was little more than a mystical arrangement of numbers. Arithmetic and other forms of mathematics were valued because they enabled one to locate the time for observance of Easter, and consequently for several holy-days. Nevertheless a mastery of mathematics might enable one to conjure with the devil. Astronomy was a mixture of astronomy and astrology.

Charlemagne was a farsighted statesman and having conquered a wide territory, he was determined to rule it. Capable man as he was, he realized how essential was some knowledge of the past. Although he never had opportunity for learning until he was a middle-aged man, and could never write his name, he was ambitious for his own children and those of his kingdom. All his life he used his influence in favor of thorough study. He exhorted the churches to be more accurate in their work—not to mispronounce words in their singing and not to allow crudities to slip into their speech. To the abbots of monasteries he sent a famous letter wherein he urged them to be more heedful themselves if they would instruct others.

"Every one should strive to understand what it is that he would fain accomplish; and this right understanding will be the sooner gained according as the utterances of the tongue are freed from error. And if false speaking is to be shunned by all men, especially should it be shunned by those who have elected to be the servants of truth. During the past years we have often received letters from different monasteries informing us that at their sacred services the brethren offered up prayers on our behalf; and we have observed that the thoughts contained in these letters, though in themselves most just, were expressed in uncouth language, and while pious devotion dictated the sentiments, the unlettered tongue was unable to express them aright. Hence there has arisen in our minds the fear lest, if the skill to write rightly were thus lacking, so, too, would the power of rightly comprehending the Sacred Scriptures be far less than was fitting, and we all know that though verbal errors be dangerous, errors of the understanding are yet more so. We exhort you, therefore, not only not to neglect the study of letters, but to apply yourselves thereto with perseverance and with that humility which is well pleasing to God; so that you may be able to penetrate with greater ease and certainty the mysteries of the Holy Scriptures."

Charlemagne founded the Palace School, maintained at his court for the instruction of his children and the children of his ministers, as well as for their parents and the great king. Alcuin, the celebrated teacher of York, was brought by him to Aachen to take control of the school. No teacher ever had a more diversified class to teach than did Alcuin when he attempted the instruction of Charlemagne and his wife and children, together with the children of his advisers with other court attendants. Charlemagne, we are told, was ever eager to learn and a most impatient pupil. Someone has said he wished to know everything and know it all at once. Surely it is safe to conclude that Alcuin was possessed of more than ordinary tact when he was able to hold pupils of such widely differing ages alike interested.

Charlemagne's interest was not for these children alone. He issued many messages concerning educational matters. He urged every parent to see that his children were sent to school and were diligent in their work. Priests were requested to maintain schools in every village for the elementary instruction of children generally, and higher schools were carried on in connection with each monastery and cathedral. The priest in the village conducted the village school and the abbot of the monastery the monastic school. No regular fee was exacted in either case, but parents paid as they were able.

After the death of Charlemagne his empire fell apart, and in the disorder of succeeding years education, like other pursuits of peace, suffered. Yet a firm foundation had been laid for the future. The work of Alcuin, the great teacher, was valuable. It had been primarily to *preserve* the learning of the time. He had books copied and mended; he collected as many as he was able. He was a teacher who sought to *preserve* rather than to create. Men followed who were greater far than Alcuin in the matter of advancing knowledge, but his work of preservation was important.

Among the great names to stand forth in the cause of learning during the Middle Ages are those of Gerbert—later Pope Sylvester II.; Abelard, and John of Salisbury. Gerbert was the greatest teacher of the tenth century. Like many another during these years, he came from poor, obscure parents. He became an expert mathematician for his age and some even surmised that he was in league with the devil because he computed the height of a tower by measuring its shadow. Gerbert was a firm churchman, but he appreciated the need of classical training for the men who were later to become priests. He was long the famous master of Rheims, and while there not only collected books and multiplied the copies of each, but beyond this his influence had the effect of broadening learning.

Abelard and St. Bernard of Clairvaux represent two prevailing and conflicting tendencies of the later Middle Ages. Abelard was the most celebrated dialectician of his age; Bernard a monk of noble qualities.

Abelard was the doubter. He said: "By doubting we are led to inquire; by inquiry we perceive the truth." He depended not upon the authority of the past, but was self-reliant. When he began to lecture in Paris his classes were crowded. The old hold of authority and the Church was already palling upon men and some gave evidence of a strong tendency for something new. *New* theories, *new* methods were appearing in the early part of the twelfth century.

Bernard of Clairvaux was absolutely the reverse of this. Living at the same time, he held Abelard in greatest reproach. He fought against him all his life. He distrusted human reason. Men were to believe in God—not to trust their own reason. Human reason, Bernard held, was something to be doubted. While he was the more successful during his lifetime, after his death all the aims for which he had labored, all the movements that he had espoused were swept away. He stood for the old order of things at a time when the new order was already imminent. It was the influence of Abelard, not St. Bernard of Clairvaux, that lived on through the ages.

"What Abelard taught that was most novel for his age was liberty, the right to consult reason and to listen to it alone. His methods were bolder than his doctrines; his influence is to be found in the impulse he gave. He imparted to minds that impulse which perpetuates itself from generation to generation."

Universities came into being during the latter portion of the Middle Ages. One of the oldest was the University of Paris. Hither students came from many countries of Europe and from several Asiatic lands. They were of many types: some the sons of nobles, others from humble walks of life. Great privileges were extended to the student then as now, and this attracted an element that probably never intended to do much studying. Safe passage was assured the student; his belongings could not be seized for debt; these protections alone moved many to register as students who never frequented class rooms. We find that in the latter years of the Middle Ages the University of Paris had 10,000 students enrolled as members. At least half the number were servants of the students, merchants who supplied their needs, and others who for different reasons found it advantageous to pass as students.

The entrance requirements were not exacting. One must be twelve years of age and understand Latin. All lectures were given in this tongue, so a knowledge of it was essential. The students heard lectures and quarreled and made merry and lived with little restraint of any sort. They were exempt from local restrictions and were often a nuisance in a town. Nevertheless, several thousand students were desirable in a city. In fact, they usually made their way, and no city ever wanted to lose a university. In days when there was no property to consider, it sometimes happened that the entire student body decamped when especially objectionable conditions arose.

We can easily imagine that the students as a whole were yet very crude when we read some of the rules laid down for them. One held that a student was not to use a knife upon the examiner after an examination, even though he failed to pass. Another forbade students to throw dice upon the altar while mass was being said. The masters continued in control in Paris, but in Boulogne the students were the stronger. The

University of Toulouse was quite popular, for sciences forbidden at Paris and Boulogne might there be studied.

Difficult questions to be settled by the king were sometimes referred to the students of Paris. The reasons offered them in support of their opinions were likely to be quite exhaustive. For example, when the king of France felt that the Children's Crusade ought to be stopped, he turned to the University of Paris for an opinion on the subject. Many similar incidents might be cited.

The students led a free, wholesome life, generally speaking. In no other age have they shown greater zeal. The masters might lecture on any subject not forbidden by the law of the university. They had to compete for their pupils and this very spirit of competition insured good instruction.

AN EARLY PRINTING PRESS.

INSTITUTIONS OF THE MIDDLE AGES.

THE Middle Ages form the transition period between Ancient and Modern times. Like all historic periods, the Mediæval cannot be confined within clearly specified dates. Although the fall of the Roman Empire is conventionally assigned to the year 476 A. D., it was in reality a long, slow process. From the days of Augustus, the empire had, in the main, ceased to try to extend its boundaries, but had been content to stand on the defensive, to guard its long frontiers, and hold at bay the seething barbarism of Northern Europe. For nearly four centuries, the Romans succeeded in this task, and time was thus given for the Greek and Latin civilizations to blend and reach their full maturity, for Christianity to arise and conquer the Roman world, for the Church to elaborate her ritual, dogma, and organization. Yet, as the fourth century advanced, there were signs to show that the barrier between the Roman and the barbarian worlds could not be permanently maintained. Behind the barrier of the Rhine-Danube frontier, the empire's strength was slowly but surely declining. The population decreased steadily in numbers, land went out of cultivation, the burden of taxation rested ever heavier on the people, yet the treasury was increasingly difficult to fill. Corruption grew ever more evident throughout the government. In addition, the empire was further handicapped by the growing separation between East and West which, ultimately, culminated in the division of the empire. Meanwhile, as the weakness within grew greater, the pressure from without increased. It had come to be only a question of time when the frontier would be broken and when the empire would be at the mercy of barbarian invaders.

Even while the frontier was still guarded by the legions, the invasion of the Germans began. At first as slaves, as captives, as colonists, they were brought or let into the empire and settled in regions more or less depopulated, to revive the declining Roman agriculture. From time to time also large bodies of Germans broke into the empire, only to be vanquished, and then settled as colonists in some devastated province. As a result of this steady influx, a strong German element found its way into the Roman world and parts of it were largely Germanized when the invasions came.

With the latter fourth century the situation changed. Under pressure of the Huns, the Goths begged admission to the empire, and the emperor Valens permitted them to cross the Danube. In no long time the government quarreled with the new settlers and found itself at war with the rebellious Goths. To fight the Goths, the troops had to be called away from the frontiers, and, these being thus left unguarded, other German peoples hastened to exchange the ruder regions of the north for the rich and cultivated fields that stretched, unguarded, to the south. And these invaders came as nations, under their kings and leaders. Henceforth the presence in the empire of organized German peoples was the dominant fact in the situation.

Yet the Germans did not come with the deliberate purpose of destroying the empire. Rather, they sought to make terms with Rome, and gain a legal sanction for their settlement. They were willing, nay anxious, to be taken into the service of the emperor, and asked chiefly for lands whereon to live. Nor did they aim at the wanton destruction of Roman civilization or the provincial population. In general, the invading barbarians looked upon themselves as an army in the service of the Empire, and quartered themselves upon the people, according to established Roman usage. As their occupation of the provinces became permanent, a division of the land and slaves between themselves and the provincials was usually made.

Yet, whatever were the conscious aims of the barbarians, slowly but surely they destroyed the machinery of the imperial government. As Goths, Vandals, Burgundians, Franks, poured into the Empire and marched here and there, seeking a settlement, the Roman emperor could no longer collect his revenues or recruit his army. Over Africa, Spain, and Gaul, his authority ceased to be effective, and various Gothic, Vandal, Frankish, or Burgundian kings, backed by the swords of their German followers, became supreme. Nominally they might rule as agents of the emperor, but in practice they were agents whom he could not control. Finally, with his territories confined to Italy, and his army recruited from the barbarians, the emperor in turn came under the control of the Germans, and in 476 Odoacer, a German soldier, deposed the last Roman emperor in the West, and ruled Italy, nominally as an agent of the Eastern emperor, but really as a German king.

Thus in the course of a century—from 376, when the Goths crossed the Danube, to 476, when the last Western Emperor was deposed—a great change was wrought in Western Europe. In 376 the West was still held in the grip of a great centralized Roman despotism. In 476 it was divided into a number of independent states, ruled by German kings. Yet the memory of the empire lived on through the weary struggles of the various German kings for the supremacy. From the midst of division and war, men looked back at the unity and splendor of the past, as to a sort of golden age.

At length, after many divisions and bloody wars, through much confusion and disorder, the Franks emerged victorious over the other German peoples. First under the leadership of the house of Clovis, then under that of the Carolingians, they united France, Germany, and Italy under the sway of one man—Charlemange. And, as in men's eyes he had renewed the unity of the West, it seemed but fitting that he should revive the imperial title which expressed that unity. After his death, however, his territories were divided among his grandsons, and the war and turmoil was renewed, with the Carolingian sovereigns constantly less and less able to control affairs within their normal kingdoms, where their officers and nobles more and more ignored or defied their authority. At length, amid wars, invasions, and anarchy, the Feudal system slowly shaped itself. Growing up out of both Roman and German institutions, and taking shape under the stress of the practical necessities of the time, it gave a frame-work to European society and history for a millennium, and contributed much to shape the institutions of the modern world.

The Middle Ages are, therefore, in a sense, an Age of Feudalism. As is only natural in a system growing up gradually over Western Europe, it is impossible to describe the Feudal System in such a way that the description will be true for all times, or all places. One feature, however, found in greater or less degree everywhere, is the decline of the power of the central government and the close association between the powers of government and the ownership of land. In the days of confusion following the break-up of the Roman empire, land was well-nigh the only form of wealth. Under these circumstances, the rich man was necessarily a great land-holder, and as the central power grew weaker and weaker, these great land-holders by one means or another possessed themselves more or less completely of the powers of government within their neighborhood.

The result of this development was completely to transform the face of Europe. Instead of one great centralized despotism, such as had existed in the time of Rome, Europe was divided into several nominally independent states, which, in turn, were made up of a myriad of still smaller states, over which the king's authority was hardly more than nominal. Thus in France, after 987, when one of the great feudal nobles seized the throne (to the exclusion of the last of the descendants of Charlemagne), the king had real authority only around Paris and its vicinity, where lay the royal domain. Outside of this domain, the various great dukes and counts, though nominally holding their lands from the king, were practically independent. Nor was this the worst. Many of the dukes were in their duchies in much the same position that the king was in his kingdom. Their power was in turn limited, indeed oftentimes defined by *their* vassals, the lesser lords of various degree. Generally these states, great and small, and states within states, were subject to conflicting claims, and hence war was the normal condition of things. The feudal lords— great and small alike—fought with one another or their king, as the occasion or their interests dictated; and all—king and lords alike—sought, as opportunity offered, to extend their power.

In some countries the kings, being more advantageously situated than the feudal lords, began in the end to get the upper hand. Thus in France the king was able slowly to overcome the nobility. Taking advantage of the mistakes of his opponents and adroitly using for his purposes the feudal law he gradually added one territory after another to his royal domain until at last his power had so increased that he could impose his will upon all his subjects and organize an efficient government for his kingdom.

In Germany and Italy, however, this tendency toward the formation of a national monarchy out of the discordant atoms of Feudalism was checked and hindered by the conflict of two great institutions, each of which continued the traditions of universal sovereignty which had been characteristic of the Roman Empire. In 800, Charlemagne, then master of Western Europe, had revived the title of Emperor. After his time, the unity of his empire had indeed been broken up, but the title still lived on, borne now by one king and then by another, until at length Otto the Great, king of Germany, invaded Italy, and, in 962, was crowned emperor in Rome. Henceforth, the title remained associated with the German kingship, and in the end the universal dominion, which the imperial title implied, proved fatal to a national monarchy, both in Germany and in Italy. For this failure there were many reasons. For one thing, the geographical formation of the two countries rendered their union under one sovereign impracticable. It was physically impossible for one man to watch closely the course of events in both. Then, too, the emperor was often forced to make concessions to the nobles in Germany, in order that he might turn his attention to an invasion of Italy. The invasion undertaken it not infrequently happened that events in Germany recalled the monarch before his task in Italy was thoroughly accomplished. Thus each of the two countries served to distract the emperor's attention from the other and in the end he was unable to establish a firm control in either. Yet, undoubtedly, the greatest obstacle of all lay in the Papacy.

Varied, indeed, were the fortunes of the bishops of Rome during the Middle Ages. At one time at the mercy of the neighboring feudal lords, they had seemed to have reached the nadir of their fortunes. Yet they never renounced their high claims to an universal authority and jurisdiction and at length a time arrived when they could effectively assert these claims. Rescued from the hands of the feudal lords by the emperors, the popes were for a time reduced in fact to a close dependency on the empire. Finally, however, under the powerful influence of Hildebrand—afterwards Gregory VII.—they succeeded in escaping from the imperial control, and in putting themselves at the head of a great movement for reform which was then agitating the church, and, indeed, all Europe. Over this question of reform the popes and the emperors came into violent collision, and a desperate struggle ensued between the two powers. Even after this had ended in a compromise, the war between them speedily broke out again. There was not room in Europe for two universal monarchies, and emperors and popes alike laid claim to that position. In the end the empire was defeated, and, though it continued to exist, with its high-sounding titles and pretensions, yet it was henceforward a mere name, justifying indeed the well known epigram of Voltaire, that the Holy Roman Empire (as it continued to be styled) was so called because it was neither holy, nor Roman, nor an empire.

Yet the claims to universal sovereignty which the popes put forth were in the end no more successful than those of the empire. For a time, under Innocent III., the papacy was able to make itself the head of Europe, setting up and deposing monarchs, and laying down the law for nations. Yet, long before the Reformation, the rising spirit of nationality had proved fatal to these claims, and the kings, as they grew stronger, rejected the pope's temporal authority. Thus, in the end, both papacy and empire, representing, as they did, the universalism of Rome, failed to impose their control on Europe. The day of world monarchies had past. Henceforth the history of Europe was to develop along national, not universal, lines. The Middle Ages may then be said to be the period of transition, when Europe passed from the world empire of Rome, through feudal anarchy, to the nations of the modern world.

Although, in the long run, the papacy was unable to enforce its control upon the nations, yet in the Middle Ages the Church played a great and useful part. It was far, indeed, from confining itself to religious functions, but entered into every phase of men's lives. Its courts administered justice in a large class of cases; it monopolized education and the arts. It was the indispensable aid on which kings and nobles alike relied, not merely for their soul's salvation, but, as well, for the conduct of their daily business. In the earlier Middle Ages only the clergy could read or write, and hence all business requiring these two arts had of necessity to be performed by them. Hence the Church sat at the king's council, kept his accounts and drew up his charters. In its performance of its innumerable tasks, the Church rendered an important service to the world. Arising in the Roman Empire, it had taken up into itself a large part of the Graeco-Roman civilization. Thus in its theology it embodied much of Greek philosophy; and in its law many of the principles of the Roman legal system. This civilization the Church not only preserved from destruction in the fierce rush of the invasions and the long disorder of feudal anarchy, but it definitely transmitted much of it to the future. Thus of the three chief elements that have gone to make up modern culture, the Christian Religion, the Graeco-Roman civilization, and the manners and institutions of the Germans, the two first were transmitted chiefly through the Church.

In yet another way and indirectly the Church aided Europe to recover the civilization of the past. When the barbarian invasions had submerged the Western Empire, the Eastern had survived. By hurling Europe against the East in the great movement of the crusades the Church brought the West into a fruitful contact with this Eastern or Greek Empire. That this contact had much to do with quickening the intellectual life of Europe there can be no doubt, although this was far from being the motive which led the Church to instigate the movement. But the crusades had other results as well. By opening a field attractive to the adventurous they gave an outlet to the energies of the feudal lords. They aided powerfully in promoting commerce and this in turn made possible the development of the towns. In many ways therefore they mark a turning point in Mediæval history.

But the Middle Ages were not only a period of transition: they were a period of beginnings as well. As out of the feudal anarchy the new nations were slowly built up, the foundations were laid of many of the institutions that still exist. Thus feudalism not only affected us through chivalry, wherein its ideas reached their highest expression, but it impressed on men a new view of government. The feudal lord no longer looked upon his sovereign as a Roman had regarded the emperor, as a divine and sacred personage whose will was law. Rather, the king was looked on as subject to the law equally with his subjects. The vassal was bound to his lord only so long as the lord observed the terms of the contract. If the vassal failed to perform his duties the lord could deprive him of his land, but on the other hand, if the lord failed of *his* duties, the vassal might rebel against him.

Moreover, it was during the Middle Ages that representative government was first devised. The Ancient World knew little or nothing of the principle of representation. It was during the Middle Ages that this new device was first seriously applied to government. It came to be an accepted maxim that one of the duties of the vassal was to give to his lord advice and counsel, and that it was the duty of the lord, on his side, to seek such advice. It is on the basis of such principles that, in all the feudal monarchies of the Middle Ages, some form of *National Assembly* arose. As illustrations of these, we need only note the parliament in England, the states-general in France, and the cortes in Spain. However much they might differ in their forms and powers, yet these assemblies, by their existence, testified to the principle that the people must be to some extent consulted by the government, and that some things required their consent. It is true that the people were not viewed in any democratic sense, but rather signified the various *classes* which had made themselves sufficiently powerful to count in politics; that is to say, the nobles, the clergy, and the people of the towns. Still, when all reservations are made, it is none the less true that the foundations, of modern representative government were laid in the Middle Ages—that the very idea first conceived during that period.

There was indeed much war and barbarism in the Middle Ages, but they have played a decisive part in the making of the Modern World. During this long period, it was not all confusion or ignorance. It was a time when important work was done. In the turmoil of this period, three great elements of our modern civilization were welded together. The classic culture, taken up and preserved in the vast organization of the Mediæval Church, Christianity, itself, and the Germanic ideas and customs all met and were, at length, more or less perfectly harmonized. Then, after a long period of feudal anarchy, built up out of feudalism itself, and using it as in part a means, arose the modern nations. The Europe of the Roman Empire is a Europe welded into one vast centralized despotism, having a single civilization. The Europe that emerged from the Middle Ages was a Europe divided into separate nations, each having its own culture, life and institutions.

DESCRIPTION OF ILLUSTRATIONS
IN PART IV

THE COLISEUM.

This great building was also known as the Flavian Amphitheater. The Flavian house was of humble origin and by gigantic building enterprises sought to win popular favor. This vast amphitheater covered nearly six acres, the walls rising to the height of 160 feet. Eighty entrances led to various parts of the building, which had a seating capacity of 80,000 and afforded standing room for 20,000 more. Underneath were subterranean chambers for gladiators, beasts, all kinds of apparatus, particularly water equipment adequate for the immediate conversion of the whole into a lake or to quickly carry off the water. Every day for months at a time scenes of murder and slaughter went on for the amusement of Rome's idle upper scum, as well as for pleasure seekers of all classes.

BATHS OF CARACALLA.

These were the largest and most magnificent of all the Roman baths. Caracalla was one of the later emperors and never saw his gigantic building completed. With its pleasure grounds, these baths covered thirty-three acres, and combined all the advantages of a modern club house with a gymnasium, lectures, discussions and social enjoyments. There were many halls, courts, galleries, etc., under one roof, the great hall or Tepidarium being 170 feet long, 82 feet wide, and 108 feet high. Adjacent were cold rooms and hot rooms, warm rooms and sun rooms, swimming pools, visitors' galleries, and many retiring rooms, for what particular purposes none at present can tell. Sixteen hundred bathers could be accommodated at once, while others waited their turn, attendants gave assistance, directors of the gymnasia instructed, philosophers lectured, and crowds disported themselves in the spacious parks. For beauty of finish and elegance of decoration these baths had no equal.

ARCH OF TITUS.

Triumphal arches were distinctively Roman. At least thirty-eight of them were erected in the course of Roman history. The Arch of Titus was raised in honor of Titus' victory over the Jews and his destruction of Jerusalem. In course of time much of this arch was destroyed and in 1823 Pope Pius VII. caused it to be restored. Two extensive reliefs have deep interest for the student: the portrayal of Titus' triumph, and the spoils of war that graced it. In the first the emperor is shown in his triumphal car, while above Victory holds the crown on his head. The golden table for the shew-bread, the silver trumpets and the seven-branched candle stick were carried along in the procession and are believed to have been faithfully represented in the relief.

TEMPLE OF VESTA.

The worship of Vesta was probably brought into Rome by the Sabines, and the first temple was erected in her honor by the early kings. During the greater portion of Roman history, the temple of Vesta stood on its early site—the extreme eastern end of the Forum. When destroyed by the Gauls and again by the great fire of Nero's time, it was always immediately rebuilt.

Within this temple the sacred fire was always kept burning. The custom originated in a remote age when it was most difficult to rekindle an extinguished flame. Six Vestal Virgins were entrusted with the care of Vesta's fire and they were severely punished if it was allowed to go out. The House of the Vestal Virgins was discovered in 1883 by those carrying on excavations in behalf of the Italian government.

Panorama of Rome from St. Peter's.

We often think of the ancient city of Rome, forgetting that Rome is again a great throbbing city of today. This view is taken from the top of St. Peter's, overlooking a considerable portion of the capital. One great difficulty confronting the modern explorer is the fact that the modern buildings stand on the site of those long since fallen into decay and life of the present prevents extensive examination into life of the past.

Death and the Plowman.

This is one of a long series of illustrations popular in the Middle Ages and known collectively as the Dance of Death. Poets sang the story and artists painted it. By either poem or picture Death was represented as coming unexpectedly to king, cardinal, peasant, bridegroom—to men of every station. (Refer to the Dance of Death, Part VI., page 178.)

> "Lo! I am Death! With aim as sure as steady,
> All things that are and shall be I draw near me.
> I call thee,—I require thee, man, be ready!
> Why build upon this fragile life? Now hear me!"

Mosaic—Worship of the Magi.

It is scarcely possible to give an adequate conception of mosaic pictures by reproductions of this kind. This is a copy of a wall picture made in mosaic in a church of Ravenna. The three wise men, guided by the star are clearly shown; Christ and His mother are fashioned after the Byzantine School—elongated, expressionless figures. While this belongs to the sixth century, in the uppermost tier may be seen the ship, which symbolized the Church. However, the use of symbols was not so great as in centuries earlier.

Plowing in Luzon—As in Middle Ages.

Here we see the farmer scratching the ground, preparatory to planting the seed. This is a daily sight in the Philippines, in many oriental lands and in the Middle Ages might have been seen in Europe. Methods of farming have advanced rapidly in progressive countries during the past hundred years, but even yet in Mohammedan lands and wherever the strong hand of custom prevents rapid innovations, early methods still continue to be used.

Miniature—Queen of Sheba Before Solomon.

This is one of a collection of miniatures treasured today in the Library of St. Mark, Venice, and adorning the Grimani Breviary. This particular miniature is believed to have been done by Hans Memling. If so, it is of comparatively late date, but nevertheless, it conveys certain distinct impressions of the illuminated work done by centuries in the monasteries by painstaking monks. Memling was a Flemish artist who lived in the fifteenth century.

Knight in Armor.

While the weapons and equipment of any armed knight might offer many distinguishing characteristics, this illustration gives a fair idea of the appearance of Mediaeval knights in general. Until the use of gunpowder, such protection rendered one practically secure. However, the weight of the iron was unwieldy and once unhorsed, a knight rose with difficulty. The decoration and elaborate detail of the workmanship depended wholly upon the purse and preference of the knight.

Political and Social Life of Rome

I. The Principate

1. Why do modern historians prefer the name Principate to that of Empire for the government instituted by Octavius Caesar? IV:1

2. For a fair understanding of ideas and ideals prevalent at this time, read The Deeds of Augustus. IV:7

3. What kind of rulers were the Julian princes? IV:15

4. Why did the government of Rome gradually decline? IV: 27

5. For what reasons did Constantine decide to found a new capital? IV:37

6. Under what circumstances did the forces of Rome suffer total defeat? IV:49

7. Why did Rome fall? IV:53

II. Social Life and Custome

1. Compare the Roman and the American family. IV:59

2. What position was accorded the woman? IV:60

3. Describe a Roman wedding. IV:62

4. Does Pliny's letter, IV:63, indicate that marriages resulted from romantic love or from convenience? IV:63

5. Was Roman life pure or not in early times? IV:65

6. What about the furnishment of Roman homes? IV:69

7. Were the villas attractive or not? IV: 71

8. When and by whom was the toga worn? IV: 73 The palla? IV: 75

9. What precious stones were popular among the Romans? IV: 76

10. Compare the articles of food common in our country with those of ancient Italy. IV:77

11. Were Roman banquets more or less costly than those given today? IV: 80

12. Read The Banquet of Trimalchio. IV:348

13. For the training of Roman children, see IV: 87

14. What sports were in favor among Romans? IV:93

15. How did the custom of giving gladiatorial exhibitions arise? IV: 98

16. See the illustration of an ancient gladiatorial school in ruins.

17. No people have ever carried the matter of public baths to greater lengths than the Romans.
IV:100

18. How were copies of books obtained? IV: 104

19. What professions were sought by Roman youths? IV:106

20. How did the system of slavery arise? What was its condition? IV:116

21. What were the Sumptuary Laws established by Augustus?

22. Why did the economic reforms attempted by Diocletian fail? IV: 36

23. What was the condition of the common soldier in the Roman army? IV:122

24. Did the Romans place more or less stress upon their tombs than modern nations? IV: 125

Books for Further Reading

Histories

Greatness and Decline of Rome, Ferraro 5 volumes

History of Rome, Mommsen, 5 volumes

History of Rome, How and Leigh, 1 volume

For Children: Story of the Romans, Guerber

Social Life

Roman Life Under the Caesars, Thomas

Private Life of the Romans, Johnston

Roman Life in Pliny's Time, Pellison

Books of Travel

Rome of Yesterday and Today, Dennie

Days Near Rome, Hare

Walks in Rome, Hare

"The first thing naturally when one enters a scholar's study or library, is to look at his books. One gets a notion very speedily of his tastes and the range of his pursuits by a glance around his bookshelves." –Oliver Wendell Holmes

ROMAN LITERATURE AND ART

"Roman literature, while it lacks the brilliant originality and the delicate beauty which characterize the works of the great Greek writers, is still one of the great literatures of the world, and it possesses an importance for us which is even greater than its intrinsic merits (great as they are) would naturally give it. In the first place, Roman literature has preserved to us, in Latin translations and adaptations, many important remains of Greek literature which would otherwise have been lost, and in the second place, the political power of the Romans, embracing nearly the whole known world, made the Latin language the most widely spread of all languages, and thus caused Latin literature to be read in all lands, and to influence the literary development of all peoples of Europe.

"The Romans were a practical race, not gifted with much poetic imagination, but with great ability to organize their state and their army and to accomplish whatever they determined to do.... Their language is akin to Greek, and like Greek is one of the Indo-European family of languages, to which English and the other most important languages of Europe belong. It started with the same material as Greek, but while Greek developed constantly more variety, more delicacy, more flexibility, Latin is fixed and rigid, a language adapted to laws and commands rather than to the lighter and more graceful kinds of utterance. Circumstances, aided no doubt by the natural bent of their minds, tended to make the Romans political, military, and practical, rather than artistic." –Dr. H. N. Fowler: History of Roman Literature

I. DEVELOPMENT OF LATIN LITERATURE

1. Is there much remaining of early Latin literature? For what reason? IV:130

2. Who were the Arval brothers? IV: 130, 163

3. Of what subjects did every Roman literature treat? IV:132

4. The writings of Catallus have much to commend them. IV: 135

5. Cicero's writings fall into what classes? IV: 181

6. What did he do for the literature of his country? IV: 185

7. Virgil had what object in writing the Georgics? IV: 233

Note: This was the age in which Augustus was doing all in his power to restore conditions which had prevailed in Rome in the early republic.

8. Of what does the Aenied treat? IV: 235

9. How do the writings of Horace rank? IV: 236, 261

10. Ovid's life presents strong contrasts. IV: 236

11. How much of Livy's historical writing remains to us? IV: 238

12. The life of Seneca was in many respects a pathetic one. Of what made emperor's caprice was he victim? IV: 269

13. What Latin writer wrote extensively of the Germans–little known then to the Romans? IV:271

14. Were the Greeks or Romans more prolific in literary production?

II. MASTERPIECES OF LATIN POETRY

1. Lucretius has influenced several modern writers. Read his Invocation to Venus; also his poem on Epicurus, a Greek philosopher. IV:187, 189

2. Catullus has been considered Rome's greatest lyric poet. The short poem written upon his return home is attractive. IV:204

3. Virgil's version of Orpheus and Eurydice is interesting. IV:249; also Laocoon, IV:251

4. Read a selection from the Aenied, IV:259, which is illustrative of his style.

5. Horace repeatedly sang of the pleasures of the simple life, as lived by the peasant or small farmer. Read the ode quoted on page 262, IV.

6. Other illustrative texts are Daily Life in Rome and The Literary Bore, IV:264, 266

7. Ovid related many stories of mythology. Note his Niobe and Baucis and Philemon, IV:277, 286

8. What were the three chief periods of Latin satire? IV:323

9. The Slothful Pupil may be noted in this connection, IV:326

10. The satires of Juvenal are well known. See page 368, IV.

11. The Romans used the art of writing as a medium of expressing their ideas of political and governmental affairs rather than for the development of a literature pleasurable for itself alone. In this respect they stand in strong contrast to the Greeks. Note for example the subjects of their poems. Lucan writes on the Rivalry between Pompey and Caesar–IV:338–instead of upon some noble theme. This may be paralleled by many illustrations.

12. The epigram was given a point–a shaft of wit, by Martial. Read some of his epigrams, IV: 363-4

III. MASTERPIECES OF LATIN PROSE

1. Cicero's I am a Roman Citizen illustrates well this great orator's powers. IV:194

2. Sallust's style is exemplified by his selection entitled Jugurtha at Roma, IV:216

3. Each year students of Latin are set to read Caesar's Commentaries which recount his campaigns in Gaul. Their direct and lucid style renders them comparatively easy reading. See Caeser's account of this expedition into Britain, IV: 223

4. Livy compiled and wrote extensively concerning Roman history. Read his treatment of Brutus and His Sons, IV:297

5. Very interesting indeed may we find an old Roman Debate on Women's Rights, IV:305.

6. For an illustration of Tacitus' writing, see IV:317

7. Seneca was a Stoic. For one who lived in the troublous times in which his career fell, it was well that Stoicism could lend some comfort. The nature of this philosophy is somewhat indicated by Anger and Its Remedies, IV:330

8. Greatest of Roman writers on Natural History was Pliny the Elder. We read his writings today for their general style rather than for their scientific value. However, during the Middle Ages his scientific treatises were highly valued. IV:355, 357

9. Suetonius wrote concerning the Lives of the Caesars. Read extracts given from the lives of Titus and Caligula. IV:375, 377

IV. ROMAN ART AND ARCHITECTURE

NOTE: For many years the fine arts were not developed by the Romans, who were too absorbed in maintaining themselves against their neighbors and in gradual expansion to find opportunity for such refinements. Lacking the artistic temperament of the Greeks, art and architecture were only valued during the later republic and the principate. To be sure this is only relatively true, public buildings were constructed and were adorned perhaps from early times. However, efforts along these lines were only partially successful. As the cultural influence were imported into Italy from the East, more attention was given them and a higher value placed upon art. Roman architecture was given a great impetus by Augustus, and was encouraged by many of the princes; Roman sculpture likewise belongs properly to the principate.

1. What was the general style of the Roman house? IV: 67

2. What building materials were available in Rome? IV:68

3. What buildings were located in the Forum? IV:380

4. The Cloaca Maxima, Rome's great sewer, may still be seen. IV: 382

5. What uses did the basilica serve? IV:383

6. Why is there so little remaining today of Roman architecture? IV:385

7. Were Roman contributions in this field equal to those in others?

8. What purpose did the triumphal arches serve?

Books for Further Reading

History of Roman Literature, H. N. Fowler

Latin Literature, J.W. Mackail

Latin Poetry, Tyrell

Translations of all improtant Latin writers

Roman Art and Architecture

Architecture of Greece and Rome, Anderson & Spiers

Ancient Rome, Lanciani

Destruction of Ancient Rome, Lanciani

Greek and Roman Sculpture, Perry

Pompeii, its Life and Art, Mau

Architectural History of Rome, Parker

Roman Sculpture, Mrs. Arthur Strong

Roman and Mediaeval Art, W.H. Goodyear

SUGGESTED OUTLINE FOR STUDY OF ANY AUTHOR

The Man

1. Portraits
2. Personal appearance
3. Comments
4. Topical Study of Life
5. Home
6. Friends
7. Personal character

Literary Career

8. Works
9. Studies of Chief Writings
10. Characteristics as a Writer
11. Literary Style

12. Contemporary Writers

13. Book so reference

V. RELIGION AMONG THE ROMANS

1. What is said of an early statue made of Saturnus? Who was Janus? Terminus?

2. When Augustus wished to restore the early religion of the Romans and discourage the worship of foreign gods, what measures did he take to accomplish this? IV:5. Can you tell why?

Early Christianity

1. What determined that Christianity should be universal rather than local? IV:40

2. What is meant by the waiting age? IV:41

3. How do you account for the separation which gradually grew up between clergy and laity? IV:41

4. Where was the first Ghetto? IV: 42

5. To what class of society did Christianity first appeal? Why? IV:43

6. What conditions made the rapid spread of the new faith possible?

7. What change took place when Christianity spread to the upper classes? IV:43

8. Viewed from the standpoint of the Romans, what justification was there for the early persecutions? IV:43

9. Who converted a religion of peace into one of war? IV:44

10. In the beginning, had the Christian Church an organized form? IV:418

11. When was toleration extended to the Christians? IV:419

12. Note how the credulity of the age made possible the introduction of the miraculous into the new faith. IV:420

13. The Romans, Greeks and Hebrews contributed much to the faith in the years when it was taking definite form. Many of the forms and ceremonies incorporated into it were borrowed from antiquity. IV:420

14. How did it develop that the bishop of Rome became head of the Universal Church? IV:421

15. Account for the rise of monasticism in the early Christian Church. IV:422

16. What does our present civilization owe to the monks of the Middle Ages? IV:424

17. How do you account for the change that converted a religion of peace into one that summoned the faithful to the wars of the Crusades? IV:451

18. What was the theory of the trial by ordeal? IV:451

19. Why were pilgrimages undertaken by pious Christians in the Middle ages? IV:453 Are such excursions still made today?

VI. EDUCATION

1. What was the early conception of one's duty to the state, in Rome? IV:87

2. What training did the Roman youth receive to fit him for manhood? IV:88

3. The Roman daughters were educated along what lines? IV:89

4. With the influx of Greek ideas, how were Roman conditions modified?

5. What opportunities were open to the favored few? IV:90

6. Travel played what part? IV:92 Is there today any greater means of broadening the mind?

7. What steps were finally taken to provide a uniformity in education? IV:92

Education in the Middle Ages

8. Were there schools in the first centuries after the fall of Rome? IV:469

9. What was the attitude of the Church toward learning?

10. How did St. Augustine help to save classical learning?

11. How did learning happen to survive at all? IV:470

12. In what ways was freedom of thought hampered?

13. What subjects were taught in the Mediaeval schools? IV:470

14. Note that Charlemagne did all that he could to foster and encourage learning. IV:471

15. In view of a letter sent to abbots by the great Charles, what can we judge of the conditions of the times?

16. Who was the celebrated teacher of the Palace school? IV:472

17. What did Alcuin do for education?

18. Compare the teachings of Abelard and St. Bernard of Clairvaux. IV:473

19. Which had greater influence?

20. What was Abelard's favorite saying?

21. For one who would enter a university, what were the requirements? IV:474

22. What is said of student life? IV:475

LIFE DURING THE MIDDLE AGES

"That is a good book which is opened with expectation and closed with profit." –Alcott

Mediaeval history opens with the introduction of a new and useful race upon the stage–a race destined to take up the work of the ancient world and to carry it on. But they are at the beginning upon a far lower stage of civilization than antiquity had reached. In order to comprehend its work and continue it, they must be brought up to that level. This is necessarily a long and slow process, accompanied with much apparent loss of civilization, much ignorance and anarchy, and many merely makeshifts in ideas and institutions. But gradually improvement begins, the new society comes to comprehend more and more clearly the work it has to do and the results gained by its predecessors, it begins to add new achievements to the old ones, and the period closes when at last the new nations, in fairly complete possession of the work of the ancient world in literature, science, philosophy, and religion, open with the greatest energy and vigor a new age of progress. This is mediaeval history, the first part of it–the 'dark ages,' if it is right to call them by that name–when ancient civilization fell a prey to savage violence and superstition; the last part of it, the recovery of that civilization, with some important additions, by the now transformed barbarians–the period which we call, when it has fully opened, the age of the Renaissance." –George Burton Adams: Civilization During the Middle Ages

VII. THE MIDDLE AGES

1. What is the story Kingsley wrote of the Troll-garden, and what does it mean? IV:398

2. For an account of the invasion of Italy by the Teutons, see IV:49

3. Why have the centuries following the fall of Rome been called the time of the Wanderings of the Nations? IV:51

4. Which of these early German tribes soon became strongest? IV:409

5. Charlemagne was the hero of the Middle Ages. What did he accomplish for Europe? IV:411

6. Read Einhard's description of Charlemagne, IV:414. This is valued particularly because Einhard was a contemporary of the great Charles.

7. Political and social life was long founded upon feudalism. What is mean by the Feudal system? IV: 442

8. The particular case cited, IV:444, will help to make the matter plainer.

9. What were some of the advantages and some of the disadvantages of this system? IV:449-50

10. What was the Peace of God? The Truce of God? IV:452

11. What motives led men to undertake the Crusades? IV:452

12. How can you explain the Children's Crusade? Would such a movement be possible in our age? IV:456

13. How did the children spend the days on the march? IV:459

14. The Germans brought the custom of trial by ordeal into Southern Europe. Read an account of a trial by the ordeal of hot water, IV:464

Made in the USA
Middletown, DE
16 October 2023

40492267R00298